Cross-Cultural Perspectives on Quality of Life

Edited by

Kenneth D. Keith, PhD
University of San Diego

and

Robert L. Schalock, PhD
Hastings College

David Braddock, PhD
Editor, Research Monographs & Books

AAMR
American Association on Mental Retardation

Published by
American Association on Mental Retardation
444 North Capitol Street, NW
Suite 846
Washington, DC 20001-1512

The points of view expressed herein are those of the authors and do not necessarily represent the official policy or opinion of the American Association on Mental Retardation. Publication does not imply endorsement by the editor, the Association, or its individual members.

Printed in the United States of America

Library of Congress Cataloging-in-Publication Data

Cross-cultural perspectives on quality of life / edited by Kenneth D. Keith and Robert L. Schalock.
  p. cm.
  Includes bibliographical references.
  ISBN 0-940898-70-5
  1. Mentally handicapped—Cross-cultural studies. 2. Quality of life—cross-cultural studies. I. Keith, Kenneth D. II. Schalock, Robert L.

HV3004 .C76 2000
362.3—dc21
                  00-055835

Contributors

Giorgio Albertini, MD
Casa di Cura San Raffaele
Rome
Italy

Ana Maria Barreira, MSc
Department of Psychology
Federal University of Pernambuco
Jaboatão, Pernambuco
Brazil

Nehama T. Baum, PhD
Muki Baum Association
    for the Rehabilitation
    of Multi Handicapped, Inc.
North York, Ontario
Canada

Ivan Brown, PhD
Centre for Health Promotion
University of Toronto
Toronto, Ontario
Canada

Roy I. Brown, PhD
School of Special Education and Disability
    Studies
Flinders University of South Australia
Adelaide, South Australia
Australia

Monica González Buján
Buenos Aires
Argentina

Diego González Castanón, MD
Buenos Aires
Argentina

Louise Doré, BA, BEd
Carrefour d'Education Populaire de Pointe
    St. Charles
Montreal, Quebec
Canada

Robert Doré, PhD
Department of Education
University of Quebec at Montreal
Montreal, Quebec
Canada

Javier Elorriaga
Fundación Tutelar Gorabide
Bilbao
Spain

David Felce, PhD
Welsh Centre for Learning
    Disabilities Applied Research Unit
University of Wales College of Medicine
Cardiff
Wales

Loreto Garcia, MA
Fundación Tutelar Gorabide
Bilbao
Spain

Sushil Kumar Goel, PhD
Regional Institute of Education
Bubaneswar
India

Tibi Goldman
Association of the Handicapped
    of Haifa and the North
Haifa
Israel

Robert Groulx
People First of Montreal
Montreal, Quebec
Canada

Sami Helle
Projektityöntekijä
Finnish Association on Mental Retardation
Helsinki
Finland

Jennifer Denise James, MS
Community Mental Health Counselor
Foundations for People With a Physical
    Disability
Curaçao
Netherlands Antilles

Kenneth D. Keith, PhD
Department of Psychology
University of San Diego
San Diego, CA
United States

Hung-Chih Lin, PhD
Department of Special Education
National Changhua University of Education
Changhua
Taiwan

John Lobley, MSc
Practice Development Centre
Calderstones National Health Service Trust
Walley, Clitheroe
England

Jorge Martinez, MA
Postgraduate Course on Social Services
Fundación Tutelar Gorabide
Bilbao
Spain

Leena M. Matikka, Lic. Psychol.
Finnish Association on Mental Retardation
Helsinki
Finland

David Matsumoto, PhD
Department of Psychology
San Francisco State University
San Francisco, CA
United States

Roy McConkey, PhD
School of Health Sciences
University of Ulster at Jordanstown
Newtownabbey, County Antrim
Northern Ireland

**Akiie Henry Ninomiya,
MDiv, MSW, MTh**
School of Policy Studies
Kwansei Gakuin University
Hyogo-ken
Japan

Brian O'Toole, PhD
School of the Nations
Georgetown
Guyana

Wojciech Otrębski, PhD
Department of Rehabilitation Psychology
Catholic University of Lublin
Lublin
Poland

Lilah Morton Pengra, PhD
Multicultural Consulting Services
Buffalo Gap, SD
United States

Dennis Raphael, PhD
Department of Public Health Sciences
University of Toronto
Toronto, Ontario
Canada

Mark Rapley, PhD
School of Psychology
Murdoch University
Murdoch, Western Australia
Australia

Rebecca Renwick, PhD
Quality of Life Research Unit
University of Toronto
Toronto, Ontario
Canada

Robert L. Schalock, PhD
Department of Psychology
Hastings College
Hastings, NE
United States

Patrick Schelfhout
Anderlecht
Belgium

Marie José Schmitt
European Group for the
    Employment of People
    With Mental Disabilities
Aix En Provence
France

Judy Smith-Davis, PhD
Division of International Special
    Education and Services
The Council for Exceptional Children
Reston, VA
United States

Akio Tachi, MA
The Institute of Vocational Training
National Polytechnic University
Sagamihara, Kanagawa
Japan

iv

Elvira Unamunzaga, MA
Fundación Tutelar Gorabide
Bilbao
Spain

Geert Van Hove, PhD
Department of Special Education
University of Ghent
Ghent
Belgium

Miguel A. Verdugo, PhD
Facultad de Psicologia
Universidad de Salamanca
Salamanca
Spain

Patricia Noonan Walsh, PhD
Centre for the Study of
   Developmental Disabilities
University College Dublin
Dublin
Ireland

Nancy Ward
TARC
Tulsa, OK
United States

Silvana Maria Russo Watson, PhD
Department of Education
Nebraska Wesleyan University
Lincoln, NE
United States

Timothy C. Watson, BS
Facilities Management Department
University of Nebraska-Lincoln
Lincoln, NE
United States

Dedication

We dedicate this book to the memory of our friends Tom Houlihan and Clyde Block. Let their lives symbolize the movement of their generation out of the darkness and into the warm light of community.

Contents

ix

Tables

Figures

Preface

The concept of *quality of life* exists in an increasingly culturally divergent and international environment. This global orientation necessitates increased cultural exchanges and greater cross-cultural research to understand better both the emic (culture-bound) and etic (universal) nature of the quality-of-life concept.

Our desire to edit this book, *Cross-Cultural Perspectives on Quality of Life,* stems from three sources. First, for more than 15 years our work on the conceptualization and measurement of quality of life has strongly suggested that the concept of quality of life is used in three significant ways throughout the world, as

- *a sensitizing notion* that gives us a sense of reference and guidance from the individual's perspective, focusing on the person and the individual's environment;

- *a social construct* that is used as an overriding principle to improve and enhance a person's perceived quality of life;

- *a unifying theme* that provides a systematic framework to apply the quality-of-life concept.

Second, our cross-cultural work has suggested the potential universality of a number of key quality-of-life concepts. For example, in a 1996 study (Keith, Heal, & Schalock) we investigated the meaning attributed to 10 common quality-of-life concepts that have evolved during the last decade: rights, relationships, satisfaction, environment, economic security and well-being, social inclusion, individual control, privacy, health, and growth and development. Our approach was to ask mental retardation professionals from seven nations (Australia, England, Finland, Germany, Japan, Republic of China, and the United States) to rate the meaning of these 10 concepts using nine semantic differential items, three from each of the dimensions of value, potency, and activity. Across the seven countries, all 10 of the quality-of-life concepts tested received strong positive ratings on the value dimension and lower (but positive) ratings on the potency and activity dimensions. Additionally, the profiles across the seven countries were remarkably similar.

Our third reason for this book stems from our firm belief that the concept of quality of life will continue to influence social policy in one or more of the following ways:

- as a social construct impacting program development and provision of services and supports;

- as the criterion for assessing effectiveness of services to people with disabilities;

- as a personal and social pursuit that is reflected in individuals who desire a life of quality; service or support providers who want to deliver a quality product; and evaluators (policy makers, funders, and consumers) who want quality outcomes.

Once we decided to develop the book, the second step was relatively easy: contacting people in 25 countries whom we knew had a personal interest in—and commitment to—a better cross-cultural understanding of the concept of quality of life. During the fall of 1996, we contacted these colleagues and asked for suggestions of people within their respective countries who might be interested in contributing a chapter from one of three perspectives: the individual person, the community or organization, or the larger cultural or sociopolitical level. Our request has resulted in 31 chapters representing 21 countries, with 6 chapters reflecting the personal perspective, 8 the community or organizational perspective, and 17 representing the larger cultural perspective. Our contributors represent South America (Argentina, Brazil, Guyana), the Caribbean (Netherlands Antilles), Asia and the Pacific (Australia, India, Japan, Taiwan), the Middle East (Israel), Europe (Belgium, England, France, Finland, Ireland, Italy, Poland, Russia, Spain, Wales), and North America (Canada, United States).

In reading these authors, we have been struck by the extent to which they reflect an ecological perspective on the concept of quality of life. Thus we have adapted Bronfenbrenner's (1979) ecological model in editing and presenting these 31 chapters. Part 1 will focus on the microsystem; part 2, the mesosystem; and part 3, the macrosystem. Our definitions are as follows:

- *microsystem:* the immediate social setting, including the person, family, and/or advocate(s);

- *mesosystem:* the neighborhood, community, or organizations providing education or habilitation services or supports;

- *macrosystem:* the overarching patterns of culture, society, larger populations, country or sociopolitical influences.

Throughout this book, the reader will encounter the challenges posed by (a) the concept of quality of life, (b) the efforts made throughout the world to understand the concept better and to use the concept to enhance the lives of people with disabilities. Chief among these challenges are

- *conceptual issues* regarding how we should refer to the term *quality of life:* is quality of life a single, unitary entity, or a multidimensional, interactive concept; how is it best to conceptualize indicators of quality of life; and is quality of life the same for all individuals?

- *measurement issues:* what should be measured; what psychometric standards need to be considered; and how do we overcome measurement challenges?

- *implementation issues* regarding how to change social policy and organizations to take account of quality of life; how to implement programs focused on its core dimensions (emotional well-being, personal development, self-determination, interpersonal relations, social inclusion, rights, material well-being, and physical well-being); and how to demonstrate that quality enhancement techniques really do enhance the perceived quality of life.

Completing this book has been both a challenge and a rewarding experience. In editing each chapter, we have attempted to maintain carefully the author's intent, and in many cases have worked jointly with the author(s) to ensure accurate translation and the best meaning of the terms and concepts presented. The task has been most rewarding because it has given us continued opportunity to work with valued colleagues from around the world who are jointly attempting to conceptualize, measure, or apply the concept of quality of life across a wide range of challenging and disparate environments. To each contributor, we say thank you for a job well done; to each reader, we promise an exciting, thought-provoking, and enjoyable read.

Kenneth D. Keith, PhD
Robert L. Schalock, PhD

References

Bronfenbrenner, U. (1979). *The ecology of human development.* Cambridge, MA: Harvard University Press.

Keith, K. D., Heal, L. W., & Schalock, R. L. (1996). Cross-cultural measurement of critical quality of life concepts. *Journal of Intellectual and Developmental Disability, 21,* 273-293.

Acknowledgments

We are grateful to the many colleagues whose work appears in this book. We value their efforts on behalf of people with developmental disabilities around the world, and their dedication is evident in the chapters they have written. It is our hope the book will contribute both to our understanding of the concept of quality of life and to its cross-cultural properties.

We are indebted to series editor David Braddock, and to David Matsumoto and Efren Carbonell for their comments on an earlier draft of the book. It is better than it would have been without their help. Thanks are due Rhonda Lakey, Jay Kahler, and Darlene Buschow for technical support; Cathy Vaughn and Evelyn Bence for humane, capable editorial assistance; and Connie Keith for contributions too numerous to name. Finally, our work would not have been possible without generous support from Nebraska Wesleyan University, Hastings College, and the University of San Diego.

Foreword

David Matsumoto
San Francisco State University
San Francisco, California, United States

As I write this introductory piece, it is the last month of the last year in the 20th century. In a short time, we will welcome not only a new year, but also a new millennium. As we close the chapter on what has got to be one of the most amazing centuries in the history of civilization, we can only look forward to new beginnings, new outlooks, and new perspectives on life.

Reflecting back on the last 100, 50, and even 20 years, the world has undoubtedly changed dramatically and dynamically. Technological advances have made it possible for us to communicate with each other faster and more efficiently than ever before. E-mail, cellular phones, and wireless pagers have quickly replaced letters, telegrams, and the good old telephone. Likewise, advances in transportation technology have made it easier than ever to go from place to place. Cars, planes, and trains all move people faster than ever, allowing us to be in Asia, Europe, Africa, or Oceania in just a few hours.

These changes mean that the world is smaller than ever before. Of course the physical size of the world has not changed. Distances remain the same, and the circumference of the planet, at least to my knowledge, is not appreciably shorter or longer. Yet the world is definitely *functionally* smaller, with people of all different races, nationalities, genders, lifestyles—cultures—coming together to work, live, and play more today than ever.

This trend promises to continue well into the future. Tomorrow brings with it technological advances in communications and transportation technology that we can only dream of. What takes hours for us to accomplish today will take only minutes and even seconds in the future. Borders will become increasingly porous, and national economies and businesses will become even more interlinked than now. The spread of English as the international language, the standardization of world currencies such as the Eurodollar, and other such developments promise to connect people around the globe in even greater and more complex ways than today.

These changes mean that we—the people of the world—have also changed how we view one another, our countries, our cultures, and ourselves. The 20th century was a time of renewed commitments, struggles, and identification with our nations and countries; as we enter the 21st century, we find ourselves increasingly recognizing that we are citizens not only of our own nation states, but also of the world. In today's world, we are not only Americans, Canadians, Brazilians, Chinese, or German; we are also members of a single global community. As we emerge from the end of this century into the new, we do so not only being solely concerned with what is in our own best interests, but also what is in the best interest of those all around us.

These changes bring with them one inevitable fact: that we are interdependent on each other today more than ever, and will even be more so in the future. Day to day we need to work and live with people highly diverse—in thought, language, custom, and lifestyle—from ourselves. International and intercultural marriage is on the rise, and businesses are increasingly becoming more international and intercultural in scope, ensuring a steady influx and outflux of workers from distant lands to come together for a common goal. National economies and currencies are tied together in ways more complex than I can ever imagine. Cross-national and cross-cultural interdependence is personal, professional, and a welcome challenge.

This increased interdependence necessitates our concern for the health, welfare, and safety of the people immediately around us and ourselves as well as for our more distant neighbors. As we more fully realize that we are *all* cohabitants of the same living space—planet Earth—we are slowly awakening to the fact that we must be concerned for the welfare of our fellow cohabitants, in lands near and far. This is because we know that what is good for all is also good for "me"; harmony, stability, and cooperation among our neighbors means peace, satisfaction, and productivity for us. Thus we all have a vested interest in the lives of our fellow humans, all around the world.

This interdependence has important moral as well as personal and professional implications. As the world continues to become a smaller place functionally, and as we rapidly recognize the interdependence of our lives with others, the ethical necessity to look after the welfare of our neighbors near and far becomes evident. As we come together in a new global community, this necessity looms large, as our lives are inextricably intertwined in work and play.

Of course we are talking about the concern for our fellow humans' quality of life. As social scientists we have a duty, right, and professional necessity to be concerned with our neighbors' quality of life. The knowledge we generate as social scientists—in psychology, social work, sociology, anthropology, and the like—is not meant to be an interesting theory to be placed on library shelves, never to impact people's lives. We study lives to improve them; we hope that the knowledge generated is used in positive and constructive ways to help improve people's quality of life. In fact, as scientists why study anything if we are not interested in the generated knowledge ultimately being used to improve the quality of life of the people around us?

Beyond our professional and social roles as scientists and teachers, indeed, as citizens of the world of the new millennium, it is also our moral obligation to be concerned with the quality of life of those neighbors. As we have the skills and tools necessary to generate knowledge that can further our understanding of the quality of life of our neighbors and ourselves, we have the ability to provide the basis for the improvement of those lives.

If you study culture long and hard enough, you generally come to two realizations. The first has to do with the enormous and amazing impact of culture on people's lives, no matter where in the world they come from. Culture provides the platform by which differences among groups of people in customs, heritage, tradition, and values arise. Culture affects our self-concepts, language, and behaviors. Culture is our worldview, our perspective, and it is as unique to each person as it is to each cultural group around the world.

Yet one comes to the equally amazing realization of the inherent universality of some of the most basic human qualities. A mother's love for her child; the good times, camaraderie, and friendship of loved ones; and the striving for self-integrity are all universal aspects of humans that transcend differences in custom, tradition, race, gender, or heritage. While cultural differences are important, pancultural similarities are also important.

Among these, we find that the search for a better quality of life is perhaps one of the most endearing of human traits, one that we share with all people all around the world. Whether African, European, or Asian, gay or straight, living with disabilities or not, the search and striving for a better quality of life is a goal for all of us. This striving separates us from our primate ancestors and all other animals. This striving is the most human of all strivings.

At the same time, we find that we often differ in exactly how we attain a better quality of life. The road toward quality is different for every culture, as it is for every person. It differs by context, place, and time. Thus while there are inherent similarities in quality of life, there are inherent differences as well.

If we are to live out our professional, personal, and moral

obligation to improve the quality of life of our neighbors and partners in our global village, we need to accept and understand both these levels in the people around us. We need to be more aware of and better understand exactly what quality of life is for *all* people in *all* cultures; what factors influence it, both positively and negatively? We have to capture all the facets of quality of life, in its enormity. We may not be able to swallow it whole, but we can certainly put the feast of quality of life on our table.

This volume does just that. It is, for all intents and purposes, perhaps the greatest compilation of stories of quality of life from many different people from many different cultures with many different perspectives. These stories not only celebrate the quality of life of so many of our neighbors; they also highlight the challenges, pitfalls, and obstacles that we all face in improving the quality of our lives. Each story has its own message, and collectively they provide meaning on several levels for laypeople, educators, administrators, and scientists alike. It is this multifaceted message that is so important for all of us as we close this century and open a new one.

As social scientists, students, teachers, and, more important, partners in tomorrow's interdependent global community, I ask you to share with me the excitement, interest, and indeed challenge that this volume brings to the table. If you read it closely, it will change your perspective on life. It surely did so for me.

The Microsystem: Quality of Life From the Individual's Perspective

During the last two decades, the field of mental retardation and closely related disabilities has embraced the concept of quality of life as both a sensitizing notion and an overarching principle for service delivery. Why? Probably because the concept has captured the changing vision of people with disabilities and has also provided a common language across disciplines and functional statuses. More specifically, over the last two decades, there has been a significant change in the way we view people with disabilities. This transformed vision of what might constitute the life possibilities of people with mental retardation is reflected in terms familiar to the reader: self-determination, strengths and capabilities, normalized and typical environments, individualized support systems, equity, and enhanced behavior and role status. As a term and concept, *quality of life* has become a social construct that has captured this changing vision, and thus has also become the vehicle through which consumer-referenced equity, empowerment, and increased life satisfaction for citizens with mental retardation can be achieved. The term is also consistent with the individualized and person-centered focus of education and (re)habilitation services that are rapidly emerging throughout the world.

The last two decades have also been a time during which the field of mental retardation has expanded rapidly, trying to adapt successfully to major upheavals caused by deinstitutionalization, normalization, mainstreaming, and economic constraints. As important as these movements have been, they are more process than outcome oriented, and thus have failed to provide a clearly articulated goal for the people involved. So the concept of quality of life has become attractive as a universal principle that provides a common goal across environments and across people. This sensitizing notion goes beyond the processes of systems change to the outcomes of those processes. The desire for a life of quality is characteristic of everyone; as a result, a common language has been born.

It's that common language, and the sensitizing aspect of the quality-of-life concept, that the reader is introduced to in this first section of the book. In chapter 1 Renwick, Brown, and Raphael consider the concept of person-centered quality of life within the

1

context of recent international trends in disabilities and the development of a broader understanding of quality of life. These authors argue that ultimately the central issue in trying to understand and apply the quality-of-life concept is improvement or maintenance of enjoyment of life at the individual level.

Quality of life from the individual's perspective is the theme of the next three chapters, which stress the important role that self-advocacy plays in a life of quality. In chapter 2 Robert Groulx, president of the People First Movement of Montreal, explains what he means by the expression *quality of life*. Groulx gives a very personal account of his earlier experiences that resulted in what he describes as a "mediocre quality of life." His perceived quality of life improved significantly after he became actively involved in the People First Movement and simultaneously became more independent, productive, and integrated into his community, where he has received recognition and validation for his work. Groulx also discusses the impact of labels and segregation, the importance of supports, and the need for people to "be as happy as possible."

The focus on self-advocacy and equity is further developed in chapter 3, in which Sami Helle of Finland shares the experience and frustration of being a person with mental retardation, and the importance of family, friends, and work. Helle further expresses hope that people throughout the world will understand him and the fact that people with mental retardation are "the same kind of people like everybody else."

In chapter 4 Nancy Ward of the United States recounts her experience with self-advocacy groups at the local, state, national, and international levels. Today Ward is employed as an organizer for self-advocacy groups, but says this about her work: "Finally, my dream for the future is that I work myself out of a job, because there will be no need to have organizations that work with people who have a disability. People with a disability will be accepted like anybody else, so there won't be a need for those kinds of organizations. That is my dream."

In chapter 5 Geert Van Hove and Patrick Schelfhout of Belgium give a personal account of the development of the People First program in Flanders. They discuss the theoretical framework and phases in development, along with the initial problems regarding roles, logistics, finding coaches, and training for self-advocates. They conclude with a number of challenges associated with establishing people's rights and tactics to live in "two worlds."

Finally, in chapter 6 Tibi Goldman of Israel describes the development of a self-help organization committed to improving the quality of life of people with disabilities. Goldman summarizes the organization's structure, organizational principles, and quality-of-life-oriented projects.

Throughout these six chapters, the reader will note the following common themes:

- the emergence of self-advocacy and People First organizations;

- a person-centered approach to understanding and applying the concept of quality of life;

- the importance of friends, family, and associates;

- the key role that dignity and meaningful work play in a person's perceived quality of life.

Person-Centered Quality of Life: Contributions From Canada to an International Understanding

Rebecca Renwick
Ivan Brown
Dennis Raphael
University of Toronto
Toronto, Ontario, Canada

Quality of life is a powerful and potentially transformative concept. It has the power to redirect our focus *from* a piecemeal view of the issues that influence people's lives *to* a holistic perspective on the lives of individuals. Such refocusing is possible and particularly effective when a person-centered approach is taken. Adopting a person-centered approach can transform our understanding of what quality of life means and how this concept may be used proactively to facilitate and mobilize truly meaningful change at the personal level and, less directly, at the social level.

This chapter considers the concept *person-centered quality of life* within the context of (a) recent international trends in developmental disability and (b) the development of a broader understanding of quality of life. It argues that ultimately the central issue in trying to understand and apply the quality-of-life concept is maintaining or improving enjoyment of life at the individual level, as each person sees and experiences it. The chapter provides an example of how a person-centered approach can be applied at the service-provider level. This application is based on the work associated with the Quality of Life Project being carried out at the Quality of Life Research Unit of the Centre for Health Promotion at the University of Toronto. The chapter presents a case for taking a person-centered approach to quality of life and suggests that such an approach is especially useful for practitioners attempting to support improved life for people with developmental disabilities. It concludes with a discussion of some future directions.

Emergence of the Quality-of-Life Concept in Response to International Trends

Recent International Trends in Developmental Disabilities

Over the past 25 years, several important principles have emerged in the field of developmental disabilities. The most noteworthy include normalization, community living, independence, individual attention, and inclusion. Although each of these principles developed at the same time in many countries, regions of Canada have often led the way in initiating and promoting their use.

These principles have altered both the way we view developmental disability and the ways in which we support people who have developmental disabilities. At the same time, they have contributed to a wider recognition of the needs of people with developmental disabilities. For example, in Ontario, Canada's most populous province, services that embody these principles have been greatly expanded, rights have been recognized, and access to education has been guaranteed (e.g., Woodill, Renwick, I. Brown, & Raphael, 1994).

The ultimate goal of these changes has been to improve attitudes toward, treatment of, and environmental conditions for people with developmental disabilities. Although the practical objectives of these changes have not yet been fully realized, considerable progress has been made. In fact, sufficient progress has been made to move away from the question "Can the objectives be realized?" to the question "How are the lives of people with developmental disabilities affected as these objectives are being realized?"

The Emergence of the Quality-of-Life Concept

The concept of quality of life has attracted interest and is being explored in various parts of the world (Goode, 1994a, 1997). The field of developmental disabilities has been, and continues to be, extremely fertile ground for developing an understanding of quality of life (I. Brown, 1994; I. Brown & Renwick, in press). The tremendous growth in the number of publications on quality of life that have appeared in the disability and health literatures in the past few years underscores the increasing interest in, and attempts to understand, quality of life as a concept.

Quality of life has emerged as a concept in large part because it is considered to be a useful concept for responding to the question posed above: How are the lives of people with developmental disabilities affected as these objectives are being realized? Quality of life shifts our main focus away from working toward objectives supporting principles that others consider to be good for people with developmental disabilities (e.g., normalization) and away from objectives that support what others consider to be good group processes (e.g., inclusion, community living). Instead, it redirects our attention to considering how the applications of these principles and processes can improve, and actually have improved, people's lives. Quality of life is a useful concept that builds on other concepts that have already gained international recognition (e.g., inclusion, normalization). However, it also offers greater potential for addressing questions such as: Are people really happier? Are they better off? Are their lives more fulfilling? If so, what makes them happier, better off, and more fulfilled?

Consideration of the intrinsic meaning of quality of life highlights its usefulness and potency. *Quality* makes us think of the excellence or "exquisite standards" associated with human characteristics, and of positive values such as happiness, success, wealth, health, and satisfaction (Lindstrom, 1992). *Of life* indicates that the concept concerns the very essence or essential aspects of human existence. Lindstrom has suggested that, from a semantic point of view, the concept *quality of life* encompasses the values that are central to human life and that constitute the essence of our existence. To understand the concept *quality of life* at this semantic level is to attach to it the utmost importance in all human endeavors: What can be more highly valued than that which makes us consider, and perhaps even aspire to, the exquisite standards of human existence?

A Broader Conceptualization: Three Levels of Understanding

At the same time that such thinking has clarified our understanding of what quality of life *means,* other work has contributed to an emerging international consensus concerning a conceptual structure through which to apply our understanding of the essential meaning of quality of life (e.g., R. I. Brown, 1997; Goode, 1994a, 1994b; Renwick, I. Brown, & Nagler, 1996; Schalock, 1996, 1997a). This work suggests that a full picture of quality of life includes the interrelationship among factors at various degrees of immediacy to individuals. For the sake of simplicity, such factors can be grouped into three levels, as follows:

- the microlevel: the individual;
- the mesolevel: communities, institutions, or programs;
- the macrolevel: culture, society, or large populations.

Goode's (1994b) thorough description and analysis of the lives of children with disabilities constitutes a strong argument that ultimately quality of life must be considered at the microlevel, that is, from the perspective of, and within the world of, the individual. The numerous conceptualizations of quality of life describing factors at the individual level are well served by Goode's work (e.g., R. I. Brown, Bayer, & MacFarlane, 1988; Ouellette-Kuntz & McCreary, 1996; Renwick & I. Brown, 1996; Schalock, Keith, Hoffman, & Karan, 1989). Felce and Perry (1996, 1997) have shown that there is an emerging international consensus among these microlevel approaches. They have organized the various aspects of life that have been addressed in the quality-of-life literature into four major domains: physical well-being, psychological well-being, social well-being, and material well-being.

Factors associated with the environment at the level of community, institution, or program (mesolevel) have been identified (Green & Kreuter, 1991; Roeher Institute, 1996). Major factors associated with quality of life from a macrolevel perspective have also been examined (Bach & Rioux, 1996; Lindstrom, 1992; Parmenter, 1996; Rioux, 1996).

Several attempts have been made to combine factors associated with quality of life at the individual level with factors at the two broader levels. A conceptual model developed in Canada by R. I. Brown et al. (1988) included "quality of environment" and "economic stability" alongside microlevel factors. In the United States Schalock (1997b) identified eight core domains of quality of life at various levels of immediacy to the individual (e.g., self-determination, social inclusion, interpersonal relations, and rights). In Europe Lindstrom (1992) described four spheres associated with quality of life: the personal (physical, mental, and spiritual resources), the interpersonal (family, friends, and social networks), the external (work, income, and housing), and the global (culture, rights, and social welfare). Collectively, this work highlights the recognition that quality of life is something that is very appropriately thought of, and ultimately *has* to be thought of, at the individual level. However, it also emphasizes that people do live within environments that have many aspects: physical, social, economic, political, and cultural. Each aspect of an environment has its own "quality" which influences the quality of life experienced by individuals.

The Emergence of Person-Centered Quality of Life

A person-centered approach to quality of life focuses on the individual but recognizes the importance of the interrelationship among all three levels of factors associated with quality of life. It emphasizes that individuals live within environments: their physical surroundings, their social and cultural groups, and their societies. Thus the person's quality of life and needs related to quality of life are best understood in a holistic way (Timmons, 1997) which takes account of individuals within their environments. Holism implies that the various aspects of individuals (e.g., physical, psychological, and spiritual) are in continuous, dynamic transaction with the various aspects of the environment (e.g., physical, social, political, cultural, and economic). Consequently, over time, individuals and their environments continue to influence and change each other to varying degrees (Renwick & I. Brown, 1996). So from a person-centered perspective, individuals are best understood in the context of their environments. Further, their quality of life is viewed as a complex, integrated whole that arises from the relationship between individuals and their environments (I. Brown & Renwick, in press; Renwick & I. Brown, 1996; Renwick et al., 1994). In essence, the person-centered approach to quality of life conceptually connects all three levels of factors associated with quality of life by taking account of their collective impact on individuals' lives.

The core domains of human life are remarkably consistent across cultures and across time. These domains are well documented in the literatures of fields such as sociology, anthropology, and psychology, and, more recently, in the literature on disability. Core life domains are merely social constructs, but they are given shape by our knowledge of common characteristics that underlie these domains.

Yet the ways in which excellence (or "exquisite standards," referred to earlier) is realized and expressed within these core domains differs, from one cultural group to another, from one group of people to another within cultures, as well as from one person to another (I. Brown, 1994; I. Brown, Renwick, & Nagler, 1996). These differences occur in family life, manners, leisure activities, work habits, religious practices, care of one's physical health, dress, and virtually all other areas of life. It is this very richness of variation in expressing the value of the same core human characteristics that makes cultural differences so interesting and intriguing and sometimes even shocking to us. So as much as quality of life needs to focus on the core domains of life that are common to the existence of all human beings, it needs equally to recognize that there are a vast number of ways that people express and realize the human characteristics that give substance to the core domains.

As a concept, person-centered quality of life focuses attention on core life domains, but it also recognizes that the human characteristics that underlie the core life domains are expressed in as many ways as there are people to express them. Each person finds his or her own ways to express needs and goals associated with core human domains. Each individual knows best which ways are most suited to his or her life and circumstances. And these individual expressions of needs and goals comprise a person's uniqueness and define a person's individuality. A person-centered approach to quality of life holds that (a) there are vast numbers of individual means to the same ends (I. Brown, 1994) and (b) the value of human individuality lies in accepting that different means can be equally valuable in attaining the same ends. The valuing of human individuality that follows from this principle is a necessary and important step toward achieving human equality.

This perspective also embraces several principles of social justice (Renwick, in press; Townsend, 1993). Social justice, as it is currently understood, implies that all individuals are worthy and have value. It also implies that individuals must have self-determination; that is, they need to make their own choices and decisions (Townsend). It emphasizes that individuals should direct and participate in planning for their own lives and futures. It also holds that individuals must have real access to resources and opportunities to exercise their choices and decisions from among a range of real alternatives. Further, the individual's values, decisions, and personal choices are worthy of respect by others. These principles of social justice, by definition, apply to all citizens in a society, whether or not they have disabilities.

Person-centered quality of life has emerged as an essential concept that underpins efforts to support individuals in making real improvements in their lives. This approach can be useful when those who apply the concept to improve people's lives:

- understand clearly and value each person's ways of expressing needs and goals related to core life domains;

- understand that the expressions of needs and goals are unique to the person and *should not* be the same as those of others;

- understand how a person's unique expressions of needs and goals add to, or detract from, quality within his or her life.

Any attempt to support improvements in people's lives using a person-centered quality-of-life approach requires, first, carefully observing and listening to what each individual shows (i.e., through actions and nonverbal behavior) and has to say about his or her life. This process involves actively seeing and hearing what makes life good and not so good, and what unique aspects of life give importance and meaning to each person. It means hearing what important life plans and visions for the future the person has (Butterworth, Steere, & Whitney-Thomas, 1997; Goode, 1997). A person-centered approach to quality of life requires as active participation as possible by the individual as the principal source of information about what he or she deems important and enjoyable (Renwick et al., 1994).

Next, those who attempt to use this approach to improving people's lives must tailor supports, from both natural and professional sources, to the specific unique characteristics, needs, and goals of the individual. By using what is important and meaningful to the person to guide the process, service providers can assist the development of personal plans that come close to the person's own perception of the world and better facilitate quality within that individual's life.

Ontario's Quality of Life Project

The authors have developed a person-centered approach to quality of life in their work with Ontario's Quality of Life Project, carried out (since 1991) at the Quality of Life Research Unit of the Centre for Health Promotion (CHP), University of Toronto. This research has been influenced by work from several countries, and by other work that has emerged from within Canada (e.g., R. I. Brown et al., 1988; Day & Jankey, 1996; Lord & Farlow, 1990; Ouellette-Kuntz & McCreary, 1996; Timmons, 1997).

The overall purpose of the project was to evaluate the policy directions of Ontario's Ministry of Community and Social Services, the branch of government that funds almost all services to people with developmental disabilities living in the province. The original project has evolved and also stimulated related work that includes several other populations, such as seniors, adolescents, people using mental health services, people with HIV, children with and without disabilities, adults with physical and sensory disabilities, and families of people with disabilities. (For more detailed descriptions of this work, see Raphael, I. Brown, Renwick, & Rootman, 1996; Renwick & I. Brown, 1996; Renwick, I. Brown, Rootman, & Nagler, 1996; Renwick et al., 1994; Woodill et al., 1994.)

One of the most important accomplishments of the project with regard to adults with developmental disabilities is the application of a person-centered approach to assisting people to improve their own lives. This application uses a quality-of-life conceptual framework designed to maximize the involvement and perspective of the person. The framework and its application are discussed in the next sections of this chapter. The concepts associated with this framework are applied to the processes of assessment, planning, intervention, and evaluation. (See Renwick et al., 1994; Renwick & I. Brown, 1996, for a full description.) The goal of the application is to use these quality-of-life concepts to draw out the uniqueness of each person's life. To achieve this goal, our quality-of-life concepts are adapted to the individual circumstances of each person in an attempt to hear about and see what is real to people, what things are important in their lives, and what things make life truly enjoyable for them.

Major Features of the CHP Conceptual Framework

The CHP framework views quality of life as arising out of the continuous interrelationship between personal characteristics of an individual and the characteristics of his or her environment. Many personal characteristics occur by chance; many others result from life choices or from both factors. These characteristics change to varying degrees over time and the lifespan. Similarly, environmental characteristics that affect a person's life occur by chance or by choice, or a combination of the two factors, and are also subject to change over time. Therefore, quality of life is a fluid and flexible phenomenon that is uniquely experienced by each individual.

Quality of life is formally defined within the CHP framework as "the degree to which the person enjoys the important possibilities of his/her life" (Renwick et al., 1994, p. 35). In everyday terms, it means "how good your life is for you." As the three major areas (i.e., being, belonging, and becoming) and the nine subareas of quality of life associated with the CHP model are discussed elsewhere (Renwick & I. Brown, 1996), they are only summarized here in Table 1.1.

Table 1.1

The Centre for Health Promotion
Conceptual Framework for Quality of Life

Domains and Subdomains	Brief Description of Aspects of Life
Being	
Physical Being	Physical health, mobility or agility, fitness, appearance, nutrition
Psychological Being	Feelings about self, self-confidence, self-control, initiating positive behaviors, coping with anxiety
Spiritual Being	Having values to live by (e.g., sense of right and wrong), transcending daily life experiences (e.g., through music, nature), celebrating special life events (e.g., birthdays, Thanksgiving, and other cultural or religious holidays or events)
Belonging	
Physical Belonging	Feeling "at home" with one's physical environment, having and displaying personal possessions, having safety and privacy
Social Belonging	Having meaningful relationships with others (e.g., partner or close other, friends, family, coworkers, neighbors)
Community Belonging	Having access to public events or resources available to members of one's community (e.g., work, education, money, services, stores, entertainment)
Becoming	
Practical Becoming	Doing practical, purposeful activities (e.g., household chores, paid or volunteer work, school or other programs, self-care, looking after others)
Leisure Becoming	Doing leisure recreational or social activities (planned or unplanned), engaging in hobbies, having breaks from daily routines, going on vacations
Growth Becoming	Learning new information, improving or maintaining existing skills, coping with life, adapting to changes in one's life

Determinants of and Influences on Quality of Life

The degree to which a person experiences "quality" or "goodness" in each of the nine subareas is determined jointly by how much *importance* and how much *satisfaction* (enjoyment) the person attaches to each one (see Figure 1.1). How good, or not good, life is for the person is also jointly affected by two moderating influences: *decision making* (choices) and the *range of opportunities available* from which to make decisions and choices (see Figure 1.1). Together, these two moderating influences constitute the degree of *personal control* the person perceives he or she has over his or her life (Renwick & I. Brown, 1996).

Unique Aspects of the CHP Conceptual Framework

The content of several of the nine domains in the CHP conceptual framework is similar to content of other conceptual approaches that focus on individuals (e.g., R. I. Brown,

---

Determinants
Perceived Importance + Perceived Satisfaction => Quality of Life
Moderating Influences
Decision Making + Opportunities Available => Personal Control

---

Figure 1.1. The Centre for Health Promotion conceptual framework for quality of life: Determinants and moderators of quality of life.

1996; Felce & Perry, 1996). However, two domains, spiritual being and community belonging, are emphasized less within other conceptual frameworks and merit special mention here. (Other distinctive aspects of this approach are noted in Renwick & I. Brown, 1996.)

Spiritual Being. Spirituality is a complex but essential dimension of a life that is experienced as good and fulfilling (Kroeker, 1997). Yet it has received very little direct attention in the quality-of-life literature (Coulter, 1997). Accordingly, the CHP framework includes spirituality as a central dimension of the "being" area of life.

As summarized in Table 1.1, spiritual being encompasses those aspects of life associated with personal spirituality. It includes moral and ethical principles (i.e., values), celebration of significant life events, and transcending experiences. In essence, spiritual being focuses on four major intertwining strands of an individual's unique, personal experiences in his or her world: (a) standards to live by, (b) a deep sense of connectedness, (c) a sense of place, purpose, and meaning in life, and (d) engagement in rituals that celebrate life (Aune & De Marinis, 1996; Bell, 1992; Bellingham, Cohen, Jones, & Spaniol, 1989; Frankl, 1968; Kroeker, 1997).

The feelings of peace, comfort, harmony, and hope for the future that usually accompany the positive experience of spirituality add enrichment to the person's life. An individual's experience of spirituality may or may not be associated with the practice of a formal religion or religious tradition. However, it is usually strongly influenced by the person's culture or society (Kroeker, 1997; Mandy, 1997; Algado, Gregori, & Egan, 1997). For example, Mandy discusses the medicine wheel, a spiritual symbol sacred and meaningful to some First Nations people of Canada. Algado et al. note that *cosmovision*, "an ancient system of beliefs which describe the place and purpose of all things in the universe" shared by many Mayans, "informs [individuals] of essential values and ways of living" (p. 140).

Most individuals have standards or values that guide the ways in which they live. These standards include moral and ethical principles that are typically influenced by their society, culture, and life experiences (Kroeker, 1997) and often (though not necessarily) by their religious traditions. These standards may take many forms and range from simple to elaborate. A common one is telling the truth most of the time but suspending this standard, on occasion, to spare the feelings of a loved one in relatively harmless matters (e.g., a new haircut). Another example of a standard to live by was clearly articulated by a young woman with a developmental disability who participated in the early developmental stages of our conceptual model: "Everyone makes mistakes, so always give the other person a second chance." Altruistic behavior, such as helping strangers in troubled or extreme circumstances (e.g., due to poverty, accidents, fires, and floods) also exemplifies such personal values.

Spirituality is characterized by a profound sense of connectedness. For an individual this may mean connectedness at one or more levels, namely, with oneself, others, nature, the cosmos, and to a creator or a higher power (Algado et al., 1997; Unruh, 1997). This sense of close linkage often gives the person an appreciation of his or her place in the world. It also contributes to a sense of meaning and purpose in life. This feeling of connectedness is achieved in different ways by individuals, often through activities that allow one to "stand apart from everyday life and to reflect on one's place in that life" (Unruh, p. 157). For some people this may mean sitting on the dock at the lake watching the sunset; for others it may mean tending a garden, playing the piano, or participating in a religious service.

Spirituality is often experienced in the context of rituals that observe important life events and occasions. For some people, in some cultures, this involves celebrating national holidays such as Thanksgiving and Labor Day (i.e., in North America). Many people celebrate birthdays, wedding anniversaries, and school graduations, and also observe the death of loved ones with rituals. Religious festivals such as Ramadan, Yom Kippur, and Christmas involve religious ritual practices and services. Rituals usually require the inclusion of special foods, activities, and the company of special others as a way of distinguishing significant life occasions and events from ordinary life events. Such rituals can foster or reaffirm a sense of connectedness, meaning in life, continuity between one's past and present life, and hope for the future (Aune & De Martinis, 1996; Bell, 1992).

Community Belonging. Several other conceptualizations of quality of life include some attention to community participation, integration, or inclusion. (For a review, see Hughes & Hwang, 1996.) Typically these approaches focus on access and use of community activities, services, and resources. The CHP framework proposes a somewhat different approach to this aspect of quality of life.

The area of life encompassed by community belonging emphasizes the *quality of the relationship* the individual experiences between him- or herself and particular aspects of the community environment. Community belonging refers to how much the person feels a sense of real attachment to, stake in, or is a part of all the places, events, services, and resources that help define his or her particular community. This domain is concerned with how much the individual views the local park as "his" park, and the neighborhood stores as "her" stores. It is concerned with the person's sense of connectedness with the same resources (i.e., services, events, programs, public places, and activities) that anyone else (with or without disabilities) in the community could have information about and be able to access. The range of these resources is quite broad and includes: social and health services, educational and recreation programs and facilities, adequate income and employment, and community events and activities (e.g., eating in a restaurant, attending a movie or concert, shopping, and going to a hockey or baseball game) (Renwick & I. Brown, 1996).

Person-Centered Measures

The *Quality of Life Instrument Package* (CHP, 1997) for adults with developmental disabilities, like the CHP conceptual framework, embodies a person-centered approach to quality of life. As material related to the instrument package is presented elsewhere (Raphael et al., 1996; Renwick & I. Brown, 1996) and is in preparation for publication, it is only briefly outlined here.

The measures of quality of life included in the package have a strong theoretical basis. They are derived directly from the concepts summarized in Table 1.1, Figure 1.1, and in the previous sections about the CHP framework.

This package reflects an endeavor to maintain a person-centered focus by considering, as its central and most important sources of information, the Interview and Personal Control Questionnaire carried out with the person with disability. These two structured sets of items address key aspects of life and provide both qualitative and quantitative data. Two other measures are also used. The Other Person Questionnaire is a subjective measure completed by one or more others who well know the person with disability. The Assessor Questionnaire, a more objective measure, is completed by a trained assessor. These measures each provide information about the person being assessed from two other perspectives.

The instrumentation preserves the emphasis on the perspective of the person with developmental disability in another way. The individual's quality-of-life scores consist of the satisfaction (enjoyment) the person experiences in each life domain weighted by the importance to the individual of the concerns associated with that domain. Qualitative information that is collected is also weighted in a similar way. The concept of importance blends two interconnected ideas that are central to the person-environment interaction: (a) how relevant each aspect of life is to the person's own characteristics, the characteristics of the environment in which the person lives, and to the ways in which life is lived; and (b) the degree to which the person values that aspect of life. This kind of weighting (see Stanley & Ashok, 1988) is now considered to be characteristic of good quality-of-life measurement methods (Cummins, 1996). The degree to which the individual exerts personal control over life is based on information concerning the person's decision making and opportunities within each of the nine life domains. The instrumentation taps into the person's own views of how much personal control he or she has in daily life activities and concerns.

The person-centered approach embodied in this instrument package allows for aggregation of individuals' data. For instance, aggregation of information can be appropriate when assessing how good life is for people living in a group home, when evaluating programs that include people with disabilities, or when using data from large-scale studies to estimate the effects of governmental policy on individuals' lives. However, because of the way in which the instrument package is designed and scored, the potential to identify and examine the subjective view of each individual is preserved and represented within the aggregated information.

Using a Person-Centered Approach to Enhance Quality of Life

When using a person-centered approach to improve quality of life, an individual's *personal* quality of life becomes the ultimate goal of the endeavor. The very reason for all plans and interventions is not just to attempt to help improve the person's life overall, but rather to help the person consider and experience that his or her life has been improved. If plans or interventions are offering inadequate support to the person such that the person does not experience life as improved (or at the very least, as being as good as it was), this goal is not being achieved.

One method of applying a person-centered quality-of-life approach is outlined in Table 1.2, which summarizes the application of the CHP framework to facilitate quality enhancement. This four-step method combines information from a person-centered quality-of-life assessment and information from various other sources collected by practitioners and applies it to person-centered planning, intervention, and evaluation. The method is by no means unique, but the details of the method will be as different for each person as each person's life is different from the lives of others.

Details concerning the application of all four steps outlined in Table 1.2 are discussed by Renwick et al. (1994). Several general guidelines for using this person-centered process are summarized in Table 1.3.

Future Directions

There has been a tremendous growth of interest in the concept of quality of life in recent years. The field of developmental disabilities appears to have provided particularly fertile ground for nurturing this emerging concept. Still, meaningful applications of the quality-of-life concept to social and health services are only beginning to emerge. One method to help improve lives has been outlined here, but credible, specific methods to help improve the lives of people with developmental disabilities have not yet been sufficiently developed and evaluated (Renwick, Brown, Rootman, & Nagler, 1996). A person-centered quality-of-life approach can be very helpful in developing new applications of this kind. Quality of life of children with disabilities, family quality of life, and quality of life of adults moving from institutions to communities are only a few of the areas that can potentially benefit from the development and application of a person-centered approach to quality of life.

Adopting a person-centered approach to quality of life does weight the various levels (i.e., micro-, meso-, and macrolevels) for considering and understanding quality of life in favor of the microlevel. Nevertheless, it recognizes the necessity of understanding how factors at all levels affect how individuals experience quality of life. Thus it serves as an entry point for studying the linkages among factors, at all three levels, that influence "goodness" within people's lives. This kind of research appears to involve a complex set of questions and methods that remain to be explored. One example would be to examine the linkages between individual quality of life, the quality of family life, and the community environment in which the family lives (e.g., attitudes toward people with disabilities, extent of natural and professional supports, availability of and accessibility of resources needed by the individual and family). These new areas for research are interesting and promising from a theoretical point of view, but they also have a great deal of potential for practical applications that can add enrichment to the lives of people, with or without disabilities.

Table 1.2

Applying the Centre for Health Promotion Conceptual Framework

Overall Goal	**Increase quality within the life of the individual from his or her own perspective**
Step 1:	
Assessment	**Determine for the nine areas of life and associated aspects of life (see Table 1.1):**

1. What is important in the person's life
2. How satisfied the person is now with the areas and aspects of life important to him or her
3. (a) The extent to which the person makes choices and decisions in the areas important to him or her
   (b) The extent to which the person wants to make choices and decisions in the areas important to him or her
4. The range of opportunities now available in the areas important to him or her

Step 2:	
Program Planning	**Set out:**

1. Methods to help the person increase satisfaction in the areas of life important to him or her
2. Methods to help the person decrease dissatisfaction in the areas of life that are not important to him or her
3. (a) The extent to which the person wants to or can deal with decisions and choices in areas important to him or her
   (b) Methods to help and support the person in making decisions and choices in the areas important to him or her
4. Methods of making available other opportunities within areas important to him or her which can be explored (with or without assistance or support)

Step 3:	
Intervention	**Implement:**

1. Methods to increase satisfaction in the areas of life that are important to the person
2. Methods to decrease dissatisfaction in the areas not important to the person
3. Methods to achieve the degree of decision making and choices the person wants in the areas important to him or her
4. A variety of opportunities within the environment that the person may explore (with or without assistance or support) in the areas important to him or her

Step 4:	
Evaluation	**Address the following questions:**

1. Has satisfaction increased in the areas of life important to the person?
2. Has dissatisfaction decreased in areas of life not important to the person?
3. Has making decisions and choices increased to the extent that the person wants?
4. Have a variety of opportunities been made available that the individual might explore, with or without assistance or support?

Note: From "Linking a Conceptual Approach to Service Provision," by R. Renwick, I. Brown and D. Raphael, 1994, *Journal on Developmental Disabilities, 3*(2), p. 39. Copyright 1994 by Ontario Association on Developmental Disabilities. Adapted and used with permission.

Table 1.3

Enhancing Quality of Life:
Guidelines for Using a Person-Centered Approach

1. For each of the four steps (in Table 1.2), the person is as active a participant as possible and his or her perspective is most important.

2. The person is understood in the context of his or her environment. Thus it is important to evaluate (a) to what extent the person's environment contributes to and promotes quality of life and (b) how the environment can be used or changed to enrich the person's quality of life.

3. As well as noting areas of life needing quality enhancement, it is important to identify, maintain, and support (as appropriate) those areas currently important or very satisfying to the person.

4. Increasing satisfaction within areas important to the person is often difficult and achieved over a long period of time. Giving some attention to goals more easily achieved (e.g., decreasing dissatis-faction in areas less important and/or more easily changed) may be rewarding in the meantime.

5. Individuals differ with respect to how much they want to or can handle decision making and choices in the various areas of life. In addition, people also differ considerably in their comfort with choosing from among many (or few) alternative opportunities. It is important for the person and the service provider to recognize and accommodate the person's level of comfort with these issues of personal control.

References

Algado, S. S., Gregori, J. M. R., & Egan, M. (1997). Spirituality in a refugee camp. *Canadian Journal of Occupational Therapy, 62,* 138-145.

Aune, M. B., & De Marinis, V. (1996). *Religious and social rituals: Interdisciplinary explorations.* Albany: State University of New York Press.

Bach, M., & Rioux, M. H. (1996). Social well-being: A framework for quality of life research. In R. Renwick, I. Brown, & M. Nagler (Eds.), *Quality of life in health promotion and rehabilitation: Conceptual approaches, issues, and applications* (pp. 63-74). Thousand Oaks, CA: Sage.

Bell, C. M. (1992). *Ritual theory, ritual practice.* New York: Oxford University Press.

Bellingham, R., Cohen, B., Jones, T., & Spaniol, L. (1989). Connectedness: Some skills for spiritual health. *American Journal of Health Promotion, 4,* 18-31.

Brown, I. (1994). Promoting quality within service delivery systems [Editorial]. *Journal on Developmental Disabilities, 3*(2), i-iii.

Brown, I., & Renwick, R. (in press). Understanding what we mean by quality of life. *Journal on Developmental Disabilities.*

Brown, I., Renwick, R., & Nagler, M. (1996). The centrality of quality of life in health promotion and rehabilitation. In R. Renwick, I. Brown, & M. Nagler (Eds.), *Quality of life in health promotion and rehabilitation: Conceptual approaches, issues, and applications* (pp. 3-13). Thousand Oaks, CA: Sage.

Brown, R. I. (1996). People with developmental disabilities: Applying quality of life to assessment and intervention. In R. Renwick, I. Brown, & M. Nagler (Eds.), *Quality of life in health promotion and rehabilitation: Conceptual approaches, issues, and applications* (pp. 253-267). Thousand Oaks, CA: Sage.

Brown, R. I. (Ed.). (1997). *Quality of life for persons with disabilities.* London: Chapman & Hall.

Brown, R. I., Bayer, M. B., & MacFarlane, C. (1988). Quality of life amongst handicapped adults. In R. I. Brown (Ed.), *Quality of life for handicapped people: A series in rehabilitation education* (pp. 107-123). London: Croom Helm.

Butterworth, J., Steere, D. E., & Whitney-Thomas, J. (1997). In R. Schalock (Ed.), *Quality of life: Vol. 2. Application to persons with disabilities* (pp. 5-23). Washington, DC: American Association on Mental Retardation.

Centre for Health Promotion. (1997). *Quality of life instrument package.* Toronto: Centre for Health Promotion, Quality of Life Research Unit, University of Toronto.

Coulter, D. L. (1997). Health-related application of quality of life. In R. Schalock (Ed.), *Quality of life: Vol. 2. Application to persons with disabilities* (pp. 95-103). Washington, DC: American Association on Mental Retardation.

Cummins, R. A. (1996, July). *Quality of life measurement: Generic and psychometric issues.* Paper presented at the 10th World Congress of the International Association for the Scientific Study of Intellectual Disabilities, Helsinki, Finland.

Day, H., & Jankey, S. G. (1996). Lessons from the literature: Toward a holistic model of quality of life. In R. Renwick, I. Brown, & M. Nagler (Eds.), *Quality of life in health promotion and rehabilitation: Conceptual approaches, issues, and applications* (pp. 39-50). Thousand Oaks, CA: Sage.

Felce, D., & Perry, J. (1996). Exploring current conceptions of quality of life: A model for people with and without disabilities. In R. Renwick, I. Brown, & M. Nagler (Eds.), *Quality of life in health promotion and rehabilitation: Conceptual approaches, issues, and applications* (pp. 51-62). Thousand Oaks, CA: Sage.

Felce, D., & Perry, J. (1997). Quality of life: The scope of the term and its breadth of measurement. In R. I. Brown (Ed.), *Quality of life for persons with disabilities* (pp. 56-71). London: Chapman & Hall.

Frankl, V. (1968). *Man's search for meaning: An introduction to logotherapy* (I. Lasch, Trans.). Boston: Beacon Press. (Original work published 1946)

Goode, D. (Ed.). (1994a). *Quality of life for persons with disabilities: International issues and perspectives.* New York: Brookline.

Goode, D. (1994b). *A world without words: The social construction of children born deaf and blind.* Philadelphia: Temple University Press.

Goode, D. (1997). Quality of life as international disability policy: Implications for international research. In R. Schalock (Ed.), *Quality of life: Vol. 2. Application to persons with disabilities* (pp. 211-221). Washington, DC: American Association on Mental Retardation.

Green, L. W., & Kreuter, M. W. (1991). *Health promotion planning: An educational and environmental approach.* Mountain View, CA: Mayfield.

Hughes, C., & Hwang, B. (1996). Attempts to conceptualize and measure quality of life. In R. Schalock (Ed.), *Quality of life: Vol. 1. Conceptualization and measurement* (pp. 51-61). Washington, DC: American Association on Mental Retardation.

Kroeker, P. T. (1997). Spirituality and occupational therapy in a secular culture. *Canadian Journal of Occupational Therapy, 62,* 122-126.

Lindstrom, B. (1992). Quality of life: A model for evaluating health for all. *Soz Praventivmed, 37,* 301-306.

Lord, J., & Farlow, D. (1990). A study of personal empowerment: Implications for health promotion. *Health Promotion, 29,* 2-8.

Mandy, P. (1997). Traditional medicine and practices for native people [Letter to the editor]. *Canadian Journal of Occupational Therapy, 64,* 106.

Oullette-Kuntz, H., & McCreary, B. (1996). Quality of life assessment for persons with severe developmental disabilities. In R. Renwick, I. Brown, & M. Nagler (Eds.), *Quality of life in health promotion and rehabilitation: Conceptual approaches, issues, and applications* (pp. 268-277). Thousand Oaks, CA: Sage.

Parmenter, T. (1996). The use of quality of life as a construct for social and health policy development. In R. Renwick, I. Brown, & M. Nagler (Eds.), *Quality of life in health promotion and rehabilitation: Conceptual approaches, issues, and applications* (pp. 89-103). Thousand Oaks, CA: Sage.

Raphael, D., Brown, I., Renwick, R., & Rootman, I. (1996). Assessing the quality of life of persons with developmental disabilities: Description of a new model, measuring instruments, and initial findings. *International Journal of Disability, Development, and Education, 43*(1), 25-42.

Renwick, R. (1998). Quality of life: A guiding framework for practice with adults who have developmental disabilities. In S. Bachner & M. Ross (Eds.), *Adults with developmental disabilities: Client-centered treatment with functional occupational therapy outcomes* (pp. 23-41). Rockville, MD: American Occupational Therapy Foundation.

Renwick, R., & Brown, I. (1996). The Centre for Health Promotion's conceptual approach to quality of life: Being, belonging, and becoming. In R. Renwick, I. Brown, & M. Nagler (Eds.), *Quality of life in health promotion and rehabilitation: Conceptual approaches, issues, and applications* (pp. 75-86). Thousand Oaks, CA: Sage.

Renwick, R., Brown, I., & Nagler, M. (Eds.). (1996). *Quality of life in health promotion and rehabilitation: Conceptual approaches, issues, and applications.* Thousand Oaks, CA: Sage.

Renwick, R., Brown, I., & Raphael, D. (1994). Linking a conceptual approach to service provision. *Journal on Developmental Disabilities, 3*(2), 32-44.

Renwick, R., Brown, I., Rootman, I., & Nagler, M. (1996). Conceptualization, research, and application: Future directions. In R. Renwick, I. Brown, & M. Nagler (Eds.), *Quality of life in health promotion and rehabilitation: Conceptual approaches, issues, and applications* (pp. 357-367). Thousand Oaks, CA: Sage.

Rioux, M. H. (1996). Overcoming the social construction of inequality as a prerequisite to quality of life. In R. Renwick, I. Brown, & M. Nagler (Eds.), *Quality of life in health promotion and rehabilitation: Conceptual approaches, issues, and applications* (pp. 119-131). Thousand Oaks, CA: Sage.

Roeher Institute. (1996). *Disability, community, and society: Exploring the links.* North York, Ontario: Author.

Schalock, R. L. (Ed.) (1996). *Quality of life: Vol. 1. Conceptualization and measurement.* Washington, DC: American Association on Mental Retardation.

Schalock, R. L. (Ed.). (1997a). *Quality of life: Vol. 2. Application to persons with disabilities.* Washington, DC: American Association on Mental Retardation.

Schalock, R. L. (1997b). Can the concept of quality of life make a difference? In R. Schalock (Ed.), *Quality of life: Vol. 2. Application to persons with disabilities* (pp. 245-267). Washington, DC: American Association on Mental Retardation.

Schalock, R. L., Keith, K., Hoffman, K., & Karan, O. (1989). Quality of life: Its measurement and use. *Mental Retardation, 27,* 25-31.

Stanley, B., & Ashok, R. (1988). Evaluating the quality of life of people with mental handicaps: A social validation study. *Mental Handicap Research, 1,* 197-210.

Timmons, V. (1997). Quality of life—issues for children with handicaps. In R. I. Brown (Ed.), *Quality of life for people with disabilities* (pp. 183-200). Cheltenham, United Kingdom: Stanley Thornes.

Townsend, E. (1993). Occupational therapy's social vision. *Canadian Journal of Occupational Therapy, 60,* 174-184.

Unruh, A. M. (1997). Spirituality and occupation: Garden musings and the Himalayan blue poppy. *Canadian Journal of Occupational Therapy, 62,* 156-160.

Woodill, G., Renwick, R., Brown, I., & Raphael, D. (1994). Being, belonging, becoming: An approach to quality of life of persons with developmental disabilities. In D. Goode (Ed.), *Quality of life for persons with disabilities: International issues and perspectives* (pp. 57-74). New York: Brookline.

Author Note

The Quality of Life Project is funded by the Ministry of Community and Social Services, Government of Ontario, Canada. However, the views expressed in this chapter are those of the authors and do not necessarily represent the views of the Ministry or the Government of Ontario.

My Quality of Life as I See It

Robert Groulx
People First of Montreal

Robert Doré
University of Quebec at Montreal

Louise Doré
Carrefour d'Education Populaire de Pointe St. Charles
Montreal, Quebec, Canada

Editors' Note: In his interview with Louise Doré and Robert Doré, Robert Groulx, president of the People First Movement of Montreal, explains what he means by the expression quality of life, *compares the quality of life experienced during different periods in his life, presents the principal aspects of his current quality of life, and finally identifies some elements to consider in order to improve the quality of life of people with intellectual disabilities.*

Louise: What do the words quality of life mean to you, Robert?

Robert: To me, quality of life means to feel good and to have what is needed to cope with your life in the best way possible, like, for example, having the right to go to school, to be able to work, to live in a decent dwelling that is not too expensive (not a slum), and to have rights to health care. (In Canada and in Quebec, every citizen is covered by Social Security and Public Health Care, which means that everyone has a right to welfare and to free medical care.) It's having enough to eat.

To me, quality of life is also being able to live in peace and harmony with others, without discrimination, without feeling differences between the races or the sexes or between handicapped and nonhandicapped people. It is to feel accepted as we are. It is also to have the greatest control possible over our own lives.

Louise: You are now 53 years old. Can we say that your quality of life has changed a lot or evolved over the course of your life?

Robert: I was placed in an institution (what in Quebec was called a crèche) when I was born in 1944. My mother was what was called a fille-mère (an "unwed mother"), and she was pushed to abandon me to the care of the Hôpital de la Miséricorde where she gave birth to me. Until the age of 19, I lived in different institutions and also in a foster home from the ages of 9 to 12.

When I think of those years and of my quality of life then, I must say that it was not worth much. It's true that we were housed, fed, washed, and nursed by the nuns who ran the institution where we lived, but the education we received was worth nothing. In other words, we did not receive any education. They taught us nothing really. We remained seated in classrooms for entire days. We waited for time to go by.

Sometimes, we went into the courtyard, but it was walled in, and we could not leave or go out. We were all the same and all treated the same. There were some people with intellectual disabilities and others who were mentally ill, and we were all mixed together. There were many people who screamed and yelled, and they were placed in cells. Days were long and extremely boring, and there was no hope in any of our lives.

At 19, I could not take this life anymore, locked up this way in an institution. I began to try to escape. To me, it was like a prison. I escaped three times, and each time the police brought me back, until they decided finally to move me to another institution. Then they placed me in a college where I lived and worked at the same time. I worked at the kitchen and in the laundry. It was my social worker who decided to change my place of residence. But he did not help me with this transition. So it was very stressful and painful for me. I developed stomach ulcers. Sure, it was less boring, because at least my days were occupied with work. But it was all new to me, and it happened too quickly. It was too big a change. I did not know anything and it made me tense and vulnerable and I had no one to talk to. Sometimes I asked myself if in the end it had been a good idea to change. It seemed as though I had only changed from one bad place to another. I found my life as difficult to live as before and I felt depressed. Finally they suggested that I leave the college and live somewhere else (room and board) for small periods of time. I accepted. Those periods away from the college helped me. It was like taking a vacation. And I lived this way for 5 years.

At 24, I tried something new. I moved into my first apartment. I lived alone, without anyone telling me what to do, but also without any help. It was a new life for me, and I wanted to try it—to live on my own. But it was hard, very hard because everything was new to me. I knew nothing of real life or how to do the things that an ordinary adult does, and I had no one to show me. I managed as well as I could, but my quality of life was just as mediocre as before.

Finally I entered a work program [protected workshop] where I was taught woodwork, and there were people who helped me learn to function better in my day-to-day life. It was finally an improvement, the beginning of a normal life. But I was alone. I had no friends at all. When I was young, the nuns had given me affection and replaced the parents I did not have. But now my life was empty, as empty as the apartment in which I lived.

After 5 years I quit the program, because I wanted to do something else. I received welfare and a work supplement that I earned, but it was not enough for my needs (rent, food, clothing, medication, etc.). So I looked for other work. But for more than 5 years, I found nothing. I found myself without work, living alone in an apartment, without a social life, without anything. My quality of life was truly mediocre. I continued to have stomach ulcers. My life was hell.

I lived that way for a long time, over a number of years. I passed my time in the doctor's office, curing my ulcers, and I couldn't work because of that. I was going in circles.

One day I met someone who, like me, had lived in an institution, had a similar history to mine, and understood me. He was an activist in an association and suggested that I join the Quebec Association for the Mentally Retarded. There I felt welcomed and respected for the first time in my life. I felt validated. I joined an advisory committee formed of people who, like me, had lived in an institution, and we shared our experiences. We proposed changes to the association in the way of seeing the work that needed to be done with the people with intellectual disabilities to improve their quality of life. We participated in conferences and all kinds of meetings where we met many interesting people with whom we developed friendships. That was a big improvement in our own quality of life. To me, it was a gift: all these people who respected me and exchanged ideas with me and who included me in their activities.

Since this time I can say that I have had some quality in my life. I was doing something I enjoyed. I shared my experiences and my thoughts, and I worked for a future, not just for me but also for the others.

At that time [beginning of 1980], with others like me, I worked to start the People First Movement in Canada and in Quebec. Today, I am the president of the People First Movement of Montreal. Our role is to be the spokesperson for people who have intellectual handicaps and to defend their rights. We try to bring public awareness, and we do promotion work. I work hard in this movement, and this brings me a lot of personal satisfaction.

When I think of my quality of life today, I can say that it is like night and day compared to what it was. I feel that I have come out of the darkness. I feel that I have taken my own place in life, and I am happy with the life I live now. Of course I am not rich. I am on social welfare. I work at the movement, and I get an income supplement for my work. I have enough to eat. I have a home that I like, comfortable without luxury. I have a TV, a VCR, a sound system. I listen to music, and I am happy in my home.

I have many friends, especially within the movement. But I also have other friends with whom I go to restaurants or shopping centers. They come to my place, we play cards, we watch videos, we have a lot of fun together. At the age of 51, I reconnected with my mother, and I see her regularly. And this is a great joy for me. On the love front, I am not looking for an intimate relationship. At 25 years of age, I had a broken heart which left its mark, but I am satisfied with other types of affection that I have in my life now.

Finally, I can say today that I am a happy man and that I am satisfied with my quality of life. Of course, like everyone else, there are some things I would like to improve. But that is OK.

Sometimes I feel a little insecure in the metro [public transportation]. For example, sometimes I feel like people are staring at me; that hurts. As far as work goes, I am interested in what I do, but I would rather have a real salary than supplemental measures of employment from the government. It would make me feel more validated.

These last few years, I have received recognition and validation of my work from the people who are active in the associative movement. I have received prizes at conferences. This gives me great pride and joy. It does some good to feel appreciated and feel that the work we do has some value for others. It motivates me to continue and to excel.

Louise: As a human rights advocate within the People First Movement, describe what aspects you want us to pay attention to when we think of the quality of life of people with intellectual disabilities.

Robert: I would like people to realize how much it hurts us to be "labeled" and to be told things like "you are an imbecile," "you are mentally deficient," "you are retarded," or "you are crazy." When I was young, it happened to me many times, but it also happened when I was an adolescent or an adult. Today it happens less often, but sometimes I feel like people are staring at me thinking these things in their head; it hurts me every time. I experience that often in public places, restaurants, stores, buses. I also often see such stares or hear these expressions from those who are around people even more handicapped than I, and this discourages me and takes away any means I have to defend myself or the others against this. I feel it inside and it hurts. I feel diminished and humiliated without knowing why.

When professionals [psychiatrists, psychologists, social workers, doctors, teachers], all those who work with people like me who have learning difficulties or adaptive problems, and when, in addition, parents talk about us as "mentally retarded" persons, it's as though they block our entrance to society. When you think of the work environment, for example, if you carry the label "mentally retarded," there's a strong chance that you will find yourself in a work program. Or the employers might say to themselves, "Oh no, I don't want a mentally retarded employee," or some might say, "OK, I accept this person," but they will not treat you like any other employee, and you can also be isolated by the other workers.

To carry the label "mentally retarded" is very hard. Often you even start to think you really are. This happened to me. You tell yourself that you are handicapped, and this stops you from trying things, from taking the first step. It takes your self-confidence away.

Another example is in the area of education. Children who carry the label "mentally retarded" are refused from classrooms and regular schools. They are segregated. Today there are many parents who struggle and fight so that their child can go to the same school as the others or in the same classrooms as the "normal" children (who are not always that "normal," in my opinion). But it doesn't amount to much, and these children continue to be separated from the others.

To me, it is as if the label makes the problem even worse. You have enough to handle, just having difficulties in learning, in functioning, or in adapting. The fact of carrying this label adds a huge weight on your shoulders. It does not help you to advance. So, when I think of quality of life, the fact of carrying that label is a negative element. One has the impression that attached to the label "mentally retarded" is the idea of "burden on society" or "burden on parents and on professionals." That does not help you to feel good and to have a positive self-image. And I would really like it if people paid attention to that and to what it feels like to be labeled.

In regards to quality of life, I would say that what we really want is to live like other people, to work, to have a real salary, and to have recreational activities with others, not just with handicapped people. We want to be able to develop our talents and capacities and to have projects. We want to have the respect of others and also help or support when we need it. Because sometimes, without this help, we are blocked. We can't manage or advance on our own.

Let's take transport, for example. Transport to me is very important. You need it to go to school, to go to work, to go out, to go shopping, and many other things. If you don't have a means of transport, or if you can't pay for it, or if you can't manage alone and you need help, like someone to accompany you, or again if you need special adapted services, well! You stay home, and there is nothing you can do about it. And it inhibits your personal development; it stops you from advancing.

I also think that people with an intellectual handicap, maybe more than others, need supportive people in their lives, children as well as adults. It can be concrete support to function as normally as possible and based on what the person wants. It can also be psychological support or moral support to encourage us to try things and also at times when things do not go so well. To me, one of the most important things is that the support provided by people—whether it be professionals or volunteers, parents or friends—be given with affection and love, and not with pity or charity. Because love or affection gives us a boost. It makes us feel good, and it brings us joy; it makes us cheerful and happy when we talk of quality of life. And it is what we should aim for, that the person be as happy as possible.

Quality of Life:
A Personal Perspective From Finland

Sami Helle
Finnish Association on Mental Retardation
Helsinki, Finland

My name is Sami Helle, and I am a project worker. I am 24 years old. I have been in a number of schools in France, the United States, and Finland. After school I went to work in Vaihetyokeskus for 2 years and then to where I am now, Kehitysvammaliito.

Friends

Yes, I have friends who are really important to me. Niina is my best friend, because I can talk to her about anything. She will not tell anybody else about my problems. We just talk about what happens to each other. Our friends accept us for what we are because we are the same as others, and I don't think that they are at all different from me.

Yes, I can tell them what I think about them, because I am always telling them the truth about everything I see in the world today. I see my friends a lot. They are everything to me; without them I don't get ahead in my life. They are what makes me happy. When I invite them to come to visit me, we don't always have a lot of time to see each other. Love is the number-one thing in a friendship. A good friend is one who doesn't tell lies about you behind your back; that is a friend, a really good one. Yes, I would want to have more friends.

Family and Parents

I see my parents every weekend, because they are the number-one thing in my life. My cousins I see about once a month; I miss them, because I don't see them a lot. I like my parents a lot, because they are my life. Yes, I can tell them all my problems. They do not control my life. Because I am a person, nobody will tell me what to do; it is the truth that I am my own boss. In my job I see that I can help my friends with mental retardation. That is why I am in this job, to make the world a better place for mentally retarded people. I will not rest before we have the same rights as other people have. Where I live is the best place I could be right now and for the future. If I did not have this chance, I would not have the place where I live right now.

Activities

Yes, we have some activities that we do in the house where I live. The activities are floor hockey and cruising about. Yes, I get all the help that I need in floor hockey. Yes, I am really happy in the clubs that I go to. They are really fun.

Love

Yes, loving somebody is a really important thing, because I don't have anybody right now. No, I don't have the time to go out with anybody right now, and, besides, others do not listen to what I say. That really hurts me. I am not with anybody right now. This is my answer to all the questions on relationships—that I do not have one.

I love music and theater a lot; they are close to my heart. I believe in Christ a lot, because he is the founder of the planet Earth. My life is worth living, because I have my parents and my job. That is the best thing in life to live for. My life is really lonely, because I don't have a girlfriend with whom I can share my happiness and loneliness.

Ideas of My Life

When we are happy, everybody does their job in the house where I live now. The best thing right now in my life is my job. That is all I need right now. No, I don't feel happy, because I don't have a girlfriend who would make me happy. Yes, I get hurt easily when people don't want to be with me; that hurts a lot inside of me. Yes, people like me a lot because they know me. People who don't know me do not know anything about us mentally retarded people. My life has been a lot like a road; it has its turns, and I hate it when people do not listen to us because they think that we are really stupid. That is not the truth about us. We are the same kind of people. I am mentally retarded. I am proud of what I am because I am a person with the same goals as anybody. If people do not believe what we stand for, they are really dumb. I hate people who are ignoring us because we have something wrong with us, but that does not make us different from everybody else.

I am working in an office right now. If I can work in an office, anybody else who has mental retardation should have the same chance, because I think that the world is made for everybody, not just normal people.

There should be love, not hate, between us, because that is the main reason I do not understand the human mind. When it does not understand us, who has the big problems in our lives? I hate that we are left out from all the decisions; we should make the decisions that affect our lives. I am really happy that people like my parents are willing to help me understand what is my problem. The truth about my life is that everybody has been really bad against me in school, and the kids called me names, like idiot, dummy, and many other names that I cannot now think of because they are really bad memories.

I hate these people who are against me. What I have done to these people? I hated to see things that I saw when I was put in the back of the class, because they didn't want to be with me. That is the worst kind of act that I think of. I am not an idiot who is just for amusement for the normal people to laugh at. I am not a dummy like everybody thinks of me. I do not get any respect from the idiots in politics. They think that we should be forgotten in the side or in a corner somewhere. The story of my life is everybody else thinks we are different. I think that if we are to be like everybody else, we have to see what we can do and be judged by our dreams.

My work is really important because I help people who have mental problems. What I get from work is the feeling of helping other people with the same problems as I have. I do not hate anything about my work; you don't have the time for hate. I expect to get a place in this firm. This is the best place I have ever been, because I get to be with people I like a lot. That is my future; if I cannot be with these people, I don't want to be nowhere. I want to help other people with the same problems. Rights are for everybody, not just normal people. Our rights are the same as anybody else's, so we should get the same opportunities as every other person in this world.

Human beings around the world share my hope that people will understand us better. I am really happy that people will listen to what we have to say in this book. It is a link between us and the rest of the world. What is the best thing to us is that the people will tell us what they want from us. The best thing in the world is that they just understand us. I like to think that we are the same kind of people like everybody else in this world.

The Universal Power of Speaking for Oneself

Nancy Ward
TARC
Tulsa, Oklahoma, United States

I think it is very important for people with disabilities to learn to accept and understand their disability, because when they are able to do that, they will see themselves as individuals. A few years ago, I saw a commercial on TV about Special Olympics. These kids were being paraded across a stage in a way that made people feel sorry for them in order to raise money. To me, the worst thing you can do to people who have disabilities is to pity them—you will see them as kids for the rest of their lives, and you will never let them grow up. They will never be what they can be, because you will see their disability rather than their abilities.

So I got mad, and fortunately at the same time some of my friends talked to me about becoming a member of Advocacy First, a local People First chapter. We wrote a letter to the president about our concerns regarding the commercial, and they took it off the air. This showed me how to direct my feelings in a positive way; before, I only knew how to direct them in a negative way.

Most states in the United States have a People First organization. This organization teaches people with disabilities how to speak out for themselves. It also teaches us our rights and our responsibilities. I think it is important that people with disabilities learn responsibilities as well as their rights, because we want to be treated the same as everyone else. We need to know and experience the consequences of our actions.

People First: Establishing Chapters

I also help people learn how to start chapters of People First. There are four things I think you need to have to start a chapter. First, it is really important that local people with disabilities really want it. We sometimes get used to tokenism, because it looks good for local services to have a chapter. But people with disabilities need to run their own chapters; if we can't manage our own chapters, how can we learn to be a part of society and to access our own communities?

Second, it is necessary for the chapter to have an advisor to give the chapter support. This person should not be paid, because people with disabilities need real friends. They already have enough paid people in their lives.

Third, the advisor should not be an employee of the local service agency. If the advisor works for the service agency, he or she may have a conflict of interest. Suppose, for example, that People First members decide they do not want to work in a workshop but want real jobs. But the advisor is a supervisor in the workshop. Where will the advisor's loyalty be?

Fourth, the advocacy meetings shouldn't be held in the agency. The kinds of issues that members might bring up might not be comfortable to talk about in front of agency staff. People should be able to talk about anything they want, and there should be a two-way trust between members and the advisor. Meetings can be held in libraries, churches, or any accessible community facility. Many of these meeting places can be arranged for free.

Self-Sufficiency: Conducting a State Convention

One of the things that People First organizations are most proud of is that we are self-sufficient. As an organization, it is important for us to be able to say that. The image we often have of people with disabilities is that they are constantly given money. We are proud that we do not need lots of outside money to run our convention. People who come to the convention pay their own registration costs, hotel, and meals. Income from the registration is the main source of money to support the organization.

The planning for the convention is done by the board of the state People First chapter. It has taken us a long time to learn how to do that. When we started, the advisors did everything; now the board of directors does the whole convention.

State officers are elected at the convention every 2 years, and we always have "open mike" time when people can come forward to talk about any ideas they have. They talk about jobs, about closing institutions, what it means to have their own apartments, and things like that. This is how we know what the members want, and it is where we get ideas for our goals.

We also have representatives from political campaigns as speakers at the convention. They listen to our concerns about issues like wage-and-hour laws, and they respond to our questions.

I also have to say that we have a lot of fun at the convention. We always have a dance, and many people go to the convention to see friends they haven't seen for a whole year. It's not only a business meeting but also a social event. The convention also allows the staff who accompany some people to see those people in a whole new light, in a situation where they are doing things on their own.

The self-advocacy movement in Nebraska started about 20 years ago. It was started to let people provide support for themselves. They didn't realize that they were doing self-advocacy until they saw a film about People First of Oregon. That was the beginning, and there are now 10 chapters plus 5 affiliate chapters across the state.

Self-Advocates Becoming Empowered is the name of the national self-advocacy organization started in 1989. In 1990 we had our first national conference and have had national conferences ever since. There are now more than 40 states with some kind of organized self-advocacy movement. The national steering committee is made up of 16 representatives who meet four times a year to run the national organization.

Self-Advocacy and Quality of Life

I think that people need to gain confidence in themselves first; that's where self-advocacy comes in. My self-advocacy skills are very important, for as I have gained self-confidence to speak for myself and seen myself as a person with disabilities, I have also come to realize that "that's OK." If we expect to teach others that it is OK to have a disability, then we need to learn that for ourselves. For example, it is important that people be able to say freely what kind of a job they want. To do that, however, they first need to feel confident and safe in saying what they really feel and want without getting into trouble. Our responsibility is to help change the situation and that is the connection between self-advocacy and quality of life. We have to learn to speak up for ourselves and help make our lives better. Also, we should be given the opportunities to learn from our successes and our mistakes just as anyone else. This is an important change in our thinking, for historically people thought we needed to be overly protected.

There are a number of things that I think have helped improve my quality of life. First, gaining the confidence in myself to see myself as a person who is worthwhile and who can speak for myself. Second, learning that speaking out for myself is OK, and that, if necessary, I can interrupt a conference call or meeting and say, "I don't understand." Third, having people believe in me and encourage me. For example, early on, we found language in the Nebraska statutes that still referred to people as "morons and idiots." We were very offended by this. We initially needed a push, but we went before a legislative committee and testified. We didn't know initially how to change a law. But we found out that our voice was heard. The legislators encouraged us to speak up, and, wonderfully, the language was changed. Fourth, encouraging others to speak out and not wait 5 years. That is how long it took me to learn to speak up, because I did not have a role model. And finally, seeing the light bulb go on in someone's head: "Oh, I can do that for myself." That is really cool, and to me that's worth all the money in the world.

People not believing in me, treating me as a little kid, and seeing only the labels that have been placed on me have been the biggest barriers to accomplishing what I have set out to do. People's abilities or disabilities are not the barrier: It's people's attitudes. And that's what I like about People First: We have really had a voice in changing people's attitudes about people with disabilities. And we are not done yet! But there is something else: We also need to believe in ourselves. A big barrier could be ourselves and feeling that we can't do it. We need to believe in ourselves. And that's another important thing about People First: Others provide support for us; for example, when we need to tell our parents that we want to move into our own homes.

A Cross-Cultural Future

We have had interest from other countries in the People First movement. When we had an international conference in Canada in 1993, self-advocates from 38 countries attended.

Common themes or issues discussed at the international conferences are empowerment, equity, and inclusion. These are truly international issues for people with disabilities who want to be strong self-advocates and thereby have a better quality of life.

I think future self-advocacy programs will become the next ARC [the parents' organization], because now we're starting to speak out for ourselves and are becoming stronger by working together to achieve one voice. One way we are learning to speak out for ourselves is by telling other people how we feel about things. That means that we need to be able to make decisions for ourselves and to let people know what we want. We are not saying that others should not help, but that we need to decide the end goal for ourselves, so it's what we want.

By learning how to work together, we are also learning that we can make a difference in politics. If we had all the people with disabilities banded together, we might have a majority, and we could elect our own political officials. Issues that affect people with a disability would be heard and taken seriously. That is what the future should look like.

Finally, my dream for the future is that I work myself out of a job, because there will be no need to have organizations that work with people who have a disability. People with a disability will be accepted like anybody else, so there won't be a need for those kinds of organizations. That is my dream.

The Quality-of-Life Paradigm in the Flemish-Speaking Part of Belgium: People With Mental Retardation Finally Stand Up for Themselves

Geert Van Hove
University of Ghent
Ghent, Belgium

Patrick Schelfhout
Anderlecht, Belgium

The Context

Belgium is a monarchy with a federal state structure in the center of Europe. In the Flemish-speaking part of the country, Flanders, there are about 6 million inhabitants. Flanders has a long tradition in caring for people with mental retardation. Local names such as Guislain and Geel are known throughout the world.

Within this historical and geographical context, a well-organized care system for people with disabilities was developed. The care is organized by private initiatives based on state subsidies. Ninety percent of the care is in the hands of organizations that are members of a coordinating Catholic group. For years all attention was focused on the relief and guidance of children. But in the past 20 years, a reconversion movement has developed toward adults. After a long trial period, adult services and supports are gradually taking definite shape.

An important part of this care for adults has received a "modern color." Daycare centers, services for family support, services for supported living, and services for supported employment are frequently situated far from the traditionally organized residential care.

Under pressure of parent associations and groups of people with physical disabilities, terms such as *participation* and *involvement* are gradually gaining a firm foothold. Facilities are required to provide users' boards and complaint procedures. And yet the question remains whether these initiatives are not included too easily in a system that runs the risk of serving "old wine in new bottles." We ask ourselves whether these participation initiatives really lead to something that exceeds "being consulted" (Ramcharam, Roberts, Grant, & Borland, 1997).

In this framework we, from the Department of Special Education of the University of Ghent, want to support the self-advocacy movement in Flanders. We firmly believe that quality of life is closely linked with "choice in and control over someone's life" (Brown, Bayer, & Brown, 1992, p. 1). This choosing and wanting to control often go together with dissatisfaction, criticism, and sorrow (Brown et al.). We have more faith in an independent coordinating self-advocacy movement as a factor for quality control than in rather limited internal groups that are consulted about an agenda drawn up by people without disabilities.

The Self-Advocacy Movement in Flanders: A Personal Story

I lived at home when I was young. I have a brother and a sister. I never had a nice childhood. I learned a lot at home (ironing, cooking, cleaning, washing). At school they noticed that I was slower than the other children. I was sent to a special school. In this school learning was equally difficult.

For 2.5 months I stayed at an observation center, where they looked for an adapted school for me. This new school was a boarding school where I stayed from ages 10 to 13. Afterwards I went to a special school on the secondary level during the day; at night I was at home. I studied to be a plumber. In this school, life was not always easy; some pupils pestered me.

During my first apprenticeship, my marks were insufficient. My second apprenticeship was in a sheltered workshop. For my final exam, I could start earlier than the others. When I graduated, I did not find a job immediately. I was unemployed for 8 months, then I found a job in the sheltered workshop where I had done my apprenticeship.

When I was 25, I went to live in a group home with three other people. It was difficult to live together with the others. After 3 years I went to live on my own with the aid of supported living services. I live in a flat, and twice a week the same counselor comes to visit. In the meantime I still work at the sheltered workshop; I drive the forklift truck and do sorting work.

At work I became a union representative. I am a member of the safety committee. In those meetings I learned how many problems people have at work and elsewhere. This interested me, and I had the feeling I had to do something about it. At work I have a right to educational leave. I talked to people of the Djophuis [unemployment center], who organize courses. Every Wednesday for 6 months I took a course there. I received information about self-help groups. I was invited by the parents' association to represent Belgium at a European Conference in Turin, Italy. There I learned that self-help groups already existed in the Netherlands and Germany. Here, however, nothing existed.

In 1995 the people from VMG [an adult education center] asked the supported living service whether they knew someone who could chair one of the discussion groups during the first conference of people with mental retardation. I already had the experience from the conference in Italy, so I said yes. In October 1995, 200 people met during the first conference. The whole time I chaired a group of people who talked about their living conditions. In October 1996 the conference was reconvened. During those 5 days I was chairman or speaker of the day. I talked about my dream to start a self-advocacy movement in Flanders.

In December 1996, with the help of VMG, I started Our New Future. I want to study the problems people with mental retardation in Flanders experience. It also would be good if we could find solutions together, without the counselors telling us those solutions.

Self-Advocacy in Flanders: A Theoretical Framework

From different angles, theories are woven around this movement. Undoubtedly the movement is based on the notion of empowerment (Ramcharam et al., 1997); this means creating possibilities allowing people with disabilities to acquire or produce the energy to take their lives in their own hands.

> Empowerment needs to be addressed within personal, systemic and societal contexts in ways which avoid unnecessary constraints on the individual and which maximize their human potential. This freedom can be achieved by the enhancement of competence and social image, the removal of constraints and by mobilising voluntary commitment and collective action. (Ramcharam et al., p. 225)

However, one cannot think about this loosely. The sense of empowerment is inseparably linked with the image one has about people with disabilities. We find much support in the entire movement about "inclusion" (see Pijl, Meijer, & Hegarty, 1997; Karan & Bothwell, 1997). The self-advocacy People First movement is based on the premise that all people in society have to be able to take their place. Only after this is established does one look for personal needs that possibly are linked with disabilities. From these special needs, one may develop a differentiated support model—support that has to guarantee membership in a community.

For this profile of individual needs, we find proof in the most recent American Association on Mental Retardation definition, classification, and systems of support model (Luckasson et al., 1992). Using this model, one chooses resolutely for a search for the individual's strengths and for appropriate supports and support intensities to allow people to participate in society as citizens.

Self-Advocacy in Flanders: Early Problems

Something for the Independently Functioning, Eloquent Man

We see the reality of a "possible struggle for the power" occurring in the new Flemish self-advocacy movement. As in every new and growing movement, some members explicitly put themselves forward. This became painfully obvious when the fairly independently functioning participants of the initial conference were confronted with a number of people with severe disabilities. The confrontation with wheelchairs and hampered communication resulted in a kind of shock to the original group. However, "Are these people able to join in the conversation?" rapidly became "What is the best way to communicate with these people?"

It will also become clear to what extent the "macho-element" plays a part in the new movement. In other words, will women have a role in the movement? What role can they fulfill? Will there be room for typically female problems among the goals of the self-advocacy group?

Self-Advocates and the Mobility Problem
Despite the fact that Flanders is a small federal state, we observe that the movement suffers from a mobility problem of its members. In its primal phase, the initial movement works with one central group; to have a meeting, some people have to travel a long way by public transport. A number of these people are also confronted with meetings that take place in the "big city" (e.g., Brussels), although they previously lived a rather sheltered life in the countryside. The number of kilometers, the early hour to get up, and the time lost in finding the way result in the fact that the meetings can take place only during weekends and require a lot of energy from the members. We advise the movement to lobby with the railroad company to hire rooms in a central railroad station.

Finding Coaches
In an interesting article, Cunconan-Lahr and Brotherson (1996) enumerate a number of barriers hampering a successful advocacy process. We think the same barriers exist when people with mental retardation are trying to find the right coaches. Important roles are played by the time factor (who has the time to work voluntarily for a movement in such an intensive way?), the financial factor (e.g., who will invest in transport costs that cannot be recovered?), and the emotions (who will go to battle for people with disabilities?).

In addition, we cannot underestimate the task of the coaches: They must give support to people with mental retardation, while at the same time "sitting on their hands." Thus the role of caretaker or counselor is being questioned. When do advocates act or intervene? How are agreements with self-advocates made? Where are they heard, and where do they find support for their reactions and emotions? These are problems that must not be underestimated (see De Wilde, 1997).

Training for Self-Advocates Is a Must
During a number of encounters with "advanced" self-advocates, members of the public sometimes asked whether the speaker was someone who had mental retardation. A number of these people indeed learned to speak so well for themselves that the caricature of someone with mental retardation having communication problems and being socially incompetent is forgotten. But it would be naive to believe that successful advocacy work is within reach for everyone.

Having said that, we believe that good self-advocates may be developed through a number of phases:

Phase 1: Individuals with mental retardation have their "hands tied" rigidly with the result that they cannot speak for themselves.

Phase 2: Individuals with mental retardation talk as the "dolls of a ventriloquist." They receive the consent of counselors to participate in discussion groups and are told, for instance, to talk or not talk about certain topics.

Phase 3: Individuals with mental retardation will think about their lives and pri orities.

Phase 4: Individuals with mental retardation participate in discussion groups, talk, listen a lot, and broaden their world.

Phase 5: Individuals with mental retardation overcome their problems and arrive at coordinating insights. Solidarity with others becomes possible, and mutual actions and solutions are developed.

Phase 6: Individuals with mental retardation reach with friends, a network of al lies who will coach them and support their actions and activities.

We are convinced that the chances to pass successfully through these phases become greater as self-advocates receive the opportunities in a process of permanent training (by external individuals and through peers).

They Would Be Glad to Take Over

The self-advocacy work is followed closely by different parties in the care sector. For parents, friends, volunteers, and professionals, self-advocacy is a new fact that questions the existing balances. People stand up for themselves and ask explicitly to be heard and to have their expectations and aspirations taken into account (see Dybwad & Bersani, 1996). This new fact sometimes results in certain forces organizing a kind of "song of sirens" and (often indirectly) trying to gain control over the movement. In every country in which the movement is active, we observe a kind of mother-child relation with the parents' associations and a kind of love-hate relation with organizations that represent professionals.

The movement will have to stand very firm to be able to determine independently the agenda items. Finding an office that guarantees independence and finding coaches who can work freely and independently seem to us to be basic conditions.

From My Rights to Our Rights

It is good that participants in the self-advocacy movement dare think about their personal situation and dare to find it problematic. It is only with a clear view of personal reality and challenges that some find sufficient energy, together with colleagues, to undertake action.

For a self-advocacy movement to succeed, it is crucially important that individual participants at some point make a transition toward the mutual. This transition marks the crucial change from the struggle for "my rights," and the energy one gets from this, to the struggle for "our rights," whereby one detaches oneself from narrow self-interest.

Which Tactics Will Be Used?

As in every action group, the self-advocacy movement will also have to continue to think about the way in which it wants to see its goals fulfilled. Internationally (see Dybwad & Bersani, 1996) a number of strategies become apparent: infiltrating organizations, lobbying, conducting an action campaign, fighting certain viewpoints legally, and finding strong coalition partners. To date, it is clear that the young movement in Flanders has not progressed further than using the media and exerting pressure (through lobbying) on the authorities.

The movement will need to have the courage to ask whether certain goals are reached; it will have to work with evaluation teams; and it will have to face changes in its means of action. For this last item, it is clear that the possible choice for difficult, more spectacular action is contradictory to the image that society has of people with disabilities.

Does the Self-Advocacy Movement Make Sense for Participants?

For some people with mental retardation it is not easy to be with and address a group of people. Some who need less support find it sometimes difficult to deal with colleagues who receive more support (read: have a greater or real handicap). It is also striking that some, because they stand up for themselves, are regarded by the public at large—in a kind of defensive reaction—as "people who pretend" (i.e., "they don't have disabilities").

In view of these facts, we must continue to ask what sense people with mental retardation may find in working for a movement to which they do not really want to belong, and on the other hand, are regarded often as "too good" to belong.

Life in Different Worlds

It is interesting to note that people from the movement in Flanders often live in different worlds. One moment they are very active members of a progressive movement, and in another moment, they return to the safe, often overprotecting world of residential facilities and services.

It is essential that self-advocate participants develop for themselves a congruence between those different worlds to get their positions as self-advocates and their emotional lives in the right balance.

Some Provisional Conclusions

We followed and studied the first activities of the self-advocacy movement in Flanders. We are convinced that this movement—if it conquers its growing pains—possesses all the elements to play an important role in the quality-of-life debate in Flanders (see Ward & Keith, 1996).

First, this group can be a broad forum from which the subjective perspective in the above-mentioned debate gets all the attention. There is an international consensus about the fact that quality of life is best determined as a combination of objective (measurable) and subjective (experience) aspects (see Felce, 1997; Taylor & Bogdan, 1996). Also—and this is maybe even more innovative—the entire event may be advanced further through involving members of the self-advocacy movement in cooperative research projects (Van Hove, in press; Whitney-Thomas, 1997). Only when they are involved from the moment the research agenda is determined is there a shift from the use of experience as a guidance method toward using experience as a synonym for participation. Only then is real emancipation established.

References

Brown, R. I., Bayer, M. B., & Brown, P. M. (1992). *Empowerment and developmental handicaps: Choices and quality of life.* London: Chapman & Hall.

Cunconan-Lahr, R., & Brotherson, M. J. (1996). Advocacy in disability policy: Parents and consumers as advocates. *Mental Retardation, 34,* 352-358.

De Wilde, L. (1997). *Coachen: Een andere stijl van begeleiden?* [To be a coach: A different way to support people?] Unpublished manuscript, Niet-gepubliceerde tekst, Lezing VMG-symposium, Gent.

Dybwad, G., & Bersani, H. (Eds.). (1996). *New voices: Self-advocacy by people with disabilities.* Cambridge, MA: Brookline.

Felce, D. (1997). Defining and applying the concept of quality of life. *Journal of Intellectual Disability Research, 41,* 126-136.

Karan, O., & Bothwell, J. (1997). Supported living: Beyond conventional thinking and practice. In R. L. Schalock (Ed.), *Quality of life: Vol. 2. Applications to persons with disabilities* (pp. 79-95). Washington, DC: American Association on Mental Retardation.

Luckasson, R., Coulter, D., Polloway, E., Reiss, S., Schalock, R., Snell, M., Spitalnik, D., & Stark, J. (1992). *Mental retardation: Definition, classification, and systems of supports.* Washington, DC: American Association on Mental Retardation

Pijl, J., Meijer, C., & Hegarty, S. (1997). *Inclusive education: A global agenda.* London: Routledge.

Ramcharam, P., Roberts, G., Grant, G., & Borland, J. (Eds.). (1997). *Empowerment in everyday life: Learning disability.* London: Jessica Kingsley.

Taylor, S., & Bogdan, R. (1996). Quality of life and the individual's perspective. In R. L. Schalock (Ed.), *Quality of life: Vol. 1. Conceptualization and measurement* (pp. 11-23). Washington, DC: American Association on Mental Retardation.

Van Hove, G. (in press). *Doing research together with persons with learning disabilities: Co-operative research projects.* Helsinki: Finnish Association on Mental Retardation.

Ward, N., & Keith, K. D. (1996). Self-advocacy: Foundation for quality of life. In R. L. Schalock (Ed.), *Quality of life: Vol. 1. Conceptualization and measurement* (pp. 5-10). Washington, DC: American Association on Mental Retardation.

Whitney-Thomas, J. (1997). Participatory action research as an approach to enhancing quality of life for individuals with disabilities. In R. L. Schalock (Ed.), *Quality of life: Vol. 2. Application to persons with disabilities* (pp. 181-197). Washington, DC: American Association on Mental Retardation.

AHVA: A Self-Help Organization for the Improvement of Quality of Life of People With Disabilities

Tibi Goldman
Association of the Handicapped of Haifa and the North
Haifa, Israel

Personal Background

I was born in Hungary in 1929. As a child I was stricken with polio and was among the few children who survived this illness in my hometown. Although all four limbs were severely damaged by the illness, I studied in a regular school. My education was interrupted when Hungary entered into World War II. With the assistance of two crutches, I moved around the ghettos and the concentration and death camps, until coming to live in Israel in 1948. When I first arrived in Israel, I trained as a radio technician but soon began my own business. Self-employed, I had to contend with the surprised reactions of my customers when they saw my disabilities; but once they had grown accustomed to me, the business flourished.

A polio epidemic broke out in Israel in the 1950s afflicting approximately 15,000 children and young people. I employed one of the victims of this epidemic—a young man with disabilities similar to mine—in my workshop. At the same time, I also met with other young people with disabilities at the physiotherapy clinic where I exercised. From these encounters, I became aware that treatment and rehabilitation practices in use at the time were inadequate. Service providers and professionals expressed patronizing educational attitudes.

In the early 1960s, having consolidated my business and established my family, I decided, in light of my criticisms about the attitude toward young people with disabilities, to engage in volunteer work. Together with a group of polio victims and amputees, we established the Israel Handicapped Association (IHA), the first organization in Israel to be run by the handicapped for the handicapped. The organizations that worked for the benefit of the handicapped prior to the establishment of the IHA were all run by good-hearted, but nondisabled people. The IHA was innovative because, for the first time in Israel, a group of people with handicaps had formed an organization to work for their own benefit.

As a member of the board of management of IHA, I was actively involved in lobbying members of the Knesset [the Israeli parliament] and in organizing demonstrations to promote the cause of the handicapped population and to advance legislation in this area. Although we were included in various government committees as observers or in an advisory capacity, on the whole our influence on decisions made by various government and welfare committees was minimal. The absence of a written constitution in Israel made it very difficult [this situation is still so] for individuals and organizations struggling to gain rights and benefits on behalf of minority groups (Habib, Factor, & Mor, 1985; Herr, 1992). Our main achievement was in the area of mobility; we reached an agreement with the treasury about a "mobility pension" [announced on July 3, 1977]. This legislation provided for a monthly payment to cover the cost of a private car owned by individuals with a disability, including the necessary auxiliary driving equipment.

Concurrent with my activities in IHA, I joined the Organization of All Disability Associations in Israel (RODAI), which was established in 1977. RODAI aimed to represent the different associations in Israel working on behalf of people with a variety of disabilities, such as the visually impaired and the blind, the hearing disabled and the deaf, victims of Nazi persecution, cystic fibrosis, and so forth.

After a number of years of intensive activity in the IHA and the RODAI, I realized that we need not only to fight for the rights of the disabled, but also to bring about a significant change among the people with handicaps themselves. Because they perceived themselves as unfortunates who were hidden away from society and accustomed to receiving favors and gifts, it became very clear to me that we could achieve this essential change only after we had brought about a positive shift in the individuals' self-perception.

I discontinued my activities in both organizations at this point, but I remained in close contact with my friends in the context of the sports club where I exercised. A number of friends approached me about starting a local group, and I thus became the head of Haifa's first self-organization for the disabled. My relations with people from the establishment, together with the experience I had accumulated in the course of my organizational work were advantageous. We established the Association of the Handicapped of Haifa and the North (AHVA), and since then I have been its chairman. On December 19, 1982, AHVA was officially registered as a not-for-profit organization.

AHVA: Organizational Structure

From its initiation it was decided that to prevent AHVA from becoming entangled in bureaucracy, the organizational structure should be composed of a minimal number of position-holders and subcommittees. AHVA's organizational infrastructure is therefore limited to those positions required by the law governing registered associations: board of management, book-keeping, internal and external audit, accountant, and lawyer. In AHVA all these functions are done on a voluntary basis.

The organization is headed by the board of trustees and a general assembly of the 20 executive members. The board of executives oversees a range of services including a social club, a transportation service, a computer instruction, a computer services center, and an educational project called Me and the Community. It is also involved in initiating new programs.

AHVA: Guiding Principles

The main principles, defined by AHVA's board of executives when the Association was first established, continue to provide its guidelines. The following is an outline of these principles:

Small-Organization Framework

The decision to maintain a small-organization framework was based on three points:

1. From the very beginning, we were aware that fierce power struggles over administrative positions often appear in large organizations. This kind of struggle can undermine efficient and quick decision-making processes. For this reason we decided to keep the number of executive members small (20).

2. This relatively small number was also in line with the principle of avoiding bureaucracy as much as possible.

3. From the outset we aimed to place the emphasis on the welfare and quality of life of the individual. Our first priority was the weakest group among us—the people who were leading socially isolated, housebound lives because they lacked transportation facilities, employment, and social stimulation.

Approximately 400 people with disabilities attend the variety of activities and programs run by AHVA.

Financial Resources

The financial resources of the Association come from several places: the public relations activities of the members of the executive board, a minimal fee paid by participants, an occasional fund-raising drive, the Haifa municipality, the Ministry of Labor and Welfare, and the National Health Institute. Other funds come from outside sources such as the JOINT Israel, the Jewish Agency, and others. Payment for different courses run by AHVA, its transportation service, and the AHVA computer services center contribute also to the Association's financial resources.

The Association as a Role Model for Others

Because we wish to maintain a small organizational framework, AHVA's work and activities are carried out on a local level. Unlike other organizations, AHVA has never had any desire or any intention to expand beyond the northern region. Nonetheless, the possibility of using AHVA as a model among organized groups of people with handicaps throughout Israel is being considered. Certain AHVA programs, such as Me and the Community (details will follow), are being "purchased" by the establishment and will be applied and operated throughout the country.

Flexibility in Establishing Programs and Projects

Whenever existing institutionalized services are lacking or seem to be inadequate, AHVA initiates programs and projects independently. This allows flexibility in project planning according to the needs as they arise. For example, immediately after setting up the social club, the need for a transportation service to bring in participants became obvious. AHVA acted accordingly and acquired a minibus. To meet the needs as they arise, projects such as AHVA computer services center are initiated and operated. Changes can be introduced in programs at any time. Thus AHVA initiates new and innovative programs and avoids merely expanding existing services.

Two-Way Integration

One of the principles behind AHVA's work is to address the need for activities within the community to bring both sides, people with disabilities and the people without disabilities, into contact with each other. There are a number of examples of this principle:

1. The Association held exhibitions at their social club with the intention that people with and without handicaps view the artwork together. The artists' works were sold within the framework of the exhibition.

2. People from the wider community purchase services from the AHVA computer services center, which employs mainly people with handicaps.

3. Members of the Association represent AHVA at the local municipality's committee on accessibility, advising architects and urban planners on how to improve the access in the community for people with handicaps.

AHVA as a Source of Information

AHVA has acquired considerable knowledge and experience about services, needs, barriers, and difficulties encountered by people with handicaps residing in the community. As the Association's primary concern is the benefit of these people, one of AHVA's guiding principles is to share this store of acquired knowledge and experience with the professionals and those giving services in the field. This means AHVA organizes a range of conferences in which the Association shares its philosophy and the knowledge and experience it has accumulated in the course of the organization's activities.

On the basis of our experience with the computer services center, we found that employment skills, which would not necessarily come to light during regular assessment, will be expressed when the person with a handicap is working in a productive and encouraging atmosphere. We recommended reducing the assembly piece work in the protected workshops, replacing it with regular production work where each department produces a different product. This proposal was presented to the Ministry of Labor and Welfare.

The Association's services are open to all people with a handicap and are not limited to members only; people from Haifa and the northern region are invited to participate in the Association's activities. The social club is open and free to all. People arrive spontaneously, and no questions are asked about "who and why?" There is no need for an official membership card. Participants, though, are asked to make one commitment: to be involved on a regular basis.

AHVA was established at the time when welfare policy on services for the disabled was guided primarily by the normalization principle. Today the claim is that, while the normalization principle is an essential condition for people with handicaps, it is not enough. The focus must be on the person's quality of life. The concept of quality of life is based on the assumption that the criteria for rehabilitation of people with handicaps are not to be found in social and professional norms, but rather are found deep within the person (Schalock, 1996). From its inception, AHVA's principles of action have been based on the concept of quality of life. This can be seen in the decision made by the founding members of the Association who, recognizing the problems and difficulties they and their friends encountered in their own day-to-day lives because of their disabilities, made the decision to set up an organization for themselves. The fact that AHVA's board of directors places emphasis on activities based on the principles of equality, dialogue, flexibility, personal involvement, and the contribution of each person according to his or her ability, together with the avoidance of political power struggles, is also indicative of AHVA's adherence to the concept of quality of life.

AHVA's Projects

The Social Club

The social club began operating when AHVA was established. The club, intended to contribute toward improving one's quality of life, operates all day. Every person is accepted for club membership without regard to age, gender, race, or cause of disability. At the club, the members can find other people, with or without handicaps, who are willing to listen to their problems or give advice, guidance, and assistance. They can chat over a cup of coffee and light refreshments and also participate in different group games.

Since its establishment, the number of participants has increased rapidly, and new organizational needs have arisen. The founding members, and other volunteers, took on the administrative, treasury, secretarial, accounting, and legal advice work at the club without remuneration. The Haifa municipality also provides some financial support for the club. Nonetheless, an increased budget was soon felt to be required to meet the needs of the different activities at the club. So under the auspices of the board of trustees, an independent fund-raising drive was set up. The funds raised allowed for the expansion of the club's activities to include transportation, hobby groups and lectures, trips and tours, the chess club, and use of computers.

AHVA Computer Services Center (ACSC)

Often people with severe physical disabilities, particularly those confined to a wheelchair, find it difficult to be employed, not because they lack the necessary skills but because of the lack of accessibility to the workplace, the inadequate facilities at the workplace, and the stigmatized attitudes toward them. Consequently, a decision was made by AHVA board of executives to establish an innovative framework for gainful employment that could employ the highly motivated who had already undergone computer training. AHVA computer services center (ACSC) opened in April 1993 (Reiter, Friedman, & Goldman, 1995). There were three main goals behind the establishment of this project:

1. to facilitate the integration of a group of people with severe physical handicaps into a productive framework;

2. to grant them financial independence by using their potential through the use of advanced technology;

3. to enable people with handicaps to be integrated into an occupational set-up that is creative and productive, thereby providing a role for other frameworks.

49

Eight graduates of AHVA's computer courses provided the central core for establishing this enterprise. The range of disabilities within the group was fairly extensive and included a mix of physical and emotional disabilities. The group included a manager, an expert in desktop publishing (the only person without handicaps in the group), a graphic designer, an artist who combined work on the computer with her own original art work, and three computer programmers. Following are excerpts from the personal stories of some of the members of the first group of workers:

> AHVA opened a new chapter in my life and enabled me to realize one of my greatest dreams. Up to this point (when I started working) I had been hidden between the four walls of my little studio…the idea of working in a regular work place, together with other people working to realize their own dream, was really exciting for me.

> Recently I started working at the ACSC, and I now hope to find satisfying and efficient work here in proof-reading and other word processing work.

> It was by chance that I heard about the handicapped persons club which was teaching computer courses. I was lucky enough to be able to participate in one of its courses. I successfully completed the course and really enjoy working on the computer. I continued to study new software programs on my own, and now a whole new world has been opened up to me.

During the first year of its operation, the center published weekly magazines, pamphlets, advertising material, and business correspondence. Donations covered the cost of the equipment purchased, and the profits earned covered the monthly expenses. Today ACSC is handling a number of projects simultaneously: the publication of a periodical, books, information brochures for different departments at the [Haifa] municipality, and booklets. It also provides graphic design services such as logo design for letterhead papers. The computer equipment at ACSC is used also for training people with disabilities who do not work at ACSC. This provides an additional source of income.

"Me and the Community" Project

This project grew out of meetings with young people who would eventually require preparation for an assisted living arrangement in the community. Because of the lack of community living arrangements for people with disabilities in Haifa, at present some of these young people will continue to live with their families until their parents pass away, at which point, if an alternative arrangement cannot be found for them, they will have to be institutionalized. Based on discussions with the directors of these institutions, and according to their appraisal of the situation, it seems that approximately 70% of the people with handicaps living in institutions at the moment in Israel would be capable of living independently within the community.

Lately attempts are being made by the Ministry of Welfare to fund apartments within the community for people with handicaps. A number of years ago, an attempt was made in Jerusalem to deinstitutionalize residents and place them in community apartments. From an organizational point of view, this was a success, though at the personal level, this attempt was a failure because they were isolated and lonely. In actual fact, the framework for independent living basically copied the institutionalized system and transferred it to the community. No significant changes in the lifestyle or quality of life took place (Gunzburg & Gunzburg, 1992).

When we tried to identify the source of the difficulty, we found that the problem lay both with those providing the services and with the people with handicaps themselves who had never acquired the skills required to lead an independent life. These issues were brought before AHVA's board of executives, where it was decided that, before the problem came to a head in Haifa, AHVA had an obligation to propose operating a program to help candidates prepare themselves for living within the community and for an independent and autonomous life. After numerous approaches to different governmental bodies, the financial backing for this project finally came from a voluntary organization—the Joint Israel.

It was not easy to enlist the first group. Despite awareness of the need for a program that promotes autonomy, the referring bodies found it difficult to find people who, in their opinion, would benefit from such a program. The claim was that the people with handicaps in their care are already rehabilitated, because "they know how to make coffee and to cook light meals, and this is enough."

Five people with physical and mental handicaps participated in the first group. Apart from one participant who did not fit into any rehabilitative framework and remained at home for 2 years, the others worked in rehabilitation centers. The staff running the project included an expert in special education and group therapy, a group dynamics moderator, a tutor in social education, and an instructor. Experts in enrichment studies also assisted the staff. This project was innovative, and it was necessary to prepare the initial plan for the first group. Dr. Reiter from the University of Haifa headed a team of experts who evaluated the outcomes of the project.

The goal of the project was to train adults to have a quality lifestyle, while placing an emphasis on promoting the individual's autonomy. To achieve this, two principles were established.

First, the teaching of proficiency and skills was considered as a means, and not a goal in its own right. Participants in the program selected areas in which they wanted to develop the skills they were lacking and which they would like to learn. Emphasis was placed on the processes of individual choice, group discussion, ability to reach decisions that would satisfy the whole group, ability to change a decision in the light of changing situations, self-assessment, and development of self-awareness.

Second, emphasis was placed on group experiences, including special group dynamics sessions, and on interpersonal communications. In regular activities, the guiding principle was educational-developmental. The goal was to consolidate the group. In the group dynamics activities, emphasis was placed on the ability of the individual to share life experiences with others and to receive feedback from the other group members. The goal was to assist the individual in self-analysis and growth.

The project called Me and the Community is innovative. As opposed to other projects dealing with social issues, it places emphasis on the development of the personality rather than on mere skills. In keeping with the normalization principle, which is prevalent in Israel today, most existing projects focus on the development of skills only and emphasize independence and the training of people with handicaps to "be like everyone else."

The Me and the Community project is run on a different ideological basis. It emphasizes the quality of life of the person—that is, the right to be different, to be unique, and to act according to one's own personal judgment, and not according to some outside judgment. Ed Roberts, a polio victim who developed a self-help group in the United States in the late 1960s, clearly expressed the essential difference between independence and autonomy. Roberts claimed that in the medical model independence is measured in terms of the distance a person can walk following an illness; but independence for the person with a handicap is the degree of control that person has over his or her own life. The number of activities the person can carry out on his or her own and without help is not a measure of independence; independence is the quality of life of the person who is receiving assistance (Shapiro, 1994). In this project, we have adopted this quality-of-life orientation.

To follow the processes being experienced by the participants in this program, two questionnaires were administered: The *Quality of Life Questionnaire* (Schalock & Keith, 1993) and the *Habits and Skills Questionnaire*, developed specifically for this project.

The *Quality of Life Questionnaire* was given to the participants in the project at three different stages during the program—at the beginning, 3 months later, and at the end. (The course is approximately 6 months long.) The findings indicated a general increase in the quality-of-life scores between the first and second stage, and then again between the second and third stage. This improvement took place despite disillusionment and an increased ability for self-criticism, as reflected in decreased scores in parts of the questionnaire, where some expressed dissatisfaction with their life at home or with the rehabilitation center in which they worked.

The *Habits and Skills Questionnaire* was also administered at three different points in time during the project. The findings indicated progress in the functional ability of the participants. In general, the members of the group developed skills and abilities they did not have prior to starting the course.

By the end of the first course, it seemed participants had undergone a significant process of change in terms of lifestyle. The experience had made them aware of the importance of consolidating the group; on the other hand, they had increased their awareness of self and of their own limits. At present, we are already running the second group in this project.

The Future

As previously stated, AHVA's overall philosophy is that the Association should meet the present and future needs of people with handicaps. It has a holistic perception of the needs of people with disabilities rather than concentrating on one specific area, such as sports or the arts.

During the 15 years since AHVA was established, the Association has developed different programs to meet individuals' needs. At present the quality of life of many people with disabilities has improved because of the normalization policy and the development of services available within the community. This improvement has occurred mainly in technical areas: attractively designed social clubs, more swimming pools with auxiliary equipment, larger vehicles, and demonstration apartments in special schools and in rehabilitation centers. But it is important to differentiate between the application of the normalization principle in its simplest form, which equates to "living like everyone else," and the concept of quality of life, which considers the unique personality of each individual. Quality of life refers to subjective processes that have no clear, outward manifestations. These processes are manifested in the individual's ability to give direction to his or her life, maintaining a sense of self-worth, self-respect, and respect for others that are cornerstones of a quality of life. These processes are inner to the individual and manifest themselves not only in the use of exterior equipment or in acquiring skills, but also in styles of communication between the individual and others. From the outset, AHVA's goal has been to relate primarily to the individual's quality of life and not just to his standard of living conditions.

I wrote the following letter in my capacity as chairman of AHVA and sent it to a trust fund as part of the application process requesting support for the Me and the Community project. The letter clearly expresses this focus on quality of life:

> Dear Sir,
>
> To this day, my ears are still ringing with the comment you made—"You can also find these same 'things' (meaning equipment) in other places"—when you saw our training apartment for the "Me and the Community" Project. I feel we ourselves are to be blamed, that we were unable to find the words to properly convey the disparity and the difference between the "Me and the Community" Project and other similar projects.
>
> It is true that the chairs, tables, windows, and eating utensils are exactly the same in both cases, and the people even wear the same clothes. People are accustomed to automatically seeing and relating to external technical objects. They are recognized, well-known, convenient, and do not require any special considerations because everyone else uses them. They are safe.
>
> In our opinion, it is not enough to give a person "a nice bed" or an attractive apartment, especially if he does not know how to run his own life or how to establish contacts with his fellowmen. If we

53

only give him the equipment, we have not done very much for him. We have given assistance and charity, but at the same time, have merely created yet another place where he is dependent on others.

It is not possible to "see" the new spirit. If you could only talk with just one of the graduates from the first course, or with other people who know this project close hand, you too would be able to stand before the Board of the Trust and convince them of the worth and importance of this project.

If you look at the reports of the Association, you will see that all its activities were pioneering and established "ahead of their time." It was only after some years that the official policy became "caught up" with these activities. We were the pioneers of the "integration" period; tomorrow, it will be the "quality of life" period with all its implications.

We are proposing a new approach to invest the primary effort to enable the disabled person whose life is run almost totally by others, to learn to control his own life, to choose his own lifestyle, to feel he can lead an autonomous life, and to independently manage his own life, even though he is different.

Yours sincerely,
Tibi Goldman, Chairman

References

Gunzburg, H. C., & Gunzburg, A. L. (1992). Grouphomes—Neoinstitutionalism? *Issues in Special Education Rehabilitation, 7,* 7-18.

Habib, J., Factor, H., & Mor, V. (1985). *Policies towards the disabled in Israel: A critical overview.* Jerusalem: Joint Israel.

Herr, S. (1992). Human rights and mental disabilities: Perspectives on Israel. *Israel Law Review, 26,* 142-194.

Reiter, S., Friedman, L., & Goldman, T. (1995). The self-employment option for people with disabilities: A case study on 'AHVA' Desk Top Publishing Company. *International Journal of Rehabilitation Research, 18,* 258-262.

Shapiro, J. P. (1994). *No pity.* New York: Random House Times Books.

Schalock, R. L. (Ed.). (1996). *Quality of life: Vol. 1. Conceptualization and measurement.* Washington, DC: American Association on Mental Retardation.

Schalock, R. L., & Keith, K. D. (1993). *Quality of life questionnaire.* Worthington, OH: IDS.

The Mesosystem: Quality of Life From the Community and Organizational Perspective

The quality revolution, with its emphasis on quality product and quality outcomes, has emerged rapidly during the last two decades. One of the main products of this revolution has been a "new way of thinking" in the field of mental retardation. The concept of quality of life has become the unifying theme around which programmatic changes and service delivery patterns are being organized. This new way of thinking stresses person-centered planning, the supports model, quality enhancement techniques, and person-referenced outcomes. More specifically, this new way of thinking is represented throughout the world in the following trends:

- service providers reorganizing resources around individuals rather than rearranging people into program slots;
- consumers and service providers embracing the supports paradigm;
- program evaluation shifting its focus to person-referenced outcomes that can be used to improve organizational efficiency and enhance person-referenced services and supports;
- management styles focusing on learning organizations, reengineered service delivery programs, entrepreneurship, and continuous quality improvement.

Chapters in this second part reflect these trends and provide the reader with a cross-cultural perspective on how organizations are attempting to integrate the concept of quality of life into their services and supports. To this end, in chapter 7 Silvana Watson and her colleagues examine the challenges facing special-education agencies in the context of Brazilian culture, where acceptance of individuals with disabilities depends largely upon long-standing perceptions of the place of the individual within society. Lack of knowledge, lack of financial resources, and Brazilian class structure have "made it difficult for Brazil to provide appropriate education to the majority of its citizens."

Organizations are beginning to focus on and assess the quality of life of service recipients. In chapter 8, for example, Akio Tachi provides an update on the role of the quality-of-life concept in assessment of service delivery and individual satisfaction for workers with mental retardation in Japan. Despite a number of significant problems in organizations influencing the quality of work life of Japanese citizens with disabilities, it is recognized that these problems can be viewed in light of core dimensions of quality of life—allowing examination of systems, services, and ways of thinking in a new light. Wojciech Otrębski (chap. 9) summarizes both current quality of life research in Poland and efforts to move into community-based programs for people with disabilities. Quality-of-life data are summarized in the chapter, comparing quality-of-life factor scores of people living in the community and using active treatment to those in a nontreatment-oriented institutional environment.

As one begins to integrate the concept of quality of life into services and supports, and to focus on a person's perceived quality of life, it is important to evaluate change and change strategies. For example, Nehama Baum of Canada (chap. 10) discusses the challenges to a service provider of integrating quality-of-life principles in services for people with disabilities who also have significant emotional limitations. Baum then describes her agency's use of a multifocal approach based on a psychotherapy and supportive environment combination, stressing the importance of a partnership between service providers and service recipients in their joint pursuit of an enhanced quality of life for people with a dual diagnosis of mental retardation and mental illness.

In chapter 11 we return to Japan with Akiie Ninomiya, who describes quality-of-life issues facing another specific population: aging people with mental retardation. With the projected aging of the Japanese population in the coming decades, both laws and organizational efforts need to be examined and changed to assure quality of life of older citizens with mental retardation.

Application of the core dimensions of quality of life to such efforts toward organizational change is the focus of a group of Spanish authors headed by Javier Elorriaga (chap. 12). Their model proposes a hierarchical arrangement of the relative importance of core quality-of-life dimensions: physical well-being, material well-being, interpersonal relations, social inclusion, rights, self-determination, personal growth, and emotional well-being. Using the model, they then summarize the current status of the service delivery system and suggest ways that quality-of-life enhancement techniques can be built around these core dimensions.

Jennifer Denise James (chap. 13) details rapid changes in both community and organizational structures in Curaçao. She describes the evolution of a service system over the past 25 years and also reports that much remains to be done if individuals with disabilities are to enjoy productive, integrated lives of quality.

Finally, evidence that quality of life is influenced by organizational culture and leadership style is presented by John Lobley (chap. 14). He sets forth the possibilities for productive organizational change through transformational leadership and shows that such leadership may occur at virtually any level in the organization.

Throughout part 2 the reader will find common mesosystem themes related to:

- how organizations can apply quality-of-life principles to the services and supports they provide people with disabilities;
- the impact that different environments have on perceived quality of life;
- the need to recognize individual differences in factors contributing to a positive quality of life;
- the importance of partnerships between service providers and service recipients.

To the extent that these themes are integrated into service and support planning and the lives of individual citizens, we may expect enhanced quality of life and a better future for people with developmental disabilities.

Perspectives on Quality of Life: The Brazilian Experience

Silvana Maria Russo Watson
Nebraska Wesleyan University
Lincoln, Nebraska, United States

Ana Maria Barreira
Federal University of Pernambuco
Jaboatão, Pernambuco, Brazil

Timothy C. Watson
University of Nebraska-Lincoln
Lincoln, Nebraska, United States

Quality of life is acknowledged to be an elusive concept. The term is even harder to define when culture and extreme disparity in socioeconomic status are dominant variables. The term is yet even more elusive when applied in the context of a vast developing country such as Brazil and applied to a particular special group, people with disabilities.

Although there are many ways to define *quality of life,* Schalock (1997) suggests that we agree on core quality-of-life dimensions, as proposed: (a) emotional well-being, (b) interpersonal well-being, (c) material well-being, (d) personal development, (e) physical well-being, (f) self-determination, (g) social inclusion, and (h) rights. To understand the conceptualization of quality of life and its application to Brazilians with mental retardation and developmental disabilities, we must take note of the dominant influence of culture, environment, and scarce economic resources.

In this chapter we discuss the general nature of special-education services provided to individuals with disabilities in Brazil. Based on societal factors, we examine the challenges Brazilian programs face in providing services for these individuals. We isolate a single cultural perspective as the dominant challenge to the advancement in quality of life for Brazilians who have disabilities.

The Cultural Hurdle

Brazilian culture does not mirror Western political values. The self-made man, the strongly independent, and the individual asserting personal rights at odds with the community—these are not typical Brazilian cultural heroes. The true Brazilian hero is a benefactor, a special person with the special ability to do special things for society. The Brazilian hero is much like a great king. The Brazilian word for this is *jeito* (a way of possessing things and of getting things done). The Brazilian hero does not exhibit merit; that hero exhibits natural gifts. The hero does not earn a place in society; that place is simply recognized.

The dark side of this hero is class structure with its incumbent class prejudices.

"For them, *to be* is *to have* and to be the class of the 'haves'" (Freire, 1986, p. 44). Success, and likewise failure, is not earned; it is deserved almost as a gift (or punishment) from God. If you do not have it, your only recourse is to pretend to have it. The Brazilian hero, then, degenerates into one who (a) knows well how to get out of a sticky situation (*sabe dar um jeitinho para se safar de situacoes comprometedoras*), and (b) one who succeeds in life without giving much consideration to ethics and values, because the person's main goal is to be admired for physical traits and material belongings. Such has become the famed Brazilian *jeito*. Where "being" is a gift that cannot be earned but must be bestowed, appearing to "be" is the only outlet for individual maneuvering. *Jeito* degenerates into the manipulation of outcomes (the coming up with a gift that may not have been bestowed) that, in turn, degenerates into a manipulation of appearance. Appearances, and keeping up appearances, is a strong motivating value in Brazilian society. Brazilians tend to be great pretenders. With that tendency, comes a great ability to ignore. The Brazilian shoulder is well exercised and is often turned away from society's problems.

Building on this, Brazilians give a lot of importance to what is in fashion (*o que esta na moda*). *Being with it, being in, having it, getting it*—all are phrases of value. If you are not "with it," do not "have it," are not "it," and are not "getting it," you are not valued. The structures of worth that exist in class society are exclusionary. Automatic distance, prejudice, and rejection are built toward people who are not "with it" or who do not belong. This exclusion by society certainly affects each of an individual's quality-of-life dimensions—emotional well-being, interpersonal well-being, material well-being, personal development, physical well-being, self-determination, and rights.

Simply put, Brazilians with mental retardation and developmental disabilities *nao tem jeito* (do not have "it") and are dismissed accordingly. This population is not good at appearances and has certainly never been described as fashionable. As if one disability were being compounded by the addition of another, Brazilian societal assumptions and prejudices would condemn the individual with mental retardation or developmental disability to an obscurity worse than death. That individual tends to be ignored, hidden from sight, and never discussed. Individuals with mental retardation and developmental disabilities face the prejudice and constraints of being included in a separate, and lower, class within a class-structured society.

Devaluation of individuals with disabilities by society is well discussed in the literature (Janicki, 1997; Roberto & Nelson, 1988). The Brazilian tendency is to find mental retardation and developmental disabilities different, exceptional, ugly, unpleasant, uncomfortable to be with, dependent, and "dumb." Individuals with mental retardation and developmental disabilities are often referred to as "the sick one" (*doente*) or "the crazy one" (*o doido*). These terms include an emotional dismissal when used (i.e., apply the term, forget the person; move on—there is nothing that can be done here).

In June 1997 mothers from the Grupo de Atendimento Psico-Pedagógico (GAPP) in Recife, Brazil, reported this cultural devaluation as their greatest obstacle in seeking services for their children. The mothers reported that neighbors, acquaintances, and family members all tend to single out and put down their children with disabilities. Derogatory terms and summary dismissals were commonly reported, as children with mental retardation and developmental disabilities were acknowledged only as unfortunate anomalies—not of the ever-valued norm.

As reported, "healthy" siblings were also affected. One mother of a daughter with mental retardation reported that classmates of her healthy child refer to her as "the child who has a sick and crazy sister." How society perceives disabilities strongly affects how society will treat those people and their families (Janicki, 1997). Class society heightens this hurdle.

There are, admittedly, instances of compassion or philanthropic action. Seldom, however, are they accompanied by an attitude of respect in which the person with a disability is looked upon as an equal citizen, as a human being with valued rights, strengths, feelings, dreams, desires, and needs (MEC, 1994). Private and public schools continue to refuse to enroll children who have physical, cognitive, or developmental disabilities even though Article 8 of Public Law 7.853 of October 24, 1989, states that such exclusion is a punishable crime (Ministério da Justiça, 1996a). A wealthy family, again in Recife, Brazil, reported in June 1997 that one private school refused to enroll their 5-year-old daughter who was born without one jaw bone and with extra skin in one ear. When these children are not excluded from schools, they are uncompromisingly punished for failing the rigorous academic curriculum. Two middle-class families from Recife shared their frustrations with having teenage children yet in elementary classrooms. The frustration centered around ridicule and the exhaustion of being subjected to inevitable and recurring failure. The insanity of these classrooms is summarized in the following statement: If you are not doing something well, just keep doing it over and over and over (Werebe, 1997).

Devaluation is an ominous and dark screen that excludes people with mental retardation and developmental disabilities from robust society. It cuts off and prevents the understanding and compassion that come from a recognition, even a small one, of oneness or sameness. *They are different; they are not like us; they are not us*—the feelings, or lack of feelings, that accompany these phrases are the greatest obstacle to extending services to individuals with mental retardation and developmental disabilities within Brazilian society. In a society structured around haves and have nots, the quality of life of the individual with mental retardation or developmental disability is that of the have nots.

The Nature of Special-Education Services: Early Efforts

The nature of special-education services in Brazil reflects economic, political, and cultural factors, as well as societal attitudes toward disability. Perhaps because poverty (or its effects, e.g., poor nutrition and health care) is so closely connected to the majority of causes of disabilities among Brazilians, special-education services are very dependent on social services. An examination of the history of special education in Brazil suggests that there has been considerable effort from parents and members of the community to provide services for individuals with disabilities. The Associação de Pais e Amigos dos Excepcionais (APAE; Association of Parents and Friends of Exceptional People) and the Sociedade Pestalozzi (Pestalozzi Society) are examples of those efforts. Both are private organizations, with strong parental support, that provide services to individuals with disabilities. The history of Brazilian special education is directly connected to these two organizations and other philanthropic organizations founded in the 1950s (Ferreira, 1995). The education of Brazilians with disabilities has been left to the charity of nonprofit private organizations (Bueno, 1993). Today there are more than 1,500 APAE clinics in Brazil (I. M. F. P. Austran, personal communication, May 27, 1997). These organizations have provided assistance and services to those with disabilities, but they have also reinforced, even perhaps created, segregation. Nonprofit organizations have diminished the pressure on governmental intervention delaying appropriate governmental action and responsibility (Carvalho, Prudente, Cruz, Carvalho, & Blanes, 1997).

The lack of government involvement tends to reinforce the community's attitude toward people with disabilities. Society has not had access to information about disabilities, its causes, prevention, services, and education. As a result, erroneous information has been created that carries prejudice and discrimination with it. People have developed superstitions and have become afraid of those who have disabilities. Society's lack of knowledge and the poor communication among community, family, and services for individuals with disabilities and their families have strongly contributed to the social exclusion of people with disabilities (Pichorim, 1994). Disability has become synonymous with deficiency, inadequacy, bad luck, and charity. According to the Ministério da Educação e do Deporto (MEC, 1994), people with disabilities are those who have atypical conduct, mental deficiency, physical deficiency, multiple deficiency, visual deficiency, or auditory deficiency.

It is difficult to estimate the prevalence of Brazilians with special needs, because: (a) there are inappropriate assessment tools (e.g., IQ tests are merely translations of the English versions); (b) individuals are hidden by their families; and (c) the Brazilian government uses world organization estimates instead of actual data. Typical estimates are that a blanket 10% of the population of a developed or developing country has a disability. Using the 10% estimate, the Organização Mundial de Saúde/ONU reported in 1989 that the prevalence of people specifically with mental retardation in the country was 5% (Carvalho et al., 1997). It is important to notice that the estimated number of people with disabilities also varies within the regions in the country, from 2.8% to 9.6%, depending on the estimated number of people living below the poverty line in those particular areas of Brazil. Estimates build on estimates as assumptions upon assumptions. In any event, the services provided clearly do not match the needs of the regions. The majority of services are found in urban centers in southeast Brazil; the largest percentage of people in need of assistance, however, live in the vast northeast.

In the last two decades, there has been significant work to recognize the rights of people with disabilities (I. M. F. P. Austran, personal communication, May 27, 1997; M. Canzini, personal communications, July 1997, August 1997; MEC, 1994, 1996; Ministério da Justiça, 1996a, 1996b; C. M. F. Nunes, personal communication, May 24, 1997). This modest change in behavior can be documented with several examples:

1. Public Law 5.692/71, in reference to elementary and secondary education, in section 9 refers to services needed for those with exceptionalities and who are gifted.

2. The Federal Constitution, section 208, part III, guarantees specialized instruction to those with disabilities as it guarantees education to any other student. Public Law 7.853/89 of 1989, Os Direitos das Pessoas Portadoras de Deficiência, guarantees the rights of—and promises social integration to—individuals with disabilities; and in 1996, Public Law 9.424, Diretrizes e Bases da Educação Nacional, in chapter V, reinsured that special education would be available in the public schools to those children with disabilities.

3. The Centro Nacional de Educação Especial (National Center of Special Education) was created in 1973 to centralize special education and to plan better delivery of educational services. Today this responsibility is part of the Ministério da Educação e do Deporto e da Secretaria de Educação Especial (SEESP/MEC).

4. The Coordenadoria Nacional para Integração das Pessoas Portadoras de Deficiência (CORDE) was created in 1986 to coordinate government planning and services to people with disabilities. Among its many accomplishments, the CORDE has recently developed a plan of action for the integration of individuals with disabilities (Conselho Consultativo, 1994) and the publication of a specific document to regulate the right to work of people with disabilities (Ministério da Justiça, 1996c).

5. Specialized private clinics for people with disabilities were created in several parts of the country (e.g., GAPP and Associação de Pais e Amigos dos Deficientes Auditivo).

6. Universities began training professionals to work with people with disabilities as an area of specialization, though not as a major or as a degree. The Universidade Federal de São Carlos in the state of São Paulo is the only institution that offers a master's degree in special education.

7. Research in the area of special education began to be published (e.g., Bueno, 1993).

8. Luis Felippe Badin, a 26-year-old man with Down syndrome, was recently given the right to vote (Rio de Janeiro). He is the first person with Down syndrome to vote, receiving his registration to vote on March 31, 1995, and voting for the first time in the election of 1996.

9. The media are slowly beginning to present people with disabilities to their audience through television programs (e.g., "Você Decide," "A Indomada," "Direito de Vencer"), films (e.g., *O Menino Maluquinho, O Quatrilho, Terra Estrangeira*), and children's books (e.g., *Um Amigo Diferente, Meu Amigo Down na Rua, Muito Prazer, Eu Existo,* all written by Cláudia Werneck).

Despite this list of achievements and activities, the education of children with disabilities has not been well supported by the Brazilian government. Although the government, through the Secretaria de Educação Especial (SEESP/MEC) and the Coordenadoria Nacional para Integração das Pessoas Portadoras de Deficiência

(CORDE), has expressed its commitment to the principles of normalization, integration, and individualization of the education of students with disabilities (MEC, 1994; Ministério da Justiça, 1995), it has not provided the resources for their successful implementation. The majority of special-education classrooms in the public schools are for children with mental retardation and they are located in the largest urban centers, São Paulo and Rio de Janeiro. The number of classrooms grows as the number of problems in the general classrooms appears. They are, as Ferreira (1995) says, a subproduct of those problems, not the effort to provide appropriate education for those children with disabilities. Very little money is allocated to deliver the services needed. According to Lobo (1992), the principles of normalization and integration are good liberal ideas but far from reality. Ferreira has indicated that Brazilian special-education laws, which theoretically aim at the integration of children with disabilities, are, in reality, a way of legalizing their exclusion.

Private Organizations: The Clinics

Special-education services in Brazil have been provided primarily by private organizations (e.g., APAE). These organizations have historically assumed the role of the state and federal governments by providing services and attending to needs of those with disabilities (Carvalho et al., 1997). These nongovernmental organizations are specialized clinics or private institutions that today work with the state governmental agencies related to labor and social services (Ministério da Previdência e Assistência Social and Secretaria de Assistência Social—both operated by the Secretaria do Trabalho e Ação Social) to provide services for people with disabilities. Each specific clinic has its own group of multidisciplinary professionals to serve the specific group of people with disabilities they are committed to serving. Among the professionals who work with the children are pediatricians, neurologists, speech or language pathologists, psychologists, physical therapists, and occupational therapists. These clinics are not equivalent to the American institutions where individuals with disabilities have often lived. They typically provide day services only to young children, adolescents, and young adults.

Several clinics are found in the urban centers located in the states of São Paulo, Rio de Janeiro, Paraná, Pernambuco, Bahia, and Minas Gerais. Most of them struggle to get support from the government. There are, however, states in the country where people with disabilities have even fewer (not to say no) services available to them. For example, in Acre and Rondônia, two poor states located in the north, private clinics or schools for people with disabilities do not exist. The regional inequalities are evident in all aspects of people's lives, especially as they relate to education and people with disabilities. The poorer the part of the country, the greater the deprivation that can be witnessed (Werebe, 1997).

The majority of families that do take their children to specialized clinics are usually of very low socioeconomic status. Generally, the monthly family income is only about 120 reais (about $110 U.S.). The middle class and the wealthy, with few exceptions, do not patronize the specialized clinics. Poorer Brazilians more readily accept and provide for family members with disabilities. Living an oppressed life, they more readily accept the oppressions of others, while wealthier Brazilians show a tendency to distance themselves from the unfortunate. Admitting their child to a clinic requires them to acknowledge publicly that the "problem" is part of them.

In the worst case, the very rich will take their child to one of the few institutions of the country located in the south of Brazil or to an institution abroad, with no intention of ever seeing or dealing with the child again. All these behaviors may be their own way of denying the problem and refusing to accept reality. Ironically, these same families spend fortunes educating their "normal," "healthy" children in the very best schools. Refusing to provide low-cost services, financed by the government, to their children with disabilities, the wealthy compete vigorously for the country's scarce educational resources. Specialized services would probably improve the quality of life of their children with disabilities, but in their eyes it would diminish their own quality of life. In fact, admission to clinics carries a certain social stigma.

GAPP: An Example of a Specialized Clinic in the Northeast

The second author of this chapter is a service provider through a specialized clinic for children and adolescents with disabilities. In 1976 Ana Maria Barreira and Ivaneide Brito de B. Correia founded the Grupo de Atendimento Psico-Pedagógico (GAPP) in Recife, Pernambuco. In the last 21 years of service, GAPP has provided services for approximately 5,000 children and adolescents with disabilities. Of those 5,000 young people, only 0.5% are from families with yearly income of more than 30,000 reais.

GAPP serves 400 children in two different locations. In one location, GAPP I, professionals work mornings with children who have congenital or acquired (traumatic brain injury) neurological impairments (29) and afternoons with children and adolescents who have speech problems (6), learning disabilities (27), emotional and behavioral problems (14), fine and gross motor difficulties (8), and mild to severe mental retardation (67).

The other location, GAPP II, provides services for children and adolescents with emotional and behavioral disorders, including autism (132), speech disorders (43), and those with fine and gross motor difficulties (11). It follows the same schedule as GAPP I. The children attend only the morning or the afternoon sessions, and never stay overnight.

Frustrations and success have been experienced by the GAPP faculty and staff for the past 21 years of service. Several alumni have improved their life quality after receiving services or treatment, and they have come back to let the staff and faculty know what they are doing. Some (15) are married and have children; others (18 males) have become their family's major income producer; three women are employed at stores in shopping malls; two deliver food to restaurants; four work as sackers at local supermarkets; and one works at an airline company. GAPP's major success is a woman who has become the assistant, in Brasília (Brazil's capital city), of one of the members of the House of Representatives. Another graduate who has brought a lot of pride to the staff and faculty is one who has cerebral palsy and, despite significant weakness in the right upper and lower limbs, has won the swimming championship in the state of Pará.

The GAPP also provides service to the parents of their clients. They bring in professionals, such as nurses, to talk to the parents about nutrition, nursing a child, sexually transmitted diseases including AIDS, children's motor development, and so forth. They also give the parents special utensils to feed their children, such as adaptive spoons. The clinic provides professional-skill-building workshops for parents and adolescents. The purpose of these classes is to help families from low socioeconomic backgrounds gain or improve skills that will make them employable and more self-sufficient. For example, they offer cooking, sewing, paper recycling, and computer courses. These are professional skills that can assist the parent or the adolescent in competing in the job market. The goal is a better job and thus increased family income.

Given the need to receive financial assistance from the government to provide these training courses to the families, the GAPP administration created the Unidade de Educação Integrada (Unit of Inclusive Education) as a nonprofit organization. The other clinics around the country must do the same in order to qualify for grants that offer career or vocational courses to low-income families. The government pays the equivalent of $54 U.S. per month per child. The type and amount of service children with disabilities need requires significantly more money. It is impossible to pay for professionals, educational materials, utilities, maintenance of the building, and so forth, with so little money. Government grants to nonprofit groups is the source of the required additional funding.

The Families

Although rejected by society, children with disabilities are usually raised privately by their families. Institutions are almost nonexistent in Brazil and carry a social stigma. Religious values, lack of knowledge about the child's disability and out-of-home placements, compassionate support from some extended family members and (sometimes) neighbors influence Brazilian families to maintain a member with a disability at home. Strong religious orientations affect families' decisions to care for the family member with a disability. It is often believed that the person is a part of God's plan, and the family must be special people to have such children (testimony given by GAPP mothers, June 1997). It is likely that these fatalistic beliefs help the family bear the suffering of having a child with disability and soften their feelings of guilt for failure (Fitzpatrick, 1981; Heller, Markwardt, Rowitz, & Farber, 1994). These beliefs provide support to the family, not to the child. The child is typically maintained through benevolence for a dependent, desperate being.

Brazilian families that have children with disabilities fall prey to societal child-rearing beliefs. They view the child as dependent and encourage overprotection, passiveness and contentedness. If the family has any wealth (middle and high socioeconomic classes), full-time maids take care of all the child's needs (e.g., eating and dressing). These children become adults who can do little or nothing, being totally dependent on others. Middle and upper socioeconomic families come with a class prejudice toward manual labor (e.g., janitorial jobs, car wash) and do not allow their children to learn manual-skill vocations even though aptitudes exist for them. Manual labor, in general, is not valued within Brazilian culture.

As Brazilian children with disabilities grow older, they cannot and do not know how to make decisions. They have not been trained to perform a job and do not know how to advocate for themselves. Typically, they have not been taught the social skills necessary to survive in society (C. H. Copus, personal communication, November 20, 1996). Consequently, people with mental retardation in Brazil are not allowed to work on those core dimensions (e.g., material well-being, self-determination, and social inclusion) that enhance one's quality of life.

Culture also influences Brazilian parents' search for alternative ways to deal with atypical behaviors of their children (e.g., rocking or self-injurious behavior). They will visit the Mãe de Santo (Mother of the Saint) and other places of Candomblé (both are African influences on Brazilian spirituality) with the hope of removing the bad spirits *(tirar os espiritos)* that are disturbing the child (making the child exhibit those embarrassing behaviors). Only after many trials, and then only maybe, will parents look for professional help.

Brazilian parents share the same fears that other parents worldwide have in raising a child with mental retardation and other developmental disabilities. A common fear is related to sex. Perhaps Brazilian parents are more apprehensive than others because of the value their culture places on sensuality. This is evident in the way Brazilians dress, their sensual music, and the dances they have inherited from the African Brazilians. Parents of girls worry about how to prepare their daughters for menstruation and how to protect them from rape and pregnancy. The preoccupation with boys is more on controlling masturbation, because it is considered very embarrassing. Having sexual intercourse, however, is not a major concern for Brazilian boys, because culturally it is acceptable: *"afinal, são homens"* (they are men). Sometimes the father will take, or send someone to escort, the son who has mental retardation or developmental disability to a prostitute's house with the hope that the son will stop masturbation. Generally the boy becomes scared and cannot have intercourse. This resolution usually complicates even more the sexual life of boys with mental retardation and developmental disabilities. Again, Brazilian beliefs and behaviors influence perspectives on quality of life; the perspectives then strongly affect the emotional well-being of the person with mental retardation.

Brazilian parents of children with mental retardation and developmental disabilities also fear having a grandchild with disabilities. Because of this, some opt for sterilization. In other cases, the parents arrange a wedding for their child (usually for the daughter) with the illusion of transferring their responsibility to someone else.

Most parents of children with disabilities fear for their child's care after their death. They often wonder what will happen to their child when they are not there to assist. These parents, usually mothers, have dedicated their lives to their child with disability. Brazilian parents know society will not easily accept disability. A group of mothers (from GAPP) whom we interviewed stated that they could not work outside the home because no one has the patience and care to watch their children for long periods of time. They assume the worst (probably correctly) because they also have experienced the prejudice Brazilian society has toward people with disabilities.

67

Present and Future Directions

Although Brazil is a developing country with many socioeconomic problems, great efforts from parents and civil organizations have been made to change society's view on disability and, consequently, the quality of life of those with disabilities. Today we see people with disabilities on the streets and in the malls, and some private clinics (e.g., APAE) are focusing on preparing their students or clients with disabilities to be productive members of society. The students or clients are taught to make baskets, candy, bread, flower arrangements, and other products. These goods are sold by the organizations as a source of funding (MEC, 1996), and this is an important step toward improving the quality of life of those with mental retardation and developmental disabilities.

Another important stride can be observed in the urban areas (e.g., São Paulo, Rio de Janeiro, Curitiba, and Belo Horizonte). The Brazilian government has started to adapt the physical environment to accommodate those with physical and sensory disabilities (Gonçalves, 1997). For example, there are now ramps on sidewalks, easier access to Braille, buses, public telephones, and restrooms; however, according to Marcelo Rubens Paiva (testimony cited in Gonçalves, 1997), who became paraplegic at the age of 19, Brazil is 40 years behind the United States and other first-world countries.

It is important to note that Brazil is a developing country that has struggled with change in types of government, with corruption among its leaders, with great demographic growth, with vast migration of the population from rural to urban areas, and with consequent inflation and other economic ills. A huge percentage of Brazil's population lives below the poverty line (Werebe, 1997), the middle class is almost nonexistent, the low socioeconomic class has become poorer, and the poor have become miserable. Without a doubt, the financial problems that the country has encountered have influenced the quality of life of people in general and, consequently, the quality of life of people with disabilities. Nonetheless, the stage appears set for improvement in that quality of life. The nation has established goals and objectives to improve the education of people with disabilities (MEC, 1994; Pichorim, 1994). Brazilians are recognizing the rights and needs of people with disabilities (Araújo, 1994; Ministério da Justiça, 1996b). However, without a doubt this transition period is going to pose many challenges to Brazilian society and it will be a difficult road to travel.

Conclusion

The struggle for quality of life by people with disabilities has a universal element. That struggle always seeks recognition and value. No matter where they live in the world—Brazil, the United States, France, or Vietnam—people with disabilities have similar barriers to work through: prejudice, lack of money, lack of resources, and lack of support. Parents of children with disabilities, regardless of ethnic background, go through much the same grief process, encounter many of the same fears, and often wrestle with the same problems.

There are specific cultural aspects to these universal challenges, and culture strongly influences one's perspectives on quality of life and societal response to disability. This influence is extended both in identifying the issue and responding to it. In Brazil, the dominant cultural element is the very popular and pervasive Brazilian *jeito*—satisfactory being. Brazilian *jeito* does not extend to mental retardation and developmental disabilities. The Brazilian culture, defined as a specific set of shared values, beliefs, and attitudes, determines how that society treats people with disabilities. In Brazilian culture the societal belief in and pursuit of *jeito* determines people's attitudes toward individuals with mental retardation and developmental disabilities. Families are committed but not equipped (culturally, psychologically, or financially) to raise these children. The result is that children are overprotected and raised as incapable beings. These children are punished by the school system either by being denied the right to be included or by repeating the same grade level they have already completed over and over without advancement. In Brazil, class culture has determined what types of services and education are offered to people with disabilities and what recourse is available to them. Class culture directly affects the Brazilian perspective on quality of life and who is included in that picture. The cultural hurdle is enormous.

Lack of knowledge, the direct result of class sanctioned differentness, has a tremendous impact on Brazilian quality-of-life issues. Brazilian society, having so deftly ignored these issues, knows very little about disabilities. Blind to its lower classes, it does not understand the causes and characteristics of disabilities. Consequently, Brazilian society does not comprehend emotionally that people with disabilities are human beings with human (Brazilian) rights and human (Brazilian) needs. Lack of financial resources has made it difficult for Brazil to provide appropriate education to the majority of its citizens. Class structure has made it difficult for Brazil to extend its love and commitment universally to its citizens. Individuals with disabilities experience even more this prejudice and rejection of class society. Lack of knowledge influences people's perspectives on quality of life. The differentness sanctioned by class-structured society engenders a lack of understanding that accentuates isolation. Brazil would be well served by a large dose of imported awareness. From awareness will come knowledge. From knowledge will come understanding. From understanding will come compassion and love.

Quality of life for Brazilians with mental retardation and developmental disabilities will improve as the dismissals and divisions of class struggles are removed. Advancement faces that huge embankment: social prejudice. To scale this embankment, to begin to address the acknowledged core dimensions of quality of life, Brazilians with mental retardation and developmental disabilities must first gain inclusion to Brazilian society. *Se não, eles não têm jeito*—If not, they don't have "it" and are not going to get "it."

References

Araújo, L. A. D. (1994). *A proteção constitucional da pessoas portadoras de deficiência* [The constitutional protection of individuals with disabilities]. Brasília: CORDE.

Bueno, J. G. S. (1993). *Educação especial Brasileira: Integração e segregação do aluno deficiente* [Brazilian special education: Integration and segregation of the student with disability]. São Paulo: Editora da PUC-SP.

Carvalho, M. C. B. de, Prudente, C. L., Cruz, D. L. da, Carvalho, R. E., & Blanes, D. N. (1997). *Uma nova concepção de proteção as pessoas portadoras de deficiênci* [One new conception for the protection of individuals with disability]. São Paulo: IEE/PUC-SP; Brasília: Secretaria de Assistência Social, Ministéio da Previdência e Assistência Social.

Conselho Consultativo. (1994). *Subsídios para planos de ação dos governos federal e estaduais na área de atenção ao portador de deficiência.* Brasília: CORDE.

Ferreira, J. R. (1995). *A exclusão da diferença: A educação do portador de deficiência* [The exclusion of the different: The education of the individual with disability] (3rd ed.). Piracicaba, SP: Editora UNIMEP.

Fitzpatrick, J. (1981). The Puerto Rican family. In C. Mindel & R. Haberstein (Eds.), *Ethnic families in America: Patterns and variations* (pp. 189-214). New York: Elsevier North Holland.

Freire, P. (1986). *Pedagogy of the oppressed.* (M. B. Ramos, Trans.). New York: Continuum. (Original work published 1968)

Gonçalves, D. N. (1997, May 7). Primeiro passo: As metrópoles brasileiras começam a se adaptar as necessidade dos deficientes [First step: The urban Brazilian cities are starting to adapt to the needs of people with disabilities]. *Veja,* p. 78.

Heller, T., Markwardt, R., Rowitz, L., & Farber, B. (1994). Adaptation of Hispanic families to a member with mental retardation. *American Journal on Mental Retardation, 99,* 289-300.

Janicki, M. P. (1997). Quality of life of older persons with mental retardation. In R. L. Schalock (Ed.), *Quality of life: Vol. 2. Application to persons with disabilities* (pp. 105-115). Washington, DC: American Association on Mental Retardation.

Lobo, L. F. (1992). Deficiência: Prevenção, diagnóstico e estigma [Disability: Prevention, diagnosis, and stigma]. In Rodrigues et al. In H. B. C. Rodrigues, M. B. S. Leitão, & R. D. B. de Barros (Eds.), *Grupos e instituições em análise* [Groups and institutions in analysis].(pp. 113-126). Rio de Janeiro: Editora Rosa dos Tempos.

MEC-Ministério da Educação e do Deporto. (1994). *Política nacional da educação especial: Livro 1* [National politic of special education: Book 1]. Brasília: MEC/SEESP.

MEC-Ministério da Educação e do Deporto. (1996). *Educação especial no Brasil: Perfil do financiamento e das despesas* [Special education in Brazil: Profile of the finances and expenses]. Brasília: MEC/SEESP/UNESCO.

Ministério da Justiça. (1995). *Câmara técnica sobre reabilitação baseada na communidade (RBC): Resultados da sistematização* [Technical commission on rehabilitation based on the community: Results of the systematization]. Brasília: CORDE.

Minsitério da Justiça. (1996a). *Os direitos das pessoas portadoras de deficiência Lei 7.853/89, Decreto 914/93* [The rights of individuals with disabilities. Law 7.853/89, Section 914/93]. Brasília: CORDE.

Ministério da Justiça. (1996b*). Programa nacional dos direitos humanos* [National program of human rights]. Brasília: Presidência da República.

Ministério da Justiça. (1996c). *Câmara técnica sobre a reserva de vagas para portadores de deficiência—Subsídios para regulamentação do artigo 5, 2 da lei 8112/90* [Technical commission on preservation of a place for people with disabilities: Committee for regulation of article 5, Law 8112/90]. Brasília: CORDE.

Pichorim, S. (1994). *Prevenção de deficiências: Proposta metodológica em pequenos municípios* [Prevention of disabilities: Methodological proposal in small towns]. Brasília: CORDE.

Roberto, K. A., & Nelson, R.E. (1988). The developmentally disabled elderly: Concerns of service providers. *Journal of Applied Gerontology, 8,* 175-182.

Schalock, R. L. (1997). Can the concept of quality of life make a difference? In R. L. Schalock (Ed.), *Quality of life: Vol. 2. Application to persons with disabilities* (pp. 245-267). Washington, DC: American Association on Mental Retardation.

Werebe, M. J. G. (1997). *30 anos depois: Grandezas e misérias do ensino no Brasil* [30 years after: Great accomplishments and miseries of education in Brazil](2nd ed.). São Paulo: Editora Ática.

Work Life and Opinions of People With Mental Retardation in Japan

Akio Tachi
The Institute of Vocational Training
National Polytechnic University
Sagamihara, Kanagawa, Japan

Rehabilitation specialists are beginning to recognize the importance of the concept of quality of life, rather than of normalization, as a new approach to the treatment of people with mental retardation in Japan. Quality of life has been examined theoretically and conceptually (e.g., Matsui, 1992; Yamamoto, 1994), but there are only a few empirical studies based on the concept of quality of life of the physical, social, and psychological circumstances surrounding mental retardation. This is because the concept is ambiguous and incorporates diverse elements.

In this chapter I will attempt to describe briefly and objectively the background of the work life of people with mental retardation in Japan as reported in governmental statistics. Then I will outline the results of interview research supported by the Nihon Hōsō Kyōkai (NHK; Japan Broadcasting Corporation) Health, Welfare, and Cultural Foundation (Koide et al., 1996). In this interview research, opinions of individuals are revealed about working hours, noon recess, holidays, overtime work, wages, participation in a company excursion, worries and enjoyment at workplaces, fear of being fired, job changes, and the will to continue to work, which are all supposed to be variables of the quality of work life. In addition, some scandals involving mistreatment of people with mental retardation, one of the hottest social issues in Japan, will be mentioned. Finally, I will consider problems of quality of life and quality of work life in Japan.

Work Life of People With Mental Retardation

Number of People With Mental Retardation

According to a survey conducted by the Ministry of Health and Welfare in 1991, the population with mental retardation is estimated to be about 385,100 in Japan. Among them, 101,300 are institutionalized at welfare facilities (15,100 under age 18; 86,200 over 18), and 283,800 are living in their homes (100,000 under 18; 168,200 above 18; 15,700 of unknown ages). These individuals are classified as follows: profound mental retardation, 35,200; severe mental retardation, 88,300; moderate mental retardation, 76,400; mild mental retardation, 69,200; and unknown, 14,800.

Work Life Situations

There are three types of work and employment of people with mental retardation in Japan: competitive employment in private corporations and governmental agencies, segregated sheltered employment, and family- or self-employment.

Competitive Employment. Competitive employment is based on a contractual relationship with an employer, and various labor-related laws such as the Minimum Wage Law are applicable. To promote the employment of workers with mental retardation, the government (Ministry of Labor) stipulated a quota system and introduced a levy and grant system based on the Law for the Promotion of Employment of the Handicapped. But corporations are required to hire only people with physical handicaps; they have no obligation to hire workers with mental retardation, although their employment can be counted toward the company's quota.

A survey conducted by the Ministry of Labor in 1994 showed that the number of people with mental retardation hired on a full-time basis by corporations with more than 5 workers was 60,000 (full-time employment means there is no guarantee of a specific contracted period, regardless of the form of the contract) and the number hired on a part-time or some other basis was estimated to be 4,000. Sixty-five percent of the males with mental retardation are hired on a full-time basis, which is far higher than the percentage of females, and 60.7% of the males work for manufacturing industries. Half of these individuals (49.5%) work for small corporations with fewer than 29 workers, and more than half (55.8%) are individuals with moderate retardation. The average length of service of workers with mental retardation is 7.75 years (compared to 11 years for other workers). Their average monthly wage is 112,000 yen, which is much lower than the 271,000 yen paid other workers. Average working hours per month for individuals with mental retardation is 171, which is a little higher than that of ordinary workers, who work 160 hours. Generally speaking, we can understand that working conditions for employees with mental retardation are worse than those for ordinary workers. Moreover, corporations that hire workers with mental retardation account for only 1.9% of the total sample of the survey.

Sheltered Employment. Sheltered employment is provided at welfare facilities to people with severe mental retardation. As this type of employment is regarded as a welfare measure, labor-related laws cannot be applied. In addition to employment at residential and nonresidential sheltered workshops for adults with mental retardation and industrial workshops for adults with mental retardation based on welfare, employment at small workshops is included in this category. Small-scale workshops were established in the 1970s by guardians and people concerned about providing individuals with mental retardation job opportunities. Originally these facilities had no legal support, but in recent years they have become eligible for public financial support. We have seen a remarkable increase in small-scale workshops recently. However, many of them are putting more emphasis on development of physical abilities and sociability than on economic outcomes.

According to the Ministry of Health and Welfare, the number of people with mental retardation working at welfare facilities, including both residential and nonresidential sheltered workshops for adults with mental retardation and welfare factories, was estimated at 33,500 as of October 1, 1994. The number employed at small workshops was estimated to be more than 50,000 (Japan Association of Community Workshops for Disabled Persons, 1994). Although many workshops offer the same kind of work as other factories, their working conditions, such as wages, are not good except for welfare factories and some sheltered workshops. The harsh reality is that average wages per month, for example, are between 10,000 and 20,000 yen for both residential and nonresidential sheltered workshops (National Association of Sheltered Workshops, 1994) and 63.8% of workers at small workshops receive wages less than 5,000 yen (Japan Association of Community Workshops, 1989). Radical measures should be taken in the future to improve working conditions from the viewpoint of income maintenance and protection of workers with mental retardation.

Family and Self-Employment. The final type of employment is self-employment and family-employment. This includes a variety of individual- and family-owned small businesses and shops. The Ministry of Health and Welfare estimated in 1992 that 13,600 individuals with mental retardation were engaged in such work.

Problems With Work Life

As already shown, work opportunities for most people with mental retardation in Japan include private corporations, welfare facilities, and small workshops. And in the case of competitive employment, working conditions are poor in comparison with those for people without physical or mental handicaps.

Working conditions for so-called sheltered employment at welfare facilities and small workshops are very bad, particularly in terms of income. In the case of competitive employment (with generally better working conditions than sheltered employment), only 1.9% of all corporations employ workers with mental retardation. Most of them are small corporations, which some argue are better for adaptation to the workplace because close monitoring of working conditions is possible. But in many cases their working conditions, such as wages, working hours, and holidays, are inferior to those of larger corporations.

On the basis of current information, we can conclude the following:

- The number of private corporations hiring people with mental retardation is small.

- The private corporations that hire workers with mental retardation are mostly small, and in many cases working conditions are worse than those for other workers.

- Many individuals with mental retardation work at welfare facilities and small workshops for lower wages.

Views About Work Life

In this section, I introduce the employment-related part of an interview survey of workers with mental retardation in a study titled *Report on Employment and Life of Persons With Mental Retardation,* conducted under sponsorship of the NHK Health, Welfare, and Cultural Foundation. The survey's purpose was to show the conditions necessary to support the employment and life of people with mental retardation. I was one of the researchers in this project led by Susumu Koide of Chiba University.

Outline of the Research

The project surveyed 573 people with mental retardation who live in 60 regions throughout Japan, are employed in workshops, and are able to communicate verbally: 188 who live with their parents; 152 who live in group homes; 135 who live in dormitories and commute to workplaces; and 98 who live alone. Of these, 359 were male and 214 female, with 11.7% of them between ages 15 and 19; 49.0% between 20 and 29; 22.7% between 30 and 39; and 16.6% 40 and over.

The questionnaire was composed of 46 items in 8 categories: residence, marriage, daily life, work life, money management, leisure, community life, and free answer. Interviews were conducted by 107 staff members who manage career guidance at special services for people with mental retardation.

Results

Here is a summary of key work-related aspects of the survey.

Working Hours. The highest percentage (35%) of people with mental retardation answered that they "work more than 8 hours and fewer than 9 hours" per day. This is regarded as a standard schedule. Twenty-two percent work fewer hours, and 41% more.

Number of Overtime Days. Respondents were asked how many days they worked overtime work in the month just prior to the research. Sixty-five percent answered "almost none," and 15% replied "1 or 2 days a week." These results show that they did not do much overtime work. When they were asked what they thought of overtime work, 41% responded that "the present situation is proper."

Number of Days Off. When asked how many days off they took in June, just prior to the time of the research, 50% responded that they took more than 6 or 7 days off, while about half (49%) said they took fewer than 5 days. The results confirmed that, as many of them are working for small workshops, their working conditions, such as holidays, are not as good as those of other workers.

Wages and Raises. When workers were asked about their monthly wage, 33% reported earning between 90,000 and 110,000 yen. This compares to an average of about 270,000 for other workers at the time of the survey. Thirty-nine percent of the interviewees said they were satisfied with their pay, while 33% replied that it was "less than expected." In Japan the minimum wage is stipulated by law at about 90,000 yen per month; this means our best-paid interviewees received only a little more than minimum wage.

When asked whether they received raises, 46% reported wage increases on their jobs; 24% reported no increases. In Japan wage increases for most workers are generally made once a year.

Management of Income. When asked whether they manage income by themselves, 71% said they did not manage it themselves. It is assumed that parents and guardians probably manage the income of these individuals. Of this group, those who indicated that they did not want to manage their own income (54%) outnumbered those who said they would like to do so (33%).

Among those who do manage their own income, the following are the main reasons: "I can use money freely" (41%); and "I am a grown-up" (32%). Those who do not want to manage income by themselves pointed out their reasons as follows: "might spend all money" (28%); "I don't know how to save" (27%); and "I may lose money" (27%). This result suggests that some respondents lack confidence in their ability to manage money.

Workplace Problems. Nearly 39% of the respondents reported unpleasant experiences at work, with females being more likely than males to have such experiences. The most common problems included teasing or ridicule (30%) and hitting or bitter scolding (15%). Most of the problems involved physical or verbal abuse, and six women said they were sexually abused.

Other types of difficulties in the workplace were reported by 31% of the workers. Of these, the greatest number had to do with inability to work fast enough (27%) or accurately enough (27%). Quick changes of job assignments (11%) also produced difficulties for some workers. Others (18%) felt their noon recess was too short, and 10% were perplexed because they had no one to talk to during their noon recess.

Company Excursions. Employee excursions are a common practice among Japanese companies, and 62% of our respondents reported that their companies conducted such excursions. Of these respondents, 82% indicated that they had participated in such excursions. Further, more than half (52%) reported going out to drink tea or alcohol on the way home from the workplace. Overall, this suggests that their integration in the companies is fairly good. When asked whether they would like to participate in a company excursion again, 87% replied positively. Among nonparticipants, 27% said they did not wish to participate, and 14% said they were not invited.

Feelings of Job Security. A significant minority (26%) of the respondents reported a fear of being fired, with 31% of them saying this could happen because they could not do the job as well as others. Others (14%) feared being fired because they perceived their company to be in a slump. Many respondents (42%) had experienced job changes, 48% of them because they had quit their companies, and 30% because they were forced by the companies to leave.

Happiness and Desire to Continue Working. Two thirds of the workers reported enjoyable experiences at the workplace, 31% attributing happiness to learning new skills and 28% attributing happiness to being trusted to do a job. Most workers (70%) wanted to continue working, with only 17% indicating they would like to change jobs. Among those who wanted to change jobs, the major reasons included lack of interest or a poor fit to their present job (33%), low wages (29%), and difficult relations with coworkers (25%). In Japan workers with mental retardation are often engaged in simple, repetitive jobs—a fact probably reflected in the number of respondents who felt their jobs were not a good fit or not interesting.

When asked to describe their most pleasant moment, 116 of 485 respondents gave answers related to their jobs. Their specific answers included a wide range of experiences related to job recognition, social support from coworkers, wages and bonuses, and financial autonomy. These answers illustrate the importance of self-recognition of growth through jobs and positive estimation by others, acceptance by coworkers, and a sense of self-efficacy. This also indicates how closely the sense of self-fullfillment of workers with mental retardation is related to their engagement in productive activities such as jobs.

The Future. When asked what they would like to say to the people around them, and what they want to do in the future, the workers focused on familiar themes that need improvement: holidays, noon recess, wage discrimination, and recognition. They want fair treatment, recognition of their efforts, and trust in themselves as human beings by their supervisors and coworkers.

In the future these workers want economic stability, pay raises, autonomy, healthy work conditions, new skills, and independent living, among other desires. These responses showed a strong desire for growth and independence.

Summary

A number of conclusions can be drawn about quality of work life of Japanese workers with mental retardation:

- Generally speaking, these workers tend to see their work life positively.

- Working hours and the number of holidays are disadvantageous for them compared with those of other workers (due mainly to the small size of the companies they often work for).

- Many are dissatisfied with their wages.

- Some are suffering disadvantage in their treatment, positions, and work assignments.

- Many are willing to strive to achieve growth and independence through jobs.

Recent Issues in Mental Retardation

Recently several news reports have described disgraceful mistreatment of Japanese citizens with mental retardation. The Japan Association of People With Intellectual Disabilities, one of the country's most influential organizations in this field, published a special feature article titled "Never Allow Maltreatment" (Aoba et al., 1996). Such reports on treatment of people with mental retardation have given us various indications of problems with quality of work life.

Based on the above-mentioned article (Aoba et al., 1996), and another by Hasegawa (1997), I will outline the Akasu scandal. (Akasu is the name of the president of the company where the scandal occurred.) The incident happened in a small cardboard processing factory in Mito City, Ibaragi Prefecture. About 30 people worked for the factory, almost all being individuals with mental retardation. The company received a subsidy from the government, paid to workers with mental retardation, and was once awarded a prize by the municipal government of Mito as the top-rated company for hiring people with mental retardation.

In the winter of 1995, when a female worker who usually stayed at the dormitory returned to her family's house, her parents discovered bruises on her body.

Investigation by her parents revealed that the president and other workers of the company consistently applied violence to workers with mental retardation and were sexually abusive to female workers. In 1996, 14 victims brought charges to the Mito police of violence and sexual abuse against the president.

Even though the company received the governmental subsidy, workers with mental retardation were paid less than minimum wage, and they were forced to resign under threat of violence. In January 1996, the president was charged by the Public Employment Security Office in Mito for unlawful receipt of the subsidy.

According to the victims, they were tortured by the president, in one case by "being hit with a wooden chair and stick to the point of the ears almost tearing off, by being handcuffed, by being forced to sit on the concrete floor with three or four concrete blocks piled on their thighs, and by being forced to sit erect with their legs folded under a square timber put between the calves" (the testimony of one victim), when he got on the president's nerves. Female workers, including minors, were raped.

Many of these charges were rejected, because the statute of limitations had run out or it was impossible to specify the time when the violations actually happened. The local prosecutor's office in Mito filed only three formal charges for unlawful receipt of a subsidy and for cases of violence and injury supported by the confession of the accused. On March 28, 1997, the district court in Mito sentenced the defendant Akasu to 3 years imprisonment, but he was put on 3 years probation in consideration of his long-time contribution to hiring people with handicaps.

These unfortunate incidents were directly caused by the president, but, needless to say, it is obvious that various organizations and people unintentionally assisted these criminal acts. First of all, the relevant authorities such as the Labor Standard Inspection Office, the Public Employment Security Office, and the Welfare Office overlooked these crimes even though they were in charge of monitoring the situations. More regrettably, even though the victims went to these offices to ask for their advice, no one listened to them. It is beyond our understanding that the people of the schools that sent individuals with mental retardation to the workplace did not notice mistreatment and other scandalous acts.

In Japan usually various follow-up monitoring measures are taken after employment of workers with disabilities. In the Mito cases, we are led to wonder if company officials simply pretended "not to notice" in order to receive high performance ratings for employing these workers. Further, it is reported that some of the parents had a vague recognition of the violence applied to their children. Despite this, they turned their eyes away from such maltreatment of their children, perhaps because they were afraid their children might lose the jobs.

Quality of life and quality of work life must be low in the experience of these victims. If we dare make a list of factors that affect quality of work life, the following would be paramount:

- violence and sexual abuse at the workplace;
- low wages;
- exploitation of wages;

- long working hours;
- harsh working conditions;
- enforcement of retirement;
- deprivation of opportunities to change jobs;
- deprivation of freedom of personal life (e.g., by forcing workers to live together in dormitories);
- no respect for human rights.

Conclusion

The problems of workers with mental retardation in Japan can be viewed in light of the eight dimensions defined by K. Keith (personal communication, 1996)—emotional well-being, interpersonal relations, material well-being, personal development, physical well-being, self-determination, social inclusion, and human rights—although every definition does not necessarily fit perfectly here, because the focus of this chapter is on work life. Further, the eight dimensions of quality of work life specified by Walton (1975) are also a good guide in considering the problems of work life of people with mental retardation in Japan. Yet the experts on this issue in Japan seem much more concerned about the dimensions of compensation, safety, social integration, and constitutionalism (rather than about opportunity to pursue human capacities, opportunity for continued growth, work and total life space, and the social relevance of work life). It remains difficult to make a simple evaluation of the problems according to each of these dimensions, as there are differences between the social situations of people with mental retardation and those of other individuals, as well as differences in individual situations among those with mental retardation as observed in their employment.

In thinking about quality of life, I would like to point out one problem inherent in Japan that should be considered (it would be interesting to know whether this problem is unique to Japan): the relationship between the attitude of parents and other concerned people and quality of life. Readers of this chapter might find it strange that 71% of the individuals with mental retardation interviewed in the NHK survey replied that they did not manage their money and left the management to their parents or others, and that those who did not manage it by themselves did not have any will to do so.

For example, being asked whether or not they are allowed to spend 10,000 yen, 50% of the respondents said no. In Japan those over 20 years of age become eligible for the disability pension, but 87% of recipients did not have their own bank passbooks to which the pension money is remitted, and 62% did not want to have passbooks. Twenty-seven percent replied that they did not buy their clothes by themselves, with 59% explaining that their parents or guardians bought clothes for them.

The tendency to avoid self-determination or self-independence reflected in these answers is attributable to the attitude of parents in raising children and the attitude of the Japanese people toward mental retardation. According to the NHK report on people with mental retardation who live at home, when parents enter their rooms only 23% knock on the doors, and 16% are still called *chan* (a term usually used for babies). In addition, 16% had experiences involving private letters opened by their parents. These facts show the unwillingness or reluctance among many parents of people with mental retardation to regard these youth and adults as independent citizens and to guide them to become more independent. Further cultural comparative studies should be made on this subject.

Parents and other concerned people are reluctant to let family members and friends with mental retardation become independent for a number of reasons including the lack of a system to advocate for human rights, as symbolized by the Akasu case, and the lack of a supporting system in the region to help these people become independent.

As to the advocacy of human rights, the need has recently increased to build systems to protect individuals as their involvement in community life expands. For example, there is only one public organization to protect the human rights of citizens with mental retardation (named the Rights Advocacy Center "Step") in Tokyo. It is desirable to establish such organizations throughout the country, and the Deliberation Council on Legislation of the Ministry of Justice has started to consider legislation for a guardianship system for adults, the essence of which is partial guardianship based on respect for the will of the individual with mental retardation.

With regard to a regional support system, though more than 1,500 group homes are established all over the country, the number remains insufficient. And there are only about 40 facilities across the country to provide individuals who live alone with the daily necessities such as shelter, food, and clothes. Moreover, more income would be needed than the amount these individuals are now making to support their independent lives, in addition to the disability pension, competitive employment, and sheltered employment. Japan is behind Western nations in support systems to provide citizens with mental retardation with various services on the assumption that they would lead an independent community life.

In conclusion, problems in the systems, the services, and the way of thinking (of parents, other concerned persons, and ordinary people) about citizens with mental retardation are being gradually revealed through the examination of their quality of life and quality of work life in Japan. In the future, it will be necessary to make efforts to specify the concept of quality of life or quality of work life; to make it measurable by comparison with other countries; to identify the factors affecting quality of life or quality of work life; and to look at the real situations of Japanese citizens with mental retardation through the perspectives of improvement of quality of life and quality of work life in terms of services and systems.

References

Aoba, K., Kaneko, T., Kitazawa, K., Soejima, H., Nagoya, S., Aoki, T., & Matsutomo, R. (1996, August). Discussion: Never allow maltreatment. *Inclusion, 486,* 4-19.

Hasegawa, H. (1997). Hell of the Mito Industrial Workshop. *AERA, 10*(11), 18-20.

Japan Association of Community Workshops for Disabled Persons. (1994). *Phone book of community workshops for disabled persons.* Tokyo: Hon-no-ki.

Japan Association of Community Workshops for Disabled Persons. (1989). *Report of the present situations of small scale workshops.* Tokyo: Author.

Koide, S., Ozaki, Y., Katsura, K., Saito, K., Suzuki, T., Tachi, A., Nakatsubo, K., Nagoya, T., Honma, H., & Miyatake, H. (1996). *Report on employment and life of the mentally retarded.* Tokyo: NHK Health, Welfare, and Cultural Foundation.

Matsui, N. (1992). Quality of life indicators in rehabilitation program evaluation. *Bulletin of National Institute of Vocational Rehabilitation, 1,* 1-18.

National Association of Sheltered Workshops. (1994). Report of the present situations of sheltered workshops. Tokyo: Author.

Walton, R. D. (1975). Quality of work life: What is it? *Sloan Management Review, 15*(1), 11-15.

Yamamoto, M. (1994). Considering QOL of the people with handicap. *Kwansei Gakuin University Sociology Department Studies, 69,* 121-130.

Author Note

I am grateful to Professor Susumu Koide and the NHK Health, Welfare, and Cultural Foundation for their generosity in allowing me to use the data and materials.

Quality of Life of People With Mental Retardation Living in Two Environments in Poland

Wojciech Otrębski
Catholic University of Lublin
Lublin, Poland

The years since 1989 have brought to Poland, a country undergoing a vivid political, social, and economic transformation, significant changes in all aspects of social life as well as sharpening of social awareness concerning problems of people with and without disabilities. During that time the following important legal acts have been laid down: the Rehabilitation and Employment of People With Disability Bill (1991), the Protection of Mental Health Bill (1994), and the Governmental Plan of the Support of Individuals With Disability (1993). In addition, amendments were added to the Social Support Bill and to the Antiunemployment Bill—all of them reflecting clear tendencies toward changes in the social welfare policy of the Polish government that have constituted totally new legal circumstances for action to be taken by and on behalf of people with disabilities in Poland.

Changes in the functioning of the social welfare system vary, however, in respect to different groups of people with disabilities depending on the type of disability. The scope of this chapter allows only a limited analysis of the phenomenon; therefore I will concentrate on that group of people with mental retardation.

Comparing the range of social support services available for the individual with mental retardation before and after 1989, it must be stated that indeed revolutionary changes have occurred in at least some areas of life. The revolutionary character of those changes flows not only from the great efforts made to increase and improve the social welfare system in general, but also from the exposing of all sorts of negligence of the previous social policy with regard to people with mental retardation. Currently improvements are not equally strong in all life domains of individuals with mental retardation and their families, one reason being, among others, the lack of radical actions on the part of decision-making bodies. An example is in the area of housing.

At present the problem is being solved in a twofold manner: Where possible individuals with mental retardation stay with parents or relatives; otherwise in most cases they live in institutions. It should be stressed, though, that especially in larger Polish cities, group homes or supported apartments for people with mental retardation have recently appeared. Yet these cannot be perceived as a clear tendency toward deinstitutionalization, considering the fact that, alongside these, new institutions have been created. Still, however, efforts are being made to approximate the quality of living of people with mental retardation to standard characteristics of the whole society. Are the range of social services adequate to the social needs of the individual with mental retardation? The issue is being addressed.

The previously mentioned legal acts, together with the amendments to the already existing ones, give equal access for various governmental and local administrative authorities as well as nongovernmental organizations to social funds. More important, they also clearly describe standards of particular services for which the funds are to be used. The procedure is an effective means of promoting initiative, guaranteeing protection against squandering of public money, and ensuring proper standards of services.

Standardization of social services remains a vital condition of any successful social policy. However, in itself, it is an insufficient solution to particular problems of people with mental retardation and their families (Butterworth, Steere, & Whitney-Thomas, 1997). Standardization depicts and refers solely to objective life conditions. Were we to consider these only, we would overlook the important factors of subjective well-being and personal satisfaction (Borthwick-Duffy, 1996; Felce, 1997). It becomes necessary, therefore, to collect and compare subjective opinions of the person with mental retardation alongside the consolidation of standarization of social services.

The idea of measuring quality of life of the person with mental retardation, so widely discussed in scientific literature, seems to be a suitable solution that can be easily applied also in Polish conditions.

From among many important publications that appeared in English and to which I have had access, I would like to distinguish works published by the American Association on Mental Retardation and edited by Robert Schalock (1990, 1996a, 1997), which comprehensively deal with the question of quality of life and comprise full documentation of the applied methods. Similarly, Polish publications also reveal numerous theoretical findings and some research on the quality-of-life issue. I shall return to the above point later in this chapter.

To analyze the question of quality of life and its practical implications as understood and applied in Polish circumstances, I will first summarize the scientific output of Polish researchers on the subject and then define the concept of quality of life. Finally, I will present the results of the research I have done on differences in quality of life among individuals with disability living in the open community and attending day activity centers, compared to those who live in institutions without any occupational activity or therapy.

Some Examples of Research in Poland

Summarizing the Polish research on quality of life, I will concentrate only on works that directly use the term. I intend to exclude the scientific literature that thematically refers to the subject in question but does not apply the term. The criterion used entails a limited focus, work from the last 3 to 5 years. The theoretical research will be presented in chronological order and precede a short discussion on empirical work, the latter being far less abundant than the former.

Theoretical Research

Initially, theoretical research on quality of life was conducted by two Polish university sites: in Poznań by Stanislaw Kowalik and Augustyn Bańka, and in Częstochowa by Romuald Derbis. The joint interest of the two centers resulted in the 1993 conference Possibilities of Psychology and Pedagogy in Examining and Shaping the Feeling of Quality of Life. The conference not only gathered Polish scientists in the field, but it also delineated main tendencies for future research. Details can be found in Psychological and Pedagogical Dimensions of Quality of Life (Bańka & Derbis, 1994).

As far as further theoretical research is concerned, attention should be drawn to works by Stanislaw Kowalik analyzing psychological dimensions of quality of life (1993) and temporal conditions of quality of life as well as theoretical controversies on the subject (1995). Equally important is the research of Jerzy Brzeziński (1994) on methodological and ethical aspects of quality of life and Augustyn Bańka's (1994) treatment of quality of life in terms of concepts of man and work. Emerging theoretical research also makes possible the examination of quality of life in the light of responsible freedom (Derbis, 1994) and of creative activity (Pufal-Struzik, 1994).

Another branch of theoretical thought concentrates on the analysis of quality of life as seen through the prism of human suffering (Maciuszek, 1994) and the spiritual life of the dying (Stelcer, 1997), focusing on differences in quality of life among people terminally ill (Jackowska, 1997; Stelcer, 1994; Surdyka, 1997).

Empirical Findings

Some of the above-mentioned works merge theoretical thought with empirical findings (the latter being still insufficient), to which I now turn. Zbigniew Zabor (1997) initiated empirical research examining residents of institutions of Poznań province using Campbell's Scale of Quality of Life. The only criterion applied in his work was that of being a resident of an institution, disregarding the age of the people under examination and type of disability (whether physical, sensory, or developmental). The evaluation of the institutional living conditions and personal satisfaction showed quality of life to be unexpectedly high.

Juros (1997) researched quality of life among people with disability from one local community. Juros investigated a group of 152 people with disability chosen randomly from the Leczna area applying the *Quality of Life Questionnaire* by Schalock and Keith (1993)(translated and adjusted to Polish conditions by Juros). Juros examined the following subgroups: people with mental retardation ($n = 35$), with physical disability ($n = 38$), with heart disease ($n = 27$), with psychiatric disorder ($n = 23$), and with multiple sclerosis ($n = 16$).

Juros compared the results for people with mental retardation on the subscales of the *Quality of Life Questionnaire* (Schalock & Keith, 1993) to research done by Keith (1996). Juros concluded that Polish results are much below average as compared with Keith's equivalents. Additionally, Juros pointed out a number of interesting interdependencies among results achieved within separate subgroups of the examined sample.

As a complement to the above, I would like to present my own research concerning differences in quality of life among people with mental retardation living in the community and attending day activity centers, and among those living in institutions without any occupational activity or therapy.

Different Living Environments and Quality of Life

According to statistics in the middle of the 90s, about 70,000 people in Poland are estimated to be residents of institutions. Within that group, 18% at most are over 74 years of age. Reasons for residing in institutions include: illness, disability (of various kinds, including mental retardation), social maladjustment, drug or alcohol addiction, and mental disease. In addition to the above, note the prolonged residence in institutions of 9,000 people, and the 17,000 awaiting vacancies owing to social factors (Wiśniewska, 1997).

These statistics may sound alarming, especially if viewed through the prism of earlier and recent investigations on the differences between quality of life of people with mental retardation living in institutions and those living in the community (Bachrach, 1981; Bradley, Ashbaugh, & Blaney, 1994; Bruininks, 1981; Butterworth et al., 1997; Kościelska, 1987; Kowalik, 1981, 1997; Minnen, Hoelsgens, & Hoogduin, 1994; Minnen, Hoogdui, Peeters, & Smedts, 1993; Mrugalska, 1987; Olechnowicz, 1987, Otrębski, 1992, 1993a, 1993b; Scheerenberger, 1981; Witkowski, 1987). Unquestionably, the institution emerges as a necessary evil rather than a positive social phenomenon for both the people institutionalized and the whole society that sustains the institutional system. Were we to consider the financial aspect solely, the institutional system still proves a much too expensive form of rehabilitation. The social and individual expenses that the institutional system entails are comprehensively dealt with in the previously cited literature.

It is widely agreed that the most beneficial form of care and rehabilitation for individuals as well as the entire society is one that relies on the resources of a local community, in which case people with mental retardation may remain in a familiar environment and avail themselves of opportunities in due measure to their needs and requirements.

The concept of quality of life in regard to people with developmental disabilities appears to be a thoroughly studied scientific domain in terms of theory, methodology, and research practices, and is supported with broad practical application (Felce, 1997; Hughes, Hwang, Kim, Eisenman, & Killian, 1995; Schalock, 1996b). Considering the immense advantages that application of the quality-of-life approach provides in terms of remodeling the rehabilitation and care services for people with developmental disabilities, I have joined the efforts to adapt the *Quality of Life Questionnaire* (Schalock & Keith, 1993), and participate in research with people with mental retardation.

Having analyzed earlier investigations in the field, and having considered my own experience, I have posed the following question: Is there a vital difference in the perception of quality of life between Polish individuals with mental retardation living in institutions and those living in the community? To examine the problem thus formulated, I have conducted research on two groups of people with mental retardation living in two different environments. The outcome of the investigation and its analysis follows.

Individuals Studied

The study was carried out on a group of 57 individuals with mental retardation (including 25 considered "educable" and 22 "trainable"). Two subgroups were identified: subgroup A comprising 37 people (21 men; 16 women) staying either with families or in group homes and actively participating in occupational therapy led by day activity centers; subgroup B of 20 people (10 men; 10 women), residents of institutions for people with mental retardation in which no occupational therapy was offered. The average age of individuals in subgroup A was 27.8 and for subgroup B, 41.6 (see Table 9.1).

Table 9.1

Gender and Mean Ages of Two Groups

| | Gender | | M Age | |
	Female	Male	Female	Male
Group A (living in the community) (N = 37)	16	21	27.9	27.8
Group B (living in institutions) (N = 20)	10	10	41.5	41.7

Instrument

To measure and evaluate the quality of life of people with mental retardation, the *Quality of Life Questionnaire* (Schalock & Keith, 1993) was used, translated and adjusted to Polish conditions, with the authors' consent, by Juros. In adjusting the *Quality of Life Questionnaire* to Polish conditions, particular attention was paid to linguistic and cultural differences treated as important factors influencing research on people with mental retardation (Keith, 1996).

The *Quality of Life Questionnaire* allows one to establish a general level of quality of life as assessed by a person with mental retardation; it provides a description in terms of factor scores related to satisfaction; competence/productivity; empowerment/independence; and social belonging. Each of the four subscales contains 10 items that can be evaluated according to a 3-point Likert scale. The minimal score is 10 for each of the subscales, and the maximal 30. The total score can vary from a minimum of 40 to a maximum of 120.

Procedure

The investigation was carried out by a team of specialists employed in institutions and day activity centers and possessing a thorough knowledge of the applied method. The participants were examined individually and asked to choose the answer themselves or to point to it. All the examined individuals were verbal.

Results

To establish potential statistical differences in quality of life between the two groups under examination, means and standard deviations were calculated and a test of significance of differences applied (see Table 9.2).

The analysis indicated that individuals with mental retardation living in the community possess a higher level of quality of life than those living in institutions ($p < .005$). Statistically significant differences were found between the investigated groups in two subscales of the questionnaire: competence/productivity ($p < .008$) and social belonging ($p < .008$). This suggests that people with mental retardation living in the community and having access to various daily activities enjoy a higher degree of competence, as well as a stronger feeling of belonging to their community.

Table 9.2

Mean *Quality of Life Questionnaire* Scores for Two Groups

	Community		Institution		
	M	*SD*	*M*	*SD*	*p*
Satisfaction	21.49	3.99	20.50	4.37	n.s.
Competence/Productivity	21.11	6.34	12.79	3.46	<.008
Empowerment/Independence	19.70	3.37	21.05	3.17	n.s.
Social Belonging	21.54	5.25	18.30	3.60	<.008
Total Score	82.70	15.91	72.85	9.65	<.005

Discussion

The results of this pilot study call into question Zabor's (1997) view claiming a beneficial influence of the institution on its residents. Furthermore, they reveal the urgency of reorganizing the system of rehabilitation and care as well as the services rendered people with mental retardation.

Such reorganization should enable a greater number of people with mental retardation to live in their local communities, provide a broader range of daily routines, and fulfill their needs. Only then will the full development of the potential a person with mental retardation possesses be possible and the normalization of life conditions be ensured. This in turn is bound to raise the level of quality of life of this group (Otrębski, 1996, 1997).

Polish norms for quality-of-life measures have not yet been established. However, in the interest of pure comparison, I note that, according to the research by Juros (1997) and the work just described, people with mental retardation in Poland acquired lower scores on the *Quality of Life Questionnaire* (Schalock & Keith, 1993) than those reported by Keith (1996). These comparisons, in my view, provide an argument in favor of change in the Polish system of services for people with mental retardation.

Summary

In conclusion, I note that scientists in Poland approach the question of quality of life multidimensionally. They thoroughly analyze the theoretical, methodological, and ethical aspects in question and also broadly apply this new category of description of reality in empirical research. This means it is very important to establish or adopt information-gathering methods and depict objective factors and subjective evaluation of quality of life of an individual person or a social group.

It is time to recognize and accept subjective assessment of quality of life as the main factor in measuring and evaluating the standard of care and rehabilitation services so as to introduce organizational changes.

References

Bachrach, L. L. (1981). A conceptual approach to deinstitutionalization of the mentally retarded: A perspective from the experience of the mentally ill. In R. H. Bruininks, C. E. Meyers, B. B. Sigford, & K. C. Lakin (Eds.), *Deinstitutionalization and community adjustment of mentally retarded people* (pp. 51-70). Washington, DC: American Association on Mental Deficiency.

Bańka, A. (1994). The quality of life in the psychological conceptions of man and job. In A. Bańka & R. Derbis (Eds.), *Measurement and sense of the quality of life in working people and the unemployed* (pp. 19-40). Poznań-Częstochowa: Ed. UAM & WSP.

Bańka, A., & Derbis, R. (Eds.). (1994). *Psychological and pedagogical dimensions of quality of life.* Poznań-Częstochowa: Ed. UAM & WSP.

Borthwick-Duffy, S. A. (1996). Evaluation and measurement of quality of life: Special considerations for people with mental retardation. In R. L. Schalock (Ed.), *Quality of life: Vol. 1. Conceptualization and measurement* (pp. 105-119). Washington, DC: American Association on Mental Retardation.

Bradley, V. J., Ashbaugh, J. W., & Blaney, B. C. (1994). *Creating individual supports for people with developmental disabilities: A mandate for change at many levels.* Baltimore: Paul H. Brookes.

Bruininks, R. H. (1981). Recent growth and status of community-based residential alternatives. In R. H. Bruininks, C. E. Meyers, B. B. Sigford, & K. C. Lakin (Eds.), *Deinstitutionalization and community adjustment of mentally retarded people* (pp. 14-27). Washington, DC: American Association on Mental Deficiency.

Brzeziński, J. (1994). Methodological and ethical context of research on quality of life. In A. Bańka & R. Derbis (Eds.), *Measurement and sense of quality of life in working people and the unemployed* (pp. 11-18). Poznań-Częstochowa: Ed. UAM & WSP.

Butterworth, J., Steere, D. E., & Whitney-Thomas, J. (1997). Using person-centered planning to address personal quality of life. In R. L. Schalock (Ed.), *Quality of life: Vol. 2. Application to people with disabilities* (pp. 5-24). Washington, DC: American Association on Mental Retardation.

Derbis, R. (1994). Responsible freedom in shaping quality of life. In A. Bańka & R. Derbis (Eds.), *Measurement and sense of quality of life in working people and the unemployed* (pp. 53-62). Poznań-Częstochowa: Ed. UAM & WSP.

Felce, D. (1997). Defining and applying the concept of quality of life. *Journal of Intellectual Disability, 41,* 126-143.

Government Program of Action on Behalf of the Disabled and Their Integration With Society. (1993) Warsaw, MpiPS.

Hughes, C., Hwang, B., Kim, J., Eisenman, L. T., & Killian, D. J. (1995). Quality of life in applied research: A review and analysis of empirical measures. *American Journal of Mental Retardation, 6,* 623-641.

Jackowska, E. (1997). Sense of quality of life in women and men after stroke. In B. L. Block & W. Otrębski (Eds.), *The terminally ill* (pp. 333-342). Lublin: WNS KUL.

Juros, A., & Otrębski, W. (Eds.). (1997). *Integration of the disabled in the local community.* Lublin: FSCEDS.

Juros, A. L. (1997). Sense of quality of life of people with disability and image of community. In A. L. Juros & W. Otrębski (Eds.), *Integration of the disabled in the local community* (pp. 297-309). Lublin: FSCEDS.

Keith, K. D. (1996). Measuring quality of life across cultures: Issues and challenges. In R. L. Schalock (Ed.), *Quality of life: Vol. 1. Conceptualization and measurement* (pp. 73-82). Washington, DC: American Association on Mental Retardation.

Kościelska, M. (1987). Social conditions of how people with mental retardation function. In S. Kowalik, S. Nowak, & S. Waśkiewicz (Eds.), *Optimization of rehabilitative activities among the mentally retarded under PDPS* (pp. 78-86). Leszno: UW WZiOS.

Kowalik, S. (1981). *Rehabilitation of the mentally retarded.* Warsaw: PWN.

Kowalik, S. (1993). Psychological dimensions of quality of life. In A. Bańka & R. Derbis (Eds.), *Psychological thought in renewed Poland* (pp. 31-43). Poznań: Gemini.

Kowalik, S. (1995). Measurement of quality of life: Theoretical controversies. In A. Bańka & R. Derbis (Eds.), *Measurement and sense of quality of life in working people and the unemployed* (pp. 75-85). Poznań-Częstochowa: Ed. UAM & WSP.

Kowalik, S. (1997). Rehabilitation in special care homes. In S. Kowalik (Ed.), *Optimization of rehabilitative activities in the mentally retarded under PDPS* (pp. 21-35). Leszno: UW WZiOS.

Maciuszek, J. (1994). Quality of life and inevitability of human suffering. In A. Bańka & R. Derbis (Eds.), *Measurement and sense of quality of life in working people and the unemployed* (pp. 63-70). Poznań-Częstochowa: Ed. UAM & WSP.

Minnen, A. van, Hoelsgens, I., & Hoogduin, K. (1994). Specialized treatment of mildly mentally retarded adults with psychiatric and/or behavioural disorders: Inpatient or outreach treatment? *The British Journal of Developmental Disabilities, 78,* 24-31.

Minnen, A. van, Hoogdui, C. A., Peeters, L. A. G., & Smedts, H. T. M. (1993). An outreach treatment approach of mildly mentally retarded adults with psychiatric disorders. *The British Journal of Developmental Disabilities, 77,* 126-133.

Mrugalska, K. (1987). Familial ties among the mentally retarded and their stay in social care homes. In S. Kowalik, S. Nowak, & S. Waśkiewicz (Eds.), *Optimization of rehabilitative activities in the mentally retarded under PDPS* (pp. 87-95). Leszno: UW WZiOS.

Olechnowicz, H. (1987). Strategies of preventing and overcoming autistic symptoms in social care homes for children. In S. Kowalik, S. Nowak, & S. Waskiewicz (Eds.), *Optimization of rehabilitative activities in the mentally retarded under PDPS* (pp. 29-35). Leszno: UW WZiOS.

Otrębski, W. (1992). Some solutions in rehabilitation of the mentally retarded in England. In A. Januszewski, P. Oleś, & T. Witkowski (Eds.), *Lectures on psychology at the Catholic University of Lublin. Vol. 6* (pp. 461-470). Lublin: Catholic University of Lublin.

Otrębski, W. (1993a). A chance to gain subjectivity in the mentally retarded under institutionalized care. In T. Witkowski (Ed.), *Subjectivity of the mentally retarded under institutionalized care* (pp. 55-66). Lublin: WZPS.

Otrębski, W. (1993b). Contemporary forms of institutionalized care and rehabilitation of the mentally retarded. In E. M. Lorek (Ed.), *Relief in Suffering* (pp. 103-114). Częstochowa: FRDM.

Otrębski, W. (1996). An attempt to draw out theoretical context for the concept of environmental rehabilitation. *Problems of Social and Occupational Rehabilitation, 2,* 34-37.

Otrębski, W. (1997). Conception of man as a point of departure in planning management towards mentally retarded people. *Problems of Social and Occupational Rehabilitation, 3,* 61-66.

Pufal-Struzik, I. (1994). Creative activity of man and its relationship with self-assessment of quality of life. In A. Bańka & R. Derbis (Eds.), *Measurement and sense of quality of life in working people and the unemployed* (pp. 97-104). Poznań-Częstochowa: Ed. UAM & WSP.

Schalock, R. L. (Ed.). (1990). *Quality of life: Perspectives and issues.* Washington, DC: American Association on Mental Retardation.

Schalock, R.L. (Ed.). (1996a). *Quality of life: Vol. 1. Conceptualization and measurement.* Washington, DC: American Association on Mental Retardation.

Schalock, R. L. (1996b). Reconsidering the conceptualization and measurement of quality of life. In R. L. Schalock (Ed.), *Quality of life: Vol. 1. Conceptualization and measurement* (pp. 123-139). Washington, DC: American Association on Mental Retardation.

Schalock, R. L. (Ed.). (1997). *Quality of life: Vol. 2. Application to people with disabilities.* Washington, DC: American Association on Mental Retardation.

Schalock, R. L., & Keith, K. D. (1993). *Quality of life questionnaire.* Worthington, OH: IDS.

Scheerenberger, R. C. (1981). Deinstitutionalization: Trends and difficulties. In R. H. Bruininks, C. E. Meyers, B. B. Sigford, & K. C. Lakin (Eds.), *Deinstitutionalization and community adjustment of mentally retarded people* (pp. 3-13). Washington, DC: American Association on Mental Deficiency.

Stelcer, B. (1994). Quality of life in palliative care. In A. Bańka & R. Derbis (Eds.), *Measurement and sense of quality of life in working people and the unemployed* (pp. 105-112). Poznań-Częstochowa: Ed. UAM & WSP.

Stelcer, B. (1997). Quality of life and spiritual sphere of the dying man. In B. L. Block & W. Otrębski (Eds.), *The terminally ill man* (pp. 322-327). Lublin: WNS KUL.

Surdyka, D. (1997). Elements of assessment of quality of life in women with cervical carcinoma. In B. L. Block & W. Otrębski (Eds.), *The terminally ill man* (pp. 328-332). Lublin: WNS KUL.

Wiśniewska, A. (1997). Social assistance in Poland: Public responsibility, regulations, and social infrastructure. In A. Pruszkowski (Ed.), *Managing care and welfare: Education and training for the governmental and nongovernmental social services* (pp. 109-131). Lublin: NICW, LOS, WZPS.

Witkowski, T. (1987). Elements of revalidation in the institutions of the type *Home of Residence and Centre of Labour.* In S. Kowalik, S. Nowak, & S. Waśkiewicz (Eds.), *Optimization of rehabilitative management of mentally retarded people under PDPS* (pp. 14-23). Leszno: UW WZiOS.

Zabor, Z. (1997). Assessment of sense of quality of life among residents of social care homes in the Posnań voivodship. In S. Kowalik (Ed.), *From sad reality to accepted necessity* (pp. 46-52). Jarogniewice: Ed. SPiSDPS.

The Multifocal Approach and Quality-of-Life Content in the Treatment of People With Dual Diagnosis

Nehama T. Baum
Muki Baum Association for the Rehabilitation of the Multi Handicapped, Inc.
North York, Ontario, Canada

The philosophy that created the shift in society's thinking regarding deinstitutionalization has also propelled an interest in the quality of life of service recipients. However, from a service provider's perspective, some aspects of quality of life, which appear congruent in theory, are not always in sync with conditions in reality. Renwick, Brown, and Raphael (1994) assert that even though quality-of-life research has increased dramatically in recent years, little attention has been given to links between the academic defining and conceptual exploration of quality-of-life aspects and their implementation in services. Therefore the gap that exists at times between quality-of-life theory and the reality of life needs to be dealt with. Such is the primary purpose of this chapter. To demonstrate a way by which quality-of-life concepts can be transformed from theory to day-to-day reality, this chapter describes a quality-of-life-oriented treatment approach, called the multifocal approach, used with people with developmental disabilities and severe emotional or psychiatric disorders in Toronto.

Individuals with developmental disabilities and severe emotional or psychiatric disorders (i.e., dual diagnosis) present the treatment provider with special challenges. Due to the complexity and multiplicity of these people's difficulties, quality-of-life issues become more crucial, on the one hand, and more complicated to achieve and execute, on the other. Yet such complexity should not prohibit service providers and caregivers from developing treatment programs and services based on quality-of-life principles that will promote the autonomy and the well-being of the people served.

For people with disabilities to become an integral part of the community, there exists a need not only for basic services that focus mainly on physical needs; other aspects of their lives also need attention. Raeburn and Rootman (1996), for example, mention that already in 1948 the World Health Organization defined health as "a state of complete physical, mental and social well being and not merely the absence of disease."

The multifocal approach (Baum, 1980, 1994a, 1994b), which provides treatment in a humanistic, person-centered therapeutic fashion, is based on a wide definition of a life of quality. When working with people who have a developmental handicap accompanied by a severe emotional disturbance, a wide definition of health and well-being is necessary; it supports the use of treatment methods that focus on the person's emotional well-being; it can also be directly linked to a quality of life that has a wider focus than the physical environment and the person's basic custodial needs.

Aspects of Quality of Life

What does quality of life mean? Some previously prescribed definitions of quality of life for people with developmental disabilities by their caregivers included mainly the level of physical or custodial care and living environments (Goode, 1994). However, as a result of the shift in society's attitude, discussed by Menolascino (1990), many researchers and treatment-providing professionals started to include other more subjective elements, such as satisfaction, fulfillment, and emotional well-being. It was argued that though objective elements (physical and custodial) are important, the essence of quality of life is embedded in the subjective experience of the person. As a result, most quality-of-life definitions and models include two realms, both objective criteria and subjective experience and opinion.

Within these two realms, Felce and Perry (1996) evaluate the physical, material, social, and emotional well-being of the person. In the objective realm, they include the following conditions of life of the individual: accommodation, health, job, income, and social leisure activities. In the subjective realm, Felce and Perry incorporate the individual's personal satisfaction regarding the above-mentioned objective aspects of life. Others (Brown, 1993; Renwick & Brown, 1996; Schalock, 1990, 1993, 1996) regard the concept of quality of life as holistic within which empowerment and opportunity for choice making need to be incorporated.

In this chapter, I propose that other aspects be emphasized in addition to the objective and subjective domains of quality of life: It is crucial that a balance between personal needs and wishes and collective societal expectations be established. People with dual diagnosis, for example, who very often communicate their needs and difficulties in aggressive acting-out behaviors, have to learn to cope with external reality that at times might seem to contradict their personal desires (Menolascino, 1994). They also have to learn how to tolerate social expectations and cope with the ever-changing conditions of reality without losing the opportunity to express themselves and thus achieve fulfillment of their wishes and actualize life possibilities. That is, to enhance the quality of life of people with developmental disabilities (with or without mental health needs), an intentional effort has to be made to develop opportunities in both the objective and subjective domains and to create a balance between the individual and the collective realities.

For example, in the institution where he resided before moving back to a group home in the community 5 years ago, Clive spent much of his time being punished for his violent behavior. He was extremely aggressive, verbally and physically, toward staff, and through anger he would destroy his physical environment. He constantly gave strong messages of "noncompliance" by, for example, repeatedly breaking the common toilet, for which he was punished with ever-growing intrusive measures. To achieve any of his wishes, he had to fully comply with the expectations of a strict behavioral code that left no room for free choice.

His move into the community presented the Muki Baum Association with a problem both on the philosophical and treatment levels. The Association does not use behavioral methods in the treatment it provides to its clients. The multifocal approach is a person-centered humanistic approach based on in-depth psychotherapeutic interventions and quality-of-life content. So a transition process had to be established that, similar to a decompression process for a diver, would enable Clive to gradually adjust to a different way of life.

On the one hand, Clive, who craved independence all these years, pushed for a greater level of freedom. On the other hand, due to his obsessions, severe emotional disturbances, and his aggressive reactions, his well-being was at risk as well as the safety of others. Thus the question: How could a balance between the individual and collective realities be reached?

In a primary meeting, Clive expressed his wish to become totally independent, so that he would be "able to do what he wanted." Clive was able to accept that this was a long-term goal; that in the short term, if he chose to achieve it, he would need to invest his energies in acquiring the emotional and psychological skills needed to become successfully autonomous. In-depth psychotherapy provided the milieu within which Clive was able to learn new ways of expressing his feelings and wishes and to develop an ability to postpone his need for instant gratification and acknowledge and cope with his obsessions. He ascertained that great responsibility needed to be established before one can get total freedom; that independence cannot be granted unless it is learned internally. In his therapeutic process, he was able to grieve his past, expressing his pain in a direct way. He said, "My mother never taught me independence. She put me in the institution when I was in grade 1. She never had the time to teach me." Through his sandplay therapy and verbal expressions, Clive was able to gain an increased level of consciousness. He was able to accept that being controlled by his "temptations" made him engage in obsessive actions. He realized how this engagement pushed him to detach from reality and start fantasizing. Gradually Clive acquired more emotional clarity and was able to maintain a higher level of responsibility. He was able to decrease his obsessive-compulsive behavior and became more trustworthy. In regard to independence, his acquisition of decision-making skills enabled him to experience more freedom and exercise greater autonomy. Through this gradual process, full of progressions and regressions, a fine balance was created: the needs of the individual were attended to and the reality of the collective was respected.

A Continuum of Well-Being

Raeburn and Rootman (1996) elaborate on the concepts of quality of life and health promotion, suggesting that the various components of quality of life are on either a positive or a negative end of a continuum of well-being. They term the positive end as *well-being* and the negative as *ill-being*. This follows the idea of Renwick and Brown (1996) that elements of quality of life might differ from person to person. As such, quality of life is a fluid concept. According to Baum (1997), this fluidity takes place on both the interpersonal and intrapersonal levels. That is, quality of life is unique to the individual whose perceptions might differ from others. It is also unique to the situation; therefore its content might change for the same person from one circumstance to another.

From a treatment point of view, a great importance is attributed to the positive and negative polarities of the continuum Raeburn and Rootman (1996) discuss. In their conceptualization, they elaborate on another important treatment element: the determinants of quality of life. They identify two types of determinants in quality of life and in health promotion: (a) environmental determinants (family, school, governmental regulations, etc.) and (b) personal determinants (the disability, psychological processes, etc.) that are perceived to be lifelong and at times permanent. The more unchanging determinants can be affected by moderating determinants that include potential opportunities, support systems, skills, and life events. These moderating determinants have the ability to effect change and thus assist in the modification of life circumstances.

Raeburn and Rootman (1996) and Renwick and Brown (1996) comment that, in theory, quality-of-life aspects are most often treated as discrete entities. They recognize the fact that in life, however, it is almost impossible to separate the different components that comprise and determine it. So emotional agitation experienced as personal stress, which in turn may be expressed in aggressive behavior, will have an effect on the person's relationships and acceptance by the community (Baum, 1994b). This might further result in expulsion from school or employment. Within the framework of the multifocal approach, an ecological approach rather than a sole behavioral approach must be taken by caregivers. Promoting quality in specific identifiable areas of psychological well-being will effect the global change in the overall quality of life of the person.

In many of the theoretical discussions about quality of life, researchers use measurement criteria generally concrete in nature, even when talking about the emotional or spiritual aspects of a life of quality. Well-being, for example, is often evaluated on the basis of the number of days a person is sick. Although it might be easier to quantify answers based on more concrete aspects, they do not necessarily portray the whole picture. As such, emotional well-being might not be expressed solely by measurable behavioral or cognitive presentations. In many cases, it might express itself through a subtle change of feeling about oneself and others, which, especially with people with dual diagnosis, cannot be described in such a concrete manner.

The quality-of-life feedback loop, presented as Figure 10.1, shows another way of explaining the dynamics of change that occur as a result of the interaction between the determinants. This dynamic interpretation can have a positive or a negative charge. As one can see, the person at the center of the loop is in relationship not only with his or her self, but also with the environment. Within these relationships, feelings, wishes, needs, thoughts, and opinions are expressed. Often we communicate such inner aspects via our behavior, which brings about environmental reaction to these expressions. Environmental feedback further establishes our feelings and perceptions about our self. This in turn influences the way we express ourselves behaviorally and causes another reaction from the environment, in a circular manner. If this dynamic occurs with positive content, our psychological well-being and quality of life will improve. If, however, the feedback loop propels negative content, it will cause ill-being and our quality of life will deteriorate.

How does this dynamic receive the positive or negative content? People with developmental disabilities experience, for most of their lives, the stresses that their handicap creates inwardly and in the environment. The struggle to learn and develop that occurs each step of the way contributes to the stress. The feelings that evolve, the image of the self, and the perceptions of environmental attitudes also add to this stress. Different people and environments respond differently to stress. Hence the loop is positive or negative. People with dual diagnosis most often express their needs in extreme behaviors. From the feedback loop one may understand how a continuous escalation occurs in the environment's attitude toward them, and how this affects their feelings, self-image, and conduct.

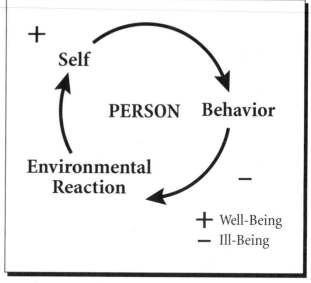

Figure 10.1. Quality-of-life feedback loop.

How can the flow of such a negative feedback loop be changed and turned into a positive direction? When he came to the Children's Program at the age of 12, George had already experienced rejection and expulsion in nine schools. His violent behavior made it impossible for him to attend regular school even within the environment of a special-education class. Being extremely verbal, he did not take any responsibility for his violent acts, constantly blaming others for his actions. He would react in an explosive manner whenever he was asked to do anything, and he would act out without any apparent reason. He would state continuously that he did not understand why he had to attend this "dumb school" and be in the same category as all "these other handicapped kids."

Frequently even the best-intended caregiver will react to such a constant barrage of violence with progressively intrusive interventions. This had been George's experience since a very early age. The message that George received at the Children's Program, however, was that this type of behavior would not bring a replication of his past experiences. The following is an example of the type of messages given to him: After kicking the director in her thigh, George felt very guilty, and in a therapy session expressed to his therapist that he wished to have a meeting with the director to apologize and discuss some of his feelings. He came to the meeting extremely anxious, fearing the consequences of his actions. After a self-initiated apology, he spoke about his feelings and stated that he did not understand why he was put in this situation and declared that he "would like to get out of this dumb school as soon as possible." The director responded by acknowledging his feelings and by stating that although she understood how he felt, she would have appreciated a verbal response rather than his kicking. She explained that she recognized that this might have been his way to make contact with her; she assured him, however, that she was also able to comprehend an oral request. He admitted that he needed to talk with her, because she "was the only person in this dumb school who could release him." They established an agreement that enabled him, after discussions with his staff and therapist, to request a meeting with the director. This was the first time in his life that George was not punished for his violence. He felt heard and understood and knew that the option of such meetings was available.

In his therapy, George dealt with feelings of inadequacy and failure. He faced the pain of being different from other children and expressed his anger at being disabled. At that point, after gaining sufficient trust in his therapist and teachers, he revealed a "big secret." He told them that he was unable to acquire reading skills and that he felt he was "stupid." Due to his violent behavior and the constant attention it received, no professional in his previous school placements considered such a deficiency. A specialized assessment confirmed a generalized, nonspecific learning disability expressed mostly, but not solely, in reading. Clarifying to him the meaning of this finding and providing him with an explanation to the nature of his learning disability and the remediation options available, he was able to slowly change the perception he had about himself. Although still feeling trapped and being concerned about "why" he was so afflicted, he no longer called himself stupid. He also stopped most of his aggressive reaction when asked to accomplish an academic task. Now that the secret was revealed and accepted by his environment, he did not need to aggress anymore to divert attention from his inability to learn how to read or to express his anger for being disabled.

After a few years of exposure to this type of support, he expressed a wish to take upon himself some responsibility in the school. From the available job options, he chose to work in the class of the nonverbal junior students, providing them with support and care. This resulted in a nomination for the 1997 Work Placement Merit Award. He received the award, which acknowledged his achievements. Though still unable to attend such a public gathering (the award was given in absentia), he had found ways to feel better about himself. He developed other modes to communicate his feelings and needs. It freed his energy, which earlier had been invested in negative content. As a result he was able to convert this energy into a more positive direction, which in turn brought about the appreciation of his human environment.

The Multifocal Approach

Challenged individuals with developmental disabilities have frequently been perceived as incapable of knowing what they need because of their intellectual limitations (Dosen, 1990; Prouty & Cornwall, 1990). Moreover, historically, when a dual combination of developmental handicaps and mental illness existed, characteristics of mental illness or severe emotional difficulties were judged to be behavioral aspects of the retardation rather than the typical expressions of a psychiatric disorder. Reiss, Levitan, and Syszko (1982) called this phenomenon "overshadowing." People with mental health needs were exposed to programs that put emphasis on modifying symptoms rather than providing them with the treatment they require. Baum (1990) observed that many caregivers, when talking about the people they serve, used phrases that described the people as not being able to make decisions due to their low intellectual ability and as unable to make choices because they didn't know how.

As a result of these beliefs, caregivers felt that their role was predominantly to care for the physical needs of the people in their charge while making sure that they complied with what the caregivers perceived to be the best for them. These perceptions created a fertile ground for the development of services that were paternalistic and tended to put emphasis on the management of behavior, which became the foundation for expected compliance. In these services there was neither room for the learning of independent choice making nor opportunities for the expression of individual wishes and wants. In such an environment a more autonomous personality could not develop; the flow of the feedback loop was most often negative.

Moreover, because our society puts great emphasis on the appreciation and valuing of intellectual ability, it relates to people with intellectual challenges as people who are deficient and without ability to become equal members in their community. This attitude becomes even more pronounced when the individual in addition to a developmental disability also manifests a psychiatric disorder. People with dual diagnosis are frequently considered as having even a lesser capacity to contribute independently to their lives.

A change in these perceptions started to emerge with the deepening of our understanding of mental retardation beyond its numerical IQ expression and the realization that people with low intellectual capacity are able to lead more normalized lives. In addition to this, and with the increased interest in quality of life, the door has been opened to the development of new concepts within the provision of services. These concepts, however, also create some difficulties and contradictions, especially in regard to choice making and independence.

The complexity of the dual diagnosis handicapping condition raises questions in regard to the gap between quality-of-life theory and its implementation in day-to-day life situations. We need to explore how we can implement quality-of-life content in treatment programs for people with dual diagnosis so as to encourage learning of choice making and acquisition of emotional skills needed to make use of available opportunities. While this learning occurs, it is important also to ensure that the needs of the people, including their safety, continue to be met, even if it infringes on their independent decision making.

Within the framework of the multifocal approach described in this chapter, which is a psychotherapeutic treatment model based on quality-of-life content and the principles of person-centered (Rogers, 1951) and person-referenced individualized programming, such empowerment takes place. To achieve this goal a mediated learning experience milieu needs to be created. Feuerstein (1980) comments that people with developmental disabilities experience difficulties in learning from direct exposure unless long-term, extensive, and suitable mediation is provided. They require, he adds, a longer process that breaks down cognitive tasks, provides ongoing specialized cognitive practice, and enables them to acquire the concepts and skills they need. Such intentional mediated learning experience provides the person with the means to expand his or her cognitive basis and learn and attain functional skills.

At the foundation of the multifocal approach is the belief that emotional blockages, which are either constitutional or have developed over the years as a result of the negative feedback loop, will prevent meaningful and significant change. The multifocal approach expands the concept of mediated learning experience to include extensive emotional mediation that "interprets the world" for the person. It enhances the development of the person's ability to understand the emotional inner reality and cope with the ever-changing content and meaning of life situations.

The question of choice in regard to psychotherapy was raised in 1996: What if a person served by the Association did not wish to receive psychotherapy? It was understood and accepted that although the fundamental principle of the multifocal approach is the emotional work deemed essential to achieving emotional stability and expanding consciousness, the imposition of psychotherapy would not accomplish this end. It was suggested that an environment that promoted respect of the person and gave opportunities for acceptance of choice would also contribute to the emotional well-being of the people served, thus providing them with a possible alternative to therapy.

To validate this idea and establish some baseline criteria, the Association took upon itself, as a first step, to conduct a survey exploring the wishes of all the people served at the Adult Program in regard to participation in psychotherapy. Nonverbal individuals were asked verbally and their responses were given either with the aids of augmentative communication devices or via gesturing. The questionnaire included questions reqarding the wish to participate or not to participate in therapy; the preferred model of therapy; the preferred setting (individual or group); and the desired frequency of therapy sessions.

Only a few of the people surveyed stated that they were not interested in participating in psychotherapy. The majority wanted to continue with their therapeutic work. They expressed, however, their choices in regard to the various available models and at times even asked for a specific therapist. Many people requested both group and individual sessions but accepted the fact that they might have to make a second choice in situations where this was not possible. The choices as reflected in the results were respected. Individuals who decided not to have psychotherapy were able to stop their participation. Others were able to receive the type of therapeutic services they requested. With one exception, the number of weekly sessions had to be restricted due to budgetary constraints.

The survey also produced one unexpected result. One participant expressed his wish to colead a peer group dealing with interpersonal conflict resolution, leisure time, socialization, and autonomy issues. He suggested as his coleader a woman, who agreed to participate. The two leaders organized the peer group, which is now running successfully for the second year. A therapist was assigned to the group as a resource person who attended the meetings as an observer, sitting outside of the group circle. The observations enabled the therapist to provide feedback and guidance when asked by the coleaders after the sessions.

At the present time, some of the people who decided to withdraw from psychotherapy have since asked to reestablish their psychotherapy engagement. Those who have not made a different decision seem to be coping well without therapy and continue to expand their physical independence and psychological autonomy. For these individuals the support received in an environment that employs quality-of-life content seems sufficient to enable them to further develop and grow.

For such flexibility to occur within a system, as shown in the above example, areas of need and difficulty have to be identified on an ongoing basis. Similarly change and growth also have to be evaluated and reevaluated, ensuring the maintenance of the resiliency of the system. In addition, caregivers need to develop awareness to the role they play and the areas of their responsibility within the relationship with the person served. Caregivers have to be able to identify, among others, boundary issues. They need to be able to provide assistance to the developing ego and to support the strengthening of ego-consciousness.

In the multifocal approach, the caregiver is perceived to be in a partnership with the person in care. As with any partnership, both partners grow, change, and learn. This partnership is not a relationship in which one partner, the caregiver, is the only one who outlines expectations of conduct and the other partner, the person in care, has only to comply. A relationship such as this one, according to the multifocal approach, perceives both partners as equal, with different responsibilities.

Conclusion

As described in this chapter, quality-of-life content manifests itself in the creation of a supportive human environment that provides the people served with the opportunity to learn, at times for the first time in their lives, how to believe in their abilities rather than focus on their disabilities. It enables them to accept themselves and to realize that they are able to actualize their human potential. Experiencing a sense of belonging provides them with the means to develop trust. This trust becomes the foundation upon which a letting go of their behavioral patterns, which served them as coping mechanisms, can take place. As a result, the direction of the feedback loop from a negative to a positive charge occurs. It enhances a more positive interaction with the environment, which further supports a stronger sense of the self.

A balance between the wishes of the individual and the demands and expectations of the collective can be attained. It contributes to a reduction in the gap between the individual's perception of the number of available opportunities for choice making and the reality of his or her objective achievements. The effect that all of the above has on the personal, subjective realm of existence enhances in the individual a general feeling of well-being and positive self-perception.

References

Baum, N. T. (1980). *A multi-focal approach in the assessment and treatment of multi-handicapped adolescents: An individual case study.* Unpublished doctoral dissertation, University of Toronto.

Baum, N. T. (1990). Therapy for people with dual diagnosis: Treating the behaviours or the whole person? In A. Dosen, A. Van Gennep, & G. J. Zwanikken (Eds.), *Treatment of mental illness and behavioural disorder in the mentally retarded* (pp. 143-156). Leiden, The Netherlands: Logon.

Baum, N. T., (1994a). *The Multi-Focal Approach.* Toronto: Muki Baum Association.

Baum, N. T. (1994b). The phenomena of playing within the process of sandplay therapy. In N. Bouras (Ed.), *Mental health in mental retardation: Recent advances and practices* (pp. 255-272). London: Cambridge University Press.

Baum, N. T. (1997). Enhancing the quality of life of people with dual diagnosis: The power of art education. *Journal on Developmental Disabilities, 5*(2), 96-111.

Brown, R. I. (1993). Quality of life issues in aging and intellectual disability. *Australia & New Zealand Journal of Developmental Disabilities, 18*(4), 219-227.

Dosen, A. (1990). Psychotherapeutic approaches in the treatment of depression in mentally retarded children. In A. Dosen & F. J. Menolascino (Eds.), *Depression in mentally retarded children and adults* (pp. 255-264). Leiden, The Netherlands: Logon.

Felce, D., & Perry, J. (1996). Exploring current conceptions of quality of life: A model for people with and without disabilities. In R. Renwick, I. Brown, & M. Nagler (Eds.), *Quality of life in health promotion and rehabilitation: Conceptual approaches, issues, and applications* (pp. 51-63). London: Sage.

Feuerstein, R. (1980). *Instrumental enrichment: An intervention program for cognitive modifiability.* Baltimore: University Park Press.

Goode, D. (1994). *A world without words: The social construction of children born deaf and blind.* Philadelphia: Temple University Press.

Menolascino, F. J. (1990). Mental retardation and the risk, nature, and types of mental illness. In A. Dosen & F. J. Menolascino (Eds.), *Depression in mentally retarded children and adults* (pp. 11-34). Leiden, The Netherlands: Logon.

Menolascino, F. J. (1994). Services for people with dual diagnosis in the USA. In N. Bouras (Ed.), *Mental health in mental retardation: Recent advances and practices* (pp. 343-352). London: Cambridge University Press.

Prouty, G., & Cornwall, M. (1990). Psychotherapy with a depressed mentally retarded adult: An application of pre-therapy. In A. Dosen & F. J. Menolascino (Eds.), *Depression in mentally retarded children and adults* (pp. 281-293). Leiden, The Netherlands: Logon.

Raeburn, J. M., & Rootman, I. (1996). Quality of life and health promotion. In R. Renwick, I. Brown, & M. Nagler (Eds.), *Quality of life in health promotion and rehabilitation: Conceptual approaches, issues, and applications* (pp. 14-25). London: Sage.

Reiss, S., Levitan, G. W., & Syszko, J. (1982). Emotional disturbance and mental retardation: Diagnostic overshadowing. *American Journal of Mental Deficiency, 86,* 567-574.

Renwick, R., & Brown, I. (1996). The Centre for Health Promotion's conceptual approach to quality of life: Being, belonging, and becoming. In R. Renwick, I. Brown, & M. Nagler (Eds.), *Quality of life in health promotion and rehabilitation: Conceptual approaches, issues, and applications* (pp. 75-86). London: Sage.

Renwick, R., Brown, I., & Raphael, D. (1994). Quality of life: Linking a conceptual approach to service provision. *Journal on Developmental Disabilities, 3,* 32-44.

Rogers, C. R. (1951). *Client-centered therapy: Its current practice, implications, and theory.* Boston: Houghton Mifflin.

Schalock, R. L. (Ed.). (1990). *Quality of life: Perspectives and issues.* Washington, DC: American Association on Mental Retardation.

Schalock, R. L. (1993). Viewing quality of life in the larger context. *Australia & New Zealand Journal of Developmental Disabilities, 18*(4), 201-208.

Schalock, R. L. (1996). Quality of life and quality assurance. In R. Renwick, I. Brown, & M. Nagler (Eds.), *Quality of life in health promotion and rehabilitation: Conceptual approaches, issues, and applications* (pp. 104-118). London: Sage.

Quality of Life of Aging Institutionalized People With Mental Retardation in Japan

Akiie Henry Ninomiya
Kwansei Gakuin University
Hyogo-ken, Japan

Following World War II, welfare for Japanese people with mental retardation was organized mainly for juveniles, according to the *Outline for Operation of Institutions for Mentally Handicapped Children* (Ministry of Health and Welfare, 1954). Later, the campaign to establish institutions for adults was started by the Nationwide Society for Mentally Handicapped Children, and its name was changed to Nationwide Society for Mentally Handicapped Adults. In 1960 the Welfare Law for Mentally Handicapped People was enacted, and institutions for adults began to provide care, mainly in the form of accommodations and protection.

In 1964 the Social Bureau of the Ministry of Health and Welfare began developing training and vocational services to enable individuals to support themselves. Institutions continued to grow, parallel to Japan's economic growth, and a number of colony-type institutions were installed nationwide during the 1970s, followed by facilities for commuters who could be served with the assistance of family members, especially parents.

The Japanese population, including people with disabilities, is aging faster than that of other developed nations. The institutions accommodating these people must be concerned not only with their aging, but with those aspects of their conditions that are worsened by aging. To date, these institutions have been concerned mainly with assistance, training, and welfare services. However, this approach is no longer good enough if the quality of life of individuals with mental retardation is to be maintained. As they age, individuals with intellectual disabilities experience deterioration in physical and social conditions and in relationships with their families. The research presented in this chapter looks at the circumstances existing in institutions for people with mental retardation; research was undertaken to support reorganization of the welfare system for aging individuals.

By 1990, the number of institutions (more than 1,000) was about 2.2 times the number existing in 1980, and they served more than 70,000 people with mental retardation. Of these people, 2.8% were over 60 years of age; more than 30% were over 40; and 50% were 30 to 60 (Statistical Association of Health and Welfare, 1991). These figures suggested that (a) the aging of these people would present major challenges in the near future and (b) the institutional population would increase as middle-aged individuals, due to the aging of their parents, have no choice but to move to institutions.

Welfare Services for People With Mental Retardation in Institutions

According to current law, the purpose of institutions accommodating people with mental retardation in Japan is to provide necessary guidance and training to protect and rehabilitate these people. Additionally, the aim of vocational-aid institutions is to provide training, guidance, and vocations to enable them to support themselves. But these services may not be applicable for aged people with mental retardation. Rather, as stated in the Geriatric Welfare Law, it is necessary to enrich the welfare services for aged citizens with mental retardation with proper methods for stabilizing their physical and mental health and their lives generally. This indicates that attention must be given to medical and nursing care, structure and accessibility of buildings and facilities, and the training and selection of staff.

Purpose of the Research

In an effort to study the issues noted above, four areas of concern were investigated in Japanese residential facilities: (a) methods of care for people with mental retardation; (b) staffing of institutions serving aged people with mental retardation; (c) service delivery for aging people with mental retardation; and (d) facilities for aging individuals.

Method

The investigation studied all institutions accommodating adults with mental retardation in Hyogo prefecture. Of the 38 Hyogo facilities, 5 were public rehabilitation programs; 27 were private rehabilitation programs; 1 was a public vocational-aid institution; and 5 were private vocational-aid institutions. Questionnaires were delivered to these 38 institutions to assess age structure, mental and physical conditions, nursing care conditions, medical care conditions, and family relations of residents. In addition, data were collected on buildings and facilities, and on staffing and program measures undertaken in response to the aging of individuals with mental retardation. The questionnaires, accompanied by a letter of support from the director of the Hyogo Prefectural Mental Retardation Association, were returned by 100% of the institutions.

In addition to the questionnaires, site visits were made to those Hyogo institutions serving significant aging populations. The visits involved week-long observations, carried out 24 hours per day, of programs and conditions in the facilities.

Findings Related to Individuals

Ages. The types of facilities and a summary of age and gender characteristics of the 2,301 clients of the Hyogo institutions are summarized in Table 11.1. The number of people with ages greater than 50 was 372 (174 males; 198 females), or 16.2% of the total. Females constituted 53.2% of the older group, compared to 40.5% of the total institutional population.

Duration of Stay. As might be expected, with increasing age people were likely to have resided in institutions longer (see Table 11.2). A separate analysis showed that duration of stay was longer in older institutions, suggesting that the number of people leaving the institutions was relatively small (9.6%). Among those who did leave

Table 11.1

Facility Type, Gender, and Mean Ages
of People Served by Hyogo Institutions

Facility Type	n	Male	Age (M)	Female	Age (M)
Total	2,301	1,268	35.60	1,033	38.23
Rehabilitation	1,934	1,063		871	
Vocational Aid	367	205		162	

Table 11.2

Duration of Institutional Residence

	Years			
	0-4	5-9	10-19	Over 20
Males Under 50	30.1%	29.8%	32.1%	7.4%
Females Under 50	29.1%	29.4%	33.6%	7.9%
Males Over 50	18.4%	35.6%	32.2%	15.5%
Females Over 50	17.6%	31.7%	42.7%	10.0%

institutions, the single largest group (39.5%) moved to other institutions. A few (5.5%) moved to geriatric institutions, a few (6.8%) moved to hospitals, and 15% died.

Prior Situations. Of those institutional residents younger than age 50, 39.2% had come from their natural homes. By contrast, 72.6% of institutional residents over age 50 had come from their homes. Of those under 50 who had come from other institutions, 27.6% came from similar types of institutions, 21.1% from nursing institutions, and 1.9% from commuter dormitories for people with mental retardation. Thus, more than half (50.6%) of those persons under 50 came from other institutions. The bulk of the remainder of younger residents came from school programs for children with mental retardation and from institutions specialized for children.

Intellectual Characteristics. Of the 2,301 people in the Hyogo institutions, 491 (21.3%) were individuals with the most significant intellectual disability (IQ below 20), an additional 1,113 (48.3%) had severe intellectual disability (IQ 20-35), and 628 (27.3%) were people with moderate intellectual disability (IQ 36-50). Mild intellectual disability (IQ above 50) was found for 155 (6.7%) of the individuals in these facilities.

While the most serious disabilities were less likely to be found among those over age 50, mild and severe disabilities were found in the same proportions among those over and under 50, and moderate disability was somewhat more likely in those over 50 (occurring in about 40% of the cases). Overall, more serious intellectual disabilities were somewhat more likely to be found in younger residents.

Physical Disabilities and Diseases. The number of residents with physical disabilities was 947 (41.2%). Of these, 391 (41.3%) had auditory or speech disorders; 126 (13.3%) had visual impairments; and 98 (10.3%) had cardiac, respiratory, kidney, or other urinary disorders. Overall, physical disabilities, particularly those involving the extremities, vision, and internal disorders, became worse after age 50.

A number of disease-related conditions were also found to increase among the aging population. For instance, neurologic disorders and diseases affecting the eyes, digestive organs, and circulatory organs increased significantly after age 50, and more than 55% of those above 50 and over 65% of those in the 55- to 59-year age group received medication for illnesses. These age-related increases are illustrated by circulatory diseases, which went from about 4% in the early 40s to more than 10% after age 55, and by digestive diseases that occurred in 6.1% of the general institutional population, but in more than 12% of the over-50 age group. Likewise, respiratory diseases occurred in only 1.2% of the residents overall, but in 15% of those over age 65. Similar trends were found for other diseases and illnesses.

In addition to the medical conditions noted here, it was found that 914 (39.7%) of the residents of the Hyogo institutions needed to see a doctor regularly. For those over age 50, the percentage requiring regular care by a doctor was 42.4.

Findings Related to Facilities and Quality of Care

Daily Care. The questionnaires addressed a number of types of care that might be considered nursing care: toilet use, eating meals, dressing and undressing, ambulation, bathing, and so forth. Respondents were also allowed to add other items as appropriate. These facilities were staffed largely by work and life instructors, with no true nursing care director, and no distinction was made between total and partial nursing care in the data collection. Except for ambulation, assistance with all the activities noted above was more necessary for those under age 50 than for those over 50, probably due to the fact that more serious disabilities were more often present in the younger group. This difference was especially true for bathing and for dressing and undressing. Overall, males required more nursing care than females, and above age 50 males (32.8%) were more likely to require assistance in toilet use than females (17.6%). Of those below age 50, 29.9% required assistance in toilet use, 44.4% in bathing, and 30.5% in dressing and undressing. These findings suggest that these individuals may need more nursing care, and that as they age the need for nursing care is likely to increase.

In addition to these daily "nursing" needs, many of these individuals (as previously noted) take medications, and many must see a doctor regularly. Nurses working in these facilities reported that they spent 17.7 to 39.0% of their working hours transporting residents to outside medical institutions—time during which they were not available to meet the needs of other residents.

Staffing. Conditions of care are related to the number of staff members. According to the *Research Report of the Social Welfare Institutions,* issued by the Statistical Association of Health and Welfare in 1991, the nationwide staffing level in facilities serving people with mental retardation was 1 staff member per 1.98 individuals served. In Hyogo prefecture, the ratio was 2.32. For the vocational-aid institutions, the national average was 2.27; the Hyogo average was 2.26.

Further, the national Health and Welfare Law of 1990 specified that "The total number of public health nurses, life instructors, and work instructors must be larger than the total number of handicapped people in the institution divided by 4.3." Hyogo prefecture used a figure of 3.03, and thus exceeded the nationwide standards. However, no physical therapist or occupational therapist was present in any institution serving adults with mental retardation in Hyogo. Additionally, it was standard for one nurse to be on duty per institution serving people with mental retardation. This is in contrast to nursing homes for the aged, where 272 full-time therapists, plus many part-time therapists, are available, and where two nurses are generally available. The national standards for staffing for nursing homes are also more stringent (requiring a ratio of 4.1:1) than those for facilities for mental retardation (4.3:1). As the population of people with mental retardation ages, and their physical functions decline, it will be necessary to make available experts on therapy, rehabilitation, nursing, and so on, to arrange programs to support physical functions.

Facilities. Most (72.2%) of the institutions studied had more than one level, and 65.8% were judged in need of improved structures. Only five of the multiple-story buildings had elevators, even though some of the others were already serving individuals in wheelchairs. National standards for nursing care facilities require that bathrooms be suitable for those with physical disabilities, and that they should be equipped with specially devised bathtubs. Among the Hyogo institutions for people with mental retardation, only two were found to be equipped with a special bathtub, despite the large number of residents who required assistance with bathing. Most (76.3%) of the institutions surveyed were equipped with handrails, but 17 of the facilities indicated the need for more handrails.

Visitors and Visits to Home. The number of visitors that individuals had was found to decrease with age. Of those below age 50, 37% had more than 11 visitors per year, while 20.6% of those over age 50 had no visitors at all. Most of the visitors to residents under age 50 were parents and siblings (47.9% of the visitors were parents); parents, however, comprised only 2.2% of the visits to people over age 50, no doubt due to the advancing age or death of the parents. The older residents, as a result, seemed to become more isolated.

Such occasions as the Bon festival or New Year festival are good opportunities for individuals to share good times with their families and to experience social life. Persons under 50 most often visited the houses where their parents and some of their siblings live (44.6%) or where only their parents live (24.3%). Those over 50 most often visited the houses where only their siblings live (54.9%), followed by houses where their parents and some of their siblings live (37.1%), with only 0.5% visiting the house where only their parents live. Also, with age the frequency of visits decreased, and with it the opportunities to participate in society.

Conclusions and Future Prospects

It is estimated that the proportion of the Japanese institutional population over age 50 will reach close to 40% in the next 10 years, and 70% within 20 years. Currently, the number of residents over 60 in Hyogo prefecture is 89—a number that is expected to grow to 372 within 10 years. Further, the number of adults with mental retardation living in their family homes is also increasing, meaning that, as their parents advance in age and it becomes difficult to care for their adult children, there will be more aging individuals in search of services. The aging of these people, if the rate with which they leave institutions does not increase, will make it necessary for their care to focus less on instruction and more on life assistance and medical concerns. Staffing may need to be more nurse-centered, staffing levels should be increased to equal or exceed those of general nursing facilities for the aged, and additional facilities may be needed.

The current method of caring for people with mental retardation in these facilities is on-the-job instruction with the aim of making them independent. However, nursing care, or so-called life instruction, becomes more necessary with age. Significant numbers of individuals in this survey required assistance with bathing, toilet use, dressing, and mealtime behavior. And, according to a report of the Osaka Prefectural Kongo Colony in 1991, the frequency of incontinence and urination during the night among this population is likely to increase rapidly after age 40. In view of the fact that more significant disabilities were actually found in the group under age 50, the next generation, as it ages, is likely to require more extensive care. Further research and planning should be carried out to determine the future needs for nursing care of these individuals.

This survey suggests that people of advancing age in the institutions studied became increasingly isolated. Their parents were deceased or unable to visit many of them, and the number of other visitors was small. For some people, their aging also made it more difficult to participate in the work offered by the institution. This is in contrast to the Japanese custom of visiting people living in community nursing homes, where relationships and connections to the local community are more likely to persist. Closer attention needs to be paid to this aspect of the life quality of individuals served by the institutions for people with mental retardation.

The rhythm of daily life provided by the institutions may also be a problem for aging individuals. In many cases, they are scheduled to wake up in early morning, wash their faces, have breakfast, exercise, work at a workshop, clean, bathe, go to bed, and so forth, on the same schedule as younger individuals. Attention to individual needs and the rhythm of aging people's lives will be necessary if they are not to be further isolated within the institutions. While enrichment of their lives, with care given to satisfaction and stability, is essential, close cooperation with nursing and medical supports is also necessary. Future work should focus on cooperation between the welfare and medical treatment systems.

To maintain life satisfaction and intellectual ability, efforts must be taken to be sure that the inside of the institution is not the sphere of the residents' activities. Interactions with the community—shopping, dining out, stimulating activities and therapies (music, art, horticulture, etc.)—need to be arranged, as well as programs to maintain contact with families and friends.

In the 21st century, Japanese society will be composed increasingly of elderly people. Current statistics indicate that 25% of the Japanese people will be above 65 years of age by the year 2025. A variety of laws have been enacted with consideration to the current age structure of people with disabilities: the Child Welfare Law, the Mentally Handicapped Welfare Law, and the Aged Welfare Law. With the aging of those with mental retardation, it is urgent that we reorganize these laws to protect the quality of life of these individuals. In this way it can be assured that future services will take account of their age, disabilities, social needs, medical problems, and facility requirements.

References

Ministry of Health and Welfare. (1954). *Outline for operation of institutions for mentally handicapped children.* Tokyo: Author.

Statistical Association of Health and Welfare. (1991). *1990 Statistics on the number of institutions and their populations.* Tokyo: Ministry of Health and Welfare.

Quality of Life of People With Mental Retardation in Spain: One Organization's Experience

Javier Elorriaga
Loreto Garcia
Jorge Martinez
Elvira Unamunzaga
Fundación Tutelar Gorabide
Bilbao, Spain

The Fundación Tutelar Gorabide is a small nonprofit social service agency devoted to the exertion of legal guardianship on behalf of disabled people who lack it. The goal of the Foundation is to provide protection and an effective guarantee of the rights of people to achieve full social inclusion and a good quality of life. The Foundation seeks to give practical answers to the needs of people under judicial "sentence of incompetence" whose abandonment situation, orphanage, and/or diminished or impoverished sociofamiliar environment prevents them from finding individuals capable of exercising the responsibility of their legal guardianship.

Taking as reference the definition of mental retardation given by the American Association on Mental Retardation (AAMR)(Luckasson et al., 1992) and the model for quality of life by Schalock (1996), our purpose is to reflect on key aspects involving the quality of life of people with mental retardation from the point of view of professionals linked to the provision of services. In this chapter we will also describe the cases of two people with mental retardation, as representative examples of the advances in the improvement of the quality of life in Spain.

The Recent Past in Spain—Antecedents

The Spanish Constitution, promulgated in 1978, was the first legal text in which the Spanish public administration was made responsible for a policy of prevention, treatment, rehabilitation, and integration of people with physical, sensorial, and psychic disabilities, as well as for paying them specialized attention and helping them exert their rights as citizens. Equally, the Constitution allocated the bulk of the social policies regarding people with disabilities to local administrations (self-governed regions and town councils). However, during the first years of democratic restoration, only the Central Administration was responsible for taking the first and basic steps on welfare policy on behalf of people with disabilities.

The Law for Social Integration of the Disabled (LISMI), passed in 1982, had the clear purpose of impelling active policies and therefore a decentralized action. Its implementation demanded some political and administrative tools that, in postdictatorial Spain, were nonexistent at either a regional or local level. This management lack was also present in the Spanish Central Administration, because the development of new programs and the setting in operation of facilities took several years and became operative only in the 1980s, with the consolidation of the National Institute of Social Services. Due to these circumstances, the implementation of this law was limited for years to the provision of monetary aids. This development was the biggest impediment to a law that was progressive and ambitious.

However, a change has occurred in the last few years. Two external factors worthy of mention besides the strong impulse given by the regional governments since 1992 determined this positive change. First, the intense lobbying carried out by parents and relatives of people with disabilities that caused their claims and proposals to be heard, finding a more receptive attitude from the local authorities. Second, the elaboration of the government's *Action Plan for People With Disabilities 1997-2002* (Institute Nacional de Servicios Sociales, 1996) had become an incentive for the regional governments. Therefore, once the transfers from the central government to the regional governments were accomplished, these regional governments became the main actors. At this point, an obvious question arose: Will a sufficient budget be guaranteed to maintain, consolidate, and increase the important changes experienced in the social policy regarding people with disabilities?

In summary, in Spain there was no welfare state until the promulgation of the Spanish Constitution in 1978. In comparison with neighboring countries, this happened late and incompletely. Some years ago we heard of the welfare state's crisis and its transformation to a "welfare society." The administration, having difficulties facing up to its social care commitments, left a wider margin to citizens' initiatives allowing a more committed society to play a more important role. This new sociopolitical arena that has been forming during the last decade, grouping many different and hardly qualifiable initiatives, lies between the public institutions and the market. It has been called the "third sector": associations, foundations, and volunteer groups.

A Model for the Study of Quality of Life

Although from antiquity people have attempted to determine how to identify and implement the necessary conditions to improve quality of life, efforts to conceptualize and measure it have a short history. In the domain of disabilities and people with mental retardation, this concept is becoming relevant and a subject for professional study.

With the assumption in Spain of normalization and the recognition of the civil rights of people with disabilities, first efforts to improve the quality of life of these people have involved community integration using a supports model. Our country is also undergoing an important ideological change, accepting the assumptions of the new paradigm represented by the latest definition of mental retardation of the AAMR (Luckasson et al., 1992). This new *Definition, Classification, and Systems of Supports* has been accepted formally by the Spanish Confederation of Federations and Associations for People With Mental Retardation (FEAPS), although the processes directed to its effective implementation have only begun.

Unfortunately, several social and cultural values have hindered the evolution of the new paradigm. For this reason it is necessary to maintain and increase the effort carried out in our country in every aspect related to the sensitization and information of the whole society. There is complete public ignorance of disability, and this simple lack of information is hindering inclusion. Fear generally brings about rejection. However, as people with disabilities participate and integrate themselves increasingly into the society, this mutual knowledge allows for a better understanding and more sensitive feelings toward them. In our society, people with mental retardation have been until not many years ago hidden away, either because of their families' attitudes, or because the facilities were scattered and distant from the urban centers. This means we need to move forward in our country on many fronts; important changes are still needed that demand that all of us commit ourselves and work together, whether we be people with retardation, their relatives, or professionals.

We propose a revised model for dealing with the quality of life of people with mental retardation. The model presented in Figure 12.1 uses the eight dimensions, with their corresponding indicators, suggested by Schalock (1996, 1997a, 1997b). We consider that such a model, besides serving as permanent reference for everything related to the quality of life in our professional field, is the most complete and innovative, and therefore is the basis of our analysis. However, in our approach, all the dimensions don't have the same value. So we have related the dimensions of the Schalock model with those of the needs theory of Maslow (1970), which allows creation of a hierarchy, although we are aware of its potential cultural bias. According to our conceptualization, the eight Schalock dimensions are categorized, in an ascending way, corresponding with the five needs of Maslow: physiological, security, belonging, esteem, and self-actualization. This classification will be maintained throughout the chapter.

Figure 12.1 shows the correlation that we have established between the eight dimensions of quality of life and the five levels of the pyramid of Maslow. The close relationship among areas of necessity, their hierarchy, and the material and interpersonal culture requires an examination and a deep knowledge of the meaning of each of these areas, and the concrete forms that they take in the country, community, or society in which measurement of quality of life is undertaken. This will allow one to classify, with some logical criteria, the goals, social concerns, and relevant realms in each of the areas of quality of life.

The following considerations on each level of the pyramid are the product of the consensus obtained after a wide debate among the group of people who took part in the elaboration of this study. Although on occasion there will be assumptions insufficiently tested, they have been positively contrasted and shared by different professionals who have contributed their work and experience as providers of services for people with mental retardation. It has been our aim to acknowledge the different opinions with bibliographical references.

Physiological Needs

In Spain, there is a remarkable absence of programs that help people with mental retardation acquire attitudes and positive lifestyles so as to maintain a healthy body

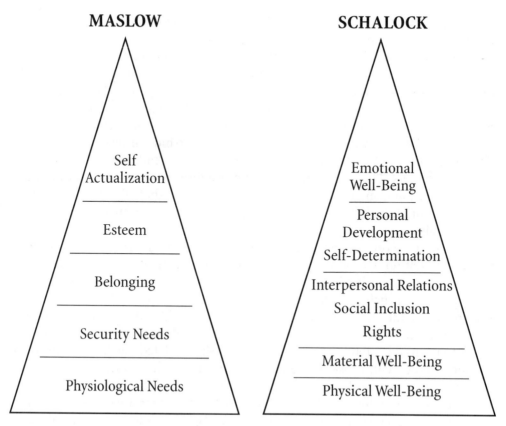

Figure 12.1. Schalock dimensions of quality of life in relation to Maslow hierarchy.

and prevent illnesses. This is so even for basic aspects, such as those related to appropriate eating habits or the habitual practice of physical exercise. A serious coordination problem exists among the systems of public health and social services that hinders proper attention to the health needs of people with more extensive support needs.

People with pervasive necessities of support no doubt suffer health problems relevant to their quality of life (e.g., constipation, generalized decay of teeth, ulcers, etc.), which receive insufficient attention from a medical-sanitary point of view. Also, even if the supports needed by a person are addressed, less attention is paid to the fact that the person could suffer so-called "minor" pains, as uneasiness, headache, back pain, stomach acid, gas pains, and so forth.

Unfortunately, few current programs address all the health needs of people with mental retardation. Specifically, there is a lack of training in specific abilities directed to people with mental retardation, and there is a complete absence of introductory units on this issue in the curriculum to prepare health professionals. In addition, challenging behaviors are often handled by means of negative contingencies, rather than being ecologically considered as behaviors might and should be. One of the consequences is the widespread use of medication.

Need for Security: Material Well-Being

Wages are the main resource of material well-being for most adults. However, it seems that our employment policy goes only to people with fewer limitations. All people, even those with more intense support needs, should have the opportunity to develop work that is significant and rewarding. To do so, it is necessary to prepare the person with mental retardation for the demands of productive activity. In the school years, there is a need for more intense training of capabilities for functioning at work and for efforts to connect people to the market demands.

Most of the adults with mental retardation continue, despite the good abilities that many possess, working in segregated labor environments. People with more intense levels of disability are deprived of being in the labor world, even the protected one, mainly if they live in institutions. The customary models of labor integration continue to be poorly developed (Elorriaga, 1996).

It is necessary to foster the transition from the current models of special employment toward ordinary supported employment as a labor modality that offers the maximum social and labor integration. Currently in Spain, some supported employment has begun, seemingly with good results.

Finally, although in our country there is the universal right to a minimum wage, we believe that it is, in most cases, insufficient for a worthy and autonomous life. Additionally, it is necessary to keep in mind that the beneficiaries of this allowance pay taxes and contribute according to their revenues.

Need for Belonging

Interpersonal Relationships. There are still people, even some professionals, who think that people with mental retardation prefer to make the acquaintance of people under the same conditions, which limits their personal growth. Consequences of this attitude are the lack of inclusion in every life domain, from educational to labor and social, and difficulties in establishing meaningful relationships with people without mental retardation, except for family and committed professionals. Their friends are generally other people with mental retardation. The maintenance of relationships among people with and without mental retardation is, in our experience, a critical matter for quality of life. Even more, it is the best interaction model, for relationships contribute to satisfying the needs of everyone and avoid discrimination.

The right to intimacy is often forgotten. People with mental retardation have their time and activities organized without consideration of their intimacy, sometimes because we think they don't need it, and sometimes because it is deemed not as important as ours. On the other hand, the happenings and feelings of people with mental retardation can often be in the public eye. In reference to intimate relationships, the public generally does not favor demonstrations of affection in people with mental retardation; nor are they educated in an atmosphere that assumes that sexuality is natural.

Concerning marriage, the Spanish society tends to deny this right in a systematic way to people with mental retardation. We authors think that this should happen only when their inability to assume the responsibilities derived from getting married is demonstrated, which is not always easy to decide (Colombo, 1997).

Regarding pregnancy and parenthood of people with mental retardation: given the lack of supports and appropriate services currently existing in our country, parenthood isn't advisable. However, this possibility is frequently left in the hands of fortune, which is paradoxical; this problem is not faced with courage but by trusting the luck or the power of prohibitions.

Last, in relation to the leisure of people with disability, the current situation is far from a normalized reality—constituting an important side of the human experience that the person with disability can exercise in equal conditions with other citizens (Gorbeña, Gonzalez, & Lazaro, 1997). And leisure programs for people with more severe disabilities are almost nonexistent.

Social Inclusion. Spanish society is far from effective social inclusion of people with mental retardation, though it is the final goal of our efforts. Residential attention to people with intensive support needs, as well as to those showing challenging behaviors, is still provided, in the best case, in residences of excessive size (in the worst case, in psychiatric hospitals). Residences are often far from local municipalities, built in isolated areas because of the low price of the land. They are planned and organized more to fulfill the staff's well-being than for concerns of the residents, resulting in living conditions that no one would wish for.

Generally, the public has a great ignorance that sometimes becomes fear of people with mental retardation. Although advances have taken place, a lot of work is necessary to modify societal attitudes, so that an effective inclusion is achieved in the community's life. Finally, people with mental retardation show little social participation and a weak connection with the social nets of mutual support. There is lack of consciousness of "belonging to the society" and therefore of active participation in the different social groups.

Rights. After 15 years, we think it sensible to highlight the lack of effective application of the dispositions contained in the LISMI, with an almost systematic nonfulfillment of some aspects, as in the recruiting of workers with disabilities. The analyses on the development of this law, elaborated by the associations of consumers and the public administrations, evaluate its impact positively, though they recognize this nonfulfillment and even some deviations. A renewed commitment is needed to complete and deepen the development of this basic law and to incorporate the new positions and the recent advances.

The rights of people with mental retardation are often damaged, as in the case of residential sites that demand a mandatory and previous judicial authorization. Also, the judicial authority is not usually informed when isolation rooms and mechanical immobilization are used.

People under judicial "sentence of incompetence" are limited in exercising their full legal rights, which deprives the individual of capability to act freely. This legal gap is filled via legal guardianship to care for people and their property, and to represent them in those cases where they cannot negotiate for themselves. But sometimes legal incompetence not only limits rights, but in fact denies them, as frequently happens even with the right to vote. The sensitization of judges concerning these themes, over the convenience of limited "incompetence sentences," must be addressed immediately especially at a time when such sentences are becoming common in our country.

Need for Esteem

Self-Determination. Because of the influence of family and the system of services, people with mental retardation have limited opportunities for decision making and freedom to choose in regard to important questions that affect their lives. The dignity of risk is rarely the basis for daily practice, so that many adults with mental retardation continue to be "children forever" who need to request permission for almost everything that affects their lives.

This attitude demands urgent changes. Opportunities to acquire functional skills should be provided people with mental retardation, so they can form their own opinions, begin activities, and have real possibilities to use those skills and preferences in every aspect of the daily life. We should guarantee for people with mental retardation the possibility of personal decision making, helped when necessary by family, friends, and professionals who avoid the widespread habit of making decisions that affect the lives of people with mental retardation without hearing them out (Elorriaga, 1996).

Self-advocacy groups are now forming in Spain; to date, these are limited groups of people with mental retardation seeking to give themselves support, to make their own voices heard, and to defend their rights without intermediaries, with the purpose of improving their quality of life.

Personal Growth. Although personal growth continues throughout one's lifetime, in its first and decisive stages the school and mainly the family are the most influential factors. Spanish families have been until the present playing a decisive role regarding the supports that their members with mental retardation can obtain. Some of their more positive characteristics, such as stability and cohesion, the protection offered to their children, and the maintenance of bonds with the extended family, play a positive role to favor the personal growth of people with mental retardation. However, there are also some negative aspects. The assumption of a wide range of responsibilities when they look after children with mental retardation, the excessive role played by the mother, and an overall absence of supports inside the family's circle often cause stress that results in a disadvantage for the personal growth of people with mental retardation.

On the other hand, balanced support for their children frequently turns into overprotection, resulting in dependency that encourages the so-called "eternal child."

In reference to the school system, students with disabilities still receive an education not according to their needs, imparted in schools far from their neighborhoods, and separated from siblings, friends, and social context.

Support is generally received outside the classroom. We recommend that it be received in the classroom; this change would imply coordination between the support teacher and tutor (Arnáiz, 1996). Many children remain in special schools or in segregated classrooms. Inclusion is difficult, especially when they enter the sec-

119

ondary school (Elorriaga, 1996). The educational process of people with mental retardation should prepare them to live, to work, and to participate in integrated environments. The educational programs should respond to the needs of the children, and should be functional and socially relevant. However, despite undeniable advances, the focus of curricula as well as educational practice is far from the demands and needs of the child, as irrelevant subjects continue to be taught.

Families must be made aware of the importance of closer monitoring of children's learning processes so that family expectations will increase as they realize that these children are able to do many things for themselves. The participation of parents in the educational process is fundamental if a constructive balance in decision making among parents, professionals, and the person with mental retardation is to occur.

Emotional Well-Being or Self-Actualization

We have located this dimension on top of the pyramid because, in our opinion, it represents the psychological and personal perspective of quality of life, as opposed to the concept of objective standard of living that has a more normative and sociological character. What's more, those who work for the benefit of people with mental retardation confront the greatest challenges in this dimension.

It is universally accepted that quality of life is a subjective experience that should be evaluated from the individual's point of view. For that reason it is necessary that people receiving services express their preferences, desires, and aspirations, so providers can (a) adapt and if necessary modify services to satisfy those desires and aspirations and (b) contribute to the attainment of an appropriate level of emotional well-being (Gardner, Nudler, & Chapman, 1997).

Currently in Spain and with the leadership of FEAPS, a considerable effort is being made so that the planners and providers of services organize them from a quality-of-life perspective and in a client-oriented way. However, there are as yet no active programs. The great majority of the existing programs concentrate exclusively on the teaching or training of abilities that the professional has unilaterally determined as goals that students should reach. This situation is reflected in the fact that the available systems of program credentials are based almost exclusively in structure-indexes that try to guarantee the basic necessities (i.e., physical needs and security). The financial sources are based on these credential systems.

One index of positive emotional well-being is the absence of challenging behaviors—minimized because of the use of proactive approaches. Although this positive approach is commonly considered the most appropriate by most professionals, its practical application continues to be minimized because of insufficient training or lack of means.

Two Cases

In summary, we are beginning to use a quality-of-life-focused public policy and intervention model. The importance of using such a multidimensional model is reflected in the following two cases. Although most of our comments thus far on the different dimensions of quality of life have criticized current practice, we now present the cases of two Spanish adults who, in the last 10 years, have experienced a considerable improvement in their quality of life and are good examples of the positive transformation in supports and services for people with mental retardation being experienced in our country.

Some readers may consider the improvements described insufficient and minimal for any citizen in the beginnings of the 21st century. But we cannot forget that Spain suffered, between 1936 and 1939, a bloody civil war that resulted in a million deaths and left the country ruined economically and isolated, both socially and politically. Our civil war was followed by a dictatorship that lasted almost 40 years; for these reasons, Spaniards with disabilities didn't reach the condition of citizens with full rights until 1978. With the brief description of these two cases, we also try to pay homage to all those people who, like María or Josu, abandoned by their parents, suffered their particular *"Christmas in Purgatory"* (Blatt & Kaplan, 1966).

María R.

María is a 45-year-old woman who has mental retardation as a consequence of a neurofibromatosis. Her childhood and most of her youth were a constant pilgrimage through a wide range of residential services in which she never stayed for long.

Finally, in 1981, she was welcomed in a residence managed by an association of parents, located in a small rural town, in which she cohabited with 50 other people, all of them with serious disabilities. There she got, for the first time in her life, the necessary stability to assert herself little by little as a person in a climate that resulted in her behavioral problems disappearing. The residence's managers encouraged María to take a step forward to better her life conditions. She has been living for 4 years with three others partners in a communal house located in a city in the north of Spain, and she works in a sheltered workshop. This allows her to carry out a wide range of activities in her new community and to take responsibility for domestic tasks. She has learned how to move around the city in the subway, and she often goes out and has a good time with her friends.

At the age of 42, María had her first opportunity to travel by plane and spend her vacation at the beach, invited by her *delegada tutelar* (volunteer who acts as personal advocate); now she has a boyfriend and, more important, she has a goal in her life: to get, as soon as possible, the personal and economic autonomy to live as a couple.

Josu

Josu is a 24-year-old youth, abandoned by his parents when he was born. He has mental retardation of unknown etiology and moderate limitations of mobility and of the use of his arms and hands. After a brief period in a rehabilitation center, he was interned in a "special" unit of an old psychiatric hospital.

In 1984 he was taken to a residential center managed by an association of parents, located in the suburbs of an intermediate-sized town, in which he lived with 70 other people, the great majority being adults with serious disabilities. Since then, he has lived there and, although he desires to live as the majority of the Spanish youths of his age do, his quality of life has improved considerably. For 7 years, he has had the possibility of going to the town school, of living with partners with or without disabilities, and to be appreciated by all. But the most significant change began, some 3 to 4 years ago, when he had the occasion to begin an intense relationship with a volunteer who acts as a personal advocate. This relationship allows him to share, not only with the volunteer, but also with her husband and daughter, his more important experiences, to feel loved in a unique and personal way, to share happiness, and to participate in a great variety of activities at home and in the community. Definitely, Josu is now considered less "special" but, more important, is accepted as a member of the family of his personal advocate.

Conclusions

The principles that have guided intervention on behalf of people with disabilities in Spain have evolved in the last two decades. There has been a transformation from charity appeals, compassion, and the policy of isolation, to the defense of normalization, integration, and personal autonomy, and especially the idea of equality of opportunities. This is the fundamental principle of the *Action Plan for People With Disabilities, 1997-2002* (Institute Nacional de Servicios Sociales, 1996), elaborated by the Central Administration; its imminent approval should guide all the policies on people with disability in the future in our country (see Verdugo, chap. 23, this volume).

The private sector is the primary provider of services in Spain. Important efforts toward "modernization" have been carried out, such as the one recently initiated by FEAPS. This nongovernmental organization is involved in an important process of organizational development. In the process almost 1,000 people have directly participated in work on some key topics and have reached the following conclusions, formulated in terms of goals to achieve in the coming years in our country. Key quality-of-life concepts include:

- People with mental retardation and their families have a meaningful life. The links between the family and their children are basic in human development. Thus public entities (the different programs and professionals) should increase the probability that family life is enhanced and supported in the best possible way.

- Children should go to their neighborhood schools and have appropriate educational programs. A variety of experiences support the idea that education in special situations or in segregated facilities prepares for "special" and nonparticipative lives in the community. In opposition, the educational programs should respond to the necessities of the children and should be functional and socially relevant. Integration should be considered an undeniable right, independent of the level of the child's capabilities.

- Individuals, when they finish the school years, should obtain and maintain meaningful work. There is no doubt that, in our society, to get and keep a job is considered one of the best means of social inclusion. As a consequence, all individuals, including those with serious mental retardation, should have the opportunity to do work that is meaningful and realistic for them. Adults should have access to a job together with partners without disabilities.

■ Every person should have a personalized plan of service. This plan should be negotiated and supported by the individual, by the family or legal guardian, and by the service, as well as by the public entities that provide the economic support.

■ The aspirations and necessities of people should be satisfied no matter what their educational, labor, or residential situation. It is essential to maintain the integrity of all the systems so that the power exerted on the lives of citizens is rational, to guarantee individuals the right to control their lives and destinies.

■ The internment of people with mental retardation in large institutions should be stopped, and annually a percentage of the residents ought to leave and be integrated into community residential facilities. This is a political decision, because, in general terms, institutionalization is the answer given by the public powers to the needs of citizens with disability. This goal requires courageous political leadership; technical activity alone is not strong enough to carry out this evolution.

In summary, life conditions, as well as the degree of satisfaction related to them by the person with mental retardation, is essential in coming years. Services and supports are only means to a more important outcome. The final result is that people with mental retardation and their families are able to live a life considered by themselves as being one of quality.

References

Anáiz, P. (1996). Las escuelas son para todos [Schools are for everybody]. *Siglo Cero, 164,* 25-34.

Blatt, B., & Kaplan, F. (1966). *Christmas in purgatory: A photographic essay on mental retardation.* Boston: Allyn & Bacon.

Colombo, J. (1997). II Jornadas sobre Fundaciones Tutelares [II Congress on Tutelar Foundation]. *Revista de la Fundación Tutelar TAU, 4,* 13.

Defensor Del Pueblo. (1996). *Atención residencial a personas con discapacidad y otros aspectos conexos* [Residential attention to people with disabilities and other aspects connected]. Madrid: Publicaciones del Defensor del Pueblo.

Elorriaga, J. (1996). Atención al cliente y calidad del servicio [Customer service and quality]. *Siglo Cero, 169,* 19-44.

Gardner, J. F., Nudler, S., & Chapman, M. S. (1997). Personal outcomes as measures of quality. *Mental Retardation, 35,* 295-305.

Gorbeña, S., Gonzalez, V., & Lazaro, Y. (1997). *El derecho al cio de las personas con discapacidad* [The right to leisure of persons with disabilities]. Bilbao: Instituto de Estudios de Ocio, Universidad de Deusto.

Instituto Nacional de Servicios Sociales. (1996). *Plan de acción para las personas con discapacidad 1997–2002.* [Action plan for people with disability 1997–2002]. Madrid: Author, Ministerio de Trabajo y Asuntos Sociales.

Luckasson, R., Coulter, D. L., Polloway, E. A., Reiss, S., Schalock, R. L., Snell, M. E., Spitalnik, D. M., & Stark, J. A. (1992). *Mental retardation: Definition, classification, and systems of supports.* Washington, DC: American Association on Mental Retardation.

Maslow, A. H. (1970). *Motivation and personality* (2nd ed.). New York: Harper & Row.

Ministerio de Asuntos Sociales. (1995). El plan de acción para las personas con discapacidad [Action plan for persons with disabilities]. *Minusval, 97,* 54-72.

Ministerio de Asuntos Sociales. (1997). El plan de acción para las personas con discapacidad [Action plan for persons with disabilities]. *Polibea, 43,* 33-39.

Schalock, R. (Ed.). (1996). *Quality of life: Vol 1. Conceptualization and measurement.* Washington, DC: American Association on Mental Retardation.

Schalock, R. (Ed.). (1997a). *Quality of life: Vol 2. Application to persons with disabilities.* Washington, DC: American Association on Mental Retardation.

Schalock, R. (1997b). Evaluación de programas sociales: Para conseguir rendimientos organizacionales y resultados personales [Evaluating social programs to achieve organizational outputs and personal results]. *II Jornadas Científicas de Investigación sobre Personas con Discapacidad. Libro de Actas,* 85-105.

People With Mental Retardation of Curaçao: Developing Toward Better Times

Jennifer Denise James
Foundation for People With a Physical Disability
Curaçao, Netherlands Antilles

Any attempt to discern the present level of the quality of life of people with mental disability in our community of Curaçao (one island of the Netherlands Antilles) would need to consider the historical background. This historical perspective is a rather short one, spanning a mere 25 years. But it is one characterized by a dynamic energy for change. It could also be typified as a frantic attempt to have to "catch up," in terms of the lack of available services and information. The field of mental retardation through the years has become synonymous with Totolika (a small popular bird in our fauna), which is the name of the organization of parents of people with mental retardation. This is due to the impact this group has had in the inception of services and the social integration for the focus group.

Totolika: Its Role in the Field of Mental Retardation

Before 1970 mental retardation was a concept about which little was known. This lack of information pervaded the public at large in our community and also most parents of children with the disability. Besides the lack of adequate information in terms of parenting a child with this disability, no structured support system was available to parents. Because of this, children with mental disability were greatly "protected" by their parents and commonly led a life of seclusion within the family home. The aspect of shame for the condition of the child was also very pronounced in our community. This could also be said of a child with a physical disability. The shame could be explained as being a result of parental ignorance of the disability or due to the lack of support from the community itself in terms of services available. As a way of filling the tremendous void that existed with regard to information, awareness, and adequate services for people with mental handicaps and their families, in 1973 a group of parents of children with a mental disability came together and started an association. It was called Totolika and set out to attain the goal of serving the interest of people with a mental disability, their parents, and their environments. This parent organization focused its work in four areas (Sprockel & Flores, 1993):

1. giving information and fostering awareness among parents and the community as a whole;

2. creating possibilities for recreation and sports for people with mental retardation;

3. advancing the establishment of necessary services for people with mental disabilities;

4. developing and maintaining contact with local, regional, and international organizations working in the field of mental retardation.

Attempts at enhancing awareness include a magazine in its 24th year of circulation through which information about the disability and other relevant issues is supplied to parents and the public at large, television programs, translation of relevant literature, and workshops and congresses. Greater awareness in the community was promoted through promotional material such as t-shirts, calendars, posters, stamps, bumper stickers, and a book of poems. Other activities included talent and fashion shows in which youth with mental disabilities took the center stage. The parent organization was also instrumental in the development of sports activities for the focus group (Sprockel & Flores, 1993). Yet a most crucial contribution made by this parent association was reviving the Foundation for the Care of the Mentally Handicapped. Through this foundation many services, before nonexistent, were born and today form the network of services available to the person with mental retardation and the family.

All these activities as well as the rather aggressive advocacy style exhibited by the parent organization Totolika greatly changed the way the parents of youngsters with mental retardation viewed themselves and related to their children. The way the community as a whole now views the individual with mental retardation, and people with disabilities in general, has also changed significantly (A. Sprockel, personal communication, August 6, 1997).

People With Mental Retardation

Demographic Data
According to the most recent available population census data (1992), there were 5,620 people with disabilities in Curaçao. Of this total, 1,086 were mentally handicapped. This figure would be higher if a fraction of those individuals denoted as "multiple handicapped" and "unknown" (894 people) is added to this total (Central Bureau of Statistics, 1993, p. 131). Of the total population of Curaçao in 1992, comprising 144,097 individuals, the 1,086 with mental retardation represent 0.75%. If the total figure of 1,086 is considered according to age groupings, 389 lie in the age group 0 to 29, which equals 35.8%; 485 belong to the age group 30 to 59, which equals 44.6%; and 212 are age 60 or above, or 19.5%. In terms of sex, 231 are male and 158 female in the age group 0 to 29. In the age group 30 to 59, 307 are male and 178 female. For the age category of 60+, 111 are male and 101 female.

Services
As mentioned earlier, the establishment of the Foundation for the Care of the Mentally Handicapped brought a significant change in the service delivery and provisions previously available to the individuals with mental retardation and their families. This foundation became the umbrella organization, in terms of day-care services and living accommodation catered to the focus group. Over the span of the last 20 years, many projects were implemented in an attempt to expand the available facilities catered to the focus group.

Day Care

Pasadia. This facility is a day-care center for 48 children with mental retardation between the ages of 3 and 6. The objective of this center is to create an environment to stimulate the child as much as possible, according to the child's ability (Sprockel & Flores, 1993).

Activity Center Inge Boutier. This center is part of the Living and Activity Center project of the Foundation for Care of the Mentally Handicapped. This facility is a day-care center for adults that daily engages a maximum of 50 adults with disabilities in a wide variety of activities (Volksgezondheid en Milieuhygiene [VOMIL],1994).

Living Accommodations

Jos Wouter Home. This 24-hour so-called "family substitution home" is an assisted residential facility that offers living accommodation, leisure time management, and guidance to 20 adults between the ages of 18 and 55 (VOMIL, 1994; Sprockel & Flores, 1993).

Supported Residential Home. Built as an annex to the Jos Wouter home, two homes provide small living quarters for two to four people. Here less guidance is given and called for, as the inhabitants are more independent. They work and earn their own living outside the facility. Approximately 45 individuals with a mental disability were registered on a waiting list for this type of living accommodation (Sprockel & Flores, 1993).

Trinitaria. This facility is a division of the governmental psychiatric hospital that houses adults with mental disabilities. In the past this institution housed individuals with mental retardation due to a lack of adequate facilities elsewhere. In 1992 an agreement was reached between the psychiatric hospital and the Foundation for Care of the Mentally Handicapped that the Trinitaria division would come under direct management of the Foundation. In 1993 when the first phase of the Foundation's Living Center (see below) was made operational, 27 Trinitaria residents were transferred and the 41 who remained are pending the finalization of the other phases of the Living Center (VOMIL, 1994).

Living Center Arco Iris. The Living Center of the Foundation for the Care of the Mentally Handicapped was partly put in operation in November 1993, housing 44 residents. The total capacity of this facility will be 125. The level of mental retardation of the inhabitants will vary from moderate to profound disability. This center is said to be a novelty in the care of the disabled in the Caribbean, in terms of both design and architecture (VOMIL, 1994).

Monseigneur Verriet Institution. This institution's goal is to nurse and care for children with physical disabilities. Through the years, however, there has been a shift in terms of the focus group. This resulted in the fact that two thirds of the actual population is individuals with mental disabilities (approximately 80 individuals). According to information furnished in the VOMIL document (1994), at present the institution is no longer admitting individuals with only a mental disability but is restricting admission to those mentally incapacitated who also have severe physical impairments.

Public Housing

As for public housing for people with mental retardation, a significant collaboration has recently been announced, involving the signing of a protocol of cooperation between the Foundation for the Care of the Mentally Handicapped and the Foundation for Public Housing (FKP) (George, 1997). The latter is the governmental agency responsible for building public housing. The protocol entails that:

- In all housing projects, FKP will include or reserve houses for the focus group.

- FKP will also contribute with building homes in any project in which the Foundation for the Care of the Mentally Handicapped indicates a need for collaboration by FKP.

- FKP will build housing complexes, so-called "family substituting" homes. The intention is that FKP will rent the houses to the Foundation for the Care of the Mentally Handicapped, and the latter, in turn, determines who will inhabit the homes.

This form of cooperation, according to George (1997), ensures that individuals with mental retardation who registered at FKP for a house would get better guidance when they are considered for a home. At the moment 25 individuals with mental retardation are registered (George). This minimal figure, however, does not give a realistic picture of the actual number of individuals with mental disabilities who are in need of adequate living accommodations, be it a supported or sheltered home or a more independent residence.

All factors considered, living accommodations catered to people with mental disabilities are said to be insufficient, given the number of individuals who could probably live more independently if such facilities were indeed available. For as noted by Sprockel (1997), lack of adequate and sufficient living accommodations for adults with mental retardation is surely a factor that obstructs overall quality of life and as such the level of integration in our society. Furthermore, the VOMIL document (1994) affirms that in terms of supported or "family substituting homes," Curaçao will need a minimum of three such facilities. These facilities should have a total combined capacity of about 75 spaces to meet the care demands that were estimated for 1994 to 1999 (VOMIL, 1994).

Education

Early Stimulation. In terms of preschool education, the Early Stimulation Program, which was introduced in Curaçao in 1977, has some relevance for children with mental retardation. The program, which is managed by the government's School Guidance and Counseling Service, caters to children ages 0 to 7 with developmental problems and their parents. Through this program parents receive guidance in stimulating the development of their child. A translation to our local language, Papiamentu, of the *Portage Guide to Early Childhood Education* (Sprockel-Da Costa Gomez, 1987) has been used as a tool for this program. The program focuses on social development, language development, motor development, cognitive skills, and self-help (K. Specht, personal communication, October 16, 1997).

According to Specht, the program director, the average monthly referrals to the Early Stimulation Program total approximately 12 cases. Between January 13 and October 13, 1997, there were 117 new referrals. She points out further that the majority of children seen recently at the agency have difficulties in language development. Although the program does not serve a majority of children with mental retardation, its implementation was said to have been a success and blessing in terms of care for such children. The previous director of the Early Stimulation Program, Sprockel (1987), reported that positive outcomes of the program included: young parents could get help, support, and guidance through the program; children with mental retardation function at a higher level than before the existence of the program; the program has allowed better integration in kindergarten of children with disabilities, as teachers and parents have become conscious of the talents and positive qualities of these children.

Special Education. Special education has existed in Curaçao for 45 years. In 1953 legislation was passed that legally anchored the then so-called "extraordinary education" (Leetz, 1977). Through the years this branch of education has developed at a slow pace. However, from fragmented efforts at furnishing some form of education and training to children with disabilities, it has transformed into a system of schools with specialized divisions. Special education at the primary school level is organized in four categories of schools, according to the assumed degree of disability of the pupil. There is one school for the child who is deaf or hearing impaired. The Leer en Opvoeding Moeilijkheden (LOM) school is for children with learning disabilities. It is assumed that after intensive individual coaching the pupil will be able to reintegrate into regular primary school. Usually children who need individual attention on specific subjects are served within this type of school. There are three schools of this kind (LOM). In addition, there are eight MLK (Moeilijk Leerende Kinderen) schools for children with learning difficulties; and three ZMLK (Zeer Moeilijk Leerende Kinderen) schools for children with extreme learning difficulties (VOMIL, 1994). Children with mental retardation are served in programs of the latter type, with a focus on self-sufficiency, and pupils remain in this type of education until they are approximately 18 years old (R. Granviel, personal communication, December 2, 1997).

Unfortunately, there is no secondary school facility or vocational training within the school system, for youths who complete ZMLK. The two secondary schools that exist within the special-education system cater to graduates of the MLK schools. Although the Tirso Sprockel Vocational Training Center (see below) somewhat fills the lack of a secondary training facility, it cannot accommodate all youngsters who complete ZMLK schools in any given year. Thus some youths with mental retardation, according to Granviel, one of the ZMLK principals, are left stranded in terms of their further development. Yet another alarming fact is that within the special-education system, both the MLK and the ZMLK schools are practically full. As Granviel further notes, there are long waiting lists to enter each of these types of schools. In the VOMIL document (1994), the lack of secondary education and the shortage of teachers for this branch were also noted. Granviel points to the lack of multidisciplinary teams to support and better equip special education. She considers the latter a dire necessity, given the characteristics of this type of education and the current social environment marred with many problems that also find their way into school.

Employment

With regard to the work situation of individuals with mental retardation, employment opportunities are very scarce. It is worth mentioning, however, that lack of employment is also a problem for the general population, especially for young adults. It is thus not limited to individuals with mental retardation. The unfortunate trend of unemployment the last few years undoubtedly exacerbates the job-market possibilities for workers with mental retardation. Notwithstanding this fact, there has been a slowly growing development in the public (and somewhat in the private) business sector toward employing individuals with disabilities. This is mainly the case for individuals with physical disabilities (VOMIL, 1994). According to A. Sprockel (personal communication, August 6, 1997), president of the parent organization Totolika, there are currently 30 young adults with mental retardation working in the private sector. Besides the employment possibilities in the public and private sector, which as noted are rather scarce, some facilities have been created to fulfill the dire need of work opportunities for the focus group.

Tirso Sprockel Vocational Training Center. This is a center with a capacity to train 50 young adults with mental disabilities. They receive vocational training to enhance their possibilities to enter the labor market and to promote their social integration. The participants range in age from 18 to 25 and generally have completed special education. The areas of training are housekeeping, cooking, needlework, carpentry, horticulture, and social skills. By the second or third year of training, pupils have the opportunity to go on an internship. When they are deemed ready for a job, the center attempts to place them. This vocational training center is housed under a foundation established by the parent organization Totolika (Sprockel, Schouten, & Peney, 1996).

Social Workplace: St. Martha and the Leather Tannery. These are divisions of the governmental department of employment, which appoint individuals with mental retardation in a "protected" work environment, to develop and promote social skills and vocational training. At the social workplace St. Martha, jobs include pottery, carpentry, mat-plaiting, and gardening. At the tannery, goat and cow skin is cleaned to make it ready for further processing. According to information included in the VOMIL document (1994), 137 individuals are employed at these two facilities.

Wasserette Valentine. In this laundry nine individuals with mental retardation who received training some years at the Tirso Sprockel Vocational Training Center are employed. In this small business venture, they are under supervision of a guide from the Training Center. This laundry falls under direct management of a foundation established to set up small businesses that would flow from the work engaged in at Tirso Sprockel. This whole set-up is an initiative from the parent organization Totolika (Totolika Year Report, 1995).

All factors considered, it should be said that employment opportunity for people with disabilities in general is very scant. There is recognition of this situation, and as proposed in the VOMIL document (1994), there should be a governmental policy that promotes increased participation of this group in the job market. Furthermore it was suggested that the government should set the example in this matter. This would be accomplished by reorganizing employment procedures in such a way that within 10 years 3% of governmental jobs are occupied by individuals with disabilities (VOMIL, 1994). Whether this recommendation will bear fruit remains to be seen, given the dire financial situation of the government at present, and the trend of greatly reducing the actual number of civil servants.

Public Policy

The area of legislation is surely one that has lagged behind in all aspects related to disabilities. In the past there have been few attempts to legally anchor issues that would have great bearing on the quality of life of individuals in this group. In terms of the right to care, control of the quality of care, rights for appropriate housing, education, and work, none are specifically anchored by law, nor are there specific accreditation requirements or specific norms for quality of care. As noted in the VOMIL document (1994), it is imperative that these issues receive attention by the government. Regulation of the above-mentioned issues would ensure better allocation of both funds and human resources. It would also ensure high quality of the care delivered.

Categories A, B, C and Care Contracts. In an attempt to bring some order to the area of funding of the various institutions, foundations, and associations by the island government of Curaçao, and yet to cut down on governmental costs, a new funding regulation was introduced in 1994. It involved organizations receiving governmental funding being divided into three categories (A, B, C). The criterion for inclusion in the various categories was the extent to which the service provided by each organization was considered a basic task of the island government. According to this standard, the level of funding was also determined. The possibilities are 100% funding, gradual decrease of funding, or no governmental funding, respectively. Category A organizations are assumed to be organizations implementing basic governmental tasks in terms of the services they provide to the community, and they receive full funding. These are organizations in the care of the elderly, general health care, child protection agencies, child day care, addiction care, after-school activities, and care for people with disabilities (VOMIL, 1994).

Besides this funding regulation, the island government has also adopted Care Contracts with these organizations that deliver services considered the responsibility of the government. These agreements establish some guidelines in terms of care to be delivered and responsibilities of both the service deliverer and the island government as the funding agent (VOMIL, 1994).

The Labizjan Law. The Labizjan law (Ordinance for General Obligatory Insurance of Special Medical Expenses), introduced at the beginning of 1997, is the national law concerning general insurance for chronic illness, psychiatric illness, and mental and physical disability. It requires that every citizen receiving an income pay a premium to contribute to the funds allocated to the care of those who receive health care and services as a result of the above-mentioned conditions (National Government Ordinance, 1996). This new law has direct bearing on those with mental retardation in terms of the funds generated and allocated to their care and service delivery. The basic philosophy of this law, a noble and social one, says that every citizen is responsible for the care of those who are chronically ill or with a disability. Thus one has the responsibility to contribute financially to the care of those who cannot provide their own care. However, the introduction of this law has met with some problems in its application, as many factors were not considered beforehand. There is also insufficient understanding of what the law does cover in terms of services in some situations.

The developments cited above could be considered a first step in attempting to control the cost of care and introduce stricter guidelines, rules, and regulation to the care of those with disabilities. However, it is clear that much more should be done in terms of laws, norms, and regulation in the health care sector of the island, to ensure better allocation and use of resources.

Quality Care Delivered

According to the VOMIL document (1994), it could be concluded that the quality of care is good and there is tremendous effort by employees and management of the various organizations within the field of care for individuals with disabilities. It is not my intention to deny that this field of work has extremely motivated individuals. It should be recognized, however, that given the lack of specific norms for quality and an official body that both establishes and monitors adherence to the latter, one could not readily conclude that all is well. Only when such mechanisms are put into operation can one evaluate the quality of service delivery and be assured of the validity of the results.

Conclusion

I have summarized the available facilities serving individuals with developmental disabilities and their families, in an attempt to look at the degree of social integration and the general quality of life attained through the existence of such services. From the above exposition, we have seen that much is still lacking in terms of the care for people with mental disabilities. This is also the case in terms of pertinent legislation that would ensure an optimal quality of life for this group of citizens.

As noted, there is a lack of housing, both supported and public, for the adult with mental retardation. Employment, which is crucial in terms of improving quality of life and the person's own sense of integration and independence, is very minimal. Efforts to create employment opportunities need to be intensified. Yet a sense of the importance of integrating individuals with disabilities in general in the work process needs still to be inculcated in the community at large.

Nevertheless, there has been a continuous drive for betterment. Notwithstanding much room for improvement in every aspect involving the care and life of citizens with disabilities, existing services could be said to have improved the overall quality of life of this population group, and a significant process of social integration has been launched, particularly as compared with the situation in the recent past. Many improvements were achieved within the last 20 years, and there are exciting developments to further ensure improved quality of life for those with mental retardation and for the general disabled population. A development that promises to become a crucial factor in advancing the plight of people with disabilities in our community is the island government's establishment of a Management Advisory Board for the Care of the Disabled (Island Council, decree 96/8/58). The Management Advisory Board consists of representatives of the Council for the Handicapped and the various governmental departments that deal with people with disabilities in their daily functioning and service delivery, and its task is to create a collaboration structure between the Council for the Handicapped and the governmental agencies. Furthermore, its principal task is to advise and give proposals to the island government that serve the interests of the disabled and promote their rehabilitation and integration in the community of Curaçao (Island Council, decree 96/8/58). With the establishment of a secretariat of this board, many issues that need to be attended to in the care of the disabled population could be attended to in a structured and well-delineated manner.

The first steps are taken. It remains to be seen if motivation, continuity, and political commitment will endure and survive the test of time. It is my fervent hope that this occurs, for so much work needs to be done, and we as a community need to have a sense that we are developing a positive path, both socially and economically. We need to counteract the power of disorder, malfunction, and social disintegration currently beating at our shores.

References

Central Bureau of Statistics. (1993). *Third population and housing census Netherlands Antilles 1992: Vol. 2.* Willemstad: Author.

George, H. (1997, June 24). *Press Release FKP.*

Island Council Territory of Curaçao, decree 96/8/58.

Leetz, M. (1977). *Enseñansa básiko ekstra-ordinario* [Primary special education]. Paper presented on occasion of the 25th anniversary of special education in Curaçao.

National Government Ordinance, P.B. 1996 no. 211 [Netherlands Antilles].

Sprockel, A. (1987). Home based programs: Early stimulation in Curaçao. In E. R. Boersma, H. J. Huisjes, H. Marius, & C. Poortman (Eds.), *A holistic approach to perinatal care and prevention of handicap* (pp. 221-223). Groningen, The Netherlands: Erven B. van der Kamp.

Sprockel, A., & Flores, W. (1993). 20 years Totolika. *Totolika, 20*(2), 5-13.

Sprockel, A., Schouten, A., & Peney, M. (1996). Vocational Center Tirso Sprockel: 10 years. *Totolika, 21*(1), 10.

Sprockel-Da Costa Gomez, A. (1987). Home based programs: Early stimulation in Curaçao. In E. R. Boersma, H. J. Huisjes, H. Marius, & C. Poortman (Eds.), *A holistic approach to perinatal care and prevention of handicap* (pp. 221-223). Groningen, The Netherlands: Erven B. van der Kamp.

Totolika year report. (1995).

VOMIL Department. (1994). *Beleidsnota zorg voor gehandicapten in de Nederlandse Antillen 1994-2004* [Management document care for the disabled in the Netherlands Antilles 1994-2004]. Curaçao: Author.

Quality of Life and Organizational Change Leadership

John Lobley
Calderstones National Health Service Trust
Walley, Clitheroe, England

As an applied researcher, I tend not to publish my work: It is meant for practical use. Consequently, I appreciate this opportunity to share some evaluative research I have conducted in a community service. I shall use the data as a vehicle for discussing an applied use of the quality-of-life concept in Great Britain. I will try to show how quality of life may be used first for evaluation and subsequently to identify areas for change in organizational behavior. Of specific interest is an observed relationship between quality of life and first-line managers' use of a recently defined leadership approach. The chapter may tell more of a story about leadership than quality of life, but paradoxically it offers an important contribution to the current state of applied quality-of-life research in Great Britain.

Quality of life for British people with intellectual disabilities resettled from large Victorian institutions and hospitals to the community has been shown to vary across and within services. Research suggests that management and leadership have a considerable influence on service success in this important area. This chapter argues that wider implementation of functional management systems and transactional leadership (contingent reinforcement), on their own, may be inadequate and may also be inconsistent with the values and organizational culture necessary for developing, maintaining, and improving responsive community services. Transformational leadership is proposed as an essential component of those processes that might bring about desired service change. This particular leadership approach can make a crucial contribution to the transmission of intended organizational culture and may be associated with increased quality-of-life outcomes.

The Changing Theory of Action Within Services for People With Intellectual Disabilities

Profound change in the aims, mission, and objectives of intellectual disability services has been engendered by a shift in beliefs about people with intellectual disabilities, their role in society, and thus the values that underpin service provision. British developments in this vein were commendably expressed by the notion of an "ordinary life" (King's Fund Centre, 1980): a set of ideas that often provided the basis for local service policy (e.g., North Western Regional Health Authority [NWRHA], 1983). A major consequence of this policy is the resettlement of people with intellectual disabilities from old long-stay hospitals into "facilities" in the community. The ordinary-life model argues that these facilities should in fact be ordinary houses, and for many people this is the case. There is an increased awareness of human rights, a concern for service quality, and, more recently, an emphasis on the quality-of-life experience of service users (Schalock, 1990).

Unfortunately these important changes in philosophy and service culture are fragmented and, as yet, only infrequently accompanied by a corresponding change in outcomes for service users. Many people have moved out of large institutions but have not experienced significant change in the quality of their lives. There are exceptions: "Houses where staff and residents like each other, treat each other with respect, have fun, and are busily engaged in the activities of the neighbourhood" (Dowson, 1991, p. 5).

Change takes time—more time in some areas than in others. For example, in 1991 Dowson reflected upon the far slower rate of change in intellectual disability services than in other areas of life in the 20 years since the Government White Paper *Better Services for the Mentally Handicapped* (Department of Health [DOH], 1971). Emerson, Hastings, and McGill (1994) observed that ideological action has had a "profound impact on the way we describe publicly the aims of services" while the assumption that changing the attitudes of staff has had an influence over service quality "has received little critical scrutiny" (pp. 1-2).

From Theory of Action to Actioning Theory

The state of theory and practice in intellectual disability services prompts many to argue that there may have been an overemphasis on service values and what might be called the "theory of action" to the exclusion of strategic, operational, and managerial issues. While accepting the general thrust of this argument, further reflection allows the possibility that "each has its day," and that the ideological level of intervention was timely and essential and has brought some services to a point where it is now necessary to consider other organizational issues. Consideration of organizational and practice issues should not, however, lose sight of the theory of action. Indeed, the fundamental value of a theory-driven approach is asserted by Rapley and Clements (1994), who argue that failings in services are related to a "retreat from theory" and that detailed thinking about what to do for people once they are in the community has been postponed.

Quality of Life: An Index of Service Effectiveness in Great Britain

"Quality of life pertains to the 'goodness' of life" (Zautra & Goodhart, 1979, p. 1). "It defines the individual's condition in positive terms, not in terms of symptoms or absence of symptoms" (Murrell & Norris, 1983, p. 89). It is an "organizing concept that can be used for . . . providing direction and reference" (Schalock, 1997, p. 246).

Improvements in objective standards do not necessarily increase one's sense of well-being, because well-being is experienced subjectively (Edgerton, 1990). Edgerton observes that there have been many attempts to measure quality of life objectively but not the more subjective components of satisfaction and sense of well-being. This has been an important omission both intuitively and philosophically and a key theme arising from Edgerton's findings. As Campbell, Converse, and Rogers (1976) observed, we tend to forget that satisfaction is a psychological experience, the quality of which may not correspond very highly with external conditions of life.

"Successful community living is complexly multivariate" and depends upon more than our present service-based conceptions of adaptation (Edgerton & Berkovici, 1976, p. 493). Quality of life is a more elusive notion than either quality of service or quality of care. There is no "gold standard" against which to measure quality of life (Sheill, Pettipher, Raynes, & Wright, 1990). Despite the difficulties in conceptualization, definition, and operation of quality of life, it offers great promise as a tool for evaluating the effectiveness of services in a way that focuses on individual people. As Landesman (1986) proposed, because quality of life is an "undeniable goal" of services for individuals, attention should be directed toward assessing outcomes in ways that "acknowledge the importance of personal values, preferences, and individual differences" (p. 1). Further, as Keith (1996) asserts: "even in a collective culture, the individual's perception of happiness in that context remains paramount" (p. 80).

Transmission of Organizational Culture

Moving to the community is no guarantee of an enhanced quality of life for people with intellectual disabilities. Variation in quality of life, as an index of service effectiveness, may be related to organizational factors and mirror the findings of, for example, Blunden (1994), who identified leadership as a crucial factor in the cultural change necessary for success. The importance of effective leadership and organizational culture is also indicated by evidence of service decay over time (Blunden, 1988). Initial improvements, while often maintained, are not always improved upon. It seems to be true that in many cases "human services are simply singing the same old song" (Rapley & Clements, 1994, p. 248). Some services, and service elements, have made less progress than others and are reported to maintain institutional practices, values, and aims for service users. Effective leadership and management may be even more important in dispersed services.

Transactional (Burns, 1978), or reactive (Farey, 1993), leadership processes tend to maintain institutional practices and values. Because of this they appear unsuited to facilitating the necessary change in organizational culture and service users' quality of life. Though, as Mansell, McGill, & Emerson (1994) warn, dissatisfaction with previous management systems can lead to new but ill-informed systems, "developed not so much in the spirit of 'we, the managers will support you moving in the directions we and you approve of,' but rather 'who knows what is supposed to happen in these services; so you can decide on your own' " (p. 79). Where such situations arise, services, staff, and clients may become isolated and inward looking. Indeed, for many people, comparative isolation within their communities remains the norm (Rapley & Clements, 1994). "The task is no less than the design of a culture which will support clients in living quality lifestyles" (Emerson et al., 1994, p. 227). The importance of organizational culture, with its attendant ideology and personal beliefs, lies in the potential to provide a day-to-day framework within which staff will operate. However, reliance on an individualized, consciousness- or awareness-raising approach has demonstrated its limitations.

Emerson and Hatton (1994) argue that the relative recency of community services suggests that they have problems similar to those typically found in growing organizations. Findings suggest that the transactional leadership, common and perhaps appropriate in long-stay institutions, does not facilitate sustained progress in community services. Where progress, and improved quality of life, is observed, it appears to be a reflection of a culture change and a new way of doing things. Pettinelli (1993) argues a key part of a leader's role is the transmission of culture, which is a critical variable and a potential barrier to the realization of strategic plans. Indeed, "the greatest challenge for any innovation lies at this point; in the move from the first exemplars to widespread implementation" (Mansell, McGill, & Emerson, 1994, p. 88).

Recent research in Great Britain into the quality-of-life experiences of people with intellectual disabilities resettled from institutions to the community shows that service success is varied. Indeed in a number of cases, it seems that resettlement must be considered a failure, as measured quality of life for some people in the community is worse than for those still in hospitals (Emerson & Hatton, 1994).

Although research confirms the importance of a positive service ideology and appropriate staff values, sole reliance on their potential for enabling positive change is questioned (Emerson et al., 1994). Lack of progress on service quality is often related to the way services are managed. For example, Hatton and Emerson (1994) cite quality-of-life research that identifies failures in deinstitutionalized services and argue that "services' failure to implement or sustain models of 'good practice' highlights the importance of leadership and management" (p. 24). Blunden (1994) also identified "mechanisms for leadership and support" as crucial factors in the success of quality action groups (Independent Development Council, 1986). Quality of life is crucially dependent on the quality of face-to-face interaction between service users and staff (Rice & Rosen, 1991), and therefore on the direction and support given to staff. Mansell, McGill, & Emerson (1994) argue that "it is in precisely this area that management is typically weakest" (p. 71).

Effective leadership and management processes are posited as essential characteristics of effective service development (Blunden, 1994; Reid, Parsons, & Green, 1989). Unfortunately, a lack of understanding about management notions such as autonomous work groups and participative approaches has permitted too many examples of poor-quality services. Consequently, some argue for a more structured, active, approach to planning client activities and managing staff (Mansell, Hughes, & McGill, 1994; Reid et al., 1989). However, the proposed leadership and management processes appear to conflict with the characteristics of an organizational culture that would support the responsiveness and risk-taking necessary to make progress on quality-of-life outcomes in an uncertain environment. A dilemma is created by the apparent conflict between a values-led approach and a structured organizational or management technology. The tactical potential of transformational leadership (Bass, 1985; Burns, 1978) may provide a means of resolving this strategic dilemma and facilitate the transmission of intended organizational culture.

Transformational Leadership

Changing staff attitudes, or the use of traditional transactional management methods, have proved to be inadequate strategies for facilitating the organizational learning and change necessary for developing high-quality community services. A different leadership approach is required. Indeed, Schein (1992) proposes: "One could argue that the only thing of real importance that leaders do is to create and manage culture" (p. 5). If the challenge is to create and manage an organizational culture that can support learning and change, it is unlikely that a simple leadership solution will suffice.

Organizational culture theories (e.g., Schein, 1992; Smith & Peterson, 1988) suggest that leadership is an integral part of an organization and its processes rather than simply a characteristic of individuals. Efforts to change the way intellectual disability services are provided are unlikely to succeed unless the organizational culture is changed (see Kleiner & Corrigan, 1989; Tichy & Ulrich, 1984). Unfortunately, culture theories of leadership are inclined to suggest a passivity except in times of initiation and change (Yukl, 1994).

Transformational leadership provides a promising improvement over culture theories, partly because it suggests that leaders are proactive and make an active contribution to the organization. It describes leadership as occurring at all levels of the organization, affected by the people involved, their situations, and their influences on each other (Van Seters & Field, 1990). Wide recognition of the importance of organizational culture to change and development perhaps partly explains the considerable interest in what appears to be a very relevant and timely leadership theory. It "is more concerned with the ends; with the direction the organization should take, its goals and values and with developing commitment to achieve these goals in the work force" (Guest, 1987, p. 191). Transformational leadership may repeat existing prescriptions "clothed in different jargon" but one unique contribution is the recognition that leadership processes "are embedded within the culture of the organization, shaping it and being shaped by it" (Yukl, 1994, p. 367).

In essence, transformational leadership differs from transactional leadership in its effect upon followers. Although it cannot stand on its own, transformational leadership is proffered as a key aspect of effective change management (Simpson & Beeby, 1993). Transformational leadership may provide an active link among the vision encapsulated within the concept of quality of life, a supporting organizational culture, and the management of appropriate staff behaviors.

Using the Quality-of-Life Concept for Organizational Research

Evaluating a Learning Disability Service

An evaluation of the Burnley Health Care Trust Learning Disability Service using the Schalock, Keith, and Hoffman (1990) *Quality of Life Questionnaire* revealed significant differences in measured quality of life (Lobley, 1994). Some of the variation in quality-of-life scores may be attributed to immutable differences such as age and, to some extent, the ability of service users. However, some differences in scores could not be explained by these variables. The management team suggested that some of the variation in service users' quality of life may be related to the leadership approach of the first-line managers (see also Reid et al., 1989). In this sense they agree with Mansell, Hughes, and McGill (1994), providing anecdotal confirmation of the importance of management, particularly with regard to the direction and support of face-to-face care staff. A second inquiry (Lobley, 1995) was designed to supplement the study by testing this hypothesis.

Quality of Life and Leadership Approach

Organizational leadership is essential for positive change. It is not necessarily observed exclusively in special or charismatic leaders. Bass (1985) identified charisma as an element of transformational leadership; however, this particular notion was omitted from the study partly because it is complex and rare (Bass) and its impact is hard to predict (Schein, 1992). Further, and of greater relevance, descriptive research suggests that transformational leaders are not necessarily perceived as charismatic by their followers (Yukl, 1994). Few of those transformational leaders studied by Bennis and Nanus (1985) fit a common stereotype of the charismatic leader; most were very ordinary in appearance, personality, and general behavior. Charisma, therefore, may not be an essential component of transformational leadership, nor a vital attribute for first-line managers.

Transformational leadership, however, Bass (1985) argues, can be found at any level. Research by Avolio and Bass (1988) in industrial, military, and educational settings indicates that transformational leadership (in contrast to charisma) is "not at all rare" and seems to exist at many levels in a variety of organizations. Further, they observe, it is "not uncommon in organizational settings nor is it limited to males, top management executives, and world class leaders" (pp. 42-43). Transformational leadership is posited to cascade from one level to the next (Avolio, Waldman, & Yammarino, 1991) and, it is claimed, can be activated from lower or upper levels in the organization (Field, 1989).

Although transformational leadership repeats themes of the 1960s (e.g., empowerment, sense of ownership, quality of work life, supportive relationships), it also provides some new contributions (e.g., intrinsic motivation and symbolic and shared leadership embedded within the culture) (Yukl, 1994). These sorts of behaviors and processes may not in themselves be new; there may have always been transformational leaders. The transformational and transactional distinction appears useful not because it necessarily explains new behaviors, but because it offers a perspective by which differences in leadership effectiveness may be better understood. Such differences in leadership processes should be determined by empirical research rather than predetermined by theoretical definitions. It is the empirical evidence for the value of these behaviors that is important. Thus I set out to investigate the value of transformational leadership processes at an important but not strategic level of a human services organization.

It is believed that leadership and management are crucial factors in quality-of-life outcomes for people with intellectual disabilities (Garner, 1989; Reid et al., 1989). This belief is supported by the findings of the second study. It was found that where first-line managers were rated by their staff as using higher levels of transformational leadership, there were also higher quality-of-life scores for the people living in that part of the service. In other words, there was a significant positive correlation between use of transformational leadership by first-line managers and quality-of-life scores for service users.

Statistical analysis disclosed significant differences between first-line managers' scores on the transformational leadership scale and a correlational relationship between first-line managers' transformational leadership scores and quality-of-life scores of service users. These results suggest that there are differences in the extent to which first-line managers use transformational leadership, and, although the scores are not high, they show a significant correlation with quality-of-life scores. This suggests an association between greater use of transformational leadership behaviors by first-line managers and higher quality of life for clients (Lobley, 1995).

Leadership, Organizational Culture, and Quality of Life

Measures of human service success are increasingly based on outcomes for service users. In the United Kingdom interest has focused on quality of life as an outcome variable in service evaluation (Emerson & Hatton, 1994; Rapley & Beyer, 1996; Rapley & Lobley, 1995). The quality-of-life studies discussed in this chapter suggest that differences in outcomes for clients of a single service can be measured.

Staff behavior is believed to be a crucial variable in outcomes and quality of life for service users (Rice & Rosen, 1991). The senior managers of the service in the present study confirm this view. The key to quality lies at the "moment of truth": the interaction between the service provider and the consumer (Dickens, 1994, p. 182).

The quality-of-life research program strives to bind outcome measurement closely to the value base of services. The importance of this connection is reinforced by Dickens's (1994) observation that the staff-client interaction is influenced by values. Organizational culture supports and directs this staff behavior (Schein, 1992). It plays two central roles in organizations: (a) employees know how to approach complex problems in the right way, and (b) it provides meaning and embodies a set of values that helps justify why certain behaviors are encouraged (Tichy & Ulrich, 1983). An organizational culture—shared values and norms—is rarely transmitted by formal written procedures but through actions (Dickens).

Much of the work attempting to bring about culture change in intellectual disability services has taken an individual focus. Attempts at consciousness change through a process of reframing—changing people's view of the world with a corresponding change in attitudes and behaviors—has had some success over the last 25 years. However, the research cited in this chapter shows that success cannot be guaranteed by this approach and suggests that a well-managed change process is necessary. It is not an uncommon assumption in organizational development attempts that "when enough organizational members change their consciousness organizational change occurs" (Porras & Silvers, 1991, p. 71). The study discussed in this chapter confirms the argument of Porras and Silvers that a combination of both individual and organizational strategies is most likely to be effective.

An organizational value system is linked to two concepts: leadership and vision (O'Brien, 1990). Using transformational leadership appears to facilitate the value change necessary to maintain transmission of an organizational culture that supports behaviors that enhance the quality of life of the service users. The results of the Burnley Health Care Trust Learning Disability Service study suggest that intended organizational culture, its values and norms, as reflected in high quality-of-life outcomes for service users, is facilitated by transformational leadership.

It should be noted that I did not set out to investigate individual first-line managers as the source of vision and organizational culture. No assumption was made that these are, necessarily, exceptional or charismatic individuals, nor that they are responsible for devising the organizational vision. The study focused on the transformational leadership processes adopted, or not, by individuals in putative leadership positions at an important level in the organization. Organizational culture and direction are variables within the context but not something that first-line managers create. The culture is largely derived from "higher up" and from the wider service environment (the "theory of action"). First-line managers may, in turn, derive their choice of behaviors (Stewart, 1982) from their managers and peers. The results suggest that leadership need not be left to other people or seen as the preserve of a few special individuals (Bryman, 1992). A relationship between leadership and service outcomes is revealed at the first-line management level. Transformational leadership appears to facilitate the transmission of organizational culture and to be associated with higher quality of life for people with intellectual disabilities.

References

Avolio, B. J., & Bass, B. M. (1988). Transformational leadership: Charisma and beyond. In J. G. Hunt, B. Rajaram Baliga, H. P. Dachler, & C. A. Schriesheim (Eds.), *Emerging leadership vistas* (pp. 29-49). Lexington, MA: Lexington.

Avolio, B. J., Waldman, D. A., & Yammarino, F. J. (1991). Leading in the 1990's: The four I's of transformational leadership. *Journal of European Industrial Training, 15*(4) 9-16.

Bass, B. M. (1985). *Leadership and performance beyond expectations.* New York: Free Press.

Bennis, W. G., & Nanus, B. (1985). *Leaders: The strategies for taking charge.* New York: Harper & Row.

Blunden, R. (1988). Programmatic features of quality services. In M. P. Janicki, M. W. Krauss, & M. M. Seltzer (Eds.), *Community residences for persons with developmental disabilities: Here to stay* (pp. 117-121). Baltimore: Paul H. Brookes.

Blunden, R. (1994). Paper presented at quality of life conference, Hester Adrian Research Centre, University of Manchester.

Bryman, A. (1992). *Charisma and leadership in organisations.* London: Sage.

Burns, J. M. (1978). *Leadership.* New York: Harper & Row.

Campbell, A., Converse, P. E., & Rogers, W. L. (1976). *The quality of American life: Perceptions, evaluations, and satisfactions.* New York: Russell Sage.

Department of Health. (1971). Better services for the mentally handicapped. London: Her Majesty's Stationery Office.

Dickens, P. (1994). *Quality and excellence in human services.* Chichester: Wiley.

Dowson, S. (1991). *Moving to the dance: Or service culture and community care.* London: Values Into Action.

Edgerton, R. B. (1990). Quality of life from a longitudinal research perspective. In R. L. Schalock (Ed.), *Quality of life: Perspectives and issues* (pp. 149-160). Washington, DC: American Association on Mental Retardation.

Edgerton, R. B., & Berkovici, S. M. (1976). The cloak of competence: Years later. *American Journal of Mental Deficiency, 80*(5), 485-497.

Emerson, E., & Hatton, C. (1994*) Moving out: Relocation from hospital to community.* London: Her Majesty's Stationery Office.

Emerson, E., Hastings, R., & McGill, P. (1994). Values, attitudes, and service ideology. In E. Emerson, P. McGill, & J. Mansell (Eds.), *Severe learning disabilities and challenging behaviour: Designing high quality services* (pp. 209-231). London: Chapman & Hall.

Farey, P. (1993). Mapping the leader/manager. *Management Education and Development, 24,* 109-121.

Field, R. G. H. (1989). The self-fulfilling prophecy leader: Achieving the metharme effect. *Journal of Management Studies, 26,* 151-175.

Garner, L. H. (1989). *Leadership in human services.* San Francisco: Jossey-Bass.

Guest, D. (1987). Leadership and management. In P. Warr (Ed.), *Psychology at work* (3rd ed.). Harmondsworth: Penguin.

Hatton, C., & Emerson, E. (1994, May 19). Moving out. *The Health Service Journal.* 23-25.

Independent Development Council for People With Mental Handicap. (1986). *Pursuing quality: How good are your local services for people with mental handicap?* London: King's Fund Centre.

Keith, K. D. (1996). Measuring quality of life across cultures: Issues and challenges. In R. L. Schalock (Ed.), *Quality of life: Vol. 1. Conceptualization and measurement* (pp. 73-82). Washington, DC: American Association on Mental Retardation.

King's Fund Centre. (1980). *An ordinary life: Comprehensive locally-based residential services for mentally handicapped people.* London: Author.

Kleiner, B. H., & Corrigan, W. A. (1989). Understanding organizational change. *Leadership and Organizational Development Journal, 10*(3), 25-31.

Landesman, S. (1986). Quality of life and personal satisfaction: Definition and measurement issues. *Mental Retardation, 24*(3), 141-143.

Lobley, J. W. (1994). *Burnley Health Care Trust Learning Disability Service: Quality of Life Survey.* Unpublished service evaluation. Calderstones NHS Trust, Research and Development Department.

Lobley, J. W. (1995). *Transformational leadership: Transmission of organizational culture and quality of life for people with learning disabilities.* London: Birkbeck College, Department of Organisational Psychology.

Mansell, J., Hughes, H., & McGill, P. (1994). Maintaining local placements. In E. Emerson, P. McGill, & J. Mansell (Eds.), *Severe learning disabilities and challenging behaviour: Designing high quality services* (pp. 260-281). London: Chapman & Hall.

Mansell, J., McGill, P., & Emerson. E. (1994). Conceptualizing service provision. In E. Emerson, P. McGill, & J. Mansell (Eds.), *Severe learning disabilities and challenging behaviour: Designing high quality services* (pp. 69-93). London: Chapman & Hall.

Murrell, S. A., & Norris, F. H. (1983). Quality of life as the criterion for need assessment and community psychology. *Journal of Community Psychology, 11,* 88-97.

North Western Regional Health Authority. (1983). *Services for people who are mentally handicapped: A model district service.* Manchester: Author.

O'Brien, J. (1990). Developing high quality services for people with developmental disabilities. In V. J. Bradley & H. A. Bersani (Eds.), *Quality assurance for individuals with developmental disabilities: It's everybody's business* (pp. 17-31). Baltimore: Paul H. Brookes.

Pettinelli, V. D. (1993). *Human services management that works.* Worthington, OH: IDS.

Porras, J. I., & Silvers, R. C. (1991). Organizational development and transformation. *Annual Review of Psychology, 42,* 51-78.

Rapley, M., & Beyer, S. (1996). Daily activity, community participation, and quality of life in an ordinary housing network. *Journal of Applied Research in Intellectual Disabilities, 9,* 31-39.

Rapley, M., & Clements, J. (1994). New song: Reflections on the inadequacy of community services for people with learning disabilities. *Care in Place: The International Journal of Networks and Community, 1*(3), 248-255.

Rapley, M., & Lobley, J. (1995). Factor analysis of the Schalock & Keith (1993) Quality of Life Questionnaire. *Mental Handicap Research, 8,* 194-202.

Reid, D. H., Parsons, M. B., & Green, C. W. (1989). *Staff management in human services: Behavioral research and application.* Springfield, IL: Thomas.

Rice, D. M., & Rosen, M. (1991). Direct care staff: A neglected priority. *Mental Retardation, 29,* 3-4.

Schalock, R. L. (Ed.). (1990). *Quality of life: Perspectives and issues.* Washington, DC: American Association on Mental Retardation.

Schalock, R. L. (1997). Can the concept of quality of life make a difference? In R. L. Schalock (Ed.), *Quality of life: Vol. 2. Application to persons with disabilities* (pp. 245-267). Washington, DC: American Association on Mental Retardation.

Schalock, R. L., Keith, K. D., & Hoffman, K. (1990). *Quality of Life Questionnaire (1990 version).* Hastings, NE: Mid Nebraska Mental Retardation Services.

Schein, E. H. (1992). *Organizational culture and leadership.* San Francisco: Jossey-Bass.

Sheill, A., Pettipher, C., Raynes, N., & Wright, K. (1990). Economic approaches to measuring quality of life: Conceptual convenience or methodological straight jacket? In S. Baldwin, C. Godfrey, & C. Propper (Eds.), *Quality of Life: Perspectives and policies* (pp. 105-119). London: Routledge.

Simpson, P., & Beeby, M. (1993). Facilitating public sector organizational culture change through transformational leadership. *Management Education and Development, 24,* 316-329.

Smith, P. B., & Peterson, M. F. (1988). *Leadership organisations and culture.* London: Sage.

Stewart, R. (1982). *Choices for the manager: A guide to managerial work and behaviour.* London: McGraw-Hill.

Tichy, N., & Ulrich, D. (1983). *Revitalizing organizations: The leadership role.* Ann Arbor: University of Michigan Graduate School of Business Administration.

Tichy, N., & Ulrich, D. (1984). The leadership challenge: A call for the transformational leader. *Sloan Management Review, 26,* 59-68.

Van Seters, D. A., & Field, R. H. G. (1990). The evolution of leadership theory. *Journal of Organizational Change Management, 3*(3), 29-45.

Yukl, G. (1994). *Leadership in organizations.* Englewood Cliffs, NJ: Prentice-Hall.

Zautra, A., & Goodhart, D. (1979). Quality of life indicators: A review of the literature. *Community Mental Health Review, 4,* 2-10.

The Macrosystem: Quality of Life From a Larger, Cultural Perspective

Quality of life exists in an increasingly culturally divergent environment that makes cultural exchange and cross-cultural understanding essential. As stated by Kuehn and McClainm (1994):

> The challenge is to develop an awareness and knowledge of the diverse cultural beliefs and behaviors. . . . And to develop an understanding of the "good life" as perceived by different racial/ethnic/cultural groups. Without such knowledge, any quantitative or qualitative analyses of quality of life will be imprecise and will limit the ability of researchers to develop a universal theory of quality of life for the purpose of research or program planning. (p. 191)

Cross-cultural research has demonstrated the presence of culturally divergent values and assumptions. Chief among these are relations with nature, time orientation, interpersonal relations, sense of self, use of wealth, thinking style, and support systems. Despite these differences, this is a reasonable question to ask: Are there some similarities across cultures in their approach to the concept of quality of life, regardless of those culturally divergent values and assumptions?

Some of our recent work suggests that there is. For example, in a 1990 study, we (Schalock et al.) administered the *Quality of Life Questionnaire* (Schalock & Keith, 1993) to a group of 92 individuals with mental retardation in four countries (Australia, the Federal Republic of Germany, Israel, and the Republic of China) and compared their measured scores to the standardization sample of 552 people with mental retardation in the United States. The *Quality of Life Questionnaire* was translated into the respective language (Australia used the English version) and then back-translated to ensure linguistic equivalence. Two results of the study stand out. First, there was considerable consistency among the specific factor scores across the five countries; second, across the five countries, measured quality-of-life scores increased as individuals lived and worked in more normalized environments.

In a second study (Schalock & Kelley, 1999), we asked colleagues in 14 countries reflecting the regions of Asia-Pacific, Europe, and North America to evaluate the influence of 10 values and 10 contextual variables on the development of integrated employment and community living programs in their respective countries. Across the 14 countries, two values (interpersonal relations and supports systems) and five contextual variables (public policies, academic or professional supports, teaching or rehabilitation staff availability, and attitudes toward people with disabilities) were rated the most influential.

These values and contextual variables are consistent with a number of principles and declarations promulgated by the United Nations. For example, during the 1970s, the United Nations General Assembly adopted two declarations that provide for a comprehensive revision of a global approach to disability legislation. The first of the two declarations, adopted in 1971, focused on the rights of people with disabilities. The Declaration on the Rights of Mentally Retarded Persons stipulated that people with mental retardation should be accorded both the same human rights as other individuals, as well as specific rights corresponding to their particular needs in medical, educational, or other spheres of life. The second declaration, adopted in 1975, encompassed all aspects of civil, political, and economic life of people with disabilities. The Declaration on the Rights of Disabled Persons proclaimed the equality of civil and political rights of disabilities and their broad social and economic rights. The Declaration places advocacy and empowerment for or of individuals with disabilities as central concerns and provides standards for equal treatment and access to services that will contribute to development of skills of people with disabilities and promote their integration into mainstreamed society.

In 1992, to mark the end of the Decade of Disabled Persons, the United Nations General Assembly adopted a resolution proclaiming December 3 as the International Day of Disabled Persons. The Day, which was initially established to commemorate the anniversary of the adoption of the World Programme of Action Concerning Disabled Persons by the international community, provides an opportunity to review annually both progress and obstacles in the implementation of actions by governments, the nongovernmental community, and private sector to further its objectives and to identify new issues and emerging trends in the disability community.

In 1994 the United Nations General Assembly adopted the *Standard Rules on the Equalization of Opportunities for Persons With Disabilities.* These rules, while not legally binding, seek to provide guidelines for efforts by governments to further opportunities for equal participation of people with disabilities in all aspects of society. The 22 Rules, listed below, represent practical tools to improve the quality of life and well-being of people with disabilities and focus on removal of barriers to their full and effective participation in social and economic development.

- Awareness raising: about persons with disabilities, their rights and responsibilities, their needs, their potential and their contributions.
- Medical care: effective medical care to persons with disabilities.
- Rehabilitation: rehabilitation services that help persons with disabilities reach and keep their highest level of independence and functioning.
- Support services: support services, including assistive devices, which help persons with disabilities increase their independence and exercise their rights.
- Accessibility: access to the physical environment (housing, buildings, transportation, streets, etc.) and access to information and communication.
- Education: equal educational opportunities for children, youth, and adults with disabilities in integrated settings.
- Employment: equal opportunities for persons with disabilities to get and keep productive and gainful employment in the community.
- Income maintenance and social security: availability of social security and income maintenance for all people with disabilities who need financial help.
- Family life and personal integrity: full participation of people with disabilities in family life, sexual relationships, marriage, and parenthood.
- Culture: equal opportunities for persons with disabilities to participate in cultural activities.
- Recreation and sport: equal opportunities for persons with disabilities to participate in recreation and sports.

- Religion: equal participation by persons with disabilities in the religious life of their communities.

- Information and research: collect and distribute information about the living conditions of persons with disabilities and conduct research on all aspects of community life, including the barriers that affect the lives of persons with disabilities.

- Policymaking and planning: include disability points of view in all relevant policymaking and planning.

- Legislation: create the legal means to achieve the full participation and equality of persons with disabilities.

- Economic policies: budget for and fund programs and measures that will create equal opportunities for persons with disabilities.

- Coordination of work: establish and strengthen coordinating committees that will serve as a focal point on disability matters.

- Organizations of persons with disabilities: recognize the rights of organizations of persons with disabilities to represent persons with disabilities at national, regional, and local levels and ask for their advice when making decisions about disability issues.

- Personnel training: provide adequate training of personnel, at all levels, involved in planning and providing programs and services concerning persons with disabilities.

- National monitoring and evaluating of disability programs in the implementation of the Rules: ensure continuous monitoring and evaluating of the implementation of programs and services concerned with creating equal opportunities for persons with disabilities.

- Technical and economic cooperation: cooperate and take action to improve the living conditions of persons with disabilities in developing countries.

- International cooperation: participate in international efforts to ensure equal opportunities for persons with disabilities. (United Nations, 1994)

Each of the chapters in part 3 addresses factors reflecting these 22 Rules that relate to specific values and contextual variables cross-cuturally or within the author's specific country. We begin with Mark Rapley's analysis (chap. 15) of the cross-cultural meaning of quality of life and its existence in the social interaction between individual and community. Rapley pursues this notion in studies conducted both in Australia and in England, while developing a particularly useful distinction between life in "the community" and life "in community," and advocating for greater awareness of this distinction on the part of researchers, clinicians, and service planners. Using data from British studies, David Felce (chap. 16) illustrates the critical importance of engagement in meaningful activity as a determinant of quality of life and explores the implications of service system training toward the end of active engagement.

Culture is a complex phenomenon, and to sensitize the reader to that complexity as it relates to the concept of quality of life, Lilah Pengra (chap. 17) examines two cultural contexts—worldview and identity—and their implications for quality of life within the culture of Native Americans (the Lakota of South Dakota) with disabilities. Pengra suggests that quality of life for the Lakota must include an understanding of their worldview, characterized by fortitude, generosity, wisdom, and respect. In a similar way, Hung-Chih Lin (chap. 18) places modern research on quality of life of individuals with disabilities in Taiwan in the context of ancient Confucian philosophy. This history provides a cultural backdrop establishing the entitlement of all citizens to respect and enjoy the basic essentials for a life of quality.

Perhaps nowhere more than in contemporary Russia is the relationship between culture and quality of life so obviously critical. Judy Smith-Davis (chap. 19) describes the efforts of the Russian people to advance quality of life for people with disabilities, even in the face of tremendous ecological, health care, and economic obstacles. Similarly, Sushil Kumar Goel (chap. 20) recounts efforts to improve economic security, employment opportunity, living standards, education, and social life of people with disabilities in India where, as he points out so poignantly, "millions and millions of Indians have been desperately struggling" to meet the basic needs of life. He proposes the need for value-oriented education, personal responsibility, parent self-help groups, and community-based rehabilitation programs in a country facing high poverty and illiteracy and limited opportunities for personal development.

Silvana Watson (chap. 21) continues discussion of the theme of cultural context, illustrating some of the unique themes inherent in Brazilian culture and their implications for social inclusion and quality of life for people with disabilities. Next, Marie José Schmitt (chap. 22) delves deeply into the historical roots of French culture to show us why the quality-of-life concept is particularly critical to modern French citizens with developmental disabilities. A focus on quality of life, she believes, will improve "real opportunities to live a full human life." Her approach is more philosophical than empirical, illustrating the essential nature of an understanding of the cultural backdrop as a foundation for current views of disability and quality of life.

The emphasis of some countries on quality of life in public policy and/or service delivery systems is illustrated in Miguel Verdugo's discussion (chap. 23) of changes in Spain in the fields of education and social service. These agencies incorporate the concept of quality of life as the basis of public policy, service delivery, program evaluation, and research. The reader will note Verdugo's optimism that current policies and practices will enhance quality of life of service recipients.

The need for—and success of—community-based programs is discussed in depth in chapter 24 by Roy McConkey and Brian O'Toole. They argue that in countries such as Guyana, South America, specialized professional services offer limited scope to generate sustained quality of life, and that alternative systems of doing this need to be structured and supported within local communities. Using their experience in Guyana, the authors share their efforts to enhance quality of life through community volunteers, health environments, poverty reduction, building solidarity and empowerment, and social inclusion. The focus on inclusion is continued in chapter 25 by Leena Matikka of Finland, who summarizes the Finnish perspective on quality of life and the basic values of the service system adopted by the Finnish Association on Mental Retardation. She proposes a framework for enhancing quality of life using different instruments at four different policy or service delivery levels: international, national, local, and individual. Like Schmitt in her earlier chapter, Matikka adopts a philosophical approach, with a particular emphasis on the legal dimensions of the cultural foundations of Finnish views of disability and quality of life.

People in many countries are working hard to change policies, procedures, and laws related to the rights and social inclusion of people with disabilities. In chapter 26 Diego González Castanón and Monica González Buján discuss the current situation regarding the rights and social inclusion of people with disabilities in Argentina. After summarizing legal rights, these authors examine four areas that reflect the current social inclusion status of people with disabilities in Argentina: work, institutional participation, collective representation, and association with peers. Castanón and Buján conclude by suggesting a number of ways that future efforts can be directed toward enhanced quality of life of people with disabilities in Argentina. The theme of legal foundations and future prospects appears again in the work of Giorgio Albertini (chap. 27), this time in the Italian context.

Patricia Noonan Walsh (chap. 28) explores recent social and political developments in Ireland that have impacted the current status (and, by inference, quality of life) of Irish citizens with disabilities. She argues strongly that opportunities for an enhanced quality of life arise at points of confluence where individuals are included in society as students, employees, and citizens.

In chapter 29 we (Schalock & Keith) delineate the evolution of the quality-of-life concept in the United States in the 1980s and 1990s, and its future role in defining lives of quality. Inevitably, implementation of the quality-of-life concept will bring challenges and, at least sometimes, conflict and confrontation. These issues constitute the theme of Roy Brown's review (chap. 30), in which he shows that cultural policies and practices will be required to change if a quality-of-life model is to be accepted.

In reading part 3, the reader is encouraged to keep two points in mind. First, the quality-of-life movement is occurring within an increasingly culturally divergent environment that necessitates cross-cultural understanding. Second, the cross-cultural study and understanding of the concept of quality of life and its application to people with mental retardation is still in its infancy. Despite this fact, the international popularity of the concept, and the calls for it to be the basis for national and international disability policy, require an increased commitment to studying its emic (culture-bound) and etic (universal) properties. This is the primary purpose of this section of this volume. Throughout your reading of these 16 chapters, note the similarity among cultures in:

- emerging changes in service delivery philosophy and techniques;

- basing services and supports on the concept of quality of life;

- understanding quality of life based on social, political, and economic factors;

- approaching quality-of-life application and evaluation from multiple levels including international, national, local, and personal;

- recognizing value and contextual variables in the conceptualization, measurement, and application of the quality-of-life concept.

References

Kuehn, M. L., & McClainm, J. W. (1994). Quality of life in the United States: A multicultural context. In D. A. Goode (Ed.), *Quality of life for persons with disabilities: International perspectives and issues* (pp. 185-193). Boston: Brookline.

Schalock, R. L., & Keith, K. D. (1993). *Quality of life questionnaire.* Worthington, OH: IDS.

Schalock, R. L., & Kelley, C. (1999). Sociocultural factors influencing social and vocational inclusion of persons with mental retardation: A cross-cultural study. In P. Retish & S. Reiter (Eds.), *Social and vocational inclusion of persons with mental retardation: An international perspective* (pp. 309-324). New York: Lawrence Erlbaum.

Schalock, R. L., Bartnik, E., Wu, F., Konig, A., Lee, C. S., & Reiter, S. (1990, May). *An international perspective on quality of life measurement and use.* Paper presented at the 104th annual convention, American Association on Mental Retardation, Atlanta, GA.

United Nations. (1994). *Standard rules on the equalization of opportunities for persons with disabilities.* New York: Author.

The Social Construction of Quality of Life: The Interpersonal Production of Well-Being Revisited

Mark Rapley
Murdoch University
Murdoch, Western Australia, Australia

There can now be little doubt that Schalock (1990a) was correct in predicting that quality of life would become "the issue of the 1990's" (p. x). Equally, as Goode (1990) suggested, it appears that the concept of quality of life is now a "permanent fixture in the field of disabilities" (p. 56). Growing out of a field inspired by the communitarian rhetoric of the normalization movement, quality of life has come to be seen by many as simultaneously both an issue about "entitlement" (Rosen, 1986) or individual human rights (Walmsley, 1991) and also as perhaps the "ultimate index" of the efficacy of human services in mental retardation (Perry & Felce, 1995).

The growth in the literature in the last decade has been, as Cummins (1995) has noted, exponential. Cummins identified in excess of 100 definitions of the term, and Hughes, Hwang, Kim, Eisenman, and Kilian (1995) and Hughes and Hwang (1996) have pointed to well over 1,000 measures purporting to quantify either quality of life or one of its putative components. Indeed it is not only in intellectual disability research that such an interest has grown; Antaki and Rapley (1996a) report having identified 1,400 papers employing *quality of life* as a key term in the broader psychological literature between 1992 and mid-1995.

As other theorists have noted (e.g., Edgerton, 1990; Taylor & Bogdan, 1990, 1996), the greater proportion of these contributions construct "quality of life" as an individual attribute or as a mental state of the individual. Such a mental state remains a private and individual possession, while also frequently construed as a function of, as consequential upon, or as an outcome mediated by, service practice. The literature constructs quality of life, like age, height, or shoe size, as a property of individuals that may be meaningfully quantified. Individuals are conceived of as being meaningfully described in terms of "having" greater or lesser amounts of quality of life, with the implicit moral position (and in the medical literature the explicit moral stance) that less quality of life is a "bad thing," and that occupation of the moral status of "having" low quality of life is indicative of a service insufficiency at best, and at worst possibly a warrant for the withholding of (life-saving) treatment.

As Wolfensberger (1994), Borthwick-Duffy (1996), and Edgerton (1990) have observed, the moral implications of this quantification of a putative mental state are extremely serious. So serious, suggests Wolfensberger (1994), that "we should hang up 'Quality of Life' as a 'hopeless term'" (p. 285). Yet as I have argued elsewhere (Antaki & Rapley, 1996a; Rapley & Ridgway, in press), and as Schalock (1990b) hints in his discussion of the "quality revolution," so potent is the quality-of-life discourse (and so interwoven with the individualistic, "quality" rhetoric of the political right) that requests for a principled rejection of the quality-of-life construct as an individual attribute appear unlikely to be heeded.

Thus despite the absolutely explicit recognition of the importance of interpersonal influences (e.g., marital relationships, family life, friendships) to personal well-being in early work on quality of life (e.g., Campbell, 1981), and the acknowledgment of "external influences" (Felce & Perry, 1996, p. 64) in recent theoretical models of quality of life, the mental retardation literature has resolutely pursued the notion that quality of life is primarily an inner state of the individual. Such a "psychologization" (Rose, 1990) of the quality-of-life construct is in keeping with broader discursive forces in Western societies (Antaki & Rapley, 1996a; Schalock, 1990b) and is visible even in areas of the field traditionally more open to a contextualist phenomenological epistemology. For example, Taylor and Bogdan (1996), champions of the qualitative evaluation of well-being, and Edgerton (1990), who cautions against the "American passion for reducing complex qualitative constructs to simple scalar instruments" (p. 150) construct quality of life as an individualized "inner state" (Taylor & Bogdan, p. 19) or as a state deriving "more from personal attributes than from the impact of [the] environment" (Edgerton, 1996, p. 87). That is to say, quality of life, or personal well-being, is, despite a nod to "external factors," constructed in the mental retardation literature as an individual property of individuals and is widely held to be determined by the inherent disposition or temperament of people with mental retardation.

Such an individualized state may too, if the literature is to be believed, be one upon which individuals with mental retardation are particularly ill-equipped or unable sensibly to report. As a consequence of widespread acceptance of supposed phenomena such as acquiescence (Sigelman, Budd, Spanhel, & Schoenrock, 1981; Heal & Sigelman, 1995), suggest Taylor and Bogdan (1996), "one cannot ask a person with mental retardation, or perhaps any one for that matter, 'How do you view your quality of life?' and expect to receive a meaningful answer" (p. 19). We thus have in the literature a rather paradoxical position. Quality of life is the dominant issue in the field, it is constructed as an individualized subjective state, and yet despite the urgings of authorities such as Heal and Sigelman (1990), who suggest that "there are compelling philosophical reasons for providing mentally retarded consumers with opportunities to tell us how they perceive their lives" (pp. 174-175), the very individuals about whose well-being we wish to enquire are constructed in the literature (indeed by the same authors) as incapable of reliably or validly reporting on it.

In this chapter I want to (a) look at quality of life not as an individualized mental state, but as an intersubjective product, a product of interaction in community with others, and (b) challenge the negativism of the literature on the interactional competence of people with mental retardation. By examining both the process and outcomes of the collection of quantitative, individualized, quality-of-life data and discussing some of the failings of the quantitative measurement paradigm, I argue that the current preoccupation with the individualized measurement of a putative internal state of individuals betrays the rhetorical and ideological commitments of what I will term here the "ordinary life" movement (from which source, at least in part, current interest in quality of life has sprung) and also misrepresents quality of life as an ontologically untroubled aspect of the psyche. I argue that the following notion must be resurrected from its current neglect: that living in community (as opposed to in the community) and the consequent quality of life are the interactional products of the everyday lives of people in their social environments.

The Rhetorical Goals of the "Ordinary Life" Movement

The establishment of residential services in community settings was, from the outset, rhetorically intended to deliver conditions in which individuals with mental retardation could live closer to the normal parameters of society, to offer an increased range of opportunities for participation in those communities, and to lay the foundations for participatory citizenship (O'Brien, 1987; O'Brien & Tyne, 1981; Wolfensberger, 1972). The aims of community-based services were clearly stated by the British King's Fund Centre in 1980. The King's Fund (1980) offers a statement of intent that is elegant in its simplicity and unequivocal in its orientation to the objective of shared membership in community. It is a statement of purpose that has yet to be bettered, with the paramount objective of assisting people to live not in the community, but in community with other, ordinary, citizens:

> Our goal is to see mentally handicapped people in the mainstream of life, living in ordinary houses in ordinary streets, with the same range of choices as any citizen, and mixing as equals with the other, and mostly not handicapped members of their own community. (p. 8)

As an explicit goal of what has come to be known in the United Kingdom as the "ordinary life movement," community integration must thus involve the social, interpersonal, and the psychological as well as the physical integration of people with mental retardation into the "mainstream," into the wider community (Dagnan, Howard, & Drewett, 1994; Emerson & Pretty, 1987; King's Fund Centre, 1988). As O'Brien (1990) has expressed it more briefly, the ultimate goal (in rhetoric at least) of the "ordinary life" movement is to "welcome people with disabilities into ordinary, rich networks of relationships" (p. 1). The specification of such a goal implies that the development by people with mental retardation of "ordinary, rich networks of relationships" is not only a necessary outcome to be sought in its own right, but also represents the vehicle by which individual well-being (or a high quality of life) is to be accomplished (O'Brien). Community integration thus constructed casts quality of life as inherently interactional, rather than individualized. As I have noted, such a focus on the interactional accomplishment of well-being appears to have been somewhat neglected in the construction of scales designed to operationalize quality of life as an individualized attribute.

Quality of Life and Social Relationships

As *quality of life* has progressed from being a descriptor of the state of states—an index of the relative comfort of large populations—to being an aspect of individual subjectivity, likewise the notion of *community* has become narrowed in its application. Community has become concretized in the literature as a place, the level or frequency of individuals' access to which has been confected as an index of their personal, or psychological, state of "social belonging[ness]."

Community, as it has been conceived in the bulk of the literature, is primarily a geographic or locality-based construct, often has been a shorthand term for "not in an institution," and, with a few exceptions such as Flynn's (1989) work in the North West has been represented as an unproblematic "good thing." Much of the mainstream literature seems not to have acknowledged the notion of relational communities, the ties and connections among individuals—who may or may not share a particular locality—by virtue of which living in community is a matter not necessarily of sharing space, but of sharing in a community of interest (Granovetter, 1982; King's Fund Centre, 1988).

Edgerton's work, for example, gives detailed attention to the crucial importance of social relationships in the determination of (in his view, temporary) subjective estimates of well-being. And existing measurement tools (e.g., Schalock & Keith, 1993; Cummins, 1993) may attribute a role to personal relationships in the factor structure of quality of life (in the social belonging/community integration subscale of Schalock & Keith and the intimacy subscale of Cummins). But scales such as these do not do sufficient justice to the importance of social influences on the subjective well-being of individuals. A body of existing work suggests that relational communities may be construed as being central to the quality of life, indeed that quality of life is inherently a socially—and hence intersubjectively—constructed object.

It is now clear that the physical aspects of community integration have been, with the notable exception of provision for people deemed "challenging," somewhat successfully managed (Emerson & Hatton, 1994, 1996; Rapley & Clements, 1994). However, a body of international research indicates that the active participation of individuals in a range of social, relational, and leisure activities within the wider community is not transpiring (Allen, 1989; Emerson, Beasley, Offord, & Mansell, 1992; Emerson & Hatton, 1994; Evans, Todd, Beyer, Felce, & Perry, 1994; Ralph & Usher, 1995; Rapley & Beyer, 1995; Sinson, 1993; Yeatman, 1996).

When researchers have looked at the social context of community-based services, at what has been termed "community participation" (O'Brien, 1987), at the neighborhood places people use (e.g., Crapps & Stoneman, 1989; Humphreys, Lowe, & Blunden, 1983; Lowe, dePaiva, & Humphreys, 1986), at levels of participation in activities in their local community (Salzberg & Langford, 1981; Saxby, Thomas, Felce, & de Kock, 1986), and their level of contact with people important to them, such as family and friends and salient others (e.g., local tradespeople, neighbors, and service providers) (de Kock, Felce, Saxby, & Thomas, 1988; Firth & Short, 1987; Malin, 1982; McConkey, Naughton, & Nugent, 1983; Reiter & Levi, 1980; Walmsley, 1996a), the verdict is nearly unanimous. Many people with mental retardation in community-based settings, either in residential services or living with their families, experience social and psychological isolation. The position is well summarized by Lowe and dePaiva (1991):

physical location alone, or even a considerable use of community amenities as in such activities as shopping and going to the pub, may not result in substantial development of social relationships or extensive participation in the normal life of a community . . . people living within their family home often remain isolated with few friends or activities. (p. 309)

Likewise de Kock et al. (1988) suggest that many people with mental retardation are "fringe dwellers" in community settings. Recent Australian research has confirmed these findings. Although people with mental retardation are located within the community, their integration into those communities is only partial (Ralph & Usher, 1995; Rapley & Hopgood, 1997). Indeed, as with studies conducted in the United Kingdom and the United States, Ralph and Usher concluded that Western Australians with mental retardation had no real choice of their coresidents; that coresidents formed an almost exclusive social network; and that structured routines with staff supervision characterized most domestic and social activities, allowing little opportunity for individuals to foster their own social networks and independence.

A large body of work suggests that people with mental retardation are both aware of and willing to express the fact that this social isolation detracts from the quality of their lives (e.g., Edgerton, 1989; Firth & Rapley, 1990; Flynn, 1989; Hoover, Wheeler, & Reetz, 1992; Malin, 1982; McConkey, Naughton, & Nugent, 1982; Reiter & Levi, 1980; Sands, Kozleski, & Goodwin, 1991; Walmsley, 1996b). Other research indicates that individuals with mental retardation perceive opportunities for social interaction and for reciprocal social relationships as of paramount importance in respect to their sense of belonging to, and integration within, the community and their degree of overall satisfaction with their lives (Atkinson & Ward, 1987; Marková, Jahoda, Cattermole, & Woodward, 1992; Rapley, 1996).

Such findings appear to be at least partly related to the nature of the community under scrutiny. Ralph and Usher's (1995) Australian study suggested that individuals in rural areas were more likely to engage in interactions with people without mental retardation than their urban counterparts. With findings comparable to Seed's (1980) research in the Scottish highlands, Ralph and Usher (1995) concluded that, as a result of the smaller size of their communities, rural respondents were more likely to come into contact with people without mental retardation and become more recognized among community members. Such recognition is clearly a desirable outcome, but it does not necessarily translate into being "known" (Evans, Beyer, & Todd, 1988; Evans, Todd, & Beyer, 1990, 1992; Todd, Evans, & Beyer, 1990) or being a member of that community with the implied reciprocity and psychological connectedness of the "ties" of membership (Granovetter, 1982; King's Fund Centre, 1988).

It is striking that sources as disparate as rural Scotland and Somerset in the United Kingdom, metropolitan Dublin, the Welsh valleys, Los Angeles, Tel Aviv, and Perth suggest that so many people with mental retardation in receipt of community-based services report isolation, a lack of friends, and loneliness. Unless we are to construe people with mental retardation as a group, across cultures and continents, as intrinsically likely to be dispositionally miserable (as an Edgertonian position would seem to imply), it seems plausible to suggest that the availability and nature of people's social relationships, rather than merely individualized dispositional factors, may be seen as constitutive of their estimations of subjective well-being.

Quality of Life and Perceptions of Social Connectedness

With criticisms of quality of life as a measurable, individualized state in abeyance for the moment, I want now to discuss further evidence, gathered by "traditional" means, that quality of life may profitably be understood as an intersubjective—or at least socially determined—product. I discuss evidence from two studies of community-based services, one in a city in northern England, the other in rural Australia, to illustrate that when construed and quantified as an individual attribute, quality of life enters into relationships with other social and interactional variables that must cast doubt upon the conceptual foundations of the construct as primarily an individual attribute.

Many studies in the United Kingdom, the United States, and Australia have studied community participation (Emerson & Hatton, 1994), but most research has generally failed to measure the quality of life of people with mental retardation, instead inferring the construct from dubious indexes (Rapley & Beyer, 1995). Cummins (1991) points out that "QOL [quality of life] for people with mental retardation has been judged either by objective criteria relating to the person's environment or by the opinions of caregivers; both highly questionable sources of data" (p. 259).

Similarly, although community participation has always been presented as a central goal of the normalization movement (e.g., O'Brien, 1990), no published work known to the author has attempted directly to capture the interpersonal sense of belonging in community settings, often referred to in the community psychology literature as a "sense of community" (McMillan & Chavis, 1986; Sarason, 1974), experienced by people with mental retardation; this might be posited as representing the most appropriate success criterion of efforts to promote community integration.

A small-scale Australian study of community-based residential services in a predominantly rural area was conducted to remedy this lack (see Rapley & Hopgood, 1997, for a more detailed report of this study). Employing well-validated instruments, the aim of the study was to (a) analyze relationships between objective measures of domestic engagement, community participation, and quality of life, and (b) examine service users' subjective perceptions of their involvement in, and connectedness to, their communities.

Although the sample size was small ($n = 34$), theoretically appropriate relationships were found between objective indexes of service quality and subjective measures. For example, both the Index of Participation in Domestic Life and the Index of Community Involvement were positively correlated with higher measured quality of life on the *Quality of Life Questionnaire* (Schalock & Keith, 1993), particularly with the satisfaction and empowerment subscales. This finding suggests, in replication of studies reported by Rapley (1996), that the more extensive the opportunities afforded by services for people with mental retardation to participate in both routine domestic activities and in community settings, the higher the service users' estimations of subjective empowerment and life satisfaction.

Scores on the social belonging subscale of the *Quality of Life Questionnaire* (Schalock & Keith, 1993) were not, however, correlated with measures of community participation and sense of community. It might theoretically be expected that this subscale should display a relationship with both the Index of Community Involvement and the Neighborhood Sense of Community Index. The absence of relationships here suggests that activity within the wider community does not automatically imply that a sense of membership in, or connectedness to, that community will develop. As community presence and participation are theoretically and empirically separable (Emerson & Pretty, 1987), so too appear to be satisfaction with levels of that participation (effectively what is measured by the social belonging subscale of the *Quality of Life Questionnaire*) and a sense of belonging within the community—an emergent property of the "connectedness" of individuals to a specific locality and its social environment.

Quality of Life and the Affective Tone of Social Contact

As has been widely noted in the literature, the behavior of staff is a critical factor in the quality of services (Felce, 1991) and, by extension, in the quality of life of service users. The second study compared the experience of people in institutional and community-based services, taking particular interest in the nature of the contact people with mental retardation routinely received from staff members. The series of studies of which this study formed a part are reported in Rapley (1996), with substudies reported by Rapley and Beyer (1995, 1998).

The experiences of a total of 67 people resident in either a large long-stay institution (33 people) or one of three satellite community-based supported housing networks (34 people) in a city in northern England were again compared on measures of the major outcome domains identified in the literature (Emerson & Hatton, 1994). A variety of data collection methods were employed: interviews with service users, staff completion of rating scales, and direct observation of activity using an established momentary time sampling protocol. Of particular interest in the results of this study was the dissociation that appeared in the relationship between different *Quality of Life Questionnaire* (Schalock & Keith, 1993) subscale scores and the type of staff contact that service users experienced.

Participants' quality-of-life scores reflected the differences in the domestic and community experience offered by the different service models. Unsurprisingly, perhaps, consistent positive associations were found between participants' residence in community-based, as opposed to institutional, housing, and higher scores on all subscales of the *Quality of Life Questionnaire*. Furthermore, differences in *Quality of Life Questionnaire* subscale scores within community-based services appeared to reflect the different emphases of the three networks studied. Thus, for example, a lower mean score on the social belonging subscale was obtained for the most domestically oriented network when compared to the network with the largest number of people involved in work or educational activities.

Of particular interest in the context of this chapter, however, was the relationship between the nature of staff contact and measured quality of life. Relationships between types of observed staff contact (coded by direct observation as positive, negative, assistance-giving, or neutral) and scores on *Quality of Life Questionnaire* subscales were examined. Statistically significant relationships were observed between higher scores on all questionnaire subscales and absolute levels of social contact from staff.

With absolute levels of contact established as being clearly related to quality of life, specific contact types were examined. The observational protocol defines positive contact as direct interpersonal contact to individuals with mental retardation by staff members, which is demonstrative of a positive affective relationship with the service user. Across service users, higher levels of positive contact from staff were associated with higher scores on all questionnaire subscales. However, while positive affective contact was strongly related to the most obviously subjective factor (satisfaction), other forms of staff contact (e.g., assistance) did not enter into relationships with the satisfaction factor, but rather showed strong significant correlations with the remaining, more "objective," subscales. Thus higher levels of neutral contact were associated with higher scores on all *Quality of Life Questionnaire* subscales other than satisfaction.

The independence of satisfaction from the other, more "objective," subscales, and from a direct relationship with staff contacts that are functional in the mediation of activity (assistance) or neutral in affective tone (neutral contact) is intriguing. Speculatively, it might be proposed that, in the associations between functional staff contact and the more "objective" subscale factors, the *Quality of Life Questionnaire* is tapping aspects of quality of life that staff can help to enhance by skills teaching or by management of the residential environment. If a primarily dispositional position on quality of life is taken (Edgerton, 1996), the theoretical reasons why the most clearly individual, dispositional indicator—satisfaction—is enhanced by positively tinged interpersonal interactions and apparently little affected by neutral contact or primarily functional assistance, remain unclear. However, in the context of a more interactional, or social, position on well-being, it is noteworthy that higher satisfaction was not only strongly related to levels of positive affective contact from staff, but also strongly related to the number of friends service users reported having and the number of community-based social activities in which they took part.

Strong relationships have been observed between (a) service users' satisfaction and levels of contact from staff (especially positive affective contact) and (b) participation in social activities and friendship networks. Considered in light of clear-cut differences in quality of life between institutional settings and community networks, as well as within community-based services, this correlation seems inconsistent with the independence of life satisfaction from objective material circumstances widely noted in the literature. These results suggest that quality of life, and specifically the satisfaction factor, is closely connected to both individual connectedness to the social environment and interpersonal affective factors in the form of the nature of relationships experienced with staff.

The Social Construction of Quality of Life: Problems With Quantification and Measurement

The studies discussed above employed a prototypical instrument designed to measure quality of life as an individualized, psychological state. Use of the instrument has suggested that the conceptual emphasis in the literature on the individualized construction of quality of life may be misplaced. These studies, albeit small in scale, have suggested that interpersonal, social, factors have much to do with "individualized" perceptions of life satisfaction. However, the discussion of these studies was predicated on the putting aside of other concerns about the process of quality-of-life measurement by means of structured instruments. These concerns can be ignored no longer.

In the studies discussed above, people with mental retardation resident in community-based supported housing in both Australia and the United Kingdom were asked to complete the Schalock and Keith (1993) *Quality of Life Questionnaire* as a structured interview in routine service evaluations. Although all participation in the evaluations was voluntary, and apparently informed consent to be interviewed was granted in all cases, many of the participants voiced concerns about a "hidden agenda." Many respondents appeared to be worried that the actual intention of the quality-of-life interviews was not an evaluation of the service being offered, but rather an evaluation of their suitability for their current residential arrangements. Many expressed fears, directly or indirectly, that "incorrect" responses to some questions may have a detrimental effect on their living situation.

From the studies discussed above among others, it is apparent that by using quantitative measurements a story can be told about services' facilitation of in-community presence of people with mental retardation and, broadly, about their quality of life and its relationship to community integration. But it is also apparent that the fears raised by respondents about the process of collecting such data highlight methodological and philosophical problems with this approach.

In the light of these fears, and to both arrive at some estimate of the validity of the data and calibrate the effects of possible social desirability influences on responses, a series of interviews were tape recorded and transcribed. Interrogation of these transcripts, using the qualitative methodology of conversation analysis, again suggests, but this time from a radically different perspective, that quality-of-life judgments are essentially interpersonally negotiated products, even (or perhaps, especially) in the context of the administration of structured quality-of-life questionnaires. While there is insufficient space here for a detailed discussion of these analyses (for further details see Antaki & Rapley, 1996a, 1996b; Rapley, 1995; Rapley & Antaki, 1996), an outline of the key findings can be sketched. Three broad observations can be made.

1. The moment-by-moment delivery and recording of quality-of-life judgments on standardized questionnaire items is a jointly negotiated, or fundamentally

intersubjective, activity. Quality-of-life scores are thus not strictly interpretable as "belonging to" the interviewee, but rather are jointly confected products of the interaction between interviewer and interviewee. In this sense quality of life is a socially constructed, rather than intrapsychic, product.

2. In the context of the administration of such measures, the interviewer disposes the power to deem as relevant or irrelevant extra-item material that the interviewee brings up as personally relevant to his or her quality-of-life construction. This power is one that interviewers were frequently seen to exercise, often to the exclusion of material obviously relevant and important to the interviewee (e.g., data about difficult relationships with parents and staff; accounts of discrimination in community settings; regrets about former friendships disrupted by the deinstitutionalization process) that occurred at the "wrong" place in the interview. Such material, significantly I would suggest, was often about interpersonal relationships but was rendered "inadmissible" in context as a direct consequence of the highly structured format of the interview schedule.

3. People with mental retardation (all interviewees were classified as having moderate to mild retardation) are ill-served by poorly constructed theoretical concepts such as "acquiescence" which portray them not only as incompetent and untrustworthy, but also as solely and individually responsible for any (and all) difficulties that arise in the collection and interpretation of interview-based data.

This third finding I want to dwell on for a moment. The widespread, uncritical acceptance of the phenomenon of "acquiescence" (most recently recycled by Heal & Sigelman, 1995) has, inadvertently perhaps, tended to discredit the views of service recipients. People with mental retardation have, in effect, been rendered incompetent to comment on their own feeling states. Yet when close and careful analyses of interviews with people with mental retardation are conducted, it becomes apparent that phenomena such as "acquiescence" are not simply a reflection of incompetence or the dispositional states of individuals; if they occur at all, they are interactional products for which interviewers are as responsible as, if not more than, their "incompetent" interviewees. Indeed Rapley and Antaki (1996) argue that, in light of developments in sociolinguistic theory (e.g., Psathas, 1995), the evidence in the literature for the notion of acquiescence is based on an inadequate picture of language and language exchange. Close examination of the actual exchange of talk between people with mental retardation and professionals in quality-of-life assessments reveals that while certain responses might look acquiescent on a superficial reading, closer inspection shows these instances to be clearly interpretable as an interplay of a range of respondents' conversation-management strategies and interviewer demands. There is no single thread that ties all the strategies together; they are all taken from the normal repertoire of conversational management. Only their surface appearance of inconsistency and agreement might tempt an analyst unfamiliar with language theory to categorize them all as "acquiescent."

It is furthermore clearly suggested in the literature that acquiescence is primarily a matter of spontaneous preference, or dispositional tendency, effectively independent of the interview situation. Such a view, I argue, is untenable. Conversation analytic studies clearly indicate that the social context of the interview situation is crucial to the joint construction of meaning within it; data suggest that quality-of-life interviews were perceived by people with mental retardation not as disinterested, well-meaning enquiries about their well-being, but rather as highly consequential tests that may have a direct and profound impact upon their living situation. Strengthening this impression were the ways in which interviewees' initial answers were subject to reformulations by the interviewer. What appeared to be perfectly acceptable answers were frequently queried, setting up a chain of (sometimes apparently inconsistent) subsequent answers. On other occasions interviewers' expectations about the "correct" answer seem to have prompted pursuit of questioning until an "appropriate" response was given. In both these circumstances, the respondent's utterances may have looked contradictory and the final utterance "acquiescent," but this is an artifact of the complex maneuvers into which both interviewer and interviewee get enmeshed.

Despite these powerful social demands, we saw many instances of resistance to interviewer-led questions and suggested response alternatives, even under conditions of severe power asymmetry. For an interviewee to "hold out" against an authority figure is in any circumstances hard, and doubly so here where interviewees with mental retardation suspect that an authority figure may be contemplating their "resettlement" on the basis of their answers.

These studies suggest that if there is inconsistency and "contradictory" agreement with interviewer suggestions in interviews with people with mental retardation, it is not a matter of general, dispositional submissiveness; rather, it is a demonstration of their attention to the manner and sequence of the way that quality-of-life questions are put and the social-interaction context into which they are embedded. In spite of any cognitive limitations they might have to overcome, people with mental retardation in the quality-of-life interviews studied demonstrably tried to make sense of what they heard the interviewer do and say, responded accordingly, and frequently could be seen to have successfully jointly negotiated with their interlocutor what subsequently became a quantified summary of "their" quality of life.

In sum these studies suggest that the long-accepted assumption that people with learning disabilities cannot respond validly in interviews is both conceptually cloudy and, where clear, empirically false. People with mental retardation can, and demonstrably do, engage in finely tuned conversational exchanges and command the use of precisely the same set of interactional competencies as others even under conditions of socially salient power asymmetry. What is produced in a quality-of-life item score, however, is not a pure reflection of a putative internal state of the respondent. Rather it is a jointly negotiated, intersubjectively constructed object; a mutually agreed upon approximation to a version of an index of a hypothetical mental state.

Concluding Comments

It would appear then that data drawn from both the quantitative and the qualitative perspectives, at both micro- and macrolevels of analysis, point broadly in the same direction. A defender of the quantitative quality-of-life measurement paradigm might point to the fact that the statistical scores obtained from the *Quality of Life Questionnaire* (Schalock & Keith, 1993) correlate with various other objective indicators: Higher scores are related to whether the interviewee is resident in a hospital ward or a house in the community; the number of friends; the frequency of use of community facilities. Yet these relationships—with interpersonal, social, and contextual variables—paradoxically act to undermine the individualized-mental-state focus of the literature. Quality of life, however it is defined, appears to be more than an individual internal mental state. It appears from these quantitative analyses to be something closely bound up with the extent and nature of interpersonal relationships: an interpersonal product of connectedness to others. Quality of life thus becomes a socially constructed something, an emergent property of the interaction of self with others in community.

From the qualitative, conversation analytic studies, the intersubjective nature of quality of life becomes even clearer. From the positivist perspective of quality-of-life quantification, for its results to be accepted as valid and reliable, any assessment interview schedule needs to show that it solicits authentic answers to clearly delivered questions. Such does not seem to be the case here. With the *Quality of Life Questionnaire* (Schalock & Keith, 1993) as an exemplar, but with the strong suspicion that any similar measure would be similarly afflicted, it seems that such measures do not support a simple run-through of questions tapping ontologically untroubled aspects of the individual's psyche. Rather, these measures occasion a complex series of maneuvers, involving significant distortions of interviewers' questions and reformulations of interviewee's answers. Analysis of these interviews shows not the collection of standardized, formalized, and generalizable numerical data representing, unproblematically and transparently, the clients' own view of the world. Instead these interviews demonstrate the social construction, jointly between interviewer and interviewee, of what is to count as representing the client's quality of life. Numerical estimations of interviewees' happiness are thus the product of a complex series of avowals jointly constructed out of what the assessor solicits, accepts, changes, or ignores, and what the client offers, reformulates, and withdraws. Certainly, it would seem, quality of life is constructed in community here, it is a socially constructed object, not a mental state located inside the head of just one of the parties to the encounter.

What does this suggest for the larger enterprise of trying to find out, without dubious inference from behavioral data or overreliance on problematic questionnaire measures, what people with mental retardation feel about the quality of their lives? Fundamentally, I would suggest, a more explicit awareness among researchers, clinicians, service planners, and others with a stake in the issue that the quality of people's lives is intimately bound up in their connectedness to, and relationships with, not only community as place, but also community as people. That a high quality of life is an emergent property of the quality of the relationship among self and others in community, and that individuals' estimations of the quality of their lives are themselves inseparable from the interpersonal and institutional context in which the questions are asked.

References

Allen, D. (1989). The effects of deinstitutionalisation on people with mental handicaps: A review. *Mental Handicap Research, 2,* 1, 18-37.

Antaki, C., & Rapley, M. (1996a). "Quality of Life" talk: The liberal paradox of psychological testing. *Discourse and Society, 7,* 3, 293-316.

Antaki, C., & Rapley, M. (1996b). Questions and answers to psychological assessment schedules: Hidden troubles in "Quality of Life" interviews. *Journal of Intellectual Disability Research, 5,* 4, 421-437.

Atkinson, D., & Ward, L. (1987). Friends and neighbours: Relationships and opportunities in the community for people with mental handicap. In N. Malin (Ed.), *Reassessing community care* (pp. 232-248). London: Croom Helm.

Borthwick-Duffy, S. A. (1996). Evaluation and measurement of quality of life: Special considerations for persons with mental retardation. In R. L. Schalock (Ed.), *Quality of life: Vol. 1: Conceptualization and measurement* (pp. 105-119). Washington, DC: American Association on Mental Retardation.

Campbell, A. (1981). *The sense of well-being in America.* New York: McGraw-Hill.

Crapps, J. M., & Stoneman, Z. (1989). Friendship patterns and community integration of family care residents. *Research in Developmental Disabilities, 10,* 153-169.

Cummins, R. A. (1991). The comprehensive quality of life scale—intellectual disability: An instrument under development. *Australia and New Zealand Journal of Developmental Disabilities, 17*(2), 259-264.

Cummins, R. A. (1993). *The comprehensive quality of life scale—intellectual disability* (4th ed.). Toorak, Victoria: Deakin University School of Psychology.

Cummins, R. A. (1995). Assessing quality of life. In R. I. Brown (Ed.), *Quality of life for handicapped people* (pp. 3-34). London: Chapman & Hall.

Dagnan, D., Howard, B., & Drewett, R. F. (1994). A move from hospital to community-based homes for people with learning disabilities: Activities outside the home. *Journal of Intellectual Disability Research, 38,* 567-576.

de Kock, U., Felce, D., Saxby, H., & Thomas, M. (1988). Community and family contact: An evaluation of small community homes for adults. *Mental Handicap Research, 1,* 127-140.

Edgerton, R. B. (1989). Retarded people of adult years. *Psychiatric Annals, 19*(4), 205-209.

Edgerton, R. B. (1990). Quality of life from a longitudinal research perspective. In R. L. Schalock (Ed.), *Quality of life: Perspectives and issues* (pp. 149-160). Washington, DC: American Association on Mental Retardation.

Edgerton, R. B. (1996). A longitudinal-ethnographic research perspective on quality of life. In R. L. Schalock (Ed.), *Quality of life: Vol. 1: Conceptualization and measurement* (pp. 83-90). Washington, DC: American Association on Mental Retardation.

Emerson, E., Beasley, F., Offord, G., & Mansell, J. (1992). An evaluation of hospital-based specialized staffed housing for people with seriously challenging behaviors. *Journal of Intellectual Disability Research, 36,* 291-307.

Emerson, E., & Hatton, C. (1994). *Moving out: Relocation from hospital to community.* London: Her Majesty's Stationery Office.

Emerson, E., & Hatton, C. (1996). Deinstitutionalization in the UK and Ireland: Outcomes for service users. *Journal of Intellectual and Developmental Disability, 21,* 1, 17-38.

Emerson, E., & Pretty, G. (1987). Enhancing the social relevance of evaluation practice. *Disability, Handicap, and Society, 2*(2), 151-162.

Evans, G., Beyer, S., & Todd, S. (1987). Looking forward not looking back: The evaluation of community living. *Disability, Handicap, and Society, 3*(3), 239-252.

Evans, G., Todd, S., & Beyer, S. (1990). The evaluation of the All-Wales Strategy for people with mental handicap. In S. Sharkey & S. Barna (Eds.), *Community care: People leaving long-stay hospitals* (pp. 211-226). London: Routledge.

Evans, G., Todd, S., & Beyer, S. (1992). *A four-year longitudinal study of the impact of the All-Wales Strategy on the lives of people with learning difficulties.* Cardiff: Mental Handicap in Wales, Applied Research Unit.

Evans, G., Todd, S., Beyer, S., Felce, D., & Perry, J. (1994). Assessing the impact of the All-Wales Mental Handicap Strategy: A survey of four districts. *Journal of Intellectual Disability Research, 38,* 109-133.

Felce, D. (1991). Using behavioural principles in the development of effective housing services for adults with severe or profound mental handicap. In B. Remington (Ed.), *The challenge of severe mental handicap: A behaviour analytic approach* (pp. 285-316). Chichester, United Kingdom: Wiley.

Felce, D., & Perry, J. (1996). Assessment of quality of life. In R. L. Schalock (Ed.), *Quality of life: Vol. 1: Conceptualization and measurement* (pp. 63-72). Washington, DC: American Association on Mental Retardation.

Firth, H., & Rapley, M. (1990). *From acquaintance to friendship: Issues for people with learning disabilities.* Clevedon, United Kingdom: BILD.

Firth, H., & Short, D. (1987). A move from hospital to community: Evaluation of community contacts. *Child: Health, Care, and Development, 13,* 341-354.

Flynn, M. (1989). *Community living for adults with mental handicaps: "A place of me own."* London: Cassell.

Goode, D. A. (1990). Thinking about and discussing quality of life. In R. L. Schalock (Ed.), *Quality of life: Perspectives and issues* (pp. 41-59). Washington, DC: American Association on Mental Retardation.

Granovetter, M. (1982). The strength of weak ties: A network theory revisited. In P. V. Marsden & N. Lin (Eds.), *Social structure and network analysis* (pp. 105-130). Beverly Hills, CA: Sage.

Heal, L. W., & Sigelman, C. K. (1990). Methodological issues in measuring the quality of life of individuals with mental retardation. In R. L. Schalock (Ed.), *Quality of life: Perspectives and issues* (pp. 161-176). Washington, DC: American Association on Mental Retardation.

Heal, L. W., & Sigelman, C. K. (1995). Response biases in interviews of individuals with limited mental ability. *Journal of Intellectual Disability Research, 39*(4), 331-340.

Hoover, J. H., Wheeler, J. J., & Reetz, L. J (1992). Development of a Leisure Satisfaction Scale for use with adolescents and adults with mental retardation. *Education and Training in Mental Retardation, 27*(2), 153-160.

Hughes, C., & Hwang, B. (1996). Attempts to conceptualize and measure quality of life. In R. L. Schalock (Ed.), *Quality of life: Vol. 1: Conceptualization and measurement* (pp. 51-61). Washington, DC: American Association on Mental Retardation.

Hughes, C., Hwang, B., Kim, J. H., Eisenman, L. T., & Kilian, D. J. (1995). Quality of life in applied research: A review and analysis of empirical measures. *American Journal on Mental Retardation, 99*(6), 623-641.

Humphreys, S., Lowe, J., & Blunden, R. (1983). *The long-term evaluation of services for mentally handicapped people in Cardiff: Research methodology.* Cardiff: Mental Handicap in Wales, Applied Research Unit.

King's Fund Centre. (1980). *An ordinary life: Comprehensive locally based services for mentally handicapped people.* London: King Edward's Hospital Fund for London.

King's Fund Centre. (1988). *Ties and connections: An ordinary community life for people with learning difficulties.* London: King Edward's Hospital Fund for London.

Lowe, K., & dePaiva, S. (1991). Canvassing the views of people with a mental handicap. *Irish Journal of Psychology, 9*(2), 220-234.

Lowe, K., dePaiva, S., & Humphreys, S. (1986). *Long-term evaluation of services for people with a mental handicap in Cardiff: Client views.* Cardiff: Mental Handicap in Wales, Applied Research Unit.

Malin, N. A. (1982). Group homes for mentally handicapped adults: Residents' views on contact and support. *British Journal of Mental Subnormality, 28,* 29-34.

Marková, I., Jahoda, M., Cattermole, M., & Woodward, D. (1992). Living in hospital and hostel: The pattern of interactions of people with learning difficulties. *Journal of Intellectual Disability Research, 36,* 115-127.

McConkey, R., Naughton, M., & Nugent, V. (1983). Have we met? Community contacts of adults who are mentally handicapped. *Mental Handicap, 11,* 57-59.

McMillan, D. W., & Chavis, D. M. (1986). Sense of community: A definition and theory. *Journal of Community Psychology, 14,* 6-23.

O'Brien, J. (1987). A guide to lifestyle planning: Using the Activities Catalog to integrate services and natural support systems. In B. W. Wilcox & G. T. Bellamy (Eds.), *The Activities Catalog: An alternative curriculum for youth and adults with severe disabilities* (pp. 175-189). Baltimore: Paul H. Brookes.

O'Brien, J. (1990). *Design for accomplishment: A workshop for people planning effective human services.* Decatur, GA: Responsive Systems Associates.

O'Brien, J., & Tyne, A. (1981). *The principle of normalisation: A foundation for effective services.* London: CMH.

Perry, J., & Felce. D. (1995). Objective assessments of quality of life: How much do they agree with each other? *Journal of Community and Applied Social Psychology, 5,* 1-19.

Psathas, G. (1995). *Conversation analysis: The study of talk-in-interaction.* Thousand Oaks, CA: Sage.

Ralph, A., & Usher, E. (1995). Social interactions of persons with developmental disabilities living independently in the community. *Research in Developmental Disabilities, 16,* 3, 149-163.

Rapley, M. (1995). Black swans: Conversation analysis of quality of life interviews with people with learning disabilities. *Clinical Psychology Forum, 84,* 17-23.

Rapley, M. (1996). *Quality of life: A critical approach.* Unpublished doctoral dissertation, Lancaster University, United Kingdom.

Rapley, M., & Antaki, C. (1996). A conversation analysis of the "acquiescence" of people with learning disabilities. *Journal of Community and Applied Social Psychology, 6,* 207-227.

Rapley, M., & Beyer, S. (1995). Daily activity, community participation and quality of life in an ordinary housing network. *Journal of Applied Research in Intellectual Disabilities, 9*(1), 31-39.

Rapley, M., & Beyer, S. (1998). Daily activity, community activity and quality of life in an ordinary housing network: A two-year follow up. *Journal of Applied Research in Intellectual Disabilities, 11*(1), 34-43.

Rapley, M., & Clements, J. (1994). New song: Reflections upon the inadequacy of community services for people with learning disabilities. *Care in Place—The International Journal of Networks and Community, 1*(3), 248-255.

Rapley, M., & Hopgood, L. (1997). Quality of life in a community-based service in rural Australia. *Journal of Intellectual and Developmental Disability, 22*(2), 125-141.

Rapley, M., & Ridgway, J. (in press). Quality of life rhetoric: The birth of a discourse. *Disability and Society.*

Reiter, S., & Levi, M. (1980). Factors affecting social integration of noninstitutionalized mentally retarded adults. *American Journal of Mental Deficiency, 85,* 25-30.

Rose, N. (1990). *Governing the soul: The shaping of the private self.* London: Routledge.

Rosen, M. (1986). Quality of life for persons with mental retardation: A question of entitlement. *Mental Retardation, 24,* 365-366.

Salzberg, C. L., & Langford, C. A. (1981). Community integration of mentally retarded adults through leisure activity. *Mental Retardation, 19,* 127-132.

Sands, D. J., Kozleski, E. B., & Goodwin, L. D. (1991). Whose needs are we meeting? Results of a consumer satisfaction survey of persons with developmental disabilities in Colorado. *Research in Developmental Disabilities, 12,* 297-314.

Sarason, S. B. (1974). *The psychological sense of community: Prospects for a community psychology.* San Francisco: Jossey-Bass.

Saxby, H., Thomas, M., Felce, D., and de Kock, U. (1986). The use of shops, cafes, and public houses by severely and profoundly mentally handicapped adults. *British Journal of Mental Subnormality, 32,* 69-81.

Schalock, R. L. (1990a). Preface. In R. L. Schalock (Ed.), *Quality of life: Perspectives and issues* (pp. ix-xii). Washington, DC: American Association on Mental Retardation.

Schalock, R. L. (Ed.). (1990b). *Quality of life: Perspectives and issues.* Washington, DC: American Association on Mental Retardation.

Schalock, R., & Keith, K. D. (1993). *Quality of life questionnaire.* Worthington, OH: IDS.

Seed, P. (1980). *Mental handicap: Who helps in rural and remote communities?* Tunbridge Wells, United Kingdom: Costello.

Sigelman, C. K., Budd, E. C., Spanhel, C. L., & Schoenrock, C. J. (1981). When in doubt, say "Yes": Acquiescence in interviews with mentally retarded persons. *Mental Retardation, 19,* 53-58.

Sinson, J. C. (1993). *Group homes and community integration of developmentally disabled people: Micro-institutionalisation?* London: Jessica Kingsley.

Taylor, S. J., & Bogdan, R. (1990). Quality of life and the individual's perspective. In R. L. Schalock (Ed.), *Quality of life: Perspectives and issues* (pp. 27-40). Washington, DC: American Association on Mental Retardation.

Taylor, S. J., & Bogdan, R. (1996). Quality of life and the individual's perspective. In R. L. Schalock (Ed.), *Quality of life: Vol. 1: Conceptualization and measurement* (pp. 11-22). Washington, DC: American Association on Mental Retardation.

Todd, S., Evans, G., & Beyer, S. (1990). More recognised than known: The social visibility and attachment of people with developmental disabilities. *Australia and New Zealand Journal of Developmental Disabilities, 16,* 207-218.

Walmsley, J. (1996a). Doing what Mum wants me to do: Looking at family relationships from the point of view of people with intellectual disabilities. *Journal of Applied Research in Intellectual Disability, 9*(4), 324-341.

Walmsley, J. (1996b). Talking to top people: Some issues relating to the citizenship of people with learning difficulties. *Disability, Handicap, and Society, 8*(2), 129-142.

Wolfensberger, W. (1972). *The principle of normalization in human services.* Toronto: National Institute on Mental Retardation.

Wolfensberger, W. (1994). Let's hang up "quality of life" as a hopeless term. In D. Goode (Ed.), *Quality of life for persons with disabilities: International perspectives and issues* (pp. 285–321). Cambridge, MA: Brookline.

Yeatman, A. (1996). *"Getting real": The final report of the review of the commonwealth/state disability agreement.* Canberra: Australian Government Publishing Service.

Engagement in Activity as an Indicator of Quality of Life in British Research

David Felce
University of Wales College of Medicine
Cardiff, Wales

Much has been written elsewhere about the breadth of what is referred to as quality of life. Commentators are agreed that it is a multidimensional construct (e.g., Campbell, Converse, & Rodgers, 1976; Cummins, 1997; Felce, 1997; Parmenter, 1988; Schalock, 1996). Encapsulation of quality of life, whether by measurement or analytic description, is therefore a challenge, one that has been taken up in a variety of ways.

One approach has been the development of quality-of-life scales with a dimensional breadth similar to the conceptualization of the term. The work of Brown, Bayer, and MacFarlane (1989), Cummins (1993), Harner and Heal (1993), and Schalock and Keith (1993) provide examples. Another approach has been to conduct ethnographic studies to reveal the nature of the everyday lives of individuals and how they experience them. The work of Edgerton (1967), Edgerton, Bollinger, and Herr (1984), Flynn (1989), Goode (1994), and Oswin (1971) provide examples. A third approach has been to measure different aspects of quality of life in different ways, exploiting the data collection method (one hopes) to suit best the nature of the quality-of-life aspect to be captured.

Some of the more comprehensive evaluations of deinstitutionalization in the last two decades provide examples of researchers establishing a multidimensional scope to their studies (e.g., Burchard, Hasazi, Gordon, & Yoe, 1991; Felce, 1989). I have argued elsewhere (Felce, 1997) that methodological pluralism is an advantage if the most sensitive ways are to be employed to capture "people's peceptions of well-being, social connectedness, opportunities to fulfil potentials and the discrepancy between what is desirable and what exists" (Goode, 1997, p. 77).

This chapter is concerned with the direct observation of engagement in everyday activity as a quality-of-life indicator. It is applicable by those wishing to follow the third approach described above, namely to reflect different aspects of quality of life by different measures, each tailor-made for the purpose. Direct observation of the extent of engagement in activity has been the most frequently used outcome measure in British deinstitutionalization research since 1980 (Emerson & Hatton, 1994). In an updated review, Hatton and Emerson (1996) considered 118 publications reporting the findings of 70 separate British research studies since the same date. Seventy-seven publications based on 47 studies provided evidence of the participation of residents in everyday activity, including indicators of participation in domestic activities (e.g., Raynes, Wright, Sheill, & Pettipher, 1994), observed engagement in a range of constructive activities (e.g., Felce & Perry, 1995), and participation in social pursuits with friends and relatives (e.g., de Kock, Saxby, Thomas, & Felce, 1988). The majority of these publications (44 of 77) and studies (27 of 47) concerned directly observed engagement in activity. As the person responsible for a good number of these studies, I feel some responsibility to justify why engagement in activity is central to the concept of quality of life and why measuring it has such practical use in evaluating the adequacy of the environments in which people with severe intellectual disabilities live, work, and recreate.

Defining Engagement in Activity

The application of direct observation of engagement in activity as a quality indicator derives from the work of Todd Risley and his colleagues (see Risley & Cataldo, 1973; Jones, Risley, & Favell, 1983). It also parallels ecological research using direct observation by Sackett and Landesman-Dwyer (1977). The central concern is with individuals' interaction with their material and social worlds. Behavior reflecting adaptive functioning, irrespective of the person or context, is characterized by the extent to which the individual is actively engaged with (attending to, interacting with, participating in) his or her environment. Introspection and casual observation led me to the conclusion that, with the exception of that small minority who choose the contemplative life, interaction with the environment is what people do, and they do it for virtually all of the time that they are awake. Unless we are traumatized, ill, chronically depressed, or withdrawn or in some other way incapacitated, human beings fill their lives by doing things. Even resting or relaxing usually involves substituting one form of activity for another—having a drink, having a good gossip, watching television, reading a novel, listening to music. Cut off from our usual sources of activity in relatively barren environments, such as when waiting alone at an airport or railway station, we take solace in whatever pursuit we can manage even to the extent of drinking or eating unnecessarily, reading magazines not normally read, or clearing up specially tedious work tasks reserved for such occasions. Exposed to truly unstimulating situations, we tend toward self-stimulation.

It is not difficult to imagine how the inclination to interact with the environment became an integral part of the human condition. It would seem to have survival value and therefore would have been selected. Selection on a different time scale is also implied by socialization. Although cultures tolerate enormous variety in individual behavior, they typically shape conformity among citizens to certain norms. Such norms may be age- and/or environment-specific. Expected engagement in activity may be differentiated across people or settings (e.g., between a toddler and an adolescent or between a church and public house), but the general concept still applies. What one sees people doing is a sample of activities that can be recognized as belonging to the population of activities connected with that age group or environment. Other forms of behavior may be seen as inappropriate for that subgroup or setting. Thus, for example, Risley and Cataldo (1973) state that:

> The direction and extent of engagement with the physical and so-
> cial environment appears to be an almost universal indication of

the quality of a setting for people. Those familiar with educational settings often evaluate a particular activity area or an entire class-room at almost a glance, without even knowing the curriculum or the goals of the program, and they usually agree with each other's independent evaluations. They are simply assessing how many of the children are looking at and/or physically interacting with materials or people at any moment. (p. 38)

Engagement in Activity as a Quality-of-Life Indicator

That the definition of engagement in activity in practice would reflect the cultural and situational context is not problematic, as quality of life itself is necessarily a culturally bound concept. Drawing together contributions from the developed world, Schalock (1996) listed eight core quality-of-life domains: emotional well-being, interpersonal relationships, material well-being, personal development, physical well-being, self-determination, social inclusion, and rights. The majority of quality-of-life concerns listed and their associated exemplary indicators are states of existence, circumstances that have developed over time or have a sense of enduring beyond the immediate activity of the moment. Here are some examples from each domain: (a) emotional well-being: spirituality, freedom from stress, contentment; (b) interpersonal relationships: family, friendships, supports; (c) material well-being: ownership, financial security, employment, possessions; (d) personal development: skills, competence, advancement; (e) physical well-being: health, nutrition; (f) self-determination: autonomy, choices, personal control, self-direction; (g) social inclusion: acceptance, status, roles; (h) rights: privacy, access, ownership, civic responsibilities. In this, they conform to the notion of accomplishment used by Gilbert (1978) and, in commenting on the goals of services for people with intellectual disabilities, by O'Brien (1987).

Gilbert's concern is to emphasize behavior that leads to accomplishment (Gilbert & Gilbert, 1992; see Figure 16.1). Not all behavior or activity is equally valued or valuable. A concern for outcome points one toward promoting behaviors that lead to or build accomplishment. O'Brien's (1987) specification of accomplishments has a similar preoccupation with enduring conditions of living (see Figure 16.1). Community presence, community participation, competence, status and respect, and choice and rights (O'Brien) refer to people having tenure within their communities, a variety of ongoing personal relationships, a range of experiences, skills, and capabilities, a social reputation, and a degree of ability to exercise control over the course of life.

Activity, however, is more transient. Purposeful activity is recognized as an exemplary indicator of personal development in Schalock's (1996) classification of quality-of-life domains. Moreover, neither Gilbert nor O'Brien suggest that accomplishment can be gained by any other route than through engagement in everyday activities. For Gilbert behavior is one side of the performance equation; not all behavior may lead to accomplishment but all accomplishments stem from or rest on behavior. Similarly, O'Brien includes a consideration of participation in valued ac-

Gilbert's Emphasis on the Behavior-Accomplishment Relationship

PERFORMANCE

Behavior   Accomplishment

Behavior you   Accomplishments
take with you   you leave behind

O'Brien's Five Essential Service Accomplishments

Participation in valued activities (engagement in ordinary living)

1. Community presence
2. Community participation
3. Competence (growth and development)
4. Status and respect
5. Choice and rights

Defining outcomes consistent with the principle of normalization

Figure 16.1. Comparison of Gilbert's (1978) and O'Brien's (1987) models of accomplishment.

tivity within the definition and discussion of all five accomplishments. Accomplishment cannot be attained in a vacuum. It is gained or conferred as a result of one's participation in everyday life. It is the long-term consequence of repeated engagement in activity. Engagement in activity could be seen from this perspective as a fundamental building block of human existence.

Although engagement in activity does not capture the qualitative nuance of many quality-of-life abstractions, it is centrally concerned with how people spend their time. Engagement in activity does not refer to a state of existence, but rather to the process of everyday living. Second by second, minute by minute, hour by hour, day by day, people interact with their social and physical environments, conducting their affairs. "I was bored; there wasn't enough to do"; "it's been a good day; I achieved a lot"; and "life is crazy at the moment; I haven't stopped all day"— these familiar commentaries on life have meaning for people. The measurement of the extent of different forms of engagement in activity, or its obverse, disengagement, can reflect important differences in how people experience life.

A Concern With Disengagement in the Exposure of the Unacceptability of Institutional Life

The interest in engagement also has its roots in the fact that services for people with pervasive disabilities have failed to provide the minimum requirements for a decent quality of life. The importance of engagement in activity is mirrored in the concern expressed about the prolonged disengagement or lack of activity that characterized the unchanging lack of stimulation within barren institutional wards. The potential of life is not being realized when people habitually spend their time isolated, unduly passive or engaging in repetitive apparently purposeless behavior. Life-long disengagement is equivalent to having life "wasted." Constructive interaction with one's material and social worlds may not guarantee the good life, but quality of life is rarely to be had without it. Two examples from British institutional research illustrate the individual and general realities of the matter:

Diary of a Weekend: A Saturday for Christopher

Christopher was nine, and badly handicapped by athetoid cerebral palsy and deafness. He could be described as totally dependent because he needed feeding. He could not walk or hold anything, and he required help with toileting. He had no speech.

At 7.30 a.m.: …Christopher was sitting in his wheelchair and a day-nurse was feeding him his hot breakfast. …Christopher could not see what was on his plate. …He finished his breakfast at a quarter to eight, and then until 8.30 he sat and waited for a nurse to take him to the bathroom. He did not have anything on his wheelchair table-tray, although at one point another child gave him a broken wind-up toy and he smiled; the toy fell to the floor as he put his hand on it, and a nurse picked it up as she passed down the ward and put it back on his tray; but five minutes later it fell down again and then remained on the floor.

At 8.30 a.m.: Christopher was wheeled into the bathroom and lifted onto the wooden 'potty-chair' (the commode) …Christopher sat in the potty-chair until 9 o'clock. Nobody spoke to him.

At 9 a.m.: Christopher was wheeled back into the ward and put on his cot, where he had his trousers put on, and his shoes and socks. Then he was lifted into his wheelchair and taken back to the bathroom, this time to have his face washed. He went back to the ward at 9.30 and was pushed into the little hobbies room for ten minutes as the ward was being swept.

From 9.40 until 12.5: Christopher sat in his wheelchair by the piano at one end of the ward. He had nothing on his chair-tray. He was given a drink just before 11 o'clock. Then for a few minutes after drinks, another child went up to him and 'wrestled' with him: this made him laugh and he waved his arms and got very excited. The same child then fetched him three torn playing cards, put them on his tray for a few minutes and then ran off with them again. Christopher spent two hours and twenty-five minutes in this same spot … during that time none of the ward staff spoke to him or put anything on his tray.

From 12.5 until 12.30 p.m.: Christopher was being fed his lunch. …The nurse did not sign to him or speak to him as she fed him. After he had been fed, he remained still sitting in the same place until 1 o'clock.

At 1 p.m.: Christopher was taken to the bathroom, toileted . . . washed and put into his pyjamas.

At 1.30 p.m.: Christopher . . . was pushed back to the ward and placed near the piano again.

From 1.30 until 4.15 p.m.: Christopher sat in the same place, by the piano. He had nothing to do and was not moved about the ward at all. Nobody spoke to him or signed to him. During this 2¾-hour period of sitting in one place with nothing to do, three children made a procession with their wheelchairs one behind the other and 'marched' down the ward between the beds. Christopher, who all the time watched the children intently, laughed at the procession and waved his arm with pleasure....

At 4.15 p.m.: It was supper time. Christopher was fed by a nurse who stood in front of him with the plate held up high; he could not see what was on the plate.... No nurse was seen to speak to Christopher at any time during supper.

At 5 p.m.: Christoper was taken to the toilet and then washed.

By 5.25 p.m.: He was lying in his cot.

From 5.25 until 7 p.m.: Christopher was lying in his cot watching the other children. Nobody gave him anything to do, nor communicated with him in any way.

At 7 p.m.: Lights were put out after the children had been given a last drink. (Oswin, 1971, pp. 81-83, reprinted by permission of author)

Life on the Ward

How did patients spend their time on the ward when not occupied elsewhere? Without any shadow of a doubt, and with the exception of the exclusively high grade wards and hostel patients, the great majority spent their day sitting, interspersed with eating. Only in very few wards (fewer than 12 out of 761 visited) did we find nurses helping patients with individual or group leisure activities.... Research workers made a note of the time each ward was observed and what was happening at that time. The result makes depressing reading: 'wandering around'; 'listening to radio'; 'sitting'; 'rocking and making noises'; 'waiting for a meal'; 'eating'.... Countless examples of inactivity could be given, but they would merely sound repetitive. (Morris, 1969, p. 169)

Quantifying Engagement in Activity

The principal dimensions of engagement in activity are time and quality of activity. The most flexible method for constructing an ecological record is time-anchored qualitative description, using the full breadth and subtlety of language to describe events. But there are advantages both for summarizing large amounts of data and for comparing across situations if behavior is coded in some standard way and its duration measured systematically. Coding schemes and category definitions can in principle reflect more or less fine-grain distinctions in the quality of different forms of activity together with cultural age-group and setting expectations, depending on the complexity of what can be achieved in practice. Time-sampling procedures have made multiple-category observation in the natural environment feasible, and now small portable computers have permitted real-time data capture on the same basis (Repp & Felce, 1990; Emerson & Felce, 1997).

Observational categories and definitions can clearly vary. For example, my colleagues and I have employed different ways of operationalizing the underlying concept to observe engagement in the home and engagement in the workplace (Beyer, Kilsby, & Willson, 1995; Felce, de Kock, & Repp, 1986;). A practical advantage is that environmental conditions and events experienced by the person being observed can be recorded at the same time. This includes the social interaction individuals receive from others. This encompasses a very important element of staff or supporter activity, namely the extent and nature of their contact with the individuals with whom they work, live, or recreate. An example of the observational framework that I and other researchers have used in residential settings is given in Figure 16.2.

Resident Behavior	**Staff or Supporter Behavior**

■ Engagement in typical activities in the home
 	
Getting ready for, doing, or clearing away a:
 	
    personal (self-care) activity
 	
    domestic (household) activity
 	
    gardening activity
 	
    leisure or educational activity
 	
■ Engagement in Social Interaction
 	
■ Engagement in challenging behavior
 	
    aggression, self-injury, destructiveness, stereotypy, other
 	
■ Disengagement or unpurposeful engagement with environment
	■ Interaction with resident
	
	Any direct verbal or physical contact with an individual:
	
	    assistance (instruction, demonstration, prompting, guidance)
	
	■ Praise
	
	■ Restraint
	
	■ Conversation
	
	■ Processing (care without resident participation)

Figure 16.2. Observation of engagement in activity in residential services.

179

Illustrative Studies

Deinstitutionalization and Relating Staff Behavior to the Residents' Activity

Felce et al. (1986) compared staff-to-resident interaction and resident engagement in activity between community and institutional residences. The community residences had been specifically set up as a research demonstration to test the feasibility of community care for adults with the most severe intellectual disabilities; they had a special emphasis on activity planning and the provision of effective assistance within the working methods that staff were trained to follow. *The Adaptive Behavior Scale (ABS)* (Nihira, Foster, Shellhaas, & Leland, 1974) scores of the total group ranged from 54 to 168 and averaged 111, with both house groups being broadly comparable. Both groups in the two community homes received significantly higher levels of instruction, physical prompting, and physical guidance than the second group did while still in institutions (see Figure 16.3). Each community

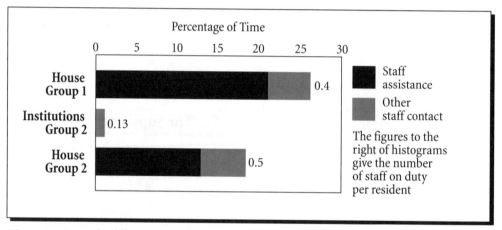

Figure 16.3. Total staff contact and staff assistance per resident in institutional and community groups.

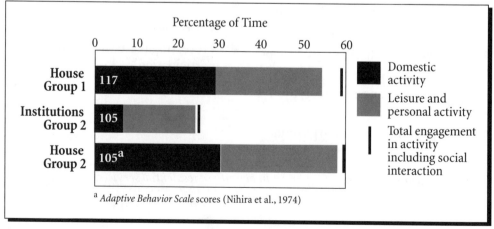

Figure 16.4. Engagement in activity in institutional and community groups.

resident received attention from staff for 24% of the time, on average, and about 75% of this attention was in the form of assistance with activities. In comparison, residents in the institutions were barely encouraged to participate in activity at all, receiving any form of attention for an average of only 1% of the time. Residents in the two homes were engaged in personal, domestic, and leisure activities for 51% and 56% of the time on average (see Figure 16.4) and social activity (mainly with staff) for 17% and 14%. Engagement in personal, domestic, and leisure activities averaged 23% in the institutions, and social engagement, 1%. Activity mainly comprised eating and drinking and other personal or self-care pursuits. On average, therefore, three quarters of the time in the institutions passed with no constructive interaction with the material or social world; even then activity range was restricted.

A correlational case can be made that the levels of resident engagement in the two houses were linked to the assistance individuals received from staff. Those with greater disabilities received more staff support. There was a perfect inverse relationship between individuals' ABS (Nihira et al., 1974) score and the amount of support they received from staff among the first group of six residents and a Spearman rank order correlation coefficient of -0.77 among the second (and an overall r_s = -0.76, p < 0.01). Moreover, as we had two sets of observations on most individuals, we could explore the correlation between the differences in support given to each person and the differences in their level of engagement in activity. A Spearman rank order correlation coefficient on these within-subject differences was near perfect (r_s = 0.97, p < 0.01). Visual inspection of the individual resident activity data suggested that the impact of high levels of staff support for those with greater disability was to bring their levels of engagement in activity up toward those with greater independence.

Such findings suggested that resident activity in these houses could be expressed as a function of resident ability and the extent of staff support (i.e., residents brought something to the equation in terms of their abilities to do various activities and staff added to this by supporting residents to be more involved than they might otherwise have been). Multivariate regression was unsatisfactory due to the high negative correlation between resident ability and staff support (r = -0.66). Therefore, the relationship between the level of resident engagement in activity and staff support was estimated first, controlling for ability, by regressing the within-subject differences in engagement level across pairs of data points against similar differences in staff support (see Felce, 1996). This produced a linear function to predict the level of activity attributable to staff support. This function produced an adjusted R Square of 0.82 (i.e., it explained 82% of the variance in the dependent variable) and an F ratio which was significant at p = 0.0002. The level of engagement not attributable to staff support was then calculated by deducting the engagement explained by the above function from the average level of engagement found for each subject. This residual engagement level was then regressed in the second stage of the analysis against resident ABS scores converted to average percentile ranks. This second function also produced a satisfactory function with an adjusted R Square of 0.72 (i.e., ability explained 72% of the variance of residual engagement) and an *F* ratio significant at p = 0.0012.

Further Analyzing Relationships Among Resident Ability, Staff-to-Resident Ratios, Staff-to-Resident Interaction, and Resident Activity

Felce and Perry (1995) further explored the relationship among resident abilities, staffing levels, staff-to-resident interaction, and resident engagement in activity in an analytic study of 15 small staffed community residences accommodating 57 people. Household groups were homogenous in terms of ability and had average *ABS* (Nihira et al., 1974) scores that spanned the range of the measure. When ordered by ascending *ABS* score, residents in Houses 1 through 6 were broadly comparable to those in the study described above. Attention received from staff per resident was variable with a mean extent of 15% of time per person (range, 2-31%) (see Figure 16.5). Slightly higher levels of contact per resident were found in the six houses serving the least-able residents (*M* 18%) compared to the remaining nine (*M* 12%). Overall, there was a near zero Spearman rank order correlation between the extent of staff-to-resident interaction per person and resident ability (r_s = -0.11). The slightly higher rates of interaction received per resident in the houses for those with the greatest disabilities were the result of considerably higher staffing levels. When the staff-to-resident ratio was taken into account, it was clear that, in common with much other research, members of staff in the houses for more

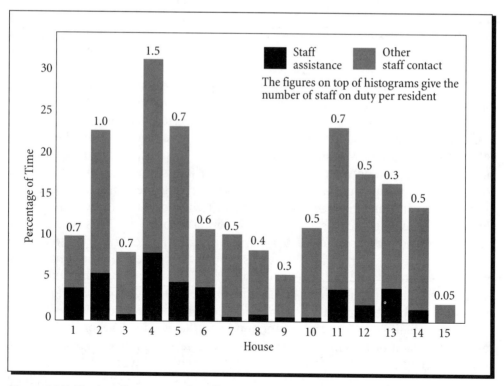

Figure 16.5. Total staff contact and staff assistance per resident in 15 staffed community residences (with numbers of staff per resident).

able people interacted more with residents than their counterparts in houses for residents with lesser abilities. Staff input did not have a reliable effect on the quality of care. The percentage of time staff spent interacting with residents varied greatly, a more than fivefold difference between the lowest and highest (range, 12%-65%).

Only a small proportion of staff attention to residents was in the form of assistance to do activities (*M* 15%, range 0%-35%). Each resident on average received assistance for only 2.5% of the time, and even those in the six houses for the least able residents received assistance on average for only 4.2% of the time, that is, for only a little over 2 minutes per hour. These levels are low in comparison to what was found in the two houses described above, where 70% and 81% of staff attention to residents was in the form of assistance. Indeed, when staff-to-resident ratios are taken into account, the comparison is made more stark. The four houses in this sample with similar or higher levels of staff-to-resident interaction compared to the earlier study had staff-to-resident ratios 75% to 375% higher. Six houses with similar or up to 75% higher staff-to-resident ratios produced only half the level of staff interaction per resident.

Average levels of engagement in activity varied sixfold across the 15 residences (range, 13%-88%) and averaged 49% (see Figure 16.6). Variation was significantly

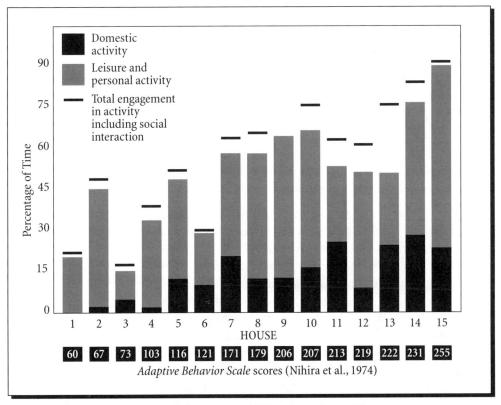

Figure 16.6. Engagement in activity in 15 staffed community residences.

related to resident ability ($r_s = 0.79$, p < 0.01), with the higher levels of occupation restricted to people who had *ABS* scores within the top decile of the scale norms. Engagement in personal activity (mainly eating and drinking) was relatively constant across houses. Participation in running their own households as evidenced by engagement in domestic activity was virtually nonexistent for residents in the four houses for the least able residents and rose to levels around 25% of the time for residents in the three houses for the most able. Engagement in domestic activity overall averaged 13% of time and was significantly related to resident ability ($r_s = 0.84$, p < 0.01). Engagement in leisure activity also tended to rise with ability; it was the largest component of activity in the majority of the nine houses for the most able residents. Much comprised fairly passive activity such as watching television. Nonetheless, the spectrum of results shows that people engage in activity for the great majority of the time when they have the skills; disengagement can be seen as a consequence of disability and inadequate prosthetic support.

Engagement in activity in houses for people of similar ability to those in the earlier study was lower, particularly participation in domestic activities. This comparison suggests that structural reform has to be complemented by procedural organization, with working methods allied to aims and values. For, in many ways, the later sample of 15 houses would be seen as having advantages over the earlier settings. They were smaller in size and much better staffed and they were more recently provided at a time when there was a more general acceptance of normalization philosophy. However, all of the houses had less well operationalized policies and less well defined outcome targets. None had any systematic approach to how staff should work with residents to support and motivate particular patterns of activity. None had any well-developed methods for activity planning or working out staff-to-resident deployment. It is perhaps not surprising, but it is still salutary in policy terms, that small, decent, homelike, architecturally typical, well-staffed, and managerially autonomous community homes do not maximize the quality of life for their residents under these conditions. It is also salutary to find repeated evidence from a number of our own studies and those of others (e.g., Hatton, Emerson, Robertson, Henderson, & Cooper, 1995) that investment in staff does not produce quality-of-care and quality-of-life changes in itself.

Evaluating Staff Training to Provide More Active Support

Jones et al. (1997) followed up the implications of these two studies by conducting an experimental evaluation of working methods designed to provide residents with severe intellectual disability more opportunities for activity and greater assistance to participate in them successfully. This Active Support training was introduced in five existing staffed community housing services for people of similar ability to those in the two houses in the first study described above and the first six houses in the second study. The central elements of Active Support are the flexible planning of resident activities, the planning by staff of how to allocate their resources to support resident activity, and practical training for staff on how to interact with residents to provide effective support.

The intervention was staggered across the five houses following a multiple

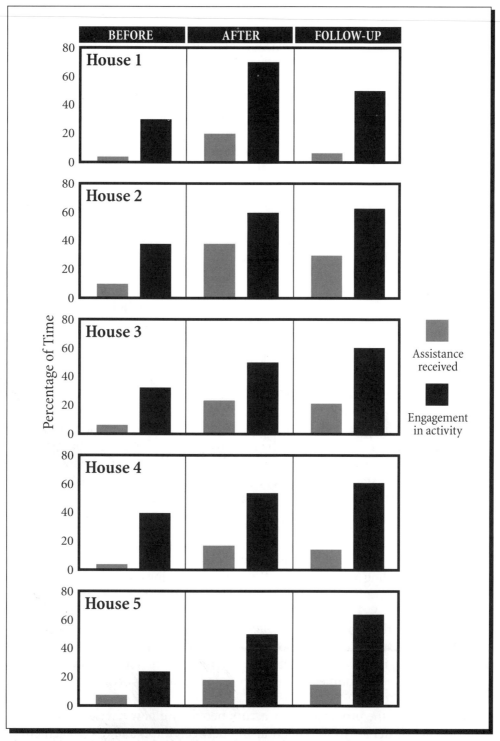

Figure 16.7. Assistance received and engagement in activity: Before, after, and follow-up.

baseline design; Figure 16.7 summarizes the data on assistance received and engagement in activity across the conditions of the study. Significant increases in the level of assistance residents received occurred in all houses following the introduction of Active Support (from 5%, 8%, 7%, 3%, and 7% to 24%, 35%, 24%, 16%, and 19% of the time). Significant increases in the level of resident engagement in domestic activities occurred in all houses following the introduction of Active Support (from 13% on average to 32% of the time). Significant increases in the total level of engagement in activity occurred in all but one of the houses following the introduction of Active Support (from 36%, 38%, 29%, and 23% to 65%, 56%, 50%, and 47% of the time). In the exception, there was still a positive effect (from 40% to 50% of the time).

Across individuals, the proportional increases in assistance and total engagement between baseline and postbaseline were significantly and positively correlated. Both were significantly inversely related to adaptive behavior. In other words, the introduction of Active Support changed the baseline pattern where staff gave more attention and assistance to people who were behaviorally more able. During postbaseline, receipt of attention was unrelated to ability and there was a tendency for those who were less able to receive more assistance. Although resident engagement in activity was significantly related to behavioral ability in both phases of the study, the change in the pattern of staff support resulted in the disparity in activity between residents who were more or less able being reduced, while the absolute level of activity increased.

Gains were fully maintained in three houses at a 6-month follow-up and partially maintained in a fourth. Assistance and engagement in activity were variable in the remaining house at follow-up, with one of the two follow-up points showing deteriorations which were predicted by negative postbaseline trends but the other showing improvement over postbaseline levels. Variability in performance may be explained by senior staff turnover or absence through sickness and the consequent loss of managerial input and increased use of untrained relief staff.

Conclusion

The research illustrated goes some way to demonstrate the relevance of engagement in activity to quality of life and the application of systematic direct observation to understanding and improving the important living conditions upon which opportunity for people with pervasive disabilities depends. The extracts from Maureen Oswin's (1971) and Pauline Morris's (1969) seminal studies illustrate the nature of life where opportunity to engage in social and nonsocial activities are not a reality. Such descriptions are echoed in the low levels of measured engagement commonly found in institutional settings. The concern then has been with the design of supportive environments that provide and realize opportunities for diverse engagement in activity.

The extent of the problem varies across people. We now have several studies that consistently demonstrate a relationship between the extent of engagement in activity and the independent skills of the person, at least when the level of assistance received from staff is low. It is an obvious result but one frequently overlooked in my experience when the design of residential services is discussed. What staff or other supporters do when supposedly enabling people with disabilities to partici-pate in ordinary living is not necessarily closely determined by the physical char-acteristics of the setting, such as its size, architectural design, and location, or by the numbers and characteristics of staff. Moreover, the nature of support and its extent needs to be differentiated across settings dependent on the degree of dis-ability of those served.

Finally, I return to the observation that people with good independent skills apparently choose to engage in activity most of the time. This was apparent in the second study described here, and we have replicated the result in two subsequent samples. The time in which people are not engaged in activity may be seen, there-fore, as the direct consequence of living with a barrier, such as a disabling condi-tion, to accessing a typical lifestyle. The adequacy of service support may be as-sessed in terms of how well it helps people overcome the barrier. Direct observa-tion of engagement and disengagement provides a sensitive measure. Even with the inclusive definitions of engagement that we employ, the indicator still has use, as only the most able among those we research and service-support approximate the fully engaged life most of us take for granted. People with greater disabilities lead lives with fewer opportunities and unfulfilled potential, even in the better ser-vices that we have observed.

References

Beyer, S., Kilsby, M., & Willson, C. (1995). Interaction and engagement of workers in supported employment: A British comparison between workers with and with-out learning disabilities. *Mental Handicap Research, 8,* 137-155.

Brown, R. I., Bayer, M. B., & MacFarlane, C. M. (1989). *Rehabilitation programmes: the performance and quality of life of adults with developmental handicaps.* Toronto: Lugus Productions.

Burchard, S. N., Hasazi, J. S., Gordon, L. R., & Yoe, J. (1991). An examination of lifestyles and adjustment in three community residential alternatives. *Research in Developmental Disabilities, 12,* 127-142.

Campbell, A., Converse, P. E., & Rodgers, W. L. (1976). *The quality of American life: Perceptions, evaluation, and satisfactions.* New York: Russell Sage Foundation.

Cummins, R. A. (1993). *Comprehensive quality of life scale—intellectual disability* (4th ed.). Melbourne: Psychology Research Centre.

Cummins, R. A. (1997). Assessing quality of life. In R. Brown (Ed.), *Quality of life for people with disabilities: Models, research, and practice* (pp. 116-150). Cheltenham: Stanley Thorne.

de Kock, U., Saxby, H., Thomas, M., & Felce, D. (1988). Community and family contact: An evaluation of small community homes for severely and profoundly mentally handicapped adults. *Mental Handicap Research, 1,* 127-140.

Edgerton, R. B. (1967). *The cloak of competence: Stigma in the lives of the mentally retarded.* Berkeley: University of California Press.

Edgerton, R. B., Bollinger, M., & Herr, B. (1984). The cloak of competence: After two decades. *American Journal of Mental Deficiency, 88,* 345-351.

Emerson, E., & Felce, D. (1997). *Hand held computer technologies for behavioral observation in residential settings.* Paper presented at the 30th annual Gatlinburg Conference, Riverside, CA.

Emerson, E., & Hatton, C. (1994). *Moving out: Relocation from hospital to community.* London: Her Majesty's Stationery Office.

Felce, D. (1989). *Staffed housing for adults with severe and profound mental handicaps: The Andover Project.* Kidderminster: BIMH.

Felce, D. (1996). The quality of support for ordinary living: Staff: resident interactions and resident activity. In J. Mansell & K. Ericsson (Eds.), *Deinstitutionalization and community living: Intellectual disability services in Britain, Scandinavia, and the USA* (pp. 117-133). London: Chapman & Hall.

Felce, D. (1997). Defining and applying the concept of quality of life. *Journal of Intellectual Disability Research, 41,* 126-143.

Felce, D., de Kock, U., & Repp, A. (1986). An eco-behavioral analysis of small community-based houses and traditional large hospitals for severely and profoundly mentally handicapped adults. *Applied Research in Mental Retardation, 7,* 393-408.

Felce, D., & Perry, J. (1995). The extent of support for ordinary living provided in staffed housing: The relationship between staffing levels, resident dependency, staff: resident interactions and resident activity patterns. *Social Science and Medicine, 40,* 799-810.

Flynn, M. (1989). *Independent living for adults with a mental handicap: A place of my own.* London: Cassel.

Gilbert, T. F. (1978). *Engineering worthy performance.* New York: McGraw-Hill.

Gilbert, T. F., & Gilbert, M. B. (1992). Potential contributions of performance science to education. *Journal of Applied Behavior Analysis, 25,* 43-49.

Goode, D. (1994) *A world without words: the social construction of children born deaf and blind.* Philadelphia: Temple University Press.

Goode, D. (1997). Assessing the quality of life of adults with profound disabilities. In R. Brown (Ed.), *Quality of life for people with disabilities: Models, research, and practice* (pp. 72-90). Cheltenham: Stanley Thorne.

Harner, C., & Heal, L. (1993). The Multifaceted Lifestyle Satisfaction Scale (MLSS): Psychometric properties of an interviewing schedule for assessing personal satisfaction of adults with limited intelligence. *Research in Developmental Disabilities, 14,* 221-236.

Hatton, C., & Emerson, E. (1996). *Residential provision for people with learning disabilities: A research review.* Manchester: Hester Adrian Research Centre, Manchester University.

Hatton, C., Emerson, E., Robertson, J., Henderson, D., & Cooper, J. (1995). *An evaluation of the quality and costs of services for adults with severe learning disabilities and sensory impairments.* Manchester: Hester Adrian Research Centre, Manchester University.

Jones, E., Perry, J., Lowe, K., Felce, D., Toogood, S., Dunstan, F., Allen, D., & Pagler, J. (1997). *Opportunity and the promotion of activity among adults with severe learning disabilities living in community housing: The impact of training staff in Active Support.* Cardiff: Welsh Centre for Learning Disabilities Applied Research Unit, University of Wales College of Medicine.

Jones, M. L., Risley, T. R., & Favell, J. E. (1983). Ecological patterns. In J. L. Matson & S. E. Breuning (Eds.), *Assessing the mentally retarded* (pp. 311-334). New York: Grune & Stratton.

Morris, P. (1969). *Put away.* London: Routledge & Kegan Paul.

Nihira, K., Foster, R., Shellhaus, M., & Leland, H. (1974). *AAMD Adaptive Behavior Scale.* Washington DC: American Association on Mental Deficiency.

O'Brien, J. (1987). A guide to life-style planning. In B. Wilcox & G. T. Bellamy (Eds.), *The Activities Catalog: An alternative curriculum for youth and adults with severe disabilities* (pp. 175-189). Baltimore: Paul H. Brookes.

Oswin, M. (1971). *The empty hours.* London: Allen Lane.

Parmenter, T. R. (1988). An analysis of the dimensions of quality of life for people with physical disabilities. In R. I. Brown (Ed.), *Quality of life for handicapped people* (pp. 7-36). London: Croom Helm.

Raynes, N., Wright, K., Shiell, A., & Pettipher, C. (1994). *The cost and quality of community residential care.* London: David Fulton.

Repp, A. C., & Felce, D. (1990). A micro-computer system used for evaluative and experimental behavioral research in mental handicap. *Mental Handicap Research, 3,* 21-32.

Risley, T. R., & Cataldo, M. F. (1973). *Planned activity check: Materials for training observers.* Lawrence, KS: Center for Applied Behavior Analysis.

Sackett, G. P., & Landesman-Dwyer, S. (1977). Toward an ethology of mental retardation. In P. Mittler (Ed.), *Research to practice in mental retardation: Vol. 2. Education and training* (pp. 27-37). Baltimore: University Park Press.

Schalock, R. L. (1996). Reconsidering the conceptualization and measurement of quality of life. In R. L. Schalock (Ed.), *Quality of life: Vol. 1. Conceptualization and measurement* (pp. 123-139). Washington DC: American Association on Mental Retardation.

Schalock, R. L., and Keith, K. D. (1993). *Quality of life questionnaire.* Worthington, OH: IDS.

Lakota Quality of Life: Mitakuye Oyasin

Lilah Morton Pengra
Multicultural Consulting Services
Buffalo Gap, South Dakota, United States

The importance of culture for the concept of quality of life is well established in the field of developmental disabilities (Keith, 1996; Schalock, 1997). Culture defines, through shared values, how one views the world, thereby providing a subjective basis for judging "the good life." And culture shapes, through shared rules of behavior, how members of society interact, thereby affecting how different groups within society are treated and how they view themselves and others.

This chapter examines these two cultural contexts—worldview and identity—with specific reference to the quality of life of Native Americans with developmental disabilities living in South Dakota. The final section of the chapter is a transcription of an interview with Cindi Roan Eagle, a Lakota woman living in Rapid City, South Dakota. She shared her thoughts on what it means to be Indian to illustrate the impact of worldview and identity on the life of one person.

Worldview and Quality of Life

In South Dakota, there are nine Indian reservations or parts of reservations where 26,522 Lakotas live. In addition, 23,847 Lakotas live in nonreservation areas of South Dakota (U.S. Census Bureau, 1990). Outsiders have called them Western Sioux, but the preferred term of self-identification is Lakota, meaning "related people" (Ross, 1989). The general term of reference accentuates shared issues (Nagel, 1996), but in some contexts talking about Lakota culture obscures significant individual variations.

Individual Differences

The most accurate generalization about contemporary Lakota people is that, although they share general values, there is great variation among them created by the choices their forebears made during the past 150 years: whether to resist or work for the army, whether to settle far from or near the reservation administrative centers, whether or not to intermarry with French fur traders and White settlers (Grobsmith, 1981), and eventually whether to stay on the reservations or move to urban areas during the post-World War II relocation programs (Starita, 1995). But the "overwhelming heterogeneity" among individual Lakotas cannot be allowed to obscure the fact that they have a shared worldview, a "uniquely Lakota attitude, philosophy, and value system" (Grobsmith, p. 3).

On the surface, it might appear that many customs and behaviors have been adopted from Euro-American culture, particularly in the areas of technology and religion, but more thorough understanding reveals that these have been "Indianized"

(W. Powers, 1977, p. 124). Individuals can behave in ways that appear to be very close to White culture when the situation demands it, but do so for very Lakota reasons and goals (Brave Bird & Erdoes, 1993). Most non-Lakota see the wide variation in behavior without understanding the underlying Lakota worldview that is distinctly different from the worldview of White America.

Lakota Worldview

The Lakota worldview, Lakolyake, is a philosophy based on four interconnected values: fortitude, generosity, wisdom, and respect (Medicine, 1987; Oliver, 1987). This worldview supports a way of life that has been described by social scientists as situational, collectivist, holistic, and noncomparative.

Fortitude. Having fortitude means that one has the strength to suffer on behalf of one's people, as in the Sun Dance where the dancer breaks free from a central pole to which he is tied by thongs piercing his skin; that one has the stamina to forgo personal pleasures in order to give one's worldly goods to others; that one has the toughness to survive the hard knocks of life and still be generous, compassionate, patient, and respectful. Fortitude guides behavior toward situational approaches: adapting to situations rather than trying to change them to meet individual needs (Lynch & Hanson, 1992); dealing with the current situation rather than planning for some imaginary future (R. White, 1970); and analyzing others' responses as due to their relationships within a concrete situation rather than to abstract personal traits (Holland, 1985).

Generosity. Having generosity means that one shares with one's family and with one's people, not just worldly goods but also one's wisdom and strength. A medicine man doesn't receive a "fee for service," because he willingly shares his knowledge and power (Mohatt, 1977). Significant life events are celebrated by giving away material possessions in recognition of the community that makes life possible. Generosity emphasizes the welfare of the whole group, a *collectivist* rather than individualist focus (Triandis, 1989), and stresses meeting one's duties to others rather than asserting one's rights as an individual (Shweder & Miller, 1985).

Wisdom. Having the value of wisdom means having knowledge as well as seeing how all things are interrelated. It is encapsulated in the phrase *mitakuye oyasin*, translated as "I am related to all that is" (Amiotte, 1987) and as "all my relatives" or "we are all related" (Ross, 1989). It is said at the end of a prayer or when friends part. It is a *holistic* explanation for an existence where there are no sharp demarcations between the living and the dead, humans and animals, or the land and the people, because everything is interconnected (Gustafson, 1997; Paige, 1987).

Respect. Having the value of respect means having the humility to live in harmony with the earth, the animals, and all people. It means cooperating rather than competing; supporting the autonomy of others rather than wielding power over them; and accepting all humans, including oneself, for what they are rather than how they compare to others (Lee, 1959). It is a *noncomparative* evaluation of people and the situations they are in, because they are not judged as better than other people or situations. After hearing a story about something John did, rather than exclaiming

"How smart!" or "How brave!" implying that John's actions were smarter or braver than someone else's might have been, a Lakota might say, "How like John!"

Quality-of-Life Measures

It is widely accepted that culture affects "notions of happiness, satisfaction, or well-being," therefore "it would be a critical mistake to believe that" different groups "are made happy by identical experiences" (Keith, 1996, p. 75). There is less recognition that the concept and measurement of quality of life itself is culture-bound (Kuehn & McClainm, 1994; Kuyken, Orley, Hudelson, & Sartorius, 1994), as the following review of several measures of quality of life relative to Lakota values show.

Situational Approaches. One measure of quality of life is whether people say they are happy or satisfied. Lakota people certainly recognize and enjoy happiness and satisfaction when those feelings are part of a particular situation, but being upset because a situation does not include them, or abstracting feelings of satisfaction or happiness as separate from the situations that contained them, would not be typical Lakota approaches. Most Lakotas would not try to change a situation in order to create happiness or satisfaction, but would adapt to the situation with fortitude and courage or withdraw from it. When interviewed by phone, one Lakota man not in the developmental disability field said, "It doesn't hurt to have things like that [happiness and satisfaction], but it's not necessary. Instead, we should have compassion for the people around us" (interview, November 19, 1997).

Collectivist Focus. Another measure of the quality of life is whether the individual is afforded the same rights as others (Turnbull & Brunk, 1997). However, a collectivist focus accentuates one's duties to the group rather than one's rights as an individual. If everyone in the group feels a duty to share with others in the group, then everyone fares equally well whether the group collectively has much or little (Shweder & Miller, 1985). Therefore, quality of life could be measured by what the group as a whole has. The man interviewed above, in response to the question "What situation do you think would provide a good quality of life for a person with mental retardation?" said, "What's good for the people would be good for him, because he is part of the community" (interview, November 19, 1997).

Holistic Explanations. Rather than approaching quality of life as a list of good things (having food and clothing), relationships (having friends and family), and internal states (being happy or satisfied) that add up to a good life for the individual, many Lakotas explain personal feelings of satisfaction as the result of harmony and balance. There is good and bad everywhere, but having all good things is just as bad as having all bad things, because "walking the Red Road" (Ross, 1989, p. 22) means finding harmony among all things.

Noncomparative Evaluation. Measuring quality of life or talking about a person's quality of life requires one to think of a person as having "a life" (Gubrium & Lynott, 1983) that can be separated from concrete situations and compared to others' lives (Nydegger, 1986). In reading Lakota biographies (Starita, 1995; St. Pierre, 1991), autobiographies (Brave Bird & Erdoes, 1993; Means, 1995), and even novels (Louis, 1995; Penn, 1995), one is struck by the similarity of form. They recount situations survived and wisdom acquired, but rarely does one read sentiments such as "Overall, I had a good life" or "I had a better life than my brother."

Mitakuye Oyasin

"The concept of quality of life has roots in the Western cultural emphasis on individualism . . . [but] in some cultures, the idea of the 'good life' could not be separated from members' moral responsibility to the society as a whole" (Taylor, 1994, p. 263). Lakota certainly are able to think about quality of life from the individualist perspective, but their inclination is to reshape the concept to fit their view of the world as a place where respect and wisdom guide people to live with fortitude and to share with generosity so that life is harmonious for all the people, a vision that is just beginning to be adopted by social scientists. As Garbarino and Garbarino (1992) argue,

> Parents need love and support in order to be loving and supporting to their children. Their ability to be good parents is not solely their own doing—their society has a great say in what stresses and supports they will encounter. . . .
>
> [Unless] a society assures that parents have the means to rear children, it will be faced with an unfortunate mixture of unhappy parents and inadequately prepared children. Both are a direct threat to the goal of quality in the human experience. (pp. 306, 310)

The focus of quality-of-life enhancement efforts should be the community, from the Lakota point of view, not because the community is the context affecting the quality of life of a particular individual, but because healthy communities are good for "all my relatives."

Identity and Quality of Life

Constructing a personal and social identity is part of normal development. As a child interacts with others, the child builds a picture of who he or she is and how he or she fits into that social group. This process can be jeopardized through distorted or inconsistent feedback from others or a lack of significant others with whom to interact. Thus identity formation can be inhibited by poverty, geographic mobility, and abuse (Garbarino & Garbarino, 1992) as well as by being a member of a group devalued by the rest of society (Gibbs & Huang, 1989) or by rejecting one's own group (Garbarino & Kostelny, 1992).

Not having a healthy social identity leads to stress, social isolation, self-hatred (Garbarino & Kostelny, 1992), poor self-esteem, and depression (O'Neill, 1996), all of which are clear threats to a good quality of life. Coping with a devalued social identity also impacts an individual's quality of life as that individual may attempt to "pass" as a member of the more valued group (Dominguez, 1986) or learn to "code switch" back and forth between behaviors appropriate for each group (M. Powers, 1988). Passing and code switching can both have deleterious effects on identity, for example, because of rejection by both groups (Ogbu, 1987) or a schizophrenic response to having two conflicting identities (O'Connor, 1993b).

Not providing services in terms of the service receiver's values results in prejudice, even if unintended, that threatens the service receiver's personal identity (Pengra, 2000) and thus the person's quality of life, because ignoring the person's values implies that his or her worldview is wrong, leading to self-doubt, confusion, and possibly anger or fear. Providing supports to a person in terms of his or her own values, on the other hand, acknowledges his or her values and, by extension, personal identity is validated. The person is in control not only of what he or she chooses to do but also of how and why.

Lakota Adults With Developmental Disabilities in Non-Lakota Environments

In South Dakota 2,348 adults with developmental disabilities receive services through one state institution and 17 private, nonprofit community agencies regulated by the Division of Developmental Disabilities, part of the South Dakota Department of Human Services. None of the agencies providing services are located on a reservation, although 232 service receivers (9.8%) are Native American, 69 of them born in a county where a reservation is located (Campbell, 1997). No official accounting of the ethnicity of staff and board members is required by the state, but observation indicates that few are Native American—not surprising in view of the fact that only one agency is located in a county where Native Americans constitute at least 7.2% of the population, the state average (U.S. Census Bureau, 1990). Therefore, Lakota adults with developmental disabilities are receiving services in environments that are predominantly non-Lakota and living in communities where prejudice against Indians, although not as overt as 30 years ago, is still not uncommon (Starita, 1995).

Service providers as a group are no more or less prejudiced than others in their communities, but the impact of prejudice on quality of life cannot be ignored, because in "situations in which a dominant ethnic group provides health care to a subordinate group . . . wider issues of political economy, racism, and exploitation" are reflected in health care interactions and affect "patient satisfaction" which can be positive when "practitioners [meet] patient perceptions and expectations" and negative when they do not (O'Neil, 1989, p. 327). Two arguments offered to deny that prejudice exists in the service system are that Lakota service receivers are not that different from others, because all people are basically the same and that cultural differences already are being supported, as service plans are based on each individual's choices and needs.

Some Lakotas are, of course, "not that different," because through the choices of their forebears, they have values more closely resembling those of the White middle-class professionals working with them than those described here as Lakota values. And it is reasonable for professionals to believe that by focusing on an individual's choices they are providing services consistent with Lakota culture; in some cases it does have this result, because the philosophy of supporting individual choices is consistent with the Lakota value on respecting personal autonomy, and because many choices offered and valued by service providers fall within the range of activities accepted and valued by many Lakotas (e.g., attending powwows, visiting sacred places), although the underlying worldviews for offering or accepting them differ. And a few Lakotas are receiving culturally sensitive supports, because some service providers are familiar with Lakolyake.

Potential Misinterpretation of Lakota Behavior

However, just because some Lakotas are receiving services that meet their perceptions and expectations does not mean that all are. Thus, to enhance quality of life and decrease unintentional prejudice against people who do embrace a Lakota worldview, it is necessary for people working with them to understand the meaning of their behavior in terms of Lakolyake. When service providers do not understand the Lakota worldview or assume that there is no difference between it and their own, they judge Lakota behavior in terms of their own non-Indian values, a form of prejudice whether it is intended or not.

Situational Fortitude. Not asking for help when assistance is needed can be attributed to a lack of initiative and negatively evaluated by non-Indian service providers. Or it can be attributed to Lakolyake and judged as a positive response, adapting with fortitude to difficult situations by not intruding on others' autonomy. When others withhold assistance or do not even notice that assistance is needed, a Lakota might see them as lacking in generosity and as having no sense of duty to others but still respect their autonomous decision to live that way.

Not choosing a goal and achieving it by eliminating barriers may be judged negatively as not planning ahead (Stewart & Bennett, 1991). On the other hand, a situational approach requires developing multiple options in the present to provide future flexibility for adapting to whatever situation occurs (Halperin, 1990). Maintaining multiple options is not evidence of indecision, but of a person prepared for whatever life may offer. Accepting one of those options at a moment's notice is a situational strategy, not impulsive decision making.

Making a decision and sticking to it no matter how the situation changes is positively judged by non-Indians as determination; it may be negatively judged by Lakotas as inflexibility. Making different decisions as the situation changes is not "changing one's mind" but adapting to the situation.

Collectivist Generosity. Fulfilling one's duties to the group rather than pursuing one's personal rights is sometimes cited as evidence of low self-esteem, dependency, or succumbing to peer pressure. Giving away all one's money or material possessions from the Lakota point of view is not a sign of abuse or lack of self-control. The difficulty occurs when a generous, dutiful individual lives in an individualist culture, where others are accumulating goods, saving for the future, and asserting their rights.

Holistic Wisdom. Making decisions through dreams or contemplation (Erdoes, 1990), interacting with one's dead relatives (St. Pierre, 1991), participating in Indian religion and one or more Christian religions simultaneously (W. Powers, 1987), and returning to a particular place (a reservation or a location in the Black Hills such as Bear Butte) to participate in a Sun Dance or a sweat lodge for group renewal (Jahner, 1987; Medicine, 1981) are all activities associated with a holistic approach to wisdom. People unfamiliar with Lakolyake may judge as fanciful or illogical making decisions through dreams and interacting with one's dead relatives; may view as lack of commitment participation in multiple religions; and may criticize as irresponsible returns to the reservation for dances and sweats when it requires time off from work for adults and time out of school for children.

Holistic thinking is nonsequential and nonlinear (Kaplan, 1988) and is sometimes judged as illogical by the nonholistic observer who is unable to see the connections, for example, between one paragraph and the next in a holistic story. Rather than using a chronology, based on the concept of linear time, holistic thinkers may use feelings (Lieberman, 1994), spatial relationships (Jahner, 1980), or qualities of recurring situations, that is, cyclic time (Shweder & Bourne, 1984), to organize their thoughts.

Noncomparative Respect. Lakota people tend to support the autonomy of others rather than wield power over them; this is accomplished by not interfering with others' decisions (Good Tracks, 1976). They respond to interference from others by withdrawing from the uncomfortable situation or by using anger to drive away the rude person (Wax & Thomas, 1961). In collectivist cultures typical behavior also includes withdrawal to handle emotional distress (Lewis, 1975) and social exclusion to punish a wrong-doer, sometimes even self-imposed by a person feeling shame from not being able to contribute to the group. Psychologists from individualist cultures may misinterpret withdrawal as resistance (Aponte, Rivers, & Wohl, 1995); anger used to control others' meddling may be mistaken as defiance or aggression (G. White, 1992).

Noncomparative respect is based on the ability to accept the ambiguity of several mutually exclusive right answers (Damen, 1987) and to use intuition and feelings, rather than a single, externally imposed, standard as a measure of rightness (Scarcella, 1990). People accustomed to comparison may disapprove of this as fuzzy thinking or see it as undisciplined or unprincipled.

Valuing cooperation facilitates a situational style of leadership that is field dependent (Hofstede, 1986) and visual (Lieberman, 1994). When Lakotas undertake a group project, the person best suited to doing a particular task begins it. But if another person joins the group who is more skilled in that task, the first person may defer. Thus who is doing what task shifts, depending on who is present at any given time. People in the group do not need to discuss assignments; visual inspection of the field of activity is enough to coordinate the project. To the outsider not familiar with this organizational style, it feels chaotic and looks as if there is no leader.

Threats to Identity

The "color blind" approach to equality, treating all people the same, can destroy the individual's identity. "In essence, people denying their race, gender, disability or whatever trait is significant to them, as though it didn't exist, or teachers and professionals saying, 'I don't see their color or disability,' only further contributes to denying who that person is" (O'Connor, 1993a, p. 11). Rejecting that there are differences in values associated with being Lakota goes one step further. Not only is the person's identity denied, but the person also may be inaccurately and disastrously judged as lacking initiative and self-control, making impulsive decisions, changing his or her mind, and being dependent, illogical, indecisive, irresponsible, defiant, aggressive, undisciplined, and unprincipled.

Supporting Lakota identity, then, means recognizing that people have their own values as well as understanding how those values give positive meanings to their behavior. This requires special vigilance and extra effort when services are provided in non-Lakota environments. But doing so affirms the Lakota individual's identity and enhances the person's quality of life.

Mitakuye Oyasin

Of the Lakotas receiving services, only 29.7% are from a reservation, although 52.6% of the Native American population of South Dakota lives on reservations. One would expect a higher rate of need for services, because of the significantly higher levels of chronic unemployment, chronic disease, and extreme poverty on the reservations (Henderson, 1991; Starita, 1995). Outsiders tend to see only the poverty (O'Connell, et al., 1987) and assume that people with developmental disabilities and their families would opt for the higher standard of living and greater services available off the reservation; but they completely underestimate the importance of social identity. The only people with developmental disabilities who leave the reservation are those who need services because of dysfunctional family situations or because of conditions requiring specialized medical and behavioral supports not available on the reservation. Social scientists and educators need to learn from the Lakota worldview (Brendtro, Brokenleg, & Van Bockern, 1990), where acceptance of people with developmental disabilities for their capabilities (noncomparative respect) and inclusion of them in the life of the community (collectivist generosity and holistic wisdom) has always been the norm (Ross, 1989) because "we are all related."

"What It Means to Be Indian" by Cindi Roan Eagle

Editor's Note: The only editing by Pengra of Roan Eagle's remarks was to delete extraneous comments about the food as the conversation occurred over lunch. Quote marks were inserted based on tone of voice. The only question asked by Pengra was the opening one, "What does it mean to you to be Indian?"

I went to Oklahoma last month with the Governor's Planning Council. I'm one of two Indians on the Council. They paid $150 to do a presentation, but I had to take off work to do it. I told them my name and how old I am and I'm from Rosebud reservation. I told them I have the fetal alcohol syndrome and that I fancy dance. I had my dress on and my eagle feather in my hair. They said, "You look pretty." And I said, "Nah. I'm just me." I was putting myself down because I didn't really want to do that presentation, but in a way I did want to do it. They wanted to know if I spoke a little Indian, and I said some words.

My mom gave me a telephone number where I could call her. So I did. I called her and told her how I'm feeling. It's hard to be that far away from Rosebud. It's hard because although I do have resentment, I still want to be there sometimes.

I had a dream about dancing at a powwow in a buckskin dress, so we had to figure out a way for me to get the dress made without the leather because it was too expensive. I made everything but the shawl. I got that at a pawn shop. I fancy dance. My grandmother taught me how to traditional dance. She's gone now. I dance for her mainly. They say you can dance for yourself, but that's kind of rude. You're supposed to dance for the elders who taught you. My grandmother and my aunt are up there now and some of my cousins. That was a shock when I found out they were dead. But I knew I should dance for them. So that's what I do. I dance.

That's the only thing I'm proud of being Indian about. I can dance. I'm not racial in any way like my family. They're very racial. They do not like my White foster family that raised me and took care of me back there when I was eight. But my mom didn't like that so she got the Social Services to give me back. But I didn't even know my family. I stayed with my mom and dad, but they fought and everything. And then, my dad started abusing me. And my mom knew about it, but she didn't really care so that's why I have a lot of resentment toward my mom. But I'm strong now. If she treats me like she did when I was younger, then I say, "Maybe I should treat you like that." But I'm not going to because that's not what I am.

I don't have to be mean, but my anger sometimes gets the best of me. I just got suspended from my job for a couple of days. I was arguing with my boss, because this girl I work with gets me mad. She says, "I'm Indian," but she's not. She's White. She just thinks she's Indian to be like me because she's jealous. But she doesn't know what it's like. A neighbor who lives behind me is always saying things like "*Them* people are mean. *Them* people are this. *Them* people are that." She hates Indians.

My boyfriend is White. I say, "Respect me. Share with me. Have a good sense of humor. Don't tell me what to do. Don't abuse me." He wants to get married in the Indian way. But he just means like what they did in *Dances With Wolves*. He says, "You don't have to have a fancy ceremony." I say, "Yeah, we don't." But it's not like it was in *Dances With Wolves*.

He asked me what Bear Butte means, and I said, "That's our sacred place. Everything that's born came from somewhere and that circle is around there." I went there and I already knew not to touch that stuff hanging on the trees [the prayer offerings]. And I felt my grandmother. And I just stood there looking up and said, "Grandma, teach me those ways. I want to be wise." I know I'll get there sooner or later. I'm just young yet. Then a buffalo came around the trees. He didn't charge me. He just sat there. Then two deer came and some eagles were flying. Everybody said I looked different. I said, "I know. It's because my grandmother and my uncles are around me."

I had to find out about my family. I told my mom I wanted to know who they are because half of them died from the alcohol. I told her, "I don't want you to be the next one."

Last Christmas I went home to visit. My sister started saying the word *retard*. But I said, "No. Get that out of your mind. I'm disabled because of the alcohol." She understood that and said she was sorry. I said it was OK.

Right now I'm pretty happy about being Indian. My brother is a Sun Dancer. He showed me the piercing ropes. He showed me his headband that he wears. He showed me the eagle bone whistle and the eagle claw. And I thought, *You really are.* We're carrying down our traditions. When I left to come back here, I hugged him and said, "Take care of us, brother." And he said, "Yes."

I want to go home again this Christmas, but I don't know. The workshop [my service provider] kind of stepped in, because they don't want me to get hurt. I might get hurt because my family doesn't know the real me. I asked my mom why she gave up the rights to me. I said, "Is it because you hate me?" She said, "I don't hate you." I said, "You gave me up. I could have been home here, taking care of you. You're getting old."

I don't use my anger against friends. When people tell me things that don't feel right, I try to tell them. When [my case manager] tells me "Oh, you can't do this. And you can't do that. And you don't have the money," that kind of upsets me, telling me what to do. And then the anger gets the better of me.

But the only thing I really want is a family. The workshop is sort of like a family. But they all have families of their own, so I'm not really theirs. And I have a foster family to talk to once in a while. But I want a real family.

My aunt was here in the [hospital] for a while. She really looks like my grandmother. I told her what's happened to me because she never used to hurt me. She always respected me. And she goes, "I really feel sorry for you. I wish I could take you in and have you as my kid."

I'm not going to move back to Rosebud. I'm going to stay up here in the Hills. It's too dangerous there. It's my home, but they gave me up into the arms of the state. So the state raised me. So now I'm here.

References

Amiotte, A. (1987). The Lakota Sun Dance: Historical and contemporary perspectives. In R. DeMallie & D. Parks (Eds.), *Sioux Indian religion: Tradition and innovation.* (pp. 75-90) Norman: University of Oklahoma Press.

Aponte, J., Rivers, R., & Wohl, J. (1995). *Psychological interventions and cultural diversity.* Boston: Allyn & Bacon.

Brave Bird, M., & Erdoes, R. (1993). *Ohitika woman.* New York: Harper Perennial.

Brendtro, L., Brokenleg, M., & Van Bockern, S. (1990). *Reclaiming youth at risk: Our hope for the future.* Bloomington, IN: National Educational Service.

Campbell, E. (1997). Management Analyst, State of South Dakota, Department of Human Services. (Responsible only for providing data, not for any interpretation given or implied here.)

Damen, L. (1987). *Culture learning: The fifth dimension in the language classroom.* Reading, MA: Addison-Wesley.

Dominguez, V. (1986). *White by definition: Social classification in Creole Louisiana.* New Brunswick, NJ: Rutgers University Press.

Erdoes, R. (1990). *Crying for a dream: The world through native American eyes.* Sante Fe, NM: Bear & Co.

Garbarino, J., & Garbarino, C. (1992). In conclusion: The issue is human quality. In J. Garbarino (Ed.), *Children and families in the social environment* (2nd ed., pp. 304-327). New York: Aldine DeGruyter.

Garbarino, J., & Kostelny, K. (1992). Cultural diversity and identity formation. In J. Garbarino (Ed.), *Children and families in the social environment* (2nd ed., pp. 179-199). New York: Aldine DeGruyter.

Gibbs, J., & Huang, L. (1989). *Children of color: Psychological interventions with minority youth.* San Francisco: Jossey-Bass.

Good Tracks, J. (1976). Native American non-interference. *Social Work, 18,* 30-34.

Grobsmith, E. (1981). *Lakota of the Rosebud: A contemporary ethnography.* New York: Holt, Rinehart, & Winston.

Gubrium, J., & Lynott, R. (1983). Rethinking life satisfaction. *Human Organization, 42,* 30-38.

Gustafson, F. (1997). *Dancing between two worlds: Jung and the Native American soul.* Mahwah, NJ: Paulist.

Halperin, R. (1990). *The livelihood of kin: Making ends meet "The Kentucky Way."* Austin: University of Texas Press.

Henderson, J. (1991). Native American health policy. *Journal of the American Medical Association, 265,* 2272-2273.

Hofstede, G. (1986). Cultural differences in teaching and learning. *International Journal of International Relations, 10,* 301-320.

Holland, D. (1985). From situation to impression: How Americans get to know themselves and one another. In J. Dougherty (Ed.), *Directions in cognitive anthropology* (pp. 389-412). Urbana: University of Illinois Press.

Jahner, E. (1980). Language change and cultural dynamics: A study of Lakota verbs of movement. In P. Schach (Ed.), *Languages in conflict: Linguistic acculturation on the Great Plains* (pp. 129-147). Lincoln: University of Nebraska Press.

Jahner, E. (1987). Lakota genesis: The oral tradition. In R. DeMallie & D. Parks (Eds.), *Sioux Indian religion: Tradition and innovation* (pp. 45-66). Norman: University of Oklahoma Press.

Kaplan, R. (1988). Cultural thought patterns in inter-cultural education. In J. Wurzel (Ed.), *Toward multiculturalism: A reader in multicultural education* (pp. 207-222). Yarmouth, MA: Intercultural Press.

Keith, K. D. (1996). Measuring quality of life across cultures: Issues and challenges. In R. Schalock (Ed.), *Quality of life: Vol. 1. Conceptualization and measurement* (pp. 73-82). Washington, DC: American Association on Mental Retardation.

Kuehn, M., & McClainm, J. (1994). Quality of life in the United States: A multicultural context. In D. Goode (Ed.), *Quality of life for persons with disabilities: International perspectives and issues* (pp. 185-194). Cambridge, MA: Brookline.

Kuyken, W., Orley, J., Hudelson, P., & Sartorius, N. (1994). Quality of life assessment across cultures. *International Journal of Mental Health, 23,* 5-27.

Lee, D. (1959). *Freedom and culture.* New York: Prentice-Hall.

Lewis, T. (1975). A syndrome of depression and mutism in the Oglala Sioux. *American Journal of Psychiatry, 137,* 753-755.

Lieberman, D. (1994). Ethnocognitivism, problem solving and hemisphericity. In L. Samovar & R. Porter (Eds.), *Intercultural communication: A reader* (7th ed. pp. 178-193). Belmont, CA: International Thomson.

Louis, A. (1995). *Skins: A novel.* NY: Crown.

Lynch, E., & M. Hanson. (1992). *Developing cross-cultural competence: A guide for working with young children and their families.* Baltimore: Paul H. Brookes.

Means, R. (1995). *Where white men fear to tread: The autobiography of Russell Means.* New York: St. Martin's Press.

Medicine, B. (1981). Native American resistance to integration: Contemporary confrontations and religious revitalization. *Plains Anthropologist, 26,* 277-286.

Medicine, B. (1987). Indian women and the renaissance of traditional religion. In R. DeMallie & D. Parks (Eds.), *Sioux Indian religion: Tradition and innovation* (pp. 159-172). Norman: University of Oklahoma Press.

Mohatt, J. (1977). Sicangu Lakota medicine men provide traditional perspective. *Sinte Gleska College News,* pp. 6-7, Rosebud, SD.

Nagel, J. (1996). *American Indian ethnic renewal: Red power and the resurgence of identity and culture.* New York: Oxford University Press.

Nydegger, C. (1986). Measuring morale and life satisfaction. In C. Fry & J. Keith (Eds.), *New methods for old-age research* (pp. 213-230). South Hadley, MA: Bergin & Garvey.

O'Connell, J., Dereshiwsky, M., Frank, L., Hodge, F., Joe, J., Johnson, M., Locust, C., Maddux, C., Martin, W., Miller, D., Morgan, J., Weinmann, S., & White, A. (1987). *A study of the special problems and needs of American Indians with handicaps both on and off the reservation.* Tucson, AZ: Native American Research & Training Center.

O'Connor, S. (1993a). *Multiculturalism and disability: A collection of resources.* Syracuse, NY: Center on Human Policy.

O'Connor, S. (1993b). "I'm not Indian anymore": The challenge of providing culturally sensitive services to American Indians. In J. Racino, P. Walker, S. O'Connor, & S. Taylor (Eds.), *Housing, support, and community* (pp. 313-332). Baltimore: Paul H. Brookes.

Ogbu, J. (1987). Variability in minority school performance: A problem in search of an explanation. *Anthropology and Education Quarterly, 18,* 312-334.

Oliver, K. (1987). Introduction to traditional Lakota religion in modern life. In R. DeMallie & D. Parks (Eds.), *Sioux Indian religion: Tradition and innovation* (pp. 211-212). Norman: University of Oklahoma Press.

O'Neil, J. (1989). The cultural and political context of patient dissatisfaction in cross-cultural clinical encounters: A Canadian Inuit study. *Medical Anthropology Quarterly, 3,* 325-344.

O'Neill, T. (1996). *Disciplined hearts: History, identity, and depression in an American Indian community.* Berkeley: University of California Press.

Paige, H. (1987). *Land of the spotted eagle: A portrait of the reservation Sioux.* Chicago: Loyola University Press.

Pengra, L. (2000). *Your values, my values: Multicultural services in developmental disabilities.* Baltimore: Paul H. Brookes.

Penn, W. (1995). *All my sins are relatives.* Lincoln: University of Nebraska Press.

Powers, M. (1988). *Oglala women: Myth, ritual, and reality.* Chicago: University of Chicago Press.

Powers, W. (1977). *Oglala religion.* Lincoln: University of Nebraska Press.

Powers, W. (1987). Dual religious participation: Stratagems of conversion among the Lakota. In W. Powers (Ed.), *Beyond the Vision: Essays on American Indian Culture* (pp. 94-125). Norman: University of Oklahoma Press.

Ross, A. (1989). *Mitakuye oyasin: "We are all related."* Ft. Yates, ND: Bear.

Scarcella, R. (1990). *Teaching language minority students in the multicultural classroom.* Englewood Cliffs, NJ: Prentice-Hall.

Schalock, R. (1997). Considering culture in the application of quality of life. In R. Schalock (Ed.), *Quality of life: Vol. 2. Application to persons with disabilities* (pp. 225-244). Washington, DC: American Association on Mental Retardation.

Shweder, R., & Bourne, E. (1984). Does the concept of the person vary cross-culturally? In R. Shweder & R. LeVine (Eds.), *Culture theory: Essays on mind, self, and emotion* (pp. 158-199). Cambridge: Cambridge University Press.

Shweder, R., & Miller, J. (1985). The social construction of the person: How is it possible? In K. Gergen & K. Davis (Eds.), *The social construction of the person* (pp. 42-69). New York: Springer-Verlag.

St. Pierre, M. (1991). *Madonna Swan: A Lakota woman's story.* Norman: University of Oklahoma Press.

Starita, J. (1995). *The Dull Knifes of Pine Ridge: A Lakota odyssey.* New York: Putnam.

Stewart, E., & Bennett, M. (1991). *American cultural patterns: A cross-cultural perspective* (Rev. ed.). Yarmouth, MA: Intercultural Press.

Taylor, S. (1994). In support of research on quality of life, but against QOL. In D. Goode (Ed.), *Quality of life for persons with disabilities: International perspectives and issues* (pp. 260-265). Cambridge, MA: Brookline.

Triandis, H. (1989). Cross-cultural studies of individualism and collectivism. In J. Berman (Ed.), *Nebraska Symposium on Motivation 1989: Cross-cultural perspectives, Vol. 37* (pp. 41-133). Lincoln: University of Nebraska Press.

Turnbull, H., & Brunk, G. (1997). Quality of life and public policy. In R. Schalock (Ed.), *Quality of life: Vol. 2. Application to persons with disabilities* (pp. 201-210). Washington, DC: American Association on Mental Retardation.

U.S. Census Bureau. (1990). *1990 U.S. Census.* Washington, DC: U.S. Government Printing Office.

Wax, R., & Thomas, R. (1961). American Indians and white people. *Phylon 4*(22), 305-317.

White, G. (1992). Ethnopsychology. In T. Schwartz, G. White, & C. Lutz (Eds.), *New directions in psychological anthropology* (pp. 21-46). Cambridge: Cambridge University Press.

White, R. (1970). The lower-class culture of excitement among the contemporary Sioux (pp. 175-197). In E. Nurge (Ed.), *The modern Sioux.* Lincoln: University of Nebraska Press.

Quality of Life of Individuals With Disabilities in Taiwan

Hung-Chih Lin
National Changhua University of Education
Changhua, Taiwan

Concern over quality of life for individuals with disabilities in Taiwan has gained increasing attention in the past decade. This concern has resulted in a strong agreement on benefits of the ancient Confucian tenet of assisting people with disabilities and their families. In his masterpiece of Li Chi, Confucius portrayed the quality of life for individuals with disabilities in terms of the aspects of a utopian commonwealth called Ta Tung in which the disabled and the ailing were well cared for from a collectivistic cultural perspective (Chen, Sietz, & Cheng, 1991). Thus quality of life was considered important and similar to the basic needs that should be met for all humans.

Even though there has been a long history of Chinese interest in the concept of, and the search for, a life of quality, the notion of subjective quality of life has only recently become an important issue in the field of disabilities on Taiwan (Lin, 1995b). More and more researchers and policy makers have become interested in quality-of-life issues and have tried to examine and understand the quality of life in Taiwan empirically (Chang, 1994; Lin, 1995b, 1996; Sun, 1997). However, the perspective that quality of life is a subjective phenomenon composed of core dimensions that may be viewed and appreciated differently by different individuals does not have a long background in Taiwan. Traditionally most research on quality of life in Taiwan was environmentally based and used social indicators such as gerontology, public policy, consumer satisfaction, advertising, health, the environment, politics, and education (Lin, 1995b, 1996) to provide empirical information on the collective quality of certain aspects of community life.

Thus to date the concept of quality of life in the field of disability has not been clearly defined or well addressed in Taiwan. Quality of life was used as a chameleon-like concept in delineating the desirable goals or standards to improve the life of people with disabilities. Most important, due to ambiguous and divergent interpretations of quality of life and lack of empirical evidence, the use of quality of life as a conceptual framework or yardstick for evaluating and improving life outcomes seems somewhat new in Taiwan.

This chapter explores philosophical and theoretical issues regarding quality of life, develops an ecological model of quality of life, and proposes future suggestions and implications that might benefit cross-national research and improve the quality of life for individuals with disabilities in Taiwan.

Philosophical and Theoretical Issues in Quality of Life

Philosophically speaking, the concept of quality of life, as seen in Taiwan, originated from Confucianism. For more than 2,000 years the Taiwanese-Chinese people have been directed by the humanistic philosophy and respect for learning that was taught by Confucius. He lived in the age of the Greek city-states and preceded Plato by more than 80 years. Based on the Confucian view, to have a life of quality, people must act reasonably, with intelligence, thoughtfulness, and virtue, and must avoid excesses of action. They must live according to a Golden Mean—the course between extremes (Legge, 1977). However, quality of life would not be viewed simply as enjoyment, pleasure, or contentment. For Confucius, it was believed that happiness, human satisfaction, and fulfillment are achieved through the power of intellect, the ability to reason, conceptualize, and make rational judgments. Furthermore, Confucius was a major revolutionary in his concepts of what kind of person a ruler or a head of family must be. The essence of his system was based on the concept of Chen Tzu, which might be translated as "a virtuous individual" (Chen et al., 1991). He believed that all people have the capacity to become such individuals through learning and education. For this reason, he opened his school to all who wished to learn and not just those born to the aristocracy. One of his most quoted phrases is "With education there is no class." Therefore, human beings are entitled to pursue good quality of life if and only if they are well educated.

However, in recent years Taiwan has been influenced by dramatic cultural, economic, social, and political changes, all of which have threatened the *traditional* Chinese quality-of-life ideology and values (Smith, 1991, 1992). Industrialization, urbanization, and Westernization have led to numerous changes in the fabric of Chinese quality of life. Currently four dichotomous interpretations of quality of life have resulted in philosophical and theoretical debate in Taiwan: (a) subjectivism versus objectivism, (b) elitism versus massism, (c) egoism versus universalism, and (d) individualism versus collectivism.

Criteria: Subjective Versus Objective

Of all the issues of quality of life, none has generated more heated discussion than how best to assess or measure a person's quality of life: subjectively or objectively. The issue is evident even in the discrepancy between "subjective" and "objective" criteria for defining and describing quality of life. Subjective definition refers to the individual's point of view, and the objective explanation refers to a societal point of view. The subjective dimensions of quality of life are idiosyncratic; the objective dimensions are normative.

For example, Confucius remarked of his disciple, the favorite Yen Hui, saying, How much heroism is in that man!!! Living on one single meal a day, with water for his drink, and living in the lowest hovels of the city, no man could have stood such hardships, yet he did not lose his cheerfulness. How much heroism is in that man! (Ku, 1976, p. 41). In other words, people would be viewed as experiencing a very low quality of life, if the criteria used for evaluation represented an environmentally objective perspective in terms of material and physical well-being, involving categories such as mobility, leisure and recreation, employment, food, clothing, and lodging. However, people may be satisfied with the quality of their life based on their own perspective.

In terms of methodology, the positivistic researchers of quality of life may often be described as "objectivist," emphasizing the objective status of knowledge of quality of life as independent of the observer. On the other hand, interpretivist researchers may be described as "subjectivist," emphasizing the subjective understandings of the actor as a basis for interpreting quality-of-life reality. In such a sense, objectivist researchers tend to exclude the qualitative variables and neglect the nonexpert perceptions, while subjectivist researchers tend to appreciate subjective feelings and personal experience about quality of life. Contemporary Taiwanese investigators tend to be subjectivist in their approach.

Approach: Elite-Based Versus Mass-Based

There are two perspectives of social, quality-of-life research: (a) social-indicators research, which considers the elites' valuation of what the people need so as to attain a better quality of life, and (b) conventional quality-of-life research, which is meant to ascertain what the people want in order to improve their quality of life (Mukherjee, 1989). The two approaches are normally considered separately. The need-based, or so called elite-based, perspective on quality of life commonly assumes a uniform valuation of social reality and considers the people's valuations of want-based, or mass-based, quality of life subsidiary. A need is a necessity for survival, whereas a want is a desire for something (Johnson & Johnson, 1991). Whereas each person basically has a unique set of wants, needs are more universal.

The elitist perspective is enforced directly by the elite in a nation or in the global context. They view the concerned social space from the top and wish to learn what the people need in order to attain a better quality of life. Therefore, they induce, or make use of, experts to provide the necessary knowledge. According to Mukherjee (1989), experts may differ among themselves in defining and projecting the needs of the people, but they assume a group character in appraising social reality for a better quality of life. The quality-of-life indicators formulated by the elite to meet the needs of the people are so-called objective social indicators (Mukherjee). Thus, in analogous or homologous group formation, the experts register commonality in their evaluation of quality of life.

The elite approach has been adopted by the Taiwanese government to evaluate current quality of life of people on Taiwan. The mass perspective, examining valuations of a better quality of life made by the masses, is preferred by Taiwanese academic researchers.

Entitlements: Egoism Versus Universalism

Philosophically and metaphorically, egoism refers to the view that one should seek as an end only one's own welfare. Universalism refers to the view that each individual should seek as an end the welfare of all. The people who believe in egoism in quality of life argue that quality of life can be a matter of individual choice. On the contrary, people supporting universal entitlements contend that each individual is entitled to minimal quality of life.

Currently, the spirit of egoism is cherished more by most Taiwanese investigators and individuals with disabilities. If one believes that quality of life is a matter of individual choice, it seems that a subjective approach is more appropriate, assuming that the ability to choose is available to everyone. However, for those who may find it difficult to conceptualize alternatives in order to make choices, the assumption seems questionable. It may be necessary to teach people how to choose. Further, the egoism of entitlement may be difficult to attain, as only governments can guarantee such basic necessities as food, clothing, and shelter to an entire population. Nevertheless, most Taiwanese caregivers, social workers, and policy makers for individuals with disabilities argue that everyone is entitled to some minimum quality of life (Lin, 1995b). This involves the equality of access to resources and the development of political policy.

Interventions: Individualism Versus Collectivism

The final area of philosophical and theoretical quality-of-life debate in Taiwan today relates to potential uses for quality-of-life information: There are two approaches: (a) personal and (b) social intervention for groups. Individualism in this context refers to the doctrine that the interests or quality of life of the individual should take precedence over the interests of the agency or social group. Collectivism, in contrast, refers to principles or systems of ownership and control of the means of production and distribution by the people collectively to pursue quality of life for a community. Even though the Confucian Golden Mean has long been embedded in Chinese culture, collectivism has dominated the disability culture of Taiwan. Individualism, on the other hand, is appreciated more by families of individuals with disabilities who advocate self-determination and self-independence.

The Ecological Multidimensional Quality-of-Life Domain

Based on the philosophical and theoretical issues of quality of life just discussed, the construct of quality of life seems not to be easily identified empirically and philosophically. Even though quality-of-life research in disability has been conducted for several decades in Taiwan, so far the parameters of quality of life have not been clearly specified (Lin, 1996). The initiation of quality-of-life constructs by different investigators, from different perspectives, different approaches, different times, and in different settings could all affect the content of quality of life. It seems that quality of life is culturally specific and should take into account ecological influences.

In Taiwan, Confucianism and family stability have been two enduring features embedded in quality of life (Chen & Chung, 1994; Chen et al., 1991). For people with disabilities especially, the family is a key determinant of healthy psychosocial adjustment and could be one of the primary influences of quality of life for Chinese with disabilities. According to Smith (1992), the Taiwanese family has developed strengths for coping effectively with the crises that all families may confront (e.g., disability, divorce, poverty) in order to maintain a certain quality of life. These specific strengths have contributed to the survival of individuals with disabilities and their families in Taiwan amid psychological, environmental, and economic stressors (e.g., substandard housing, poor traffic conditions, high crime rates) that adversely affect their quality of life.

Based on these cultural and ecological characteristics in Taiwan, an ecological multidimensional quality-of-life model has been proposed by Lin (1996) to emphasize that Taiwanese with disabilities and their families have the potential cultural and family resources needed to succeed in rehabilitation and transition and thereby improve their quality of life. The model has several central and practical factors (or "domains") contributing to one's perceived quality of life: physical and material well-being, psychological and emotional well-being, adult performance/independence, and family and community. These quality-of-life domains basically were constructed according to previous empirical studies in Western countries (e.g., Goode, 1990; Halpern, 1993; Lin, 1995a; Parmenter, 1988, 1992; Schalock, 1990). Figure 18.1 depicts these domains.

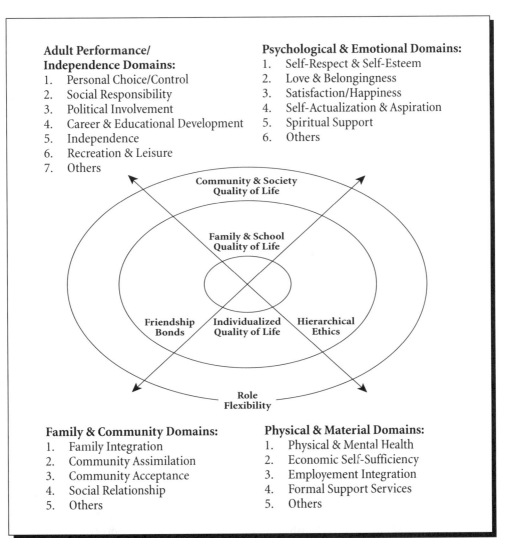

Adult Performance/ Independence Domains:
1. Personal Choice/Control
2. Social Responsibility
3. Political Involvement
4. Career & Educational Development
5. Independence
6. Recreation & Leisure
7. Others

Psychological & Emotional Domains:
1. Self-Respect & Self-Esteem
2. Love & Belongingness
3. Satisfaction/Happiness
4. Self-Actualization & Aspiration
5. Spiritual Support
6. Others

Community & Society
Quality of Life

Family & School
Quality of Life

Friendship
Bonds

Individualized
Quality of Life

Hierarchical
Ethics

Role
Flexibility

Family & Community Domains:
1. Family Integration
2. Community Assimilation
3. Community Acceptance
4. Social Relationship
5. Others

Physical & Material Domains:
1. Physical & Mental Health
2. Economic Self-Sufficiency
3. Employment Integration
4. Formal Support Services
5. Others

Figure 18.1. Dynamic quality-of-life domains in transition for youth with disabilities.

The model regards the Taiwanese-Chinese strengths of kinship bonds, role flexibility, and hierarchical ethics as particularly useful means for individual and family adaptation to better quality of life when one member experiences a disabling condition. Consequently, the model emphasizes the inclusion of the strengths in the rehabilitation and transition process. The Taiwanese-Chinese family structure usually consists of the nuclear, extended, and external family. In this model, the Taiwanese-Chinese individual with disabilities is depicted as insulated by both the nuclear and extended family. The external environment consists of those extrafamilial systems, such as the local school, church, temple, or community organizations.

Physical and Material Well-Being

This domain includes basic elements, such as food, clothing, housing, and sex life that should be available to all human beings. Even though physical and material well-being are often viewed as basic entitlements in the history of human beings' development, researchers have not agreed on what should be the minimal elements or conditions for experiencing an acceptable and reasonable quality of life. For instance, Halpern (1993) has proposed four basic outcomes that should cluster into this domain, including: (a) physical and mental health; (b) food, clothing, and lodging; (c) financial security; and (d) safety from harm. Flanagan (1978) also identified physical well-being as a primary component of quality of life. Even though different terms have been used to determine physical and material well-being, the descriptions and connotation of these terms are quite similar. There is no doubt that physical and material well-being constitute one of the multidimensional constructs, even though agreement on the subdomains of this element has not yet been achieved.

Psychological and Emotional Well-Being

This domain of quality of life is entirely person-centered and subjective from person to person. Psychological and emotional well-being reflects an individual's affective dimension, including how a person feels and experiences life. Happiness, satisfaction, and a sense of general well-being are the content areas mentioned by researchers. Contrary to what one might expect, if there is congruence between person and environment, even if the environment is substandard, the individual will experience a high state of quality of life. In Taiwan the concept of psychological and emotional well-being is strongly influenced by Confucian humanism. A spiritual and natural quality of life is much more appreciated by Taiwanese-Chinese than is materialistic quality of life.

Adult Performance or Independence Domain

The independence domain reflects an individual's "performance of adult roles" in society or independent interaction with his or her environment in a society. Eight outcomes have been identified by Halpern (1993) in his terms of performance of adult roles that seem to fit well into this domain: (a) mobility and community access; (b) vocation, career, and employment; (c) leisure and recreation; (d) personal relationships and social networks; (e) educational attainment; (f) spiritual fulfillment; (g) citizenship; and (h) social responsibility. Each of these subdomains presents opportunities for enhancing quality of life, and yet it is not essential that each person participate at similar levels of involvement within each role. Campbell (1981) also identified the following factors that related to the social, economic, and political components: education, marriage, family life, friendship, health, standard of living, the country, neighborhood, residence, and work. As Lippman (1976) suggested, such measures provided a set of indicators that could be applied to community settings, both locally and cross-culturally. Thus, this domain could also be applied to Taiwan.

Family and Community Domain or Context

This domain consists of at least four components: (a) family integration, (b) community assimilation, (c) community acceptance, and (d) social relationship. This specific domain was psychometrically found in Gossett's (1989) clustering of his Quality-of-Life Scale under the subscales of (a) choices or independent functioning and (b) friendships and relationships. By using the same procedure of principal component factor analysis, Schalock, Keith, Hoffman, and Karan (1989) also found a similar construct domain related to family and community. They grouped items composing the qualify-of-life factor scores into three factors: (a) environmental control, (b) community involvement, and (c) social relations. Similarly, these factors focused more on the relationship with others and the community. In this model, family integration emphasizes strengths of kinship bonds, role flexibility, and strong education and work ethics in Taiwanese-Chinese culture.

Recommendations and Implications

Special education in Taiwan has made great progress during the 20th century with the establishment of special schools for special-education populations. Special-education classes have been held in numerous regular schools in the country for years. There are two major types of care facilities for special populations—the medical-clinical facilities and the educational foundations. Major hospitals and counseling centers provide clinical services to special populations. Most of the facilities offer a range of service from medical diagnosis to rehabilitation, and some facilities provide counseling for individual clients, while others provide counseling services for the family. Most of the facilities are located in the city of Taipei, which creates difficulties for those in other parts of the country. Although there are a few facilities in other cities such as Tainan, Kaohsiung, and Taichung, the services are not comprehensive, and the efforts are scattered (Chen et al., 1991).

Barriers to service access are numerous and extremely difficult for families to overcome. These barriers to service delivery for special populations include: (a) scarcity of service agencies, (b) scarcity of trained service providers, (c) lack of coordinated services, (d) lack of public information, (e) cost of services, (f) lack of follow-up, and (g) the long distance one needs to travel for services (Chen et al., 1991). However, many organizations are designed to improve services for special populations. For example, the Taiwan Association for People With Mental Retardation, Taiwan Association for the Deaf, Taiwan Association for the Blind, and Taipei Association for the Deaf all provide services to designated groups. Nonprofit foun-

211

dations, such as Shuang Chi Foundation for Children With Mental Retardation, Yang Kuang Foundation, and others, also promote services for special populations. However, these organizations have small memberships and generally serve a small portion of those needing services. The foundations are few in number and have limited financial resources. Although these organizations provide an important base, more public and private services need to developed.

Considering philosophical and theoretical issues, along with the Taiwanese-Chinese cultural influence and the condition of special education concerning quality of life, it seems clear that there is an urgent need to evaluate more carefully and develop quality of life in Taiwan. To this end, several recommendations are offered concerning the implications of these findings based on the theoretical, methodological, and measurement perspectives for policy makers, service providers, and researchers.

Theoretical Implications

Even though quality of life is not a revolutionary idea, as Knoll (1990) pointed out, by definition, assessing one's quality of life is a process that transcends empiricism. This process ultimately appeals to the fundamental values of an individual, a group, or a society. The theoretical issues, such as subjectivism versus objectivism in measurement, elitism versus massism in research approach, egoism versus universalism in entitlements, and individualism versus collectivism in intervention strategies, seem to complicate the operational definition, scientific measurement, and practical improvement of quality of life for individuals with disabilities. Obviously, continuous philosophical consideration and empirical research on these issues are required. The following implications and suggestions seem appropriate at this time for subsequent work on the concept of quality of life in Taiwan.

All Entitled. *All human beings should be entitled to quality of life.* Despite the unclear definition of quality of life from academic society and the philosophical and theoretical differences discussed above, quality of life, like the basic needs (e.g., food, clothing, housing, safety), should be an entitlement for all human beings. Both Eastern and Western societies have long offered (indirectly or directly) certain rights to their citizens, even though, historically, quality of life was not viewed as a requirement for every person. But now it is recognized that all members of the human species, regardless of color, race, gender, age, disability, and so forth, are entitled to have a good quality of life.

Development Needed. Multiple and flexible models of quality-of-life approaches need to be developed. Undoubtedly, the quality-of-life construct or model must be not only adaptable to different client levels and programs, but also flexible enough to fit the needs of different cultural settings. From a societal perspective, for example, social norms perhaps are the most meaningful frame of quality-of-life reference. Social norms could be used to identify socially desirable goals for groups of people. And yet conformity with such norms may not be appropriate for any given individual within the norm group. Cultural influences and the context in which the individual acts should be considered to determine their effect on the individual. As previously noted, quality of life is specific to life settings (Goode, 1990). Thus the quality-of-life model should be multiple, flexible, and sensitive to different circumstances, such as distinct society and culture or different residential settings.

Translation Into Policies and Practices. *The concepts of quality of life should be translated into policies and practices.* No matter which approach is adopted, elitism or massism, quality-of-life research had better be practical. As Emerson (1985) has noted, the major use of research on quality of life is symbolic (i.e., using data nonfunctionally to justify predetermined positions). Due to the lack of social validity, quality-of-life research usually fulfills, in Goode's term, rhetorical, political, and professional purposes, but does not help people with disabilities achieve a better quality of life (1990, p. 5). Contemporary social policies in Taiwan have been enshrined in legislation that underpins the way services to people with disabilities are funded and evaluated. There is a need, however, for research to question the way those policies are being articulated in practice. Quality-of-life research provides a framework of concepts, orientations, and generalizations that can inform policy, identify problems and potential solutions, and set the agenda for future policy formulations. As this type of knowledge is accumulated through social validation research, appropriate recommendations should emerge concerning desirable changes in public policy and program development.

Methodological Implications

Considering the methodological issues (i.e., qualitative versus quantitative, subjective versus objective) concerning quality of life, it is clear that the challenges proposed by Landesman (1986) in defining the construct of quality of life still exist. Both qualitative and quantitative research have philosophical foundations, characteristics, and techniques that make them ideally suited for the exploration of some questions and inadequate for the investigation of others. However, the complex methodological philosophy behind qualitative and quantitative approaches and the ongoing debate between quantitative and qualitative researchers (e.g., Guba & Lincoln, 1989) still make research design difficult. Even so, the following recommendations seem to be useful in considering the use of specific methodologies as we continue to research the concept of quality of life in Taiwan.

Holistic Design. *The adoption of a specific methodology or design should be more holistic and balanced in dealing with the diverse and multidimensional aspects of quality of life.* Multiple and holistic methods may be needed to adequately assess the quality of life for individuals with disabilities. Using critical science methodology could be a viable option, because critical theory offers a multidisciplinary approach to society that combines perspectives drawn from political economy, sociology, cultural theory, philosophy, anthropology, and history (Carr & Kemmis, 1986); it overcomes the fragmentation endemic to established academic disciplines and addresses issues of broad interest. As critical theorists (e.g., Kellner, 1989; Raymond, 1994) point out, critical theory is not only an antidote to the frequently noncritical quantitative approaches within contemporary social science, but also provides a potentially more useful and politically relevant alternative than currently fashionable approaches, such as existentialism and phenomenology, poststructuralism, and postmodernism, and various versions of humanist idealism that are periodically recycled and repackaged.

Nontraditional Research Techniques. *Nontraditional research techniques that allow for rich description of context and process such as qualitative approaches should be considered for further research, as quality of life is a deeply personal and individual construct.* The nontraditional approaches are useful for documenting life outcomes both for the individual and agencies that offer services. For example, qualitative methods could provide better measures for assessing lifestyle satisfaction, independence, and anticipated service needs. As Goode (1990) has urged, researchers should place more emphasis on observational methods that may better portray the richness of the relationships a person forms with others in his or her environment than on carefully validated and reliable scientific instruments, the content of which may not be a sufficient reflection of an individual's subjective experience and "actual" or "real" social identity.

Longitudinal Designs. *The use of longitudinal designs should be taken into consideration, because outcomes associated with quality of life do not necessarily occur during or shortly after participation in a quality-of-life improvement program.* Many cross-sectional and conventional research designs are not sensitive to the true outcomes of the programs. Longitudinal designs that follow cohorts of individuals throughout a program and for several years into adult life seem most effective for this type of study (Halpern, 1990; Edgerton, 1990). They could help identify quality-of-life trends and patterns, attitudes, psychological experiences, effects of related policy and programs, and other objective quality-of-life outcomes of the past, present, and future. Applying longitudinal designs would be beneficial in examining quality-of-life factors and their relationships, transitional patterns, quality-of-life construct structure, and the causal-effect structure of quality of life.

Measurement Implications

No matter what the specific methodology, developing any reliable and valid quality-of-life measure requires considerable effort toward having a fuller understanding of the lives of individuals with disabilities. Obviously, with the development of quality of life as an all-inclusive notion, future research should include new evaluation inputs, from an exclusively quantitative and assumedly objective base to an increasingly complex blend of quantity and quality of objective behavioral and subjective perceptual variables (Mukherjee, 1989). Thus, in Taiwan, the following suggestions and implications concerning measurement seem appropriate and timely.

Objective and Subjective Outcomes. *The measurement of individual quality of life should evenly comprise both objective and subjective outcomes.* As Goode (1988) suggested, professionals and researchers must get much closer to the people they are studying, and the collection of either objective or subjective data should truly reflect the quality of life of a person's "actual" self. It is possible that a person's subjective sense of well-being may have a greater influence than objective factors on his or her quality of life (Lin, 1995a). Even though in Taiwan the cultural and ecological conditions have potential effects on quality of life of individuals with disabilities, the possibility should not be excluded that a person's subjective sense of well-being may derive more from individual attributes than from the impact of environment.

Theme Oriented. *The measurement of quality of life should be theme oriented.* Based on the literature presented, it seems the multidimensional and multivariate approach to quality-of-life research has a greater promise of capturing the complex nature of quality of life. There is evidence to suggest that well-being or quality of life may be domain specific; that is, psychological well-being may be quite different from occupational or economic well-being and from adult-independence well-being (Lin, 1995a). The development of quality-of-life measures should also reflect this concern and establish multiple indexes to examine the quality of life of individuals with disabilities.

Better Indicators. *It might be valuable to develop better indicators to more comprehensively and extensively examine the quality of life for individuals with disabilities.* The concept of quality of life is evolving; the narrow scope of indicators of quality of life used to extract the factors in past studies could be a serious drawback to the validity of these dimensions. In the future, it would be valuable to develop better indicators by using multivariate and multidimensional measurement to describe the many and varied aspects of quality of life.

Genuine Picture. *In their design of studies, researchers should be guided by the multidimensional and codetermined nature of environments—to seek a genuine picture of the degree of quality of life of people with disabilities.* Too often the superficial elements of quality-of-life living have been the focus of attention. As important as changes in the physical environment, residents' adaptive behavior, or provision of activities for daily living might be, there are more critical aspects that relate to quality-of-life outcomes (e.g., client satisfaction, happiness, family interaction, social and interpersonal relationships, activity patterns, degree of self-determination, social-economic factors, cultural influences, and access to community services). As complex as they might be to identify and measure, quality-of-life outcomes that reflect a person's interaction with his or her environment are a more valid index of the success of quality-of-life programs. Therefore, in their measurement researchers should be directed by the multidimensional and codetermined nature of ecology, so as to have a more authentic description of quality of life of individuals with disabilities.

Summary

It is apparent that gaining and using knowledge regarding quality of life for people with disabilities in Taiwan will never be an easy, uncomplicated, or value-free endeavor. Such knowledge is best derived over time not only from people with disabilities and familiar others, but also from service providers and researchers and the environmental context. We need to continually accumulate and update this knowledge to reflect changes in needs and contexts. Individuals with disabilities, familiar others, service providers, and researchers should work together to identify important quality-of-life themes that can serve as a basis and context from which to plan and evaluate programs and services. Quality policies and services developed in this context should also provide options to people to pursue their own unique quality of life and simultaneously respect the people's choice concerning their quality of life.

There is no doubt that continued research and discussion on quality-of-life issues are needed to ensure that quality-of-life concepts are socially validated in Taiwan and incorporated appropriately into planning and evaluation of services for people with disabilities. Even though philosophers and researchers cannot agree on the definition of quality of life for individuals or methodologies for studying it, undoubtedly this lack of agreement has little impact on people with and without disabilities pursuing a better quality of life and thinking about how various factors will affect it. The pursuit of quality of life by people with disabilities is no less complex than that pursuit has been for all people throughout the ages in the world. In theory, to better understand the construct of quality of life, it seems that we should avoid stereotypical assumptions about the experience and cultural values of others.

It appears that we should approach quality-of-life issues with an attitude of openness and respect for the values and needs of each individual with disabilities. In practice, to effectively affect the outcomes of program planning, it seems that the theme of quality of life should provide a context for the planning process itself. In measurement, it seems that the inquiry for an empirical definition that includes both subjective and objective outcomes of quality of life in the field of disabilities currently receives the greatest notice. In methodology, a variety of research paradigms and methods probably are needed to capture the diversity of experiences associated with the constructs of quality of life. These research perspectives should embrace a continuum of strategies that involve normative descriptions and multivariate, qualitative, and even experimental perspectives. Of critical importance to the multivariate perspectives are studies that use the indicators of validated dimensions in attempts to develop and empirically test theoretical models of quality of life.

References

Campbell, A. (1981). *The sense of well-being in America*. New York: McGraw-Hill.

Carr, W., & Kemmis, S. (1986). *Becoming critical: Education, knowledge and action research*. Philadelphia: Falmer.

Chang, Y. P. (1994). Evaluation on the life quality of people with mental retardation. *Special Education Quarterly, 51*, 29-33.

Chen, G. M., & Chung, J. (1994). The impact of Confucianism on organizational communication. *Communication Quarterly, 42*(2), 93-105.

Chen, Y. H., Sietz, M. R., & Cheng, L. L. (1991). Special education. In D. C. Smith (Ed.), *The Confucian continuum: Educational modernization in Taiwan* (pp. 317-365). New York: Praeger.

Edgerton, R. B. (1990). Quality of life from a longitudinal research perspective. In R. L. Schalock (Ed.), *Quality of life: Perspectives and issues* (pp. 149-160). Washington, DC: American Association on Mental Retardation.

Emerson, E. R. (1985). Evaluating the impact of deinstitutionalization on the lives of mentally retarded people. *American Journal of Mental Deficiency, 90*(3), 277-288.

Flanagan, J. C. (1978). A research approach to improving our quality of life. *American Psychologist, 33,* 138-147.

Goode, D. A. (1988). *Quality of life for persons with disabilities: A look at the issues.* Final report for a conference held in Washington, DC, April 30-May 1, 1988. Valhalla, NY: The Mental Retardation Institute, Westchester County Medical Center and New York Medical College.

Goode, D. (1990). Thinking about and discussing quality of life. In R. Schalock (Ed.), *Quality of life: Perspectives and issues* (pp. 41-58). Washington, DC: American Association on Mental Retardation.

Gossett, K. D. (1989). *Measuring and managing quality of life in human service organizations.* Unpublished doctoral dissertation, University of Minnesota, Minneapolis.

Guba, E., & Lincoln, Y. (1989). *Fourth generation evaluation.* Newbury Park, CA: Sage.

Halpern, A. S. (1990). A methodological review of follow-up and follow-along studies tracking school leavers from special education. *Career Development for Exceptional Individuals, 13,* 13-27.

Halpern, A. S. (1993). Quality of life as a conceptual framework for evaluating transition outcomes. *Exceptional Children, 59,* 486-498.

Johnson, D. W., & Johnson, R. T. (1991). *Teaching students to be peacemakers.* Edina, MN: Interaction Book.

Kellner, D. (1989). *Critical theory, Marxism, and modernity.* Baltimore: Johns Hopkins University Press.

Knoll, J. A. (1990). Defining quality in residential services. In V. J. Bradley & H. A. Bersani (Eds.), *Quality assurance for individuals with developmental disabilities. It's everybody's business* (pp. 235-261). Baltimore: Paul H. Brookes.

Ku, H. M. (1976). *The discourses and sayings of Confucius: A new special translation, illustrated with quotations from Goethe and other writers.* Taipei: Shean-Chue.

Landesman, S. (1986). Quality of life and personal satisfaction: Definition and measurement issues. *Mental Retardation, 24*(3), 141-143.

Legge, J. (1977). *The original Chinese texts of the Confucian Analects, the Great Learning, the Doctrine of the Mean, the Works of Mencius, & the Work of Lao-Tsze.* Taipei: East Asia.

Lin, H. C. (1995a). *Factors affecting quality-of-life outcomes for youth with severe disabilities in transition from youth to adulthood: A path analytic model of a national sample.* Unpublished dissertation, University of Minnesota, Minneapolis.

Lin, H. C. (1995b). Quality of life of individuals with disabilities: Issues and perspectives, *Proceedings of the 1995 Annual Convention of the Taiwan Special Education Association on Instruction and Research* (pp. 449-496). Taipei: Taiwan Special Education Association.

Lin, H. C. (1996). An analysis of the dimensions of quality of life for youth with severe disabilities in transition. *Journal of Special Education, 11,* 79-108.

Lippman, L. (1976). Indicators of societal concern for mentally retarded persons. *Social Indicators Research, 3,* 181-215.

Mukherjee, R. (1989). *The quality of life valuation in social research.* Newbury Park, CA: Sage.

Parmenter, T. R. (1988). An analysis of the dimensions of quality of life for people with physical disabilities. In R. I. Brown (Ed.), *Quality of life for handicapped people: A series in rehabilitation education* (pp. 7-36). London: Croom Helm.

Parmenter, T. (1992). Quality of life of people with developmental disabilities. In N. Bray (Ed.), *International review of research in mental retardation, Vol. 18* (pp. 247-287). New York: Academic Press.

Raymond, M. A. (1994). Critical theory, poststructuralism, and critical realism: Reassessing the critiques of positivism. *Current Perspectives in Social Theory, 14,* 27-51.

Rosen, M. (1986). Quality of life for persons with mental retardation: A question of entitlement. *Mental Retardation, 24,* 365-366.

Schalock, R. (Ed). (1990). *Quality of life: Perspectives and issues.* Washington, DC: American Association on Mental Retardation.

Schalock, R. L., Keith, K. D., Hoffman, K., & Karan, O. C. (1989). Quality of life: Its measurement and use. *Mental Retardation, 27*(1), 25-31.

Smith, D. C. (Ed.). (1991). *The Confucian continuum: Educational modernization in Taiwan.* New York: Praeger.

Smith, D. C. (1992, Spring). *The Chinese family in transition: Implications for education and society in modern Taiwan.* Paper presented at the Comparative Education Association, World Bank Seminar, Annapolis, MD.

Sun, S. J. (1997). The future of measuring quality of life of individuals with mental retardation: The feasibility of qualitative research. *Special Education Quarterly, 62,* 10-15.

People With Disabilities in Russia: Progress and Prospects

Judy Smith-Davis
The Council for Exceptional Children
Reston, Virginia, United States

In Western parlance, Russia and the former Soviet Union were often interchangeable. Even now, people from various former U.S.S.R. countries may be erroneously described as Russians—particularly immigrant Russian-speaking school children. Whereas some policies and conditions prevailed across all of these countries, cultural history and developments over the past several years have diverged. This chapter addresses Russia alone, with reference to new guarantees for human rights and educational rights of individuals with disabilities; health and material well-being; and initiatives for less restrictiveness in the education of students with disabilities.

For several reasons, St. Petersburg is a focus of the discussion on school and community inclusion. Although I have been to various places in Russia, I am most familiar with activities in St. Petersburg and believe that this city is ahead of the rest of the country in collective action and could become a replicable model for Russia.

Human Rights and Public Consciousness

In 1990 a declaration of sovereignty created the independent Russian Republic. In December 1993, Russia's "Second Republic" began with the adoption of a constitution (following the standoff between President Yeltsin and the Russian legislative body in September-October of that year).

> Article 2 of the 1993 constitution describes human rights as the supreme value of both the constitution and the Russian state. Articles 17 through 64 elaborate on this theme, outlining the myriad rights guaranteed under the constitution and making human rights the most prominent theme addressed therein. Protected under the constitution, among others, are the right to equality, to life, to human dignity, to freedom and human inviolability, to privacy, and to one's choice of nation and language. Freedom of movement and speech are secured, as are freedom from torture and the right to property, housing, health, education, and legal assistance. (Adhieh, 1997, p. 173)

Special-Education Legislation

The Federal Law on Education of Persons With Disabilities of the Russian Federation was approved by both legislative chambers and signed by President Yeltsin in 1995. Chapter II, Article 7, Item 1 states that "disabled persons are entitled to enjoy to the maximum extent of feasibility the same rights as the persons who do not have disabilities."Among the educational rights accorded to individuals with disabilities are: (a) free examinations and assessments; (b) free medical-psycho-pedagogical remediation of physical and/or mental disability from the moment of its identification, irrespective of its complexity; (c) preschool education from the age of 3, and general elementary and basic secondary education from the age of 7 to 8, in less restrictive educational environment, in accordance with psycho-medical-pedagogical findings and the individual education program; (d) "education at any level at a special-education institution, integrated educational institution, special-education unit of regular education institution, or at a regular education institution in accordance with psycho-pedagogical and medical indications"; (e) free education at any type of educational institutions within the state educational standards (including special-education standards); (f) provision of transportation, according to social and medical recommendations, to get disabled individuals to the nearest corresponding educational institution; (g) upon graduation, labor opportunities corresponding to the obtained education and/or vocational training in accordance with this and other legislation concerning employment (Chapter II, Article 7, Item 2). Article 8 specifies parents' rights that are similar to basic parental rights in United States law.

This legislation is a great step forward for children and youth with disabilities and their families. It is important to understand, however, that the compliance with law in Russia is not altogether uniform across the regions and provinces and that putting the law into practice is likely to be a gradual, and sometimes erratic, process over time.

Public Consciousness of Rights

During the early 1990s, the upper chamber of Russia's parliamentary body established a Human Rights Committee, and President Yeltsin created a Human Rights Commission. Both were headed by Sergei Kovalov, until his resignation over human rights violations in the first Chechnyan war. In a 1993 interview, Kovalov indicated that public consciousness had not shifted from a sense of rights that are granted by the state to a sense of inalienable rights held by the individual; thus rights consciousness is extremely weak (Adhieh, 1997).

Public memory of, or yearning for, an omnipotent state as the source of all things has not evaporated. In the centralized command system of the Soviet Union, the state regulated and provided for basic human needs, repressing individual incentive and creating passive attitudes that take time to change. The Soviet Union's system also intertwined the worksite, housing, health and social services, and schools, both economically and administratively, in ways that are difficult to dismantle without dislocation and loss among large segments of the population. These attitudinal and socioeconomic legacies are important to understand the status and progress of individuals with disabilities in the late 20th century.

Quality of Life

Ecological and Health Problems

Feshbach and Friendly (1992) published a scholarly compilation of data on the environmental degradation, and resulting health effects, brought about by exploitation and neglect in the former regime. This devastation includes: pollution of rivers and toxic drinking water supplies in many areas (including cities such as St. Petersburg); 10 times the maximum permissible concentration of harmful substances in the air in at least 125 towns and cities; soil contamination so extensive that "there exist 14 natural, permanent breeding grounds for plague ... (with) the potential for infecting a total area of 512 million acres" (p. 201); and occupational diseases caused by harmful conditions in the workplace.

The following are just a few of the sequelae cited by these authors. These data help to clarify some causes of disability and also demonstrate the additional health risks that individuals with disabilities face.

- Average life expectancy is age 62.

- Every fourth adult and every sixth child is chronically ill.

- Nearly three fourths of pregnant women have pathologies during pregnancy because of poor nutrition and poor health conditions.

- The infant mortality rate is 20 deaths per 1,000 live births and rising.

- Sixty percent of children are not born healthy, and 25% develop anemia or rickets in their first 5 years.

Speaking in 1995, the (then) Russian minister of education supplied further detail on the incidence of disabilities among children and youth. Although the damaged environment is not the only source of these conditions, it contributes prominently.

> Only 14% of Russian children are considered to be practically healthy, 45% suffer from chronic diseases....Eighty percent of children entering the first form in primary school possess different health deviations, from functional to chronic diseases....Among children attending the mass school, 4 to 12% are suffering from neurosis, approximately 8% are with learning disabilities; these numbers increase two times with children attending boarding schools; as to children living in orphanages, 90 to 96% suffer from psychic disabilities of different levels of complexity. The number of handicapped and mentally retarded children is constantly growing. Even the number of children with physical and mental disabilities attending Moscow schools is close to 20%. (Tkaveshenko, 1995, pp. 4-5)

Although some ecological problems are more pronounced in remote areas than in cities, the reverse is more likely, because industrial and automotive toxins are greater in metropolitan locations. For example, according to 1990 data, "congenitally deformed children were being born in the Soviet capital 'one and a half times more often' on average than in the U.S.S.R. as a whole. With infant mortality rates running 'two to three times higher' in Moscow than in other republic capitals, as of 1989 'more inhabitants . . . died than were born'" (Feshbach & Friendly, 1992, p. 9). Among the 87 "secret cities" of the former Soviet Union (where chemical and biological weapons were made, nuclear tests were conducted, and toxic wastes were dumped), it is believed that the incidence of congenital birth defects is elevated by 30% to 40%.

Moreover, there are the victims of the nuclear accident in Chernobyl, near Kiev in Ukraine. Radiation from Chernobyl has affected parts of Russia, but has had its greatest impact on Belarus, where 800,000 children have been directly affected by radioactivity, with all of the infant population being affected in some way (Feshbach & Friendly, 1992). Although most of the vulnerable children in affected areas of Russia are not yet regarded as ill, the Ministry of Education has developed an interagency program to study the impact of radioactivity on child development, including education.

The ecological crisis is so widespread and so extreme as to require many years and many billions of dollar value to correct it—all in the face of serious economic limitations. There is, however, growing public support and agitation for cleaning up the environment and stopping the military, industrial, automotive, and other causes of the Russian "ecocide."

Health Care
The socialized system of health care in the former Soviet Union lagged behind that of more advanced countries by about 40 years. Improvements have been occurring slowly, particularly through Western cooperation. On the other hand, there has been a flight of medical, health, social service, and many other types of professionals to other countries and into private business ventures in Russia, because most of their salaries are little higher than the official minimum subsistence level. As Feshbach and Friendly (1992) point out, medical facilities are poorly equipped, lack many medications commonly available in the West, and are less than adequately staffed; sanitary conditions also give cause for concern. Because of well-grounded fears about unsafe vaccines and unsterilized needles and syringes, many parents no longer have their children immunized. Nearly half of rural hospitals have no sewer connections and 80% have no hot water (and limitations of hot water occur even in Moscow hospitals).

Lack of faith in the healthcare system has led to decreases in the numbers of people who seek medical assistance, particularly hospitalization. "Against the background of unwillingness to seek medical advice, the incidence of cancer, contagious and other types of disease (is) shown to have become more frequent. . . . In many respects, this is due to the lack of emphasis on preventive health care within the public health care system" (Glukhovyets, 1994, p. 148). In early 1996 St. Petersburg became Russia's pilot city for a medical insurance program with features similar to the American health maintenance organization model. The impact of this pilot program on the quality of health care, preventive services, and public trust in medicine remains to be seen.

Material Well-Being

The 1990s have been marked by political, social, and economic instability as Russia moves to an open market and a different form of government. Between 1991 and 1995, inflation increased almost daily. Between September 1991 and late 1995, the value of the ruble declined from 35 to the dollar (U.S.) to 4,900 to the dollar. Then ruble value was held fairly steady until the economic crisis of summer 1998 after which there were further fluctuations. In the meantime people's life savings have become worthless, as have the monthly "pensions" historically paid to retirees and individuals with disabilities, and incomes have not nearly matched the rising cost of living. In Moscow, which has become the most expensive city in the world, a ministry official may earn the equivalent of $250 per month, for example. Teachers' salaries are much lower, and nearly everyone is scrambling for any source of supplementary income that can be found.

"The plight of the individual Russian is especially discouraging, with prices continuing to rise, wealth being distributed inequitably, corruption and profiteering growing rampant, and the social safety net falling into tatters" (Adhieh, 1997, p. 180). The early results of privatization and open markets have led to a society of a few "haves" at top income levels and great wealth, and a majority who are "have nots." Across the country as a whole, it has been estimated that 20% of the Russian population lives below the official minimum subsistence level (Adhieh), and there is no doubt that people with disabilities are largely in this category.

Debilitating poverty is more pervasive in cities than in the countryside. In St. Petersburg, "in 1991, the proportion of the population with income below the minimum subsistence level was 11.7%; by the end of 1992 it had increased to almost 30%. Some scientific measures put the 1994 figure at above 50%, of which 14% will be living below the minimum physical survival level" (Dyskin, Navrotskaya, & Nikiforov, 1994, p. 69). Further, for several years there have been delays of up to 6 months in payments of salaries and pensions across Russia. As of February 1997, the Russian government owed $7 billion in unpaid late salaries, $2.7 billion in unpaid late pensions, and more than $10 billion in late payments to government contractors (Cohen, 1997).

In late 1993, St. Petersburg's Scientific Research Institute on Work Capability and its Organization of Labor for the Disabled surveyed a representative sample of families to derive data on individuals with disabilities and retirees (Dyskin et al., 1994). The following findings pertain to individuals with disabilities of working age (and the cost of living has increased markedly since 1993):

- 18.8% were working.

- Only 49.1% had an income greater than the sum of two minimum pensions.

- 10.9% received an income equal to, or less than, the minimum pension and are "patently in need of social assistance" (p. 171).

- Individuals with disabilities of working age were primarily living with parents or other relatives.

- In 23% of families of working-aged individuals with disabilities, the monthly expenditure on food by a single family member amounted to 1.08 times the minimum pension; 1.08 to 2.16 times the minimum pension was spent on food by 21.5% of families of individuals with disabilities in all age groups, with 15% to 25% of these families spending even more.

- Two thirds of the entire sample, including people with disabilities and old-age pensioners, were in need of footwear, half needed outer clothing, and more than one third reported needing underwear and bedclothes.

During the 1980s and earlier, the government secured employment for some people with disabilities, often such work as painting toys and souvenirs at home, but also in vocations and professions. Postsecondary vocational-technical education of good quality has been available for students with disabilities in the larger cities, and computer training has led to good jobs for some graduates. Some individuals with disabilities also attend college. By and large, however, the lack of workplace accommodations would prohibit many employment opportunities.

After 1990 unemployment among individuals with disabilities rose along with unemployment in the general population. As obsolete industries have been privatized or closed down, and as some of the largest state-owned industries were converted beginning in 1995-96, not only have jobs been lost, but dramatic changes have occurred in the system of health, education, and social services for entire populations whose benefits were tied to their jobs in the "company towns" that typified the command economy. The impact of privatization on the typical worker helps to explain the longing that some express for the greater security of the old regime, and this is particularly true among the older generation.

Inclusion in Education at the Federal Level

The Soviet Union separated individuals with disabilities from society. Children with disabilities were sent to large categorical boarding institutions *(internati),* although even those placements were unavailable for some (e.g., nonambulatory children with cerebral palsy were not admitted to *internati* because wheelchairs and related devices were not manufactured in the Soviet Union until the 1980s). Across all schools, including *internati,* the Soviet Union imposed uniform curriculum and instruction, and teachers who did not follow prescribed lessons and procedures were subject to sanctions that could include arrest. This history has created a mindset that is not readily changed among longstanding members of the teaching force.

Two ministries are responsible for *internati.* The Ministry of Social Protection did and does administer *internati* for children and youth with severe mental retardation or developmental disabilities, for whom expectations are low. These individuals are sent home or to adult institutions when their adolescence ends. Conditions at the adult institutions are grim and have led some parents to organize an attempt to petition the United Nations about human rights violations.

In Russia, people with severe learning difficulties are categorized as "invalids from childhood." This term is all too precise if "invalid" is taken as meaning "not valid." From the moment they are born, such people are considered "in-valid" despite the Declaration of Rights of Mentally Retarded Persons adopted by the United Nations General Assembly. . . . Is there a solution to these problems? Undoubtedly. We must radically change state policy regarding children and young people with (severe) learning difficulties. The present policy is absurd. Billions are spent on maintenance (pensions, the construction of huge children's and adults' homes), while rehabilitation and, most important, social and professional training, attract paltry coppers. . . . For now, our children of all abilities should already start moving toward each other, so that from generation to generation the Russian consciousness will gradually re-accustom itself to a model of society where special children are cared for and not despised. (Krivochey, 1994, pp. 186-188)

The Ministry of Education continues to administer the *internati* for students with mild, moderate, and sensory disabilities. Although these boarding institutions isolate students from their homes and communities, their programs have not been poor, and there are things that we can learn from Russian instructional practice. Results are particularly good, for example, with students who have visual or hearing impairments and who are deaf-blind. Students who complete *internati* programs in late adolescence are discharged and have been eligible for small "pensions," which were minimally adequate until the inflationary era that ensued after 1991.

Since 1993 the Ministry of Education of Russia has been taking steps to encourage greater integration of students with mild, moderate, and sensory disabilities in the mass general (public) schools. Ministry of Education leadership has examined special education in many countries (notably the Flemish Community of Belgium, Great Britain, and the United States) and have used this expertise both legislatively and programmatically. Under the Federal Program of the Development of the Russian Educational System Until the Year 2000, the Ministry of Education has also been carrying out overall education reform, including decentralization of control; enabling provinces, regions, and districts to take charge of local schools and school improvement; encouraging greater autonomy and creativity among teachers and in schools; publication of new textbooks to remove ideology and to restore various scientific and literary contents that earlier had been suppressed (Lenskaya, 1994). Changes are occurring not only in city schools, but also in rural schools, which educate 40% of Russia's students and where instructional options are expanding, "allowing each school to determine optimal conditions for learning" (Suvorova, 1997, p. 49).

In the Soviet Union mass general schools were designed to educate the standard student, but more and more students, "as a result of biological, social or psychological factors, could not fit into the narrow constraints of the 'standard student.' Annual statistics show (that) . . . today, every fifth student entering school cannot adapt to the traditional educational process" (Avdeichuk, 1977, p. 5), and "individualization of education of disabled children is attracting more and more attention" (Tkaveshenko, 1995, p. 3).

For these reasons, some federal inclusionary efforts encompass not only students with disabilities but also others who need specialized interventions. This is true of a small number of pilot schools across Russia, each of which has designed its own strategies for inclusion. A separate pilot project is based on a Flemish model for bridging general and special education, with a particular focus on integration of students with hearing impairments and of preschool children with disabilities (Lasutova, 1995). Further, the Ministry has conducted seminars and engaged in several international projects to improve training at pedagogical universities, particularly to prepare teachers for inclusion of students whose disabilities or other learning characteristics diverge from the average.

Alongside these efforts, differential diagnosis of the effects of disability on learning is being reinstated in Russia. In 1936 Stalin prohibited all psychological testing in the Soviet Union. In the 1960s psychologists and diagnosticians, in selecting children for special education, resumed using the tasks for intelligence tests and other psychological measures, but could not use the scoring systems. Consequently diagnosis of disability became an intuitive, rather than a scientific, practice until recently (Lubovsky & Smith-Davis, 1996). Since 1992 the Laboratory of Psychology of Disabled Children of the Russian Academy of Education has been developing diagnostic tools that incorporate, and add dimensions to, the work of Vygotsky and Sakharov. According to the head of the Laboratory:

> We are now developing various tasks to measure the potential learning abilities of children. We start with the actual ability, but we change the context of the tasks in order to measure the effects that different approaches to each task will have on an individual child. This work has been completed for assessing students with a range of disabilities in the 6-8 year-old age group, and we now await funds to prepare this assessment manual for publication. Meanwhile, we are working on measures for the 4-5 age group, and subsequently will develop them for the 9-10 age group and others. (Lubovsky & Smith-Davis, 1996, p. 14)

Inclusion and Self-Determination in St. Petersburg

In October 1990, before the dissolution of the Soviet Union, the Congress of People's Deputies passed a Law on Public Associations, specifying procedures whereby informal citizen groups (which had been springing up in the period of *glasnost* and *perestroika*) could become registered as formal public associations, a status that included eligibility for public funding and private contributions. A vast number of groups with wide-ranging concerns—from services for veterans of the war in Afghanistan to agenda of the Cossacks, and so on—became registered associations immediately, have continued to register, and have established an important foundation for the development of civil society. In St. Petersburg, a city of nearly 5 million, and its outlying region of northeast Russia, parents of children and youth with disabilities have organized 63 associations, each concerned with a particular category of disability, and covering all severity levels. In late 1993 these associations formed a unified structure, which (though still fragile) provides central leadership for such functions as a database on children and interaction with local government and the federal Ministry of Education. Essentially these parents want a more normal life for their children, better services and education for them, and greater acceptance and opportunities in society. Their greatest concern (shared with such parents everywhere) is what will become of their children when the parents are gone. For families in Russia, this is indeed a source of anguish.

The St. Petersburg parent associations have been active in acquiring the knowledge and skills to start services for their own children in the community. Several have started their own schools for students with disabilities (usually with support of a business benefactor, under a tax-deduction code), as well as community sports and arts programs and a day program of rehabilitation for young adults with severe mental retardation. One advocacy group works with local universities to arrange for students with disabilities to enter higher education. An organization of young adults with hearing impairments has also been formed, as a spin-off of the organization of parents of children with hearing impairments.

Besides the services that parents have been instituting, other initiatives have taken shape. A boarding school in the Petrodvoretz District of St. Petersburg made plans to close its educational program, so that the developmentally delayed and orphan children from this institution could go to a regular public school each day (with their teachers) for instruction in this less restrictive setting. There is now a public self-contained day school for children with mental retardation and cerebral palsy in St. Petersburg, supported by the city government. An Early Intervention Institute operates a program that helps parents of newborns with disabilities to bond with and work with their children, thus reducing the chance that these babies will be relinquished to *internati*.

The Raoul Wallenberg International University for Family and Child has established a community-based demonstration school for students with disabilities, populated by children who have been brought out of *internati*. Faculty members from this institution, the Herzen State Pedagogical University, and St. Petersburg University have all participated in Ministry-of-Education sponsored activities designed to improve teacher education and prepare personnel for more integrated public schools.

The Mayor's Committee on Social Policies includes disabilities on its agenda, cooperates with parents and professionals, and has developed a list of programs to support inclusion in the public schools (as required by the Federal Law on Education of Persons With Disabilities of the Russian Federation). One advocacy organization disseminates positive radio and television information (which is organized by a young man with cerebral palsy). Several city services have been made available for the pension population, including free access to the public transit system and other benefits. The world-famous Marianskii Theatre (formerly the Kirov) provides free tickets for individuals with disabilities on a regular basis, and the wheelchair section is often occupied at ballet and opera performances.

All of these outcomes have been achieved by unified efforts of determined parents, by teachers, professors, agency leaders, city officials, and by people with disabilities themselves.

Conclusion

The need to fundamentally redesign and reform standing institutions and bureaucracies has been a major problem in Russia's endeavors to move toward new economic, political, and social structures. Whereas privatization of much business and industry occurred with a speed that has perhaps produced new difficulties, change in other arenas will be slower, and many institutions will not disappear in this generation, although alternatives are springing up beside them. Education for students with disabilities appears to belong to this latter category.

It is difficult to imagine that the boarding school model will be abandoned in the near future. Alternatives are only in the early and experimental stages. Systems change and public accessibility will no doubt take more than a generation. In addition, modifications in public attitudes regarding disability will not happen overnight.

At the same time, it is important to recognize the progress that is occurring, largely through the efforts of the people themselves, facing great odds in a historically unprecedented type of transition that cannot be expected to take place without upheavals. Considering the magnitude of change occurring and the massive infrastructure problems remaining to be solved, great recognition should be given to the advancements for individuals with disabilities that have been accomplished, and for many other positive developments in Russia. Despite the barriers and problems reported in this chapter, one cannot overlook the dynamism of this era. Even though this generation will not reap many benefits of Russia's transition, and even though the process often involves two steps forward and one step back, many people are participating in rebuilding, rejuvenating, and reinventing their country. As has been true for a thousand years, the strength of Russia lies in its people. That is the real story going on in Russia today.

References

Adhieh, R. B. (1997). *Russia's constitutional revolution: Legal consciousness and the transition to democracy, 1985-96.* University Park, PA: Penn State Press.

Avdeichuk, N. G. (1977). Remedial education in the Ismailovo Education Complex. In Z. I. Batioukova & T. D. Shaposhnikova (Eds.), *Innovation in Russian schools* (M. Korolov, Trans., pp. 3-16). Bloomington, IN: Phi Delta Kappa Educational Foundation.

Cohen, A. (1997, June 9). Russia's mountains of debt. *Washington Times*, p. A21.

Dyskin, A., Navrotskaya, T., & Nikiforov, V. (1994). The social status of the disabled and old-age pensioners. In *Petersburg in the early 1990s: Crazy, cold, cruel* (pp. 169-172). St. Petersburg: Nochlezhka Charitable Foundation.

Feshbach, M., & Friendly, A., Jr. (1992). *Ecocide in the USSR: Health and nature under siege.* New York: Harper Collins, Basic Books.

Glukhovyets, B., & Semyonova, O.(1994). Sickness and mortality in the population of St. Petersburg. In *Petersburg in the early 1990s: Crazy, cold, cruel* (pp. 147-149). St. Petersburg: Nochlezhka Charitable Foundation.

Krivochey, B. (1994). Special children. In *Petersburg in the early 1990s: Crazy, cold, cruel* (pp. 186-188). St. Petersburg: Nochlezhka Charitable Foundation.

Lazutova, M. (1995, November). *The Russian-Flemish joint program-special education.* Paper presented at the International Conference on Special Education, Moscow, Parliamentary Center.

Lenskaya, E. (1994, March). Education reform in progress in Russia. Address before a U.S.A.-Russia Seminar on Special Education, Moscow.

Lubovsky, V. I., & Smith-Davis, J. (1996, November). Vladimir Ivanovich Lubovsky: Reflections on my life and work. *National Association of School Psychologists Communique, 25*(3), 12-14.

Suvorova, G. F. (1997). Innovative processes in rural schools. In Z. I. Batioukova & T. D. Shaposhnikova (Eds.), *Innovation in Russian schools* (M. Korolov, Trans., pp. 47-55). Bloomington, IN: Phi Delta Kappa Educational Foundation.

Tkaveshenko, E. (1995, November). *Report of the Federal Minister of Education.* Paper presented at the International Conference on Special Education, Moscow, Parliamentary Center.

Improving Quality of Life in India: Challenges and Emerging Concerns

Sushil Kumar Goel
Regional Institute of Education
Bubaneswar, India

Since the beginning of time, improving quality of life has been a top priority for all people, including those with mental retardation. Today public policy and rehabilitation agencies are struggling to redesign themselves using a quality-of-life paradigm. In India the concept of quality of life provides a fundamentally positive and growth-oriented principle that can be the basis for developing a national policy toward people with disabilities. In India, as throughout the world, quality of life steers us toward person-centered planning, supporting people's needs and desires, and asking people what they think and how they feel. In today's changing political and economic climate in India, we all need to focus on quality-of-life principles so that people with disabilities will lead fulfilling, self-directed lives. The purpose of this chapter is to discuss these quality-of-life principles and a shift in public policy within the context of present-day India.

Present-Day India

Quality of life is a holistic concept that encompasses not only physical and economic improvements, but also the social, cultural, and even perhaps political aspects of a community (Schalock, 1996). Aspects of development that could influence the quality of life of a given community include poverty, health care indexes such as life expectancy, educational levels, communication facilities, transportation, neatness and hygiene, and energy availability. One should also consider distributive aspects that address rural-urban differences, income-level differences, gender differences, and regional differences. The socioeconomic indices of the quality of life of the Indian population are frequently very different from those of more affluent Western countries. Such differences are reflected in the following four important areas of Indian society: population, science and technology, education, and public attitudes.

Population

Three broad indicators of quality of life—needs, comforts, and luxuries—are mainly dependent upon the developmental stage of a country. In India we have no uniformity in these indicators. Most of our population is still in the need stage, while a good cross section has comfort, and a few have luxuries. The quality and per capita quantity of basic necessities vary not only from region to region in India, but also from community to community, and even from family to family. Varied ethnicities, diverse languages, and different religions are all orchestrated into the indigenous civilization of India. Thus Indian society is a plural society, and Indian civilization is a conglomeration of traditions.

We have the highest points at two extremes of our social milieu—the rich (including the upper middle class) and the poor—but no broad spectrum fills the gap in between. Thus it becomes difficult to take just one index for quality of life. For example, the gross national product or the per capita income does not truly reflect the reality of whether the basic needs of the people are met. There can be many needs besides food, shelter, clothing, education, health, and transport. Maintenance of ecological balance and human rights are as important as the other basic needs. Unless the question of population control is aggressively pursued and some stability is achieved, it is impossible to achieve in India an enhanced quality of life, including people with disabilities. Nearly 950 million people place a demand on the environment that is rapidly approaching the upper-most limits of the environment's capacity to support life. Thus overpopulation has a number of ill effects on our quality of life and on the quality of the environment. As population grows at a faster rate than the availability of land for cultivation, large numbers of people are becoming redundant and marginal.

Science and Technology

Development is intrinsically related to the advance of science and technology, which in turn leads to urbanization, environmental pollution, and now even fears of atomic annihilation. People are worried; moral and mental degradation are all challenging the very existence of human society. The accumulation of tensions and stresses results in the breakdown of health, coping abilities, impairment of judgment, and loss of enthusiasm and zest for life. Within the Indian social framework, conditions of poverty, illiteracy, and lack of opportunities for personal development seem to contribute to behavioral deviancy.

The process of urbanization and industrialization has disrupted old bonds of traditional social structure and family relations. Migration from rural to urban areas has changed the extended-family structure and its values. Older parents wish to remain in villages where they have land for agriculture, which has been their prime occupation for several generations. They also cling to their property with sentimental attachment. But children move to urban areas, primarily for education, and then for white-collar jobs. These trends have deteriorated the emotional bonds between parents and children, made the home environment deprived of interaction among the family members, and affected quality of life at family level.

Currently, quality of life is invariably considered in terms of physical comforts and mere possession of electronic gadgets and modern amenities. In other words, materialistic aspects of life and mechanical culture have usurped value systems in children and a concern for mental health and quality living. Surprisingly, in this poor country people look down on others who cannot afford these luxuries and modern amenities.

Education

There is a direct relationship between basic education and quality of life. From the days of the freedom movement, there was a strong desire among Indian people to eradicate illiteracy and to promote education suited to our needs and way of life. The pattern of education designed by the British in the preindependence era proved to be unsuitable to our conditions, as it did not foster the basic idea of universal primary education. Mahatma Gandhi was the first person to think about universalizing primary education; he thought that it would promote better life, particularly in the rural areas. Later on, in the postindependence period, the government of India made all possible efforts to make primary education compulsory. Forty-seven years after the adoption of the constitution and during the Golden Jubilee Year of Independence, the government of India has just now decided to make education a fundamental constitutional right.

To enjoy life to its fullest and face its challenges, individuals need to be equipped with value-oriented education to build self-esteem. By inculcating basic values in human beings, we can combat social evils. One ought to have faith, love, and courage to lead a quality life.

Life can become a wild chase if one's perceived needs are constantly increasing with the rising standards of civilized living; discontent makes perceived well-being recede. Mahatma Gandhi and Vinoba Bhave addressed this problem, claiming that by reducing needs to the barest minimum one can live in harmony with nature and the environment. This feeling enriches our quality of life. This level of human well-being focuses on the pursuit of social values like justice, cooperation, benevolence, social welfare, charity, organization, education, or progress. In this regard, well-being requires a self-change from need orientation to value orientation. The effort itself involves a sense of well-being. A more invigorating level of well-being consists in the kind of unique inner strength that is known as morale.

The future of humanity is each individual's responsibility. Safeguarding human dignity and creating a just society call for initiation of a concerted effort at a national level to orient parents, teachers, administrators, politicians, and other functionaries at all levels to make value-oriented education an integral part of the ongoing educational process (Sen, 1993).

Turning to higher education and its contribution to quality of life: In India there has been a spectacular expansion in the higher education system, but commoners have not reached the stage where they are able to appreciate the importance and usefulness of information technology—which would improve their quality of life. India got a late start in developing the information technology; initially we made slow progress, which was followed by phenomenal growth, and today we are using it profusely in railways, banks, industries, and weather forecasting. What's more, this technology is being used in teaching and for the eradication of illiteracy. The total literacy rate of the country by 1991 had increased to 42.49%; the male literacy rate is 52.68% and the female literacy rate 32.52%. The literacy figures for the tribal population, the handicapped population, and other weaker sectors of the society are not available. Literacy is an essential aspect of human dignity and a window on apprehension and comprehension. The country is entering the 21st century with a very high illiteracy rate. Education empowers a person to face the challenges of life, and thus it liberates him. Lack of education is a colossal deprivation and is a major deterrent of quality of life.

India has some peculiar problems. It has about 6 million villages and about three fourths of the population live in villages. To quote Mahatma Gandhi, "If the village perishes, India perishes too." Rural development holds the key for our national development. One of the most important roles of psychologists lies in educating rural people for harmonious development of their personalities, so they can be self-reliant, self-dependent, and confident to look after their own affairs. Adult education needs to be expanded to raise the literacy and health status of rural residents. The health status of a community is an index of living standard. Health for all in the new century can be achieved only if we take strong measures. Abnormal behavior, physical disabilities, intellectual disabilities, mental diseases, and other ailments are not being attended to properly in the rural areas.

Public Attitudes

The problems of definition, assessment, and personnel are also faced in the Indian context. Though changes are taking place in society and social institutions, traditions, indifference, and prejudices are not disappearing fast enough. People with mental retardation represent most poignantly the underprivileged and poorly educated of any social group. The burden of mental retardation falls not only on the parents, but on the entire nation. It is also clear that sociocultural deprivation—casteism, prejudice and discrimination, poverty, poor nutrition, inadequate health services, rural-urban discrepancy in facilities, substandard housing, inferior education, and unemployment—is one of the causes of mental retardation in the Indian context. Whether mental retardation is more prevalent among different castes or cultures is a matter to be settled by scientific inquiry. In this context, when size of the country and diversity of population with numerous languages, religions, and cultures are taken into consideration, mental retardation research is a very promising field in India (Sen, 1993).

A Shift in Public Policy

One of the most striking features of ancient Indian sociology was the hierarchy of classes, separated by birth for generations. The caste system is responsible for class consciousness among the higher castes in India. However, with the advent of British rule and with new ideas of liberty, equality, and fraternity, this old social structure has developed the first cracks. The recent modernization and industrialization have already started pulling down the old structure. Remodeling it is a very big challenge facing Indian social scientists today. The social integrating forces, such as modernization, youth movements, voluntary organizations, and educational societies, are gradually molding the society into a new shape. Of course, this kind of social reconstruction is not going to take place overnight. The dedicated, sustained, and enlightened efforts of specialists and other social workers will have to be directed toward this goal.

The Rise of Parental Involvement

The impact of the individuals with retardation on Indian society and the nation's growth can be well imagined by the fact that behind every person with mental retardation stands a puzzled, distressed, and anxious family.

There is a great need for psychological support to parents. Parental counseling has to be taken to the doorsteps of parents if it is to be successful in India. Parental cooperation is essential for successful implementation of services to the children. It has been universally accepted that parental involvement is essential in education, training, and management of people with mental retardation. The formation of parent self-help groups is the need of the hour to solve the problems, even in the remotest areas. There are about 40 self-help groups operating in the country at present. Goel (1996, 1997a) conducted three need-based Parent Training Programs with a view to investigate the misconceptions and superstition held by Indian parents, to increase the knowledge and understanding of parents about children with intellectual disability through information services and a training package, to promote positive attitudes toward their child's potential and capacity for development, to form self-help groups to provide mutual support, and to evaluate the program. The most prevalent attitude among the Indian families is a belief in the consequence of bad deeds (karma-phala). Most of the people believe that mental retardation is some sort of punishment given by God for bad deeds that a person had committed in a previous life. The ancient belief in the influence of stars and the consequent disability still persists among some people. Such negative attitudes, which are prevalent in our society, act as the main barrier in the education, training, and rehabilitation of people with mental retardation. The social stigma associated with mental retardation may lead some parents to stay away from community involvement, a danger that the professional should seek to avoid by encouraging wide community links. The emotional well-being of the parents, lack of education, and the inordinate financial strains together with the person's special needs cause innumerable problems within the family structure and adversely affect the quality of life of the whole family. In these training programs, parents were given extensive information services, support, and education to effectively care for and train their children at home.

In a developing country like India where service centers for people with mental retardation are few and far between, the role of parents in carrying out the program is vital. In contemporary India the joint family system is slowly giving way to the nuclear family. The exigencies of earning a living are splitting up the traditional joint family system. This, however, assigns the responsibility of rearing children solely to parents rather than the extended family. In the Indian context, it is necessary to emphasize preservation of families. The family is a stable social institution and the family bond is strong in India. The child with mental retardation should be absorbed in the family as far as practicable for a good quality of life, because no institution can adequately replace a good home. In such an affectionate and secure atmosphere, the person with mental retardation has fewer problems than he or she has in a monotonous and mechanical institutional atmosphere. These people need individual attention which cannot be provided by most of the institutions on account of limited resources. The concept of mother-teacher needs to be given proper consideration.

The Need for Family Support Programs

If we want to reach every family and provide quality of life to people with mental retardation in India, we have to educate their parents and other family members. The government must give some financial assistance and professional expertise to the family. The major problem is that parents do not know their rights and empowerment is a new concept to many parents in India (Goel, 1997b). The social stigma attached to mental retardation in Indian families keeps parents separate. Empowerment comes through sharing and learning through informal and formal gatherings and education. The work toward ensuring the human rights of people with intellectual disability starts with the empowerment of the parents. The parents in the home environment are the first and primary educators of the child. The promotion of inclusion, citizenship, and self-determination of a person with intellectual disability begins in the family. Special teleschool programs in different languages provide instruction to parents for home management of children with mental retardation on television on alternate Saturdays. The National Institute for the Mentally Handicapped has 12 family cottages that offer stay and training facilities to parents who come from far off places and like to consult the experts from the multidisciplinary team depending upon the nature of the problem and the requirements of their children with mental retardation. Parents who had almost given up hopes regarding the improvement of their family members with mental retardation felt that proper care, adequate information services, understanding, and patience could lead to some amount of improvement. Information services are usually neglected in such training programs. Access to precise and reliable information in a most convenient form can help to minimize the waste of resources. Information is the key for empowerment of families and communities. This situation calls for increased cooperation of subject specialists and information scientists for economy and optimal use of information (Goel, 1985, 1990). As much as any normal child, a person with mental retardation needs to enjoy the fundamental rights of existence, care, education, and other opportunities for intellectual, emotional, social, and occupational adjustment in the family and outside.

The Rise of Special Education

In a vast country like India where 75% to 80% of the population is living in villages and having limited facilities for special education, mass media, transport, and road links, one wonders how we can fulfill the cherished goal of primary education for all. The existing facilities—special training centers, daycare centers, rehabilitation centers, sheltered workshops, industrial therapy units, and other services—do not begin to meet the problem. With the high incidence of mental retardation, a limited number of special schools, shortage of trained personnel, and financial constraints, the concept of inclusive schooling is one such alternative to serve a large number of children all over the country. The objective is to integrate children with special needs with the general community as equal partners. The information available at present shows there are currently 18,289 children on the rolls, as against 1,485 special educators and 1,021 untrained assistant teachers in 482 special schools spread across the country. Keeping in view the huge magnitude of the population of children with mental retardation (approximately 22 million), even the Integrated Education for the Disabled scheme in 14 states and Project Integrated Education for the Disabled—a UNICEF-assisted project—in 10 states have not served the purpose due to lack of resources and basic infrastructure.

Community Integration and Rehabilitation

The rehabilitation problem posed by people with mental retardation is, in the fullest sense of the term, a community one. It is, therefore, incumbent on each of us to examine this problem area and determine what contribution we can make in the light of our competence and resources to bring improved quality of life and a dignified place for them in our society. Questions are often raised about the acute problem of unemployment in the country; with adequate vocational facilities not available for "normal" youth, why employ people with mental retardation? Why make facilities for vocational and institutional training available to them? Only by heightening community awareness of this problem through education and communication will the public view people with mental retardation in the same light as any other citizens.

Adults with retardation have received the least attention so far in India and facilities for them are relatively few throughout the country. Neither the private organizations nor the state authorities have dealt sufficiently with this problem. In recent years, however, attempts have been made in many parts of the country to devote some attention to them. It has been realized that they are like any of us in many respects and have a right to economic security, work and employment, decent standards of living, leisure activities, education, rehabilitation services, and protection from exploitation, abuse, and degrading treatment. This has to be done not out of pity and sympathy, but as a result of practical recognition of the fact that using the abilities of people with mental retardation will benefit the society and the nation. More than a year after the landmark Equal Opportunities, Protection of Rights and Full Participation Act, 1995, the benefits of it were yet to reach people with disabilities. On the whole, the Act exhibits more weaknesses than strengths when it concerns people with mental retardation, as the Act is totally silent about their employment and rehabilitation and providing equalization of opportunities and services. The Act has confused pertinent issues, by including people with mental illness alongside those with mental retardation. Terminology including the "mentally ill" and those of "unsound mind" should be excluded from the Disability Act, 1995 (Act No. 1 passed by president of India, January 1, 1996).

A national trust for people with mental retardation needs to be promulgated to ensure guardianship after the demise of the parents. Foster-care home set-ups ensure care and rehabilitation in the quality of services on the basis of parents' requests and affordability. Pursuant to the enactment of the Disability Act, the Indian cabinet approved the proposal to set up a National Handicapped Finance and Development Corporation to give soft loans for the self-employed projects of people with disabilities.

These legislative measures are no doubt necessary, but adults with mental retardation must be empowered in the context of the local milieu and situations. We

237

must promote inclusion of individuals with mental retardation in the world of work and their empowerment through better quality of life. We can reach the optimum level and achieve the target if we start with community-based services. In India community-based services on a large scale are required, with special concentration in the rural areas. It is up to the community to see that the lives of people with mental retardation are not wasted by living in a dim world, limited to a narrow sphere.

Mental retardation is no longer considered a social stigma in more advanced and enlightened societies. More and more parents are joining the battle for the rights of people with mental retardation, to promote their quality of life. Throughout the world a common consensus has emerged that community-based services offer the best prospect of meeting the needs of people with intellectual disabilities and their families (McConkey & O'Toole, 1996; this volume).

The vast majority of people with intellectual disabilities live in developing countries, and at present only a fraction of them receive any form of help. The most promising way of assisting many more people and their families is through community-based rehabilitation, which is a strategy for enhancing the quality of life of people with mental retardation by improving service delivery, by providing more equitable opportunities, and by promoting and protecting their human rights. Any intent to improve quality of life must attempt to bring about and focus pertinent dialogue with the individuals, discussing their complaints and wishes, dreams, and ideas about their everyday lives. Fortunately, this dialogue is increasing in today's India.

References

Goel, S. K. (1985, March). *National information system in mental retardation.* Paper presented at the Seventh World Congress of the International Association for the Scientific Study of Mental Deficiency, New Delhi.

Goel, S. K. (1990). Education, training and rehabilitation of the handicapped in India: Retrospect and prospect. *Education and Society, 8*(1), 21-29.

Goel, S. K. (1996, July). *Human resource development and family oriented services for children with mental retardation in India.* Paper presented at the 10th World Congress of the International Association for the Scientific Study of Intellectual Disabilities, Helsinki.

Goel, S. K. (1997a, July). *Information services, training and support to families having children with intellectual disability in rural India.* Paper presented at the World Congress of the World Federation for Mental Health, Helsinki.

Goel, S. K. (1997b, September). *Parents' empowerment of children with intellectual disability in India.* Paper presented at K97 Human Rights for Persons With Mental Handicap Conference, Czech Republic.

McConkey, R., & O'Toole, B. (1996, July). *A training strategy for personnel working in developing countries.* Paper presented at the 10th World Congress of the International Association for the Scientific Study of Intellectual Disabilities, Helsinki.

Schalock, R. L. (Ed). (1996). *Quality of life: Vol. 1. Conceptualization and measurement.* Washington, DC: American Association on Mental Retardation.

Sen, A. K. (1993). A decade of experimental research in mental retardation in India. In N. R. Ellis (Ed.), *International review of research in mental retardation: Vol. 4.* New York: Academic Press.

Themes Affecting Social Inclusion of Individuals With Disabilities in Brazil

Silvana Maria Russo Watson
Nebraska Wesleyan University
Lincoln, Nebraska, United States

The foundation for this chapter is that social inclusion, the feeling of belonging, will enhance the quality of life of people with disabilities. When social inclusion successfully occurs, it affects positively the recognized dimensions of quality of life: well-being, personal development, self-determination, and rights (Felce & Perry, 1996; Schalock, 1990, 1996; Snell & Vogtle, 1997). Quality-of-life dimensions must be used as a context for planning and evaluating programs and services for people with disabilities (Dennis, Williams, Giangreco, & Cloninger, 1993; Schalock, 1997a). Care, then, must be taken that the context is accurately identified and its strengths properly diagnosed. Where there is a dominant or dominating quality-of-life dimension, it must be duly noted. Social inclusion within the Brazilian society is such a dimension.

As strategies are developed and programs are planned to enhance the quality of life of people with disabilities, care must be taken to consider the influence of culture on people's values, beliefs, behaviors, and attitudes (Keith, 1996; Schalock, 1997b). The special educator consulting and/or collaborating in Brazil must comprehend and be sensitive to the cultural context in which the work will be done. Only by understanding the implications of an accurately identified social context is the special educator able to choose effective strategies; strategies that will be received positively and productively by the "locals" (Brazilians).

In one way or another, each chapter in this book attempts to accurately describe differing cultural factors affecting the quality of life of people with disabilities. In this chapter I use an ethnographic approach to introduce special educators to the major themes that will and do shape services to people with mental retardation or developmental disabilities within Brazil. To introduce the special educator to Brazil, I identify the influence of four major themes that shape the Brazilian social context: spirituality, citizenship, politics, and economy. I then broadly outline their implications for social inclusion of individuals with disabilities within Brazilian society.

As a native (born, raised, educated, and employed in Recife, Brazil), I share the perspectives of an inside informant who knows the culture well and can communicate about the culture in a nonanalytic manner (Spradley & McCurdy, 1972). I also provide an outsider's view. As an adult, I have lived, worked, and studied within the United States. I have the unique advantage of being a Brazilian American who can interpret cultural factors that a Brazilian in the local environment might not see or be conscious of. The guide that I present is drawn from my personal experiences, interviews, conversations, studies, and collaboration with numerous individuals. Among the informants were mothers of individuals with disabilities from different socioeconomic groups, service providers, researchers or academicians, private and public school personnel, Brazilians who are not connected with the education field, and especially my husband, an American who lived in Brazil for 9 months and studied Latin America as part of his political science studies. I recently visited two clinics for individuals with disabilities in two different parts of the country. I read recent literature to become familiar with new laws, goals, and objectives. The themes of Brazilian social context that I introduce here are carefully identified from these multiple sources of information.

Themes of Social Context

Identifiable themes within Brazilian society establish the macrocontext in which quality-of-life dimensions are played out. These themes must be identified for quality-of-life dimensions to be assessed. The quality of life for Brazilians with mental retardation or developmental disabilities is determined by their success at social inclusion. What are the "Brazilian" themes of social context that affect issues of inclusion of people with disabilities within the broad society? What is their impact?

Labeling something as Brazilian is inherently dangerous. Brazil comprises a vast geographical area (larger than the mainland U.S.), is diverse in topography (from expansive ocean beaches to mountainous deserts to the flooding enormity of the Amazon), and has multiple and mixed populations, economies, and politics. When asked about the cultural diversity of the United States, Brazilians can scoff, "Melting pot? What melting pot? If you want to see a kettle of cultures, visit my Brazil!" And perhaps more important, when asked to comment on progress within their nation, Brazilians may well ask, "Which century? I can comment on and show you three different centuries coexisting right now." Plagued as are most developing countries, Brazilian progress, where it has occurred, has not been uniformly shared.

There is, however, a dominant, identifiable Brazilian context—the context that is heard in the laws issuing forth under the current government, that is heard and seen in current music, art, and entertainment that is being exported by Brazilian propaganda. This context is what wells up emotionally within me when I declare, *"Eu sou Brasileira"* (I am a Brazilian woman). The feeling that comes with that identification must be acknowledged, because I sense that it wells up in the multitude who say it and directly impacts their ability to hear and respond to what the special educator may have to say.

Articulating a sociopolitical context for Brazil, then, is dangerously presumptuous but both useful and necessary for any educational strategist, especially for those whose goal it is to promote social inclusion of people with mental retardation and developmental disabilities. What is important? Not the accuracy of the context as a final object, for this will be ever changing and is never quite right. Rather, it is the identity and feeling of themes for which Brazilians must strive. The strength of cultural (sociopolitical) themes in shaping the eventual success or failure of specific educational strategies cannot be overemphasized. Cushner, McClelland, and Safford (1992) stated, "Socialization in any cultural milieu not only teaches one such things as what language to speak and what nonverbal communicative behaviors to use, but how to learn as well" (p. 108). Within the United States alone, studies show clearly the impact of culture on disabilities (Anderson & Anderson, 1983; Franklin, 1992; Gonzalez, 1995). To state that cultural differences create learning difficulties might not be too strong a statement (Mercer, 1973; Ortiz & Yates, 1983). To state that learning disabilities are highlighted and exacerbated by cultural differences is a demonstrable fact (Collier, 1988; Collier & Hoover, 1987; Cummins, 1984; Fradd & Weismantel, 1989; Grossman, 1995).

It is my belief that the tools (e.g., assessment and teaching strategies) that the study of special education has given to me have universal applicability. Whether in the United States, Indonesia, or Brazil, these tools will serve me well. This confidence comes from recognition of the universal challenges special educators face. Meyen, Vergason, and Whelan (1993) suggested that special educators are risk takers who have shown the ability to meet several challenges, such as: attain professional status; design assessment tools and interventions to help people with disabilities become effective citizens; shape public policy at the state and federal levels; promote conditions necessary to protect the rights of children with disabilities and provide them with the quality of life that everyone deserves. In the interviews conducted to prepare this chapter, I reheard the long list: Teachers are not prepared; people do not believe children with disabilities can learn; there is no access to education; families do not care; disabilities, much like disfigurements, are socially unwelcome; there is no money; the government does not care; there is no acceptance; there is no understanding; there are no tools; there are no resources; there is no hope. These are the sentiments expressed to me from Ouro Preto in mountainous, central-southern Brazil, to Rio de Janeiro in southeastern Brazil, through Recife in Brazil's expansive northeast. The challenges are universal and can therefore become familiar. The tools are universal and can be ever more developed. The specific social contexts are the surprise variables that may thwart otherwise diligent and studied educational effort. Ignoring social context will render educational strategies ineffective. It is the purpose of this chapter to place road signs at some of those hazards, particularly with regard to the dominance of social inclusion as it affects other core dimensions of quality of life, within the context of Brazilian education and society.

Themes of Social Context and Their Implications

Spirituality

Brazilian spirituality is characterized by tremendous mysticism and has an admittedly strong strain of superstition. The country is traditionally Catholic but has been strongly influenced by native and African Brazilian cultures. There is a strong belief in the magical and a corresponding respect for the magician.

This is typified best in the everyday belief in *dando um jeito* (giving it a shot). The emphasis here is not on giving diligent effort but in giving one's effort up to the *outcomes specially arranged by bargaining with or manipulating outside forces*. Under this umbrella, Brazilians look at intelligence as something other than academic performance or IQ scores. The intelligent Brazilian, as stated by Watson, Barreira,

243

and Watson (this volume), is the one who (a) knows how to get out of difficult situations, (b) succeeds in life without giving much consideration to actual processes, and (c) is particularly persuasive and/or lucky (charmed). It is an individual good at the sacrifice of compromise, as opposed to the sacrifice of hard work, who succeeds by negotiating and renegotiating the hand dealt to him. The Brazilian *jeitinho* is "the magical way" to succeed in a country where there are so many stumbling blocks to hard work.

Implication 1. The belief in supernatural powers and demonic possession influences how Brazilians look at disabilities. People with mental retardation and developmental disabilities will have difficulty manipulating outside forces. They are usually not very charming and not able to negotiate well. Consequently, they do not have "the magical way" to succeed in that community. People feel sorry for the "sick ones" and their families because they have not been able to manipulate outside forces; they have been cursed. The Brazilian *jeitinho* did not work. One must demonstrate some "magical way" to "cure the sick ones."

The special educator will gain the respect of the Brazilian audience not by talking about special-education techniques but by demonstrating special-education results. That educator will be seen as the purveyor of magical outcomes, as a holder of special powers. Brazilians will come more readily to special-education strategies not through the argument of methodology and principles, but through demonstrations of success. Brazilian culture is one of the high-context cultures that Hall (1976) described as existing along a continuum from high to low context. High-context cultures depend on information beyond the meanings of the spoken word. They rely on nonverbal cues and unspoken knowledge. Your best arguments will go unheeded, a simple success will open innumerable doors. Brazilians will believe in your magic; do not lose them in teaching them your science. Brazilians learn by watching, not by being told.

Use modeling (Bandura, 1977) as a strategy to educate your audience. Seeing is believing. If the strategies can be seen, Brazilians will believe they are plausible and feasible. The special educator will then be able to anchor theory to application. The special educator must understand the social nature of learning and that learning is a dynamic and interactive process. Skills and knowledge are gained based on observations and experiences (Bos & Vaughn, 1994). Do not try to teach strategies to promote social inclusion and disability awareness. Model those strategies to create Brazilian acknowledgment.

Implication 2. Sophistication, refinement, and intelligence are characteristics valued in this culture. People with mental retardation and developmental disabilities may not be seen as having these characteristics; consequently they are excluded, because they do not know how to use the Brazilian *jeito* to manipulate situations.

Knowing that *innovative, external,* and *new* are all words of value in this culture, the special educator can use these values to promote social inclusion of people with disabilities. Great strides can be made through attention to these values. Professionals with training in foreign countries are given great credibility. They are seen as the "magician," and Brazilians expect to see "magic." Distance learning—

bringing external expertise through innovative media—is well received in Brazilian communities. It is granted an immediate credibility that a local, traditional educator will simply never earn.

Technology, generally, is a very successful vehicle for educational strategies within Brazilian culture. The razzle and dazzle of computers and television is inherently compelling to a society steeped in the charms of the magical. Globe-spanning technology is viewed as an external power of magical (awe-inspiring) proportions—a magical problem solver. Besides being innovative, a multimedia environment creates social contexts for goal-directed activities. Several forms of technology can be used to engage learners, to provide social dialogue, demonstrate and provide multiple resources and tools, and especially to show expert teachers implementing inclusive pedagogical practices. Observing experienced professionals, through videos or simulation software, will help the Brazilian audience develop schemas they can call upon later (Schank & Abelson, 1977) in their own efforts at promoting social inclusion of people with mental retardation and developmental disabilities. Also, making a video within the community will favorably demonstrate that social inclusion is possible and that it will benefit everyone.

Citizenship

To be Brazilian is more a cultural than a political phenomenon. Brazilians are not identified by rights but by characteristics and by birth. They are sensuous, fun-loving, carefree. They are born Brazilian. Brazilians are "glad" or "joyful" rather than "proud" to be Brazilian. They have a tremendous identification with their rich geography and rich culture. It is not uncommon to hear them say, penitently, "Such natural riches, such bounty, such beauty—why have we not been more deserving of it?" Brazilians do not take credit for creating or building Brazil; rather, they feel that they were blessed with it. They blame themselves (more particularly, the Portuguese), not their beloved Brazil, for Brazil's mediocre standing in the world community. The strongest sentiment of citizenship is not pride but gratitude and love.

The first and broadest criterion for inclusion will be identification of "Brazilianship." Brazilian culture strongly merits beauty, physical perfection, and intelligence *(jeito)*. Therefore, the tendency to hide children and adults with mental retardation and developmental disabilities from society is perhaps heightened in Brazilian society. These children and adults are kept at home and out of sight. To the family, they represent embarrassment and failure to conform with Brazilian bounty and beauty *(natureza)*. They are uncomfortable to be with; they are different; they have a disability. Families from cultures other than Brazil, most assuredly, experience these same feelings. The important note for devising social inclusion strategies, however, is that this embarrassment, in Brazilian culture, is more a cultural embarrassment than a proficiency embarrassment. This embarrassment cannot be lifted by merit, but rather must be extended through acknowledgment of commonality.

Social inclusion efforts must address attractiveness and should seek to tap the strength of compassion that comes with gratitude and love. The Brazilian psyche shows an ability to love Brazil with all its societal scars, loving the country for its inherent beauty despite its glaring failings. Strategies to promote social inclusion of people with disabilities need to focus on their strengths. The special educator must seek out positive contributions, activities, or tasks that the person with disabilities can successfully do. The strategist should demonstrate to the Brazilian audience that people with mental retardation and developmental disabilities are more like than different from those without disabilities (Friend & Bursuck, 1996). The special educator can acknowledge a characteristic of beauty in the person with disability—voice, attitude, or particular aptitude—and concentrate on it. Failing that, simple, comprehensive attention to hygiene and social etiquette or simple speech may bring startling results. Drawing out and showing what their child can do (rather than hiding failures) will be the first empowerment of the family to show the inclusion and love not yet acknowledged by society. It is essential to focus on the strength of the person with disability (Aune, 1991). A gratitude felt with accomplishment will encourage further endeavor. Again, small, magical miracles should be stressed. An attractive haircut or suit of clothes recognizable as emulating a pop or sports hero may well be more important than hours of patient study of enunciation.

Politics

Politically, Brazilians live with enormous and inaccessible bureaucracy and are not equal before the law. Despite efforts at democracy, politics is openly mocked and its corruption immediately implied and accepted. Having success politically depends upon *dando um jeito* (adept manipulation) not upon pursuing one's political right. Brazilians will often state that they are successfully apolitical. They will point to the bloodless revolution that separated them from Portugal and will adamantly note that their 175 years of independence is largely uncharacterized by bloodshed and violence either through domestic revolt or external war. The emphasis of Brazilian politics is on compromise and reconciliation of social groups rather than on assertion of individual rights. Brazilians often suggest that they have the quiet virtues of peace makers.

Asserting the rights of individuals with mental retardation and developmental disabilities is hardly viable. Laws that do exist are far ahead of actual societal practices and go ignored and unenforced. For example, the principle of normalization (making available to people with disabilities patterns of life and conditions of everyday living as normal as possible; Nirje, 1985) that has been encouraged by the Brazilian government (Araújo, 1994; MEC, 1994; Ministério da Justica, 1996) is, according to Lobo (1992), just a liberal fantasy. The National Politic of Special Education, which was included in the Federal Constitution in 1988, is fiction, not reality (Lobo). In a country where political rights in general languish, arguments for the rights of special groups go unheard. Only the socially powerful are given political access.

Attempts to require inclusion through the court or legislative systems may actually create exclusion. More effective will be efforts to create inclusion within the immediate community—efforts focused on gaining the eye of a dominant group (e.g., church, clubs, major employer). Educators can create personal attractiveness and social acceptance by working on quality inclusion within the family and the family's community. I cannot overstress the importance of the family's acceptance and participation. Those involved need to understand that the individuals with disabilities are part of their lives. Involve the family in planning services for the individual with disability. The immediate family will spread the feeling of acceptance to the extended families and to the community. Point out what the family and the person with disability do well. These family-centered strategies, already advocated in the United States, will prove even more powerful in the Brazilian context of cultural citizenship. Encourage friendships among individuals with like experiences and help create parent-to-parent support groups. Involve the parents and support them. At the same time, the special educator must provide opportunities for people with disabilities to interact with their peers without disabilities. Work diligently to reduce the isolation of the person with disability. Isolated individuals never see even the rays of the legal sun. Communal individuals share the area of the beach that their group has won.

Friend and Bursuck (1996) stress the importance of promoting positive social interaction among individuals with and without disabilities. They group strategies to create positive peer relationships into three categories:

Create Opportunities. Create opportunities for people with and without disabilities to interact face to face. Face-to-face interactions are very important in high-context cultures (Hall, 1976) that tend to rely on shared, unspoken knowledge. Brazilians seem to rely on information beyond the meaning of the spoken words and to be group oriented. High value is placed on being part of a group. So it is important that people with disabilities are provided opportunities to interact with others without disabilities and be part of a social group. Playing sports, going on field trips, or attending informal, fun meetings where they can just visit and listen to music are good ways to provide togetherness and common shared experiences.

Nurture Support. *Nurture support and friendship among individuals with and without disabilities.* Use of programs like Special Friends (Voeltz et al., 1983, cited in Friend & Bursuck, 1996) will help others learn about people with disabilities and how to interact with them. Encourage love and compassion; these are strong qualities that Brazilians carry with them. In this way you will not fight for their rights, but arouse those quiet virtues, the virtues of the "peace makers" (Brazilians). Arguments, as already mentioned, go largely unheard but social influence can be very powerful. So supporting the friendship of individuals with disabilities with those without disabilities is an important strategy to promote social inclusion. In a society where inequality of rights is frequently observed, where "having is a condition of being" (Freire, 1986), strategies must focus on supporting friendships, on social dialogue, and on creating relationships that will help society become conscious of the need to include those with disabilities. As Freire suggested:

> It is not our role to speak to the people about our own view of the world, nor to attempt to impose that view on them, but rather to dialogue with the people about their view and ours. We must real-

ize that their view of the world, manifested variously in their actions, reflects their situation in the world. Educational and political action which is not critically aware of this situation runs the risk either of "banking" or of preaching in the desert. (p. 85)

Serve as a Role Model. *Serve as a role model and provide access to other positive role models.* As mentioned earlier, Brazilians learn by watching. They don't like to be preached to; they need to see the special educator being positive, supportive, and friendly to individuals with disabilities. As an educator, point out their abilities. Bring in those family members or anyone you know who can model positive and inclusive behaviors toward those with disabilities. Find out who has social prestige in that community, because such people will be politically powerful. Look for their support. Look for the support of the media to get society's attention. Pursue the rights of people with disabilities through the magic of the Brazilian jeito (creating a "why" where there is not one; creating inclusion where there was exclusion).

Economy

Brazil is separated and structured around its resources of production. Class structure has been created in large-scale agriculture, large-scale industry, large-scale (government or military or church) bureaucracy, and large-scale technology, with little movement among these sectors. Everything is large scale, and each scale is a pyramid with a few exceptionally rich and powerful at the top and a multitude of destitute and powerless at the bottom. Freire (1986) called them the oppressor and the oppressed. The closest thing to a thriving middle class with characteristic independent, competitive entrepreneurs exists only in the fields of entertainment, tourism, and small-scale shop keeping. Even there, the dominance of big players is noteworthy.

The individual sectors of Brazilian economy are further created by the strong social structure and geography that isolate sectors of Brazil. Industry is based in two large southern states. Large-scale agriculture is based in the remaining southern states. Traditional, almost feudal, agriculture persists in the north and northeast. Mining, forestry, and government dominate the underpopulated interior. Brazil exhibits deep societal divisions created by geography and vocation. These divisions are further accentuated by the prevalence in each of specific large immigrant groups.

Implication 1. Brazil is a highly structured society in which interpersonal relationships are stringently restricted through dictates of appropriateness that are based on class, wealth, ethnicity, and race (race being by far the least restrictive). Class and wealth are especially and extremely valued in Brazilian society, and people are recognized for the socioeconomic class to which they belong (Freire, 1986; Lobo, 1992). Movements across these dictates of appropriateness are difficult to impossible even for the robust. Those with disabilities experience even greater hurdles.

Efforts to foster inclusion for people with mental retardation or developmental disabilities must be sensitive to these class, wealth, ethnic, and race structures. These structures will determine social values, technical knowledge, and taste preferences, and they will be held with differing prestige (Erickson, 1997). The special educator, then, must think of culture as being "personal, familial, communal, institutional, and societal in its scope and distribution" (Erickson, p. 33) and consider the sub-cultures within the Brazilian context. Social inclusion will be immediately thwarted if we ask that someone be included in a vocation, relationship, or society for which other factors make that person unacceptable. For example, the landed wealthy of the Brazilian northeast would find a son or daughter skilled in the vocational arts every bit as unacceptable as the son or daughter who has a disability. Success within Brazilian culture requires compromise, not indignation. To identify an inclusive place for the person with mental retardation or developmental disabilities, the educational strategist must keep the person in appropriate social context. Success requires consideration of the visible or invisible, overt or covert, explicit or implicit (Erickson; Hall, 1959; 1976; Phillips, 1983) cultural differences. Educational strategy must help to identify and exercise cultural rights as opposed to inalienable individual rights. This can occur only if those visible/invisible cultural differences are identified.

In fostering interpersonal relationships, engaging vocations, and personal aptitude, educational strategies should include appropriate social choices. The special educator must perceive those unspoken, invisible, implicit, covert values. Any vocation involving manual labor (e.g., carpenter and janitor) will not carry the prize virtue in Brazilian society that it does in the United States. Teaching manual skills will not foster inclusion in most Brazilian sectors. Where it does, white collar, clerical tasks will be a more inclusive fit as opposed to janitorial, automotive, or construction-related jobs. Teaching social skills, rather than vocational skills, will prove more inclusive. Educating individuals for service to assemblies—religious, political, social—will be good prescriptions. Gathering of petitions, phone skills, or ceremonial skills attendant to Catholicism, would all be good fits where aptitudes exist or can be fostered. Again, inclusion will come best through the social, not the vocational, arena.

Implication 2. The sectors of Brazilian society, looking like giant pyramids controlled from the tiny top, are extremely paternalistic. With this paternalism comes a clearly recognized and traditional responsibility of care taking. Though this often runs directly parallel to sentiments of strong disdain, the "haves" do care for the "have nots." Wealth is the condition of "being" (Freire, 1986), but "being" includes the self-infliction engendered by feeling oneself to be essential to those who merely exist. Leaders in Brazil (blessed possessors of the Brazilian *jeito*) see themselves as caretakers of a dependent multitude. They are blessed, and they are capable of bestowing blessings. More important, it is their social responsibility to do so.

As educators, catch the eye of the all-powerful. Bring people with mental retardation and developmental disabilities out of obscurity (hidden away in individual homes), and tap the acknowledged responsibility of the "haves" to support the "have nots." Remembering not to lecture or win by argument, make this population recognizable through the miraculous results of good teaching strategies. Empower them with peer groups, parent-to-parent resources, and appropriate social skills.

Make them recognizable cultural citizens. The paternal instincts of Brazilian society will then kick in.

Paternalism within Brazilian society will strongly reinforce the strategies already outlined. Paternalism is cultural and focused by geographical and economic sectors. Work within the appropriate sector, seeking private funding and support from that sector's leaders. These leaders can be the source of money, location, vocations, and opportunities. They can grant a place of quality existence to the properly identified sector "child." Paternalism strongly supports the tendency and interest in bringing in outside, "expert" help. Teachers can be sent abroad for proper training. Experienced professionals and technology can be brought in. "Magical" outcomes are most believed in from outside forces.

Conclusion

In this chapter I have not focused on the enormity of the problems that face Brazil socially, economically, and therefore educationally. If I took the time to paint an accurate picture of the Brazilian educational landscape, a traveler could justifiably stand back in horror. The statistics on illiteracy alone are staggering, reaching as high as 65% according to some estimates. My fear is that the special educator will decide not to go to Brazil until some of these obvious ills are ameliorated. Too often special education is placed in this dependent position on general education. We reach those who are gifted and have disabilities only after we have reached to everyone else. This is directly contrary to all our efforts at inclusion, undermining them even as they are being implemented. The real contribution of special education has been the skills and insights that all education benefits from. The ultimate statement of special educators is that there is no education that is not special. Special care, special tools, attention to circumstance and to individuals pervades all good education today.

It is my hope that the special educator will go to Brazil and work educational magic there. Take a tool kit full of well-sharpened modern teaching methods and techniques. Solicit grants before you go and be prepared to do so when you get there. Be patient; think peace and compromise. Work compassionately and with undying hope. Remember, wherever you are in Brazil, when working for social inclusion, you are within the Brazilian heart. Social inclusion is the dominant quality-of-life dimension within Brazilian society.

References

Anderson, G. R., & Anderson, S. K. (1983). The exceptional Native American. In D. R. Mark and J. G. Erickson (Eds.), *The bilingual exceptional child* (pp. 163-180). Boston: College-Hill.

Araújo, L. A. D. (1994). *A proteção constitucional das pessoas portadoras de deficiência* [The constitutional protection of people with disabilities]. Brasília: CORDE.

Aune, E. (1991). A transition model for post-secondary bound students with learning disabilities. *Learning Disabilities Research and Practice, 6,* 177-187.

Bandura, A. (1977). *Social learning theory.* Englewood Cliffs, NJ: Prentice-Hall.

Bos, C. S., & Vaughn, S. (1994). *Strategies for teaching students with learning and behavior problems* (3rd ed.). Needham Heights, MA: Allyn & Bacon.

Collier, C. (1988). *Assessing minority students with learning and behavior problems.* Lindale, TX: Hamilton.

Collier, C., & Hoover, J. J. (1987). *Cognitive learning strategies for minority handicapped students.* Lindale, TX: Hamilton.

Cummins, J. (1984). *Bilingualism and special education: Issues in assessment and pedagogy.* Clevedon, United Kingdom: Multilingual Matters.

Cushner, K., McClelland, A., & Safford, P. (1992). *Human diversity in education: An integrative approach.* New York: McGraw-Hill.

Dennis, R. E., Williams, W., Giangreco, M. F., & Cloninger, C. J. (1993). Quality of life as context for planning and evaluation of services for people with disabilities. *Exceptional Children, 59,* 499-512.

Erickson, F. (1997). Culture in society and in education practices. In J. A. Banks & C. A. M. Banks (Eds.), *Multicultural education: Issues and perspectives* (3rd. ed., pp. 32-60). Needham Heights, MA: Allyn & Bacon.

Felce, D., & Perry, J. (1996). Assessment of quality of life. In R. L. Schalock (Ed.), *Quality of life: Vol. 1. Conceptualization and measurement* (pp. 63-72). Washington, DC: American Association on Mental Retardation.

Fraad, S. H., & Weismantel, M. J. (1989). Developing and evaluating goals. In S. H. Fraad & M. J. Weismantel (Eds.), *Meeting the needs of culturally and linguistically different students: A handbook for educators* (pp. 34-62). Boston: College-Hill.

Franklin, M. E. (1992). Culturally sensitive instructional practice for African-American learners with disabilities. *Exceptional Children, 59,* 115-122.

Freire, P. (1986). *Pedagogy of the oppressed.* (M. B. Ramos, Trans.). New York: Continuum. (Original work published 1968.)

Friend, M., & Bursuck, W. (1996). *Including students with special needs: A practical guide for classroom teachers.* Needham Heights, MA: Allyn & Bacon.

Gonzales, V. (1995). *Cognition, culture, and language in bilingual children: Conceptual and semantic development.* Bethesda, MD: Austin/Winfield.

Grossman, H. (1995). *Special education in a diverse society.* Needham Heights, MA: Allyn & Bacon.

Hall, E. T. (1959). *The silent language.* New York: Doubleday.

Hall, E. T. (1976). *Beyond culture.* New York: Doubleday.

Keith, K. D. (1996). Measuring quality of life across cultures: Issues and challenges. In R. L. Schalock (Ed.), *Quality of life: Vol. 1. Conceptualization and measurement* (pp. 73-82). Washington, DC: American Association on Mental Retardation.

Lobo, L. F. (1992). Deficiência: Prevenção, diagnóstico e estigma. In H. B. C. Rodrigues, M. B. S. Leitão, & R. D. B. de Barros (Eds.), *Grupos e instituições am analise* (pp. 113-126). Rio de Janeiro: Editora Rosa dos Tempos.

MEC-Ministério da Educação e do Deporto (1994). *Política nacional da educação especial: Livro 1* [National politic of special education: Book 1]. Brasília: MEC/SEESP.

Mercer, J. R. (1973*). Labeling the mentally retarded: Clinical and social system perspectives on mental retardation.* Berkeley, CA: University of California Press.

Meyen, E. L., Vergason, G. A., & Whelan, R. J. (1993). *Challenges facing special education.* Denver, CO: Love.

Ministério da Justica (1996). *Os direitos das pessoas portadoras de deficiencia* [The rights of people with disabilites]. Lei 7.853/89, Decreto 914/93. Brasilia: CORDE.

Nirje, B. (1985). The basis and logic of the normalization principle. *Australia and New Zealand Journal of Developmental Disabilities, 11,* 65-68.

Ortiz, A. A., & Yates, J. R. (1983). Incidence of exceptionality among Hispanics: Implications for manpower planning. *Journal of the National Association for Bilingual Education, 7,* 41-53.

Phillips, S. U. (1983). *The invisible culture: Communication in school and community on the Warm Springs Indian Reservation.* New York: Longman.

Schalock, R. L. (Ed.). (1990). *Quality of life: Perspectives and issues.* Washington, DC: American Association on Mental Retardation.

Schalock, R. L. (1996). Reconsidering the conceptualization and measurement of quality of life. In R. L. Schalock (Ed.), *Quality of life: Vol. 1. Conceptualization and measurement* (pp. 123-139). Washington, DC: American Association on Mental Retardation.

Schalock, R. L. (1997a). Can the concept of quality of life make a difference? In R. L. Schalock (Ed.), *Quality of life: Vol. 2. Application to persons with disabilities* (pp. 245-267). Washington, DC: American Association on Mental Retardation.

Schalock, R. L. (1997b). Considering culture in the application of quality of life. In R. L. Schalock (Ed.), *Quality of life: Vol. 2. Application to persons with disabilities* (pp. 225-243). Washington, DC: American Association on Mental Retardation.

Schank, R. C., & Abelson, R. (1977). *Scripts, plans, goals, and understanding.* Hillsdale, NJ: Erlbaum.

Snell, M. E., & Vogtle, L. K. (1997). Facilitating relationships of children with mental retardation in schools. In R. L. Schalock (Ed.), *Quality of life: Vol. 2. Application to persons with disabilities* (pp. 43-61). Washington, DC: American Association on Mental Retardation.

Spradley, J. P., & McCurdy, D. W. (1972). *The cultural experience—Ethnography in complex society.* Prospect Heights, IL: Waveland Press.

Voeltz, L. J., Hemphill, N. J., Brown, S., Kishi, R., Fruelhling, R., Collie, J., Levy, G., & Kube, C. (1983). *The special friends program: A trainer's manual for integrated school settings.* Honolulu: University of Hawaii, Department of Special Education.

Author Note

The assistance and collaboration of Timothy C. Watson in preparation of this chapter is gratefully acknowledged.

Cultural Contributions to Quality of Life in France

Marie José Schmitt
European Group for the Employment
of People With Mental Disabilities
Aix En Provence, France

This French contribution to cross-cultural study of quality of life will be short, as quality of life is not a current social-science issue in France as it is in Anglo-Saxon countries. This is true for the population in general, not only for people with disabilities. Quality standards are now a concept in industry, but we are just beginning to think that quality standards might apply to services as well. Quality standards remain linked with the concept of production of goods and are not yet applied to people's lives. The movement toward nature, natural products, and healthy life, though having some importance in the last 10 years, is far from being as important in France as in Germany, for instance. Even if it has become fashionable for a part of the population, it has no real political or social impact in France. Unemployment is a major problem, and words such as *purchasing power, disadvantage,* and *marginalization* are more likely to be found in the newspapers than in social-science discourse. This might explain why the concept of quality of life is not often used for people with disabilities.

In this chapter I will examine reasons that explain this fact, rooted in French culture as reflected in history, language, and law. Finally, I will explore the cultural features of disabled people's position in French society and look at the way of life of people with a mental disability in France.

Definition of Culture

A French researcher counted more than 150 definitions of culture—so we have a big selection. The Latin definition of individual culture is "the development of taste, critic, and judgment." From the point of view of ethics, we can read in this definition that culture is what helps people to take their place in the events occurring in their surroundings according to their own values. In other words, we could say that culture is mainly expressing the image that we have of others. And this image, in turn, is not to be separated from our self-image. So we have come to a psychological view of culture.

Applied to a population, culture becomes a civilization, a series of features that bear on our way of considering the organization of our way of living together. This raises the question of the part played by governments in cultural expressions, as for instance in laws. Some features bearing on a population's cultural expressions are quite obvious, such as geography, climate, and economy of the region where people are living. The representation of quality of life is very much influenced by sitting in the sunshine rather than sitting next to the fireplace, for example.

A Point of History

History has forged in us a common memory and has given emphasis to values that have been shared over years. In France these values, inherited from Greek democracy seen through the mirror of the French Renaissance, prompted three words at the Revolution: *freedom, equality,* and *fraternity.* Whether achieved or not, these values are still dominant in our collective way of thinking. Our society is built on these three values that combine individual freedom with our neighbours' equal right to freedom, so that the link between citizens is seen to be like that of children in a family.

The last of these three values, fraternity, was assaulted by the growth of fascism in most European countries in the 1930s. The war became a real civil war, not only in Spain, but in Italy, Germany, France, Belgium, and in the Netherlands—a war deep within the families, where brothers were divided between fascists and opponents. Civil war is the most destabilizing of all wars, because nobody really knows where the enemies are—before us, behind us, or sitting at the same table. Many mothers in Italy prepared the "black shirt" for one son by day and brought food and arms to the other son, hidden in the forest, by night. In such a context the word *fraternity* has lost its first sense. And if we look at the broader sense, that of brotherhood as members of humankind, never has there been such a disaster as in the years of fascism.

We must remember that France, if we consider its remote past, has always been centralized since the Middle Ages. *Individual freedom,* whatever the content of these words might have been over the centuries, was therefore always measured against a hierarchy, referring to a center, a vertical power represented by administrative bodies. This hierarchy is built upon a general agreement that a central power (king, emperor, president) is necessary to organize interaction among people and guarantee equality, while individuals determine their individual way of life according to their own values.

The period of fascism destroyed those usual (we could say cultural) guarantees. The central figure was no more a faithful bearer of people's values, and even the values had gone. This might explain why, during the postwar period, only one out of the three values was given some importance in the collective thought of Europe, and this value was that of freedom. Postwar anarchy worshiped freedom as a value in a population where fraternity had lost meaning and where equality was no longer an issue. Individual freedom had become a central value. This gave a new impulse to a very individualistic construction of society in France, around two complementary but distant poles: national solidarity, on one hand, and private life, on the other. There is no opposition to be found between those two trends of individualism and solidarity. In fact, we can see how they are joined in a new, albeit timid, humanism. This has been translated by governments into the Universal Declaration of Human Rights of the Council of Europe.

Human rights have been, and still are, the basis of The Council of Europe. The founding members of the Council of Europe have launched a huge change in the organization of our way of living together without fighting. Jean Monnet, one of the fathers of European thought, used to say that "Europe is a not too bad way of management of our interdependency." This word *interdependency* gives a new sense to the value of equality on which there is a strong hope that the social construction of Europe will be based.

Two Points of Language

Community and Society

In France, we don't use the word *community,* but the word *society*—the latter referring perhaps better to the way in which we organize our public matters *(res publica),* this unavoidable "outside" part of our life, while keeping a strong position for the individual part. This difference in wording is not a mere question of vocabulary, because, as a matter of fact, the two words do exist in all European languages. We can come up with a number of possible reasons for this difference. In fact, community and society are two different concepts, the first referring to a horizontal image of how to share responsibilities; the second referring to a vertical construction of the way of facing up to one's responsibilities. We can also say that the word *community* is closer to the Protestant view of human relationship to God and to the Bible, whereas the word *society* corresponds to the strong hierarchy of the Catholic church as a means of access, a mediation between God and humankind. We all know that the dominant religion directly influences the way in which people join a group, share its ethics, and take part in decision making.

The French word *society* refers to three different things: to a civilization, to a way of organizing collective life, and to commercial companies as well. It has something to do with citizenship as an individual input to a collective aim bringing results for the individual. Would it be wrong to say that *community* has more to do with the idea of output, of common aim? This difference between society and community, between collective and common, might also explain that, depending on the culture, another meaning will be given to *quality of life.*

Social Life

There is another point of language, indeed a point of culture, to be made. Sociability, or social life, seems to be a real issue in Anglo-Saxon countries. In France, social life is not considered to be an aim as such. It is a means, a necessary common standard to be reached for the management of public life, the main value still remaining private life.

We have to be careful not to think of one term necessarily opposed to another, as *public* to *private,* or *collective* to *individual.* We know that this is never true in human life. Black and white do exist of course, but most realities are embedded in a wide range of grays. Language is an ever-changing means of communication that reflects our different approaches to reality, and sometimes it is useful to ask ourselves why two different words are used for saying (apparently) the same thing. For example, I noted that freedom is an accepted, important value in our society. But we also use the word *independence.* Does independence then have another meaning and does it have a link with freedom? How would such a link be shaped? This could be an endless philosophical debate on the essential features of being human.

But let us come back to our subject and simply transpose the question in matters of social policy for people with disabilities. We must consider whether independence is, in itself, a guarantee of individual freedom. And this immediately raises questions, at least in Europe, as to where *independent living*—a key phrase in social policy—is coming from. Is it really a result of free choice of people with disabilities? Or of a need to face up to economic restrictions? I believe that fashionable concepts such as independent living and integrated employment should be seriously examined. Reflecting on the words that are used, we face another question: What is the link between independence and interdependence? This leads to the third point to be explored in culture: the translation of cultural trends into laws.

Laws

The combined move of history and values has always been translated into this tool for management of population that is called laws. France, as most European countries, has directly inherited aspects of the tradition of *agora* and *forum*—places where everyone could have a say in this Mediterranean civilization, where the servant often used to speak on behalf of his master, and sometimes louder. The Romans, reaching back to the old Jewish tradition, considered a written law necessary. Law was the fixed and stable counterpart to the ongoing debate at the forum. Thus there was a guarantee of balance between spoken words and written words, between creation and conservation, between change and permanence. From Roman law to Napoleon's code, written law has kept its symbolic value of strength, of a word given to people so that they can live. It is a binding word and as such is constitutive of society. Law has been, and still is, established by the legislative body with a double function: On the one hand, it has to strengthen and protect individual rights; on the other, it has to protect the society from individual behavior that might be dangerous for the society as a whole or for one of its members.

The evolution of these laws reflects the evolution of the peoples' way of thinking, as perceived by the legislative body. In written law a rule changes only when a new rule is given; interpretations of a law can lead to different judgments, but not to a change in law. The written text remains binding so long as the legislative body has not changed it.

The present shift from social laws (collective rights) to a human rights perspective (individual rights), as in the 1992 Americans With Disabilities Act or in the English law, is coming from the area of jurisprudential law and reaches continental Europe through the European Court of Justice. The Napoleon Code must integrate this new input, and huge changes might be expected in the coming 20 years. We now observe the influence of international input, with or without compulsory application, on our local written law. For example, *the Standard Rules on the Equalization of Opportunities for Persons With Disabilities* (United Nations, 1994), once adopted and translated, came to Europe either directly through governments (although they generally did not care very much) or through nongovernmental organizations working together with European bodies. This illustrates the very interesting way in which interdependence (among member states and/or among groups) is now becoming a reality.

Equalization of opportunities carries with it the need to measure inequalities and lacks. And who could perform such measurements better than people themselves? This is why we expect quality of life very soon to become an important tool in France, particularly for people with mental disabilities. We now must examine the cultural aspects of the concept of mental disability if we want to show the French.... and, more generally, the Latin.... position with regard to these individuals.

The Concept of Mental Disability

As long as disability is a minor difficulty, or a slight difference, French society is usually very helpful and open-minded; however, severe mental disability is seen as a radical difference. There are, of course, reasons for such a cultural trend. Let us start with an optimistic view: People, at the individual as well as the collective level, like to help each other. We help the old man to get up the stairs; we help the person with visual impairment to cross the street; in so doing we find a satisfactory answer to our inner questions about being old or being blind. It is the same with governments; politicians feel satisfied with all the rules on accessibility (even though insufficient or not put into practice), because they think they have solved a problem.

For people with a mental disability, there is no obvious available technical help to compensate for or to solve the problem, and our ever-speeding information-based society seems to become more and more hostile to these people. Integration becomes a real challenge, even though we know that when these people are given a real opportunity to live in the society, to earn their living, and to participate in a productive way, they find their own way, according to their own logic. Does this mean that what we take to be an impossibility is merely a difference? Does it mean that people with mental disabilities can better cope with life than we can cope with their difference?

Where is this old fear of differences rooted? Society seems to fear mental disability, because the very nature of this disability appears to lead to the terrible doubt that these people are perhaps not really human beings. The collective thought, since far remote times, contains this idea of beings similar to but not really human beings. We can read this in Greek literature, in the belief in possession by the devil, and in positivism and Darwinism. This radically questions human identity.

In France, in humanistic Europe, we are still living under the dominant ideas of Descartes, of his *"cogito ergo sum,"* the production of thought creating the evidence of being human. We quickly jump to the conclusion that thoughts are inherently expressed and communicated, and in this way those people who do not express their thoughts, or do not express them in the socially expected manner or in a manner that we can understand, are excluded from communication and (by implication) from humankind. This may explain why, in the period when the organization of society was mainly agricultural, people with mental disabilities often lived with farm animals, tolerated in their mysterious difference as was the house cat. They were not considered real human beings.

We could say that the great fear raised by people with severe mental disabilities has something to do with our own fear for our fragile identity when faced with difference. Such fear exists, deeply rooted in collective thinking, despite major cultural changes. We can find it in the laws, where the ordinary labor relationship remains unavailable to individuals with mental disability; and in education, where recognition of achievement without assessment in abstract fields such as mathematics or grammar seems impossible. Full participation is considered essential and is desired all over the world. For example, in the ongoing revision process of the *International Classification of Impairments, Disabilities, and Handicaps* (World Health Organization, 1980) we observe a shift from integration (being there) toward participation (contributing). But even there, limits, barriers, and some "loud" silences demonstrate that participation is not meant for "these" people.

Acting and reacting to one's environment and changing it is perhaps the most important feature of being human. But people with severe mental disability can become actors in their surroundings only if we provide them with the help they need. This help is not to be found in technical devices; it is human help. Policy makers, when dealing with social costs, are reluctant to include human helpers' training as an investment on the usual balance sheets. Accustomed as we are to the principle that losses must be assessed and gaps filled, there is a somewhat sad and desperate conclusion that, for people with severe mental disabilities, there is nothing to be done. And it is true that there is no technical device that would compensate for the difficulties of these people. We feel puzzled, unable to cope with an image of humanity that does not correspond to our established standards. As a result, the image that these people see reflected in our eyes is a very disabling one. Action and reaction thus work in a destructive sense, not a creative sense. We all seem unable to forget differences and to make a space for hope and faith, the two powerful energies that can elevate people with mental disabilities to the place they have a right to occupy as full citizens in French society.

Hope and Faith

Hope and *faith* are the key words of parent organizations in France. Since the end of World War II, and because of the holocaust suffered by people with mental disabilities during the War, parents have formed strong organizations struggling for disabled children's rights to education. The starting point was refusal of institutional care for their children, leading to creation of small special schools all over France (some of them boarding schools). The government was alternately reluctant and helpful, finally accepting the following arrangement: Parent organizations would create and manage the special schools, and the state would provide the money for the settings and operating costs.

As the children have grown up, parent organizations have had to face new needs, resulting in creation of a range of vocational training units, adapted enterprises providing work opportunities, and small group homes. In France economic life is mainly organized into small enterprises with 20 to 50 workers, and this pattern is reflected in the adapted enterprises. The large group homes, serving 20 people or more in the 1950s, began to be split up in the 1960s. Now, according to degree of disability, people are living in small homes, from 3 to 6 people together, in independent houses or flats. Sometimes, when more care is needed, two groups may live together on the same site. Today then, most people with severe mental disability in France live with friends, work every day of the week in adapted enterprises, and go to their homes (or are brought there) in the evening. Leisure time and weekend activities are organized in the home.

In France, due in part to the role of psychoanalysis in the organization of care, there has long been a general practice of weekly group therapy or group sessions in which staff listen to people with disabilities. By law (since 1975), in each unit there is an elected committee with representatives of professionals, parents or relatives, and of people with disabilities living or working there. These committees meet at least once every 3 months (and usually monthly) to make practical decisions. Participation, in this sense, has been organized for more than 20 years. It can thus be said that people with mental disabilities are accustomed to having their say in their daily surroundings. In some cases it works quite well, and in others it does not. Empowerment is not an issue or a strategy in France; it is a result of the general way of living. However, those working in adapted enterprises and living with their families face the challenge of remaining a child in their parents' eyes and being an adult with a personal say—a balance that is perhaps more difficult to find for people with mental disabilities than for other adult children who share a portion of their lives with their parents.

In France, we strongly believe that we must take the opportunity presented by new trends toward quality standards and try to investigate each person's real, individual opportunities to live a full human life. And if hope and faith need a tool, the concept of quality of life, as it has been developed in the United States and in other Anglo-Saxon countries, will be well adapted for improving the right of people with mental disabilities to have their say. This would be a very healthy and useful contribution to humankind.

References

United Nations. (1994). *The standard rules on the equalization of opportunities for persons with disabilities.* New York: Author.

World Health Organization. (1980). *International classification of impairments, disabilities, and handicaps.* Geneva: Author.

Quality of Life for People With Mental Retardation and Developmental Disabilities in Spain: The Present Zeitgeist

Miguel A. Verdugo
Universidad de Salamanca
Salamanca, Spain

People associate the idea of quality of life with various notions that, in turn, have a clear positive emphasis: nice life, to feel good, to have a good living standard, to have well-being, to be satisfied, to be happy (Casas, 1993). Such notions of "good living" have long been disregarded as a topic of scientific study, because their subjective character seemed to make it impossible to analyze them from a scientific approach. With the passage of time, however, the expression and its meaning have ended up as one of the key concepts in planning and evaluating the professional actions and services for people with disabilities, together with other population groups.

The term *quality of life* has been used in Spain from different perspectives related to the individual's living conditions and their improvement, rather than the individual's personal satisfaction with those living conditions. This last aspect, which is one of the most common approaches to the definition of quality of life in other countries (Borthwick-Duffy, 1992; Edgerton, 1990; Felce & Perry, 1995), has begun to be taken into account in the last few years in Spain, because of great stress on the consumer's perspective about health services, social services, and education. But generally one's quality of life has been defined from the professional's point of view; the main interest has been on defining quantitative parameters related to social indicators (i.e., health, living standards, education, security, etc.), and not so much on psychological (i.e., well-being and satisfaction) or ecological aspects (i.e., the individual's needs and wishes, environmental demands, and the resources of the individual). These psychological and ecological aspects should be borne in mind in trying to make *quality of life* an operational term (Dennis, Williams, Giangreco, & Cloninger, 1993).

The purpose of this chapter is to present a current overview of the quality of life of people with disabilities in the Spanish society. First, I give a general presentation of the use of the term in the fields of public policies and service delivery. Second, I review the most important studies on quality of life, focusing on the interpersonal relations dimension, according to the model proposed by Schalock (1996, 1997). Finally, I draw some conclusions as a summary of the existing intellectual climate in terms of the concept of quality of life and its use for people with disabilities.

Public Policy and Service Delivery

The significant changes in the Spanish social policy in the last two decades have their origins in the 1982 Spanish Law for Social Integration of the Disabled (Ley 13/82 de Integración Social de Minusválidos; LISMI). This law was the general framework for the introduction of the massive reforms of public services, including health and education, and it encouraged development of regional regulations in the various Spanish autonomous communities. The LISMI meant that a constitutional mandate (the Spanish Constitution was enforced in 1978) was achieved. And it defined the duty of the public authorities of affording special protection measures for the disabled.

Changes in the Education System

The education system existing in Spain during the last 15 years has experienced a significant change. The educational reform has invested ample means and human resources to improve educational services. Particularly, since 1985 the students with special needs have received special measures to support their integration (mainstreaming) in ordinary schools. The education reform has changed concepts and practices, bringing to schools the "supports" approach, interdisciplinary work, and an interactional conception of disability. From a technical point of view, the education system in Spain has advanced to a leadership role in Europe and in many parts of the world. The Spanish reform has influenced other countries' reforms, mainly in Latin America, as one can see in the *Salamanca Statement and Framework for Action on Special Needs Education* (United Nations, 1994).

Curricular development is one of the main changes that the educational reform has brought into the schools. Every school is required to provide special measures in its curriculum for students with special educational needs. The educational levels and each classroom should subsequently establish the specific characteristics for the student's curricular adaptations (Ministerio de Educación y Ciencia, 1992a, 1992b). Although curriculum adaptations refer to any aspect in the curriculum, including nonschool factors, the current emphasis is on skill acquisition. In this sense, and to pave the way for the approaches derived from the concept of quality of life, it is important to assess and include specific aims and objectives related to improved social and interpersonal relations, enhanced self-esteem, satisfying emotional well-being, and the development of self-determination.

Teachers and other educational professionals are implementing some quality-of-life techniques (i.e., mainstreaming, assessment based on life activities, provision of community-based activities and experiences), although the use is not yet common. The recent curricular changes and the dynamics of change in the educational system are in the right direction, but now it is time to confirm those changes. These efforts are not enough to assure the maintenance of the changes, and the advances are currently being seriously questioned due to political changes. Besides, we should make an additional effort to develop a consumer perspective and to analyze satisfaction with the services provided. The increasing participation of users and relatives of students with special needs in the processes of planning, teaching, and personal assessment of the student would be a great step forward.

Quality of Life in Public Policy

During the last few years, the development of plans and regulations both in the state and in the regions (autonomous communities) has begun to take into account a quality-of-life perspective.

In 1992, to mark the 10th anniversary of the enforcement of the LISMI, the lower chamber of the Spanish Parliament assessed the law's status. The Chamber stressed the substantial achievements in the recognition of the rights of people with disabilities in various contexts, but it also pointed out the deficiencies and limitations in the law's implementation. To overcome the shortcomings in the development of the law, a new *Action Plan for People With Disabilities 1997-2002* (Instituto Nacional de Servicios Sociales, 1996) was developed by the National Institute of Social Services in the Department of Social Affairs, called today the Institute of Migrations and Social Services. It is the national plan developed to establish common guidelines and principles in the plans of all the regions in Spain; it assumes specific principles and goals directly related to quality of life. The Plan covers the years 1997-2002 and includes a proposal for a comprehensive social policy for people with disabilities.

The *Action Plan* consists of five sectorial plans: health promotion and disability prevention; health assistance and comprehensive rehabilitation; school integration and special education; participation and integration in the economic life; and community integration and autonomous living. There are two general objectives of the *Action Plan:* in the personal sphere, to achieve maximum autonomy and independence of the disabled person; and in the social sphere, to promote a more active role and participation of the disabled person in the social and economic life. There are five basic principles: (a) to promote individual rights and freedom of the individuals involved; (b) to promote independent living, personal autonomy, and self-sufficiency; (c) to stress quality of life; (d) to guarantee equal opportunities for people with disabilities; and (e) to foster integration and normalization. The *Action Plan* includes a set of strategies about how to organize and manage resources. The strategies include equal opportunities, regional equity, institutional cooperation, participation of the people, and support to quality.

The term *quality* appears in the *Action Plan* associated with various concepts and different roles. First, it appears as "quality of life" among the basic *principles* that are the basis of the plan's actions. Regarding this issue, the person's search for satisfaction with living conditions at home, school or workplace, and community is the driving force for the specification of objectives that include the wishes of the person and the promotion of services. It focuses on user satisfaction and the management of the resources in such a way that resources will be used not only to fulfill physical needs, but also to promote the general well-being of the individual.

Second, the word *quality* is also associated with services when trying to improve their efficiency and user satisfaction. Quality of services is one of the *strategies* common to the five sectorial plans. The aim of the strategy is to promote research projects; to promote, develop, and disseminate innovative experiences and programs; to plan ar d develop the training and retraining of the professional staff;

to develop studies and methods for the continuous assessment of service and program processes and results; to devise quality guides for service accreditation and assessment; to encourage meetings of those bodies responsible for service research, training, and assessment; and to devise a statistical system allowing the continuous monitoring of current policies.

Finally, *quality* appears in expressions such as "the improvement of the quality of teaching, training, and services" in the *objectives* that make up the 20 programs of the *Action Plan* and in the specific *measures* to achieve those objectives.

Although the term *quality of life* appears several times in the Spanish *Action Plan,* it seems that the normalization philosophy, and not quality of life, is the driving force of the plan. There is not a single operational definition of the concept of quality of life that might favor its implementation and assessment. A solution to this problem might be found in the development of a specific plan in the autonomous communities. However, the existing plans in the autonomous communities are not following this line. Only some plans of the autonomous communities include quality of life as a general criterion that should be taken into account when developing the areas and intervention programs in the plans for people with disabilities (Junta de Castilla y León, 1995). Other regional plans being developed, as in Castilla La Mancha, stress the use of quality of life as a guiding principle for the planning and assessment of social policies.

The specific principles that direct the social policies for the disabled in Spain basically follow the Recommendation No. R(92) 6 of the European Council (Consejo de Europa, 1992). The recommendation favors the adoption of a coherent policy for the rehabilitation of people with disabilities stating several objectives, based on every aspect of life, taking into account the stages of personal development. The principles include: to prevent or to eliminate the disability, its deterioration, and consequences; to guarantee that the people with disabilities have an active and global participation in the social life; and to help the people with disabilities to lead an autonomous life, according to their own wishes.

Quality of life is explicitly included in the national *Action Plan* as a driving concept of public policies, but its actual implementation is insufficient for a proper development of the concept. Hence, in contrast to what Goode (1997) stated, the concept of quality of life does appear in the official policies for disabilities in Spain. However, this new situation is a result of the work done in the late 90s. Goode's statements followed a book by Daunt (1991) which did represent the European situation in the 1980s, but things are changing very fast. The attention given to the concept of quality of life, however, still is fairly general and has not been thoroughly defined.

Quality of Life as a Crucial Task in Private Organizations

The National Confederation of Federations and Associations in Favor of People With Mental Retardation (FEAPS), which is the main nongovernmental organization working with people with mental retardation, is involved in a process of organizational development and has recently adopted a new perspective and orientation of the goals of its work. The FEAPS includes 585 associations, and 17 federations of associations, with 1,700 centers, 12,000 professionals, and 67,000 individuals assisted. This totals 125,000 people associated with FEAPS and includes more than 90% of the private programs, services, and activities developed to support people with mental retardation in Spain. The associations that make up FEAPS have been established by parents and relatives of people with mental retardation.

In 1997 FEAPS approved a strategic plan for the organization that establishes the organization's mission: to improve the quality of life of people with mental retardation and their families. Thus quality of life is the main focus of the efforts of all the organizations in FEAPS. The strategic plan is developed around five different axes: (a) the cultural process—the quality plan; (b) the communication plan; (c) an efficiency plan; (d) organizational development, and (e) the leadership of FEAPS in the environment. In the first axis, the American Association on Mental Retardation definition of mental retardation (Luckasson et al., 1992) has been adopted, and thus a new paradigm for the achievement of quality of life has been established. Moreover, another strategic line in the first axis is the reinforcement of the role of the family as a key factor in the process of quality-of-life enhancement for people with mental disabilities. In the second axis, there are three strategic goals: to define FEAPS quality; to develop a plan for its implementation; and to put in motion quality-of-life assessment systems.

At the moment, FEAPS is developing its strategic plan using a combination of various aspects of quality in organizations (total quality management) and is also focusing on the quality of life of the individual. The quality-of-life definition proposed by Schalock (1996), with its eight core dimensions and indicators, together with his proposals of how to measure them, is being analyzed and debated for use by every organization. Schalock's proposal is so flexible that it can be used by different organizations with diverse aims and by different organizational dimensions.

Research on Quality of Life

In the recent past, much attention in Spain has been drawn to the concept of quality of life. Most of the research studies come from the field of health psychology, and areas that have received the most interest have included rehabilitation (Cuervo-Arango, 1990; Fernández, Covas, & Moreno, 1996; Moreno Gea, 1996; Verdugo, 1995), the elderly (Fernández-Ballesteros, Zamarrón, & Maciá, 1996; Martorell, Gómez, Cuenca-Campillo, & Weber, 1995) and the person with mental retardation (Grupo de Investigación en Medicina Psicosocial, 1995; Verdugo, Canal, & Bermejo, 1997; Verdugo et al., 1996; Verdugo, Canal, & Gómez, 1997).

In the last few years, the Institute for Community Integration (INICO) of the University of Salamanca has been developing a research line on quality of life for people with mental retardation and other disabilities (Verdugo et al., 1996; Verdugo, Canal, & Gómez 1997). Research developed from 1994 to 1996 attempted to show that ordinary housing positively influenced the living conditions of five adult people with mental retardation and pervasive support needs, improving their well-being (Verdugo, Canal, & Bermejo, 1997). Different indicators were used to compare the quality of life of these people to other people with mental retardation living in a large residence owned by the same agency. A questionnaire was developed to assess the quality of life, physical well-being, personal safety, social relationships, choice, and quality-of-life promotion. Studies of reliability and validity of the questionnaire were positive. The questionnaire was completed by 100 people independent of the agency, randomly distributed to two groups that visited and inspected during one complete day either the ordinary housing or the large residence. Statistical analyses of the responses showed that visitors of ordinary housing gave higher scores in all quality-of-life indicators than visitors of the large residence. All the differences in the indicators were statistically significant, except physical well-being.

At present, we are developing a quality-of-life assessment instrument for people with mental retardation based on Schalock's eight core-dimensions model (1996, 1997). It covers the individual's perceived satisfaction with living conditions so as to know what constitutes the person's quality of life (Verdugo, Canal, & Gómez, 1997). The instrument includes three questionnaires: one for service users, another for their families, and the third for professionals.

Interpersonal Relations

Some of the most remarkable and differentiating aspects of quality of life in the Spanish culture can be traced to the interpersonal relations context (i.e., family, friends, and neighbors) and to the availability of time and leisure opportunities. In contrast to other European countries and the United States, Spain is known for its important outdoor social life. The "street" is a common and daily meeting point with other people (i.e., relatives, friends, neighbors, workmates). Cafeterias, bars, restaurants, parks, squares, and other outdoor spaces are meeting and recreation places. Spaniards enjoy those moments together with other people. This is a major contribution to our specific well-being and life satisfaction.

In Spain there are cultural variations depending on the geographical area, but in contrast to other countries the outstanding factor is our having fun together with other people: something basically done outdoors. This situation may also be characteristic, and even more marked, of the Latin American countries in contrast to the social behavior of the Anglo-Saxon societies. Further cross-cultural quality-of-life research should answer such presuppositions.

This differentiating cultural feature can be verified by the observation of social behaviors in different cultures and social groups and by the analysis of opinions. For example, analysis of the leisure activities and preferences of people with visual impairment and blindness in Spain would confirm some of the ideas stated above. According to EDIS (1993), the activities preferred in their spare time, and done by at least 80% of those polled, were listening to the radio, talking with friends, and talking with their family. The same activities (in the same order) were their preferences for the future. Although these are passive leisure activities, they confirm the hypothesis stated above about the predilection for relations with other people. In their daily life, 8 out of 10 people with visual impairments have contact with their family, and 6 out of 10 with their friends. In the field of mental retardation, due to the special characteristics of a higher family dependence, it is very likely that contacts with friends do not reach those levels. Gender differences can also be significant. Research should answer such questions. Cultural features of the Spanish society compared to other societies and cultures, and differences within Spain, are not reflected in group support activities already implemented. Thus our future efforts should be focused on the verification of those peculiarities in the understanding of quality of life in different cultures. Then we should develop educational and rehabilitation strategies to enhance the quality of life of every individual according to the special features of the cultural context in which the person lives.

Sexuality, Affect, and Intimacy

Everyone has social, affective, and sexual needs that must be satisfied and are linked to emotional security, social support, and physical intimacy. The family, the school, and peer groups fulfill those needs (López, 1997). Emotional security contributes to a better feeling of personal well-being and emotional stability. Social supports, with friends, peer groups, neighbors, and others, help build the personal identity and allow communication, cooperation, and natural development within the community.

Sexuality in people with mental retardation has recently been given special attention in Spain not only by parents and professionals, but also by researchers (Barbero & González, 1993; Belmonte, 1993; Crespo, 1993; Instituto Nacional de Servicios Sociales, 1993; Jiménez, 1995; López, 1993; Martín, 1995; Miguel & Ortega, 1995; Verdugo, 1993). Despite the interest in a better knowledge of the sexual needs and how to better address the issues within the family and services, there still is a lack of systematized teaching and some shortcomings in the development of attitudes that favor sexual development according to the individual's preferences and decisions. It is very normal to find restrictive approaches in parents and professionals in terms of the person with mental retardation's development of sexual manifestations. The childish image that many people have of the individual supports these approaches. Sometimes, the parent's fear of pregnancy or other unwanted consequences favors such restrictive and limiting behaviors. Women with mental retardation usually suffer a double discrimination, in their right to have sexual expression and in the development of friendships.

The research conducted in the recent past is especially focused on descriptive studies of the attitudes of parents and professionals (Jiménez, 1995; Martín, 1995) and of the individuals with mental retardation themselves toward sexuality (Miguel & Ortega, 1995). However, some educative and intervention experiences have also been developed (Barbero & González, 1993; Belmonte, 1993; Crespo, 1993; Verdugo, 1989a, 1989b, 1997). Currently, the key factor would be to support prevention, teaching, and intervention in order to admit and to favor the individual's ability to make a decision.

It is commonplace to deal with sexuality as a separate aspect differentiated from other behaviors of the individual. The links of "sexuality" with friendship, affect, and intimacy should be the appropriate educational context. The educational reform includes sexual education contents in the field of education for health. Such contents should be developed within attitudinal and practical contexts. From the second half of the 1980s, professionals have been able to promote a great activity and interest of services to follow this line (Instituto Nacional de Servicios Sociales, 1993). A better knowledge of research and innovations on the concept of quality of life can help to make progress in this field. Sexuality, affect, and intimacy are closely linked to some of the quality-of-life dimensions: interpersonal relations, self-determination, and rights (Schalock, 1996, 1997). Behavioral problems related to sexuality are one of the main worries in the Spanish services for the people with mental retardation. The lack of action-norms shared by all professionals and the lack of awareness of assessment and intervention techniques have meant there are no standard criteria to approach these problems. In recent years some community perspectives have been developed. On the one hand, they lead to serious reflection on the difficulties (and the need to find a solution) that people with disability meet when wanting to express their sexuality; on the other, they develop procedures to assess and change maladjusted behaviors.

Professionals and researchers interested in this issue met in the First National Conference on Sexuality in People With Mental Disability in 1992 (Instituto Nacional de Servicios Sociales, 1993). In the meeting they wrote a summary, drawing conclusions from all the studies and papers presented, with the following recommendations to:

- implement the normalization principle;
- defend the individual, asking pluralism;
- link the family network to educational tasks;
- promote trainer training;
- use more of the legal possibilities given by the current improvements of the legal protection;
- expand interprofessional effort in research, intervention, and prevention.

Leisure and Recreation

Leisure is crucial to establishing adequate interpersonal relations and to one's perceived quality of life. Interaction with other people and contact with others can be enjoyed at their best in leisure and recreational activities. Nevertheless, the sort of activities developed by people with mental retardation is very limited in this area. We have long talked about the importance of those activities, but they have mainly been undertaken by volunteers and have been given a secondary role in objective planning. Organized activities have often lacked long-term planning and logical structure. Such a situation began to change in Spain in the 1990s with a substantial increase of specific professional work in these tasks and with a progressive strengthening of the organizations specifically dealing with this objective.

Some crucial problems must be addressed in the future role of leisure activities. One major task is to increase leisure options to allow individuals to have a choice. As proposed by Hawkins (1997), free time is closely related to freedom of choice. It is commonplace to leave decisions related to the use of spare time in the hands of professionals or the family, with little reference to the opinions and decisions of the individual. Quality of life might also be improved by linking activity planning with friendship development and increasing interactions of people with and without disabilities. This enhances the individual's social life and personal network, having a direct effect on quality of life. Finally, learning independent leisure skills must be a fundamental educational objective for the person with disabilities.

Social Inclusion and Social Skills

School integration has meant social integration of students with special educational needs. This new step forward can clearly be seen in the achievement of social objectives as compared to students in more segregated educational options. Nevertheless, the integration process shows some contradictions, because the student's social acceptance by classmates leaves much to be desired. Although significant efforts have been made in the training of and skill acquisition by students with disabilities, very little has been done to change classmates' attitudes toward them (Arias, Verdugo, & Rubio, 1995).

The improvement in social acceptance in schools is more evident in students with physical and sensory disabilities than in students with mental retardation (Arias et al., 1995). Social acceptance of students with disabilities, especially mental retardation, as shown in sociometric status (number of choices, rejection, negative and positive ratings by their peers) is not quite positive yet. Students with special needs are not chosen as much as their classmates, suffer more rejection, get low positive ratings and, particularly, more negative ratings than their classmates without disabilities. This shows the need to implement strategies devised to change stereotyped conceptions that students without disabilities have about their classmates with disabilities. If we do not follow this line, interpersonal relations will be completely limited by a lack of understanding and ignorance.

Interpersonal relations and the improvement of the social acceptance of students with special educative needs has been addressed by programs of adaptation skills and social skills. Such programs have been an alternative to educative approaches that focused exclusively on school or labor activities. Such a prevention and support perspective in social skill development is related directly to interpersonal relations in factors such as intimacy and affect, the development and maintenance of friendships, and the encouragement of interactions in various community contexts. Other aspects addressed are leisure, use of community resources, and participation in social acts (Verdugo, 1989a, 1989b, 1997).

In the recent past, school-based research on social skills for students with special needs has examined several innovative teaching procedures such as teaching through peers, starting training as soon as possible, even in kindergarten (Monjas, 1992, 1996; Monjas, Verdugo, & Arias, 1995), and encouraging horizontal rather than vertical interventions, which seems to facilitate "friendlier" interactions (Díaz-Aguado, Royo, & Baraja, 1995). Research in Spain regarding this issue resembles that conducted in other countries (Snell & Vogtle, 1997). Previous research has resulted in expansion of services following this line.

Family and Supports

The Spanish family plays a crucial role in the supports provided to family members. In fact, most of the services and programs for people with mental retardation were created thanks to parental and family initiatives. In the field of education, public administrations subsequently took on those tasks despite the fact that many people with broader support needs still are in a private context. In the field of employment and community services, private- and parent-related services and programs are the main solution.

Some characteristics of the Spanish family such as stability (with a low level of separations and divorces compared to other countries), low geographical mobility in the course of life that propitiates a supportive family and neighbor network, and the traditional protective role of the family, can be very positive for stable supports. It is quite normal to discover that sons and daughters stay with their parents well into adult life. The relationship between brothers is often positive and supportive. Parents assume responsibility for the economic maintenance of their children until they leave the family. And the broad family, other than father, mother, brothers, and sisters, maintains ties and is in contact quite often. Analysis of the importance of such factors in the support of people with mental retardation should be done in cross-cultural studies.

Families are very often subject to stressful situations caused either by the personal features of the individual with disabilities (e.g., behavioral problems, functional level, intensity of support) or by inadequate or nonsupportive answers from the environment. And structural factors related to unemployment, poverty, or social isolation situations suffered by the parents may trigger a stressful situation within the family.

Family stress is important to understand due to some stressful situations that might lead to the maltreatment of the person. Some families suffer problems of stress and situation adaptation, but many other families don't. Which factors in such families are playing an absorbing role and which a triggering role?

In a study regarding maltreatment of people with mental retardation in Spain, a great number of abuse and neglect practices were detected (Verdugo, Bermejo, Fuertes, & Elices, 1993; Verdugo et al., 1995). These studies report in a sample of 445 people with mental retardation that 11.5% suffer maltreatment; of this, physical neglect is the most frequent. Emotional neglect was especially emphasized as it is a less evident aspect of maltreatment and thus more difficult to detect. The studies also report that problems among the parents and the behavior of the child and the interaction between the parent and child were significant factors in situations of maltreatment.

Attitudes and actions of the professionals in the defense of the rights of people with disabilities are the key to identifying situations of maltreatment in the family, the institution, and the social environment. However, the lack of courage of many people in facing such situations leaves the person's position unrecognized and therefore untreatable. Present services should include among their priorities the development of programs addressed at mitigating stressful situations often suffered within the families of people with mental retardation or individuals with serious developmental disorders. Early professional intervention, support groups, and the development of family assistance services and resources are some of the necessary factors. Moreover, all this will resound to the benefit of the person with mental retardation in a better service and support delivery system.

Conclusions

The 1980s and the 1990s have brought to Spain a dramatic change in the moral, cultural, and intellectual climate regarding attitudes toward people with disabilities. Institutional changes brought by democracy have favored the introduction of important changes that have contributed significant human and material resources to the fields of education and social services. Social policies, service delivery, research, and professionals have become more productive, taking into account advanced technical approaches. These new approaches have allowed Spain to deal seriously with the quality of life of the people with disabilities and the quality of activities to support them. But the fundamental shifts have been done in the sphere of better public attitudes, and "in the long run, the quality of life of a retarded person is far more dependent on these general attitudes of society than it is on whatever specific programs happen to be in effect at any given time" (Ingalls, 1978, p. 442).

Quality of life is present in social policy planning and in service delivery, but it has been defined primarily from a general perspective. Private agencies and the public administration should increase their efforts to define explicitly the applicability of the concept in their plans and in service and program evaluation. Although there have been several major breakthroughs in the research on disabilities in the Western world and in Spain, Spanish society still has to consolidate the innovations and experiences. Current initiatives allow us to be optimistic about the future.

Quality of life, and particularly the model proposed by Schalock (1996, 1997), presents a general outlook that covers the whole life span of the person. Such an outlook links the efforts and advances in the different elements of professional work and research done in the recent past. The concept of quality of life can help greatly change current practices, moving forward to an individual-focused conception (Butterworth, Steere, & Whitney-Thomas, 1997).

The quality of life of people with mental retardation in Spain will improve rapidly thanks to the gradual steps being taken to define the planning of public policies according to the concept of quality of life and the adoption of a uniform model of quality of life for nongovernmental organizations. The concept of quality of life, which was preceded by the mainstreaming movement and the supports paradigm in the 1980s, has played a major role in the area of social planning and in the mission of private organizations. These institutions are beginning to consider its use in education, rehabilitation, health, employment, and every context of the life of individuals with mental retardation. We still lack the fundamental part, however: to achieve a true comprehensive application of the concept of quality of life in one's daily life. The years to come will be crucial to address that issue.

References

Arias, B., Verdugo, M. A., & Rubio, V. (1995). Evaluación de la actividad modelo local de Valladolid (Programa Helios). [Evaluation of the Valladolid Local Model Activity (Helios Program)]. Madrid: Ministerio de Educación y Ciencia, Centro de Investigación y Documentación Educativa.

Barbero, L., & González, F. (1993). La sexualidad en centros e instituciones de atención a deficientes mentales: La experiencia del C.O. "Juan de Austria" de Madrid [Sexuality in centers and institutions dedicated to mentally retarded: the experience of occupational center Juan de Austria of Madrid]. In Instituto Nacional de Servicios Sociales (Ed.), *Sexualidad en personas con minusvalía psíquica* [Sexuality in people with mental retardation]. [Proceedings of the First National Convention on Sexuality in People With Mental Disability.] Madrid: Editor.

Belmonte, R. (1993). La sexualidad en personas con minusvalía psíquica: Principales problemas y estrategias de intervención en un centro de educación especial [Sexuality in people with mental retardation: Main problems and treatment issues in a special education center]. In Instituto Nacional de Servicios Sociales (Ed.), *Sexualidad en personas con minusvalía psíquica* [Sexuality in people with mental retardation]. [Proceedings of the First National Convention on Sexuality in People With Mental Disability.] Madrid: Editor.

Borthwick-Duffy, S. A. (1992). Quality of life and quality of care in mental retardation. In L. Rowitz (Ed.), *Mental retardation in the year 2000* (pp. 52-66). Berlin: Springer-Verlag.

Butterworth, J., Steere, D. E., & Whitney-Thomas, J. (1997). Using person-centered planning to address personal quality of life. In R. L. Schalock (Ed.), *Quality of life: Vol. 2. Application to persons with disabilities.* (pp. 5-23). Washington, DC: American Association on Mental Retardation.

Casas, F. (1993). El concepto de calidad de vida en la intervención social en el ambito de la infancia [Quality of life concept in the social intervention in infancy]. In Colegio Oficial de Psicólogos (Ed.), *III Jornadas de Psicología de la Intervención Social* (Vol. 2, pp. 649-672). Madrid: Ministerio de Asuntos Sociales, INSERSO.

Consejo de Europa. (1992). *Una política coherente para la rehabilitación de las personas con minusvalía* [A coherent policy for the rehabilitation of persons with handicaps]. Recomendación nº R(92) 6 adoptada por el Comité de Ministros el 9 de abril de 1992 durante la 474 reunión de Delegados de Ministros [Recommendation no. R(92) 6 adopted by the Committee of Ministers on April 9, 1992, during the 474th meeting of Ministers' delegates]. Estrasburgo: Ediciones del Consejo de Europa.

Crespo, G. (1993). Sexualidad y deficiencia mental: Algunos datos de AFANIAS [Sexuality and mental retardation: Some data of AFANIAS]. In Instituto Nacional de Servicios Sociales (Ed.), *Sexualidad en personas con minusvalía psíquica* [Sexuality in people with mental retardation]. [Proceedings of the First National Convention on Sexuality in People With Mental Disability.] Madrid: Editor.

Cuervo-Arango, M. A. (1990). *Satisfacción residencial. Una aproximación psicosocial a los estudios de calidad de vida* [Residential satisfaction. A psychosocial approach to quality of life studies]. Madrid: Universidad Complutense de Madrid.

Daunt, P. (1991). *Meeting disability: A European response.* London: Cassell Educational Limited.

Dennis, R., Williams, W., Giangreco, M., & Cloninger, C. (1993). Calidad de vida como contexto para la planificación y evaluación de servicios para personas con discapacidad [Quality of life as context for planning and evaluation of services for people with disabilities]. *Exceptional Children, 59*(6), 499-512.

Díaz-Aguado, M. J., Royo, P., & Baraja, A. (1995). *Programas para favorecer la integración escolar de niños ciegos: Investigación* [Programs to facilitate school mainstreaming of blind boys: Research]. Madrid: Organización Nacional de Ciegos Españoles.

Edgerton, R. B.(1990). Quality of life from a longitudinal research perspective. In R. L. Schalock (Ed.), *Quality of life: Perspectives and issues* (pp. 149-160). Washington DC: American Association on Mental Retardation.

EDIS. (1993). *Las necesidades en servicios sociales de los afiliados a la ONCE* [Social services needs of ONCE affiliates]. Madrid: Organización Nacional de Ciegos Españoles, Departamento de Servicios Sociales para Afiliados.

Felce, D., & Perry, J. (1995). Quality of life: Its definition and measurement. *Research in Developmental Disabilities, 16*(1), 51-74.

Fernández, M. J., Covas, M., & Moreno, P. (1996). Valoración de la calidad de vida en personas con traumatismo cranoencefálico y sus familiares [Evaluation of quality of life in people with brain impairment and their families]. In Fundación Mapfre Medicina (Ed.), *Daño cerebral traumático y calidad de vida* [Traumatic brain impairment, neuropsicology, and quality of life] (pp. 493-498). Madrid: Editor.

Fernández-Ballesteros, R., Zamarrón, M. D., & Maciá, A. (1996). *Calidad de vida en la vejez en los distintos contextos* [Quality of life in aging in different contexts]. Madrid: Ministerio de Trabajo y Asuntos Sociales, Instituto Nacional de Servicios Sociales.

Goode, D. A. (1997). Quality of life as international disability policy: Implications for internatioal research. In R. L. Schalock (Ed.), *Quality of life: Vol. 2. Application to persons with disabilities* (pp. 211-221). Washington, DC: American Association on Mental Retardation.

Grupo de Investigación en Medicina Psicosocial. (1995). *Evaluación psicosocial del retraso mental. Conceptos, metodología e instrumentos* [Psychosocial assessment of mental retardation. Concepts, methodology and instruments]. Madrid: Minsterio de Asuntos Sociales, Instituto Nacional de Servicios Sociales.

Hawkins, B. A. (1997). Promoting quality of life through leisure and recreation. In R. L. Schalock (Ed.), *Quality of life: Vol. 2. Application to persons with disabilities* (pp. 117-129). Washington, DC: American Association on Mental Retardation.

Ingalls, R. P. (1978). *Mental retardation: The changing outlook.* New York: John Wiley.

Instituto Nacional de Servicios Sociales. (1993). *Sexualidad en personas con minusvalía psíquica* [Sexuality in people with mental retardation]. [Proceedings of the First National Convention on Sexuality in People With Mental Disability.] Madrid: Author.

Instituto Nacional de Servicios Sociales. (1996). *Plan de acción para las personas con discapacidad 1997-2002* [Action plan for people with disability 1997-2002]. Madrid: Author, Ministerio de Trabajo y Asuntos Sociales.

Jiménez, J. (1995). Encuesta sobre la sexualidad en los centros de atención a personas con minusvalía psíquica [Survey about sexuality in centers dedicated to people with mental retardation]. *Siglo Cero, 24*(1), 25-30.

Junta de Castilla y León. (1995). *Plan sectorial para personas con discapacidad en Castilla y León* [Partial plan for people with disability in Castilla y León]. Valladolid: Author, Dirección General de Acción Social.

López, F. (1993). Criterios de salud y minusvalías. In Instituto Nacional de Servicios Sociales (Ed.), *Sexualidad en personas con minusvalía psíquica* [Sexuality in people with mental retardation]. [Proceedings of the First National Convention on Sexuality in People With Mental Disability.] Madrid: Editor.

López, F. (1997). Relaciones entre iguales [Peer relationships]. *Cuadernos de Pedagogía, 261,* 44-48.

Luckasson, R., Coulter, D. L., Polloway, E. A., Reiss, S., Schalock, R. L., Snell, M. E., Spitalnik, D. M., & Stark, J. A. (1992). *Mental retardation: Definition, classification, and systems of supports.* Washington, DC: American Association on Mental Retardation.

Martín, E. (1995). Encuesta sobre actitudes, conocimientos, problemática y comportamientos en torno a la sexualidad en un grupo de deficinetes mentales ligeros y medio de un centro de empleo protegido de Fuenlabrada [Survey on attitudes, knowledge, problems, and behaviors about the sexuality of a workshop group with mild and moderate mental retardation in Fuenlabrada]. *Siglo Cero, 24*(1), 43-47.

Martorell, M. C., Gómez, O., Cuenca-Campillo, A., & Weber, V. (1995). Quality of life: Physical and psychological health in elderly. In Rodríguez Marín, J. (Ed.), *Health psychology and quality of life research* (pp. 862-868). [Proceedings of the eighth annual conference of the European Health Psychology Society.] Murcia: University of Alicante.

Miguel, E., & Ortega, B. E. (1995). Resultados del cuestionario de actitudes psicosexuales [Results of the psychosexual attitudes questionnaire]. *Siglo Cero, 24*(1), 35-39.

Ministerio de Educación y Ciencia. (1992a). *Alumnos con necesidades educativas especiales y adaptaciones curriculares* [Students with special education needs and curriculum adaptation]. Madrid: Author, Dirección General de Renovación Pedagógica.

Ministerio de Educación y Ciencia. (1992b). *Alumnos con necesidades educativas especiales y adaptaciones curriculares. Propuesta de documento individual de adaptaciones curriculares (DIAC)* [Students with special education needs and curriculum adaptations. Individual document proposed for curriculum adaptation]. Madrid: Author, Dirección General de Renovación Pedagógica.

Monjas, I. (1992). *La competencia social en la integración escolar de los alumnos con necesidades educativas especiales* [Social competence in school integration of students with special education needs]. Unpublished doctoral dissertation, University of Salamanca.

Monjas, I. (1996). *Programa de enseñanza de habilidades de interacción social (PEHIS) para niños y niñas en edad escolar* [Program to teach social interaction skills (PEHIS) for school boys and girls]. Madrid: CEPE.

Monjas, I. Verdugo, M. A., & Arias, B. (1995). Eficacia de un programa para enseñar habilidades de interacción social al alumnado con necesidades educativas especiales en educación infantil y primaria [Efficacy of a program for teaching social interaction skills to primary and secondary students with special education needs]. *Siglo Cero, 26*(6), 15-27.

Moreno Gea, P. (1996). Trastornos psíquicos y calidad de vida en los traumatismos cranoencefálicos [Mental disorders and quality of life in brain impairments]. In Fundación Mapfre Medicina (Ed.), *Daño cerebral traumático y calidad de vida* [Traumatic brain impairment and quality of life]. (pp. 161-168). Madrid: Editor.

Schalock, R. (1996). Reconsidering the conceptualization and measurement of quality of life. In R. L. Schalock (Ed.), *Quality of life: Vol. 1. Conceptualization and measurement* (pp. 123-139). Washington, DC: American Association on Mental Retardation.

Schalock, R. L. (1997). Can the concept of quality of life make a difference? In R. L. Schalock (Ed.), *Quality of life: Vol. 2. Application to persons with disabilities* (pp. 245-267). Washington, DC: American Association on Mental Retardation.

Snell, M. E., & Vogtle, L. K. (1997). Facilitating relationships of children with mental retardation in schools. In R. L. Schalock (Ed.), *Quality of life: Vol. 2. Application to persons with disabilities* (pp. 43-61). Washington, DC: American Association on Mental Retardation.

United Nations. (1994). *The Salamanca statement and framework for action on special needs education.* Paris: Author, Educational, Scientific, and Cultural Organization.

Verdugo, M. A. (1989a). *La integración personal, social y vocacional de los deficientes psíquicos adolescentes* [Personal, social and vocational integration of mentally retarded adolescents]. Madrid: Ministerio de Educación y Ciencia, Centro de Investigación y Documentación Educativa.

Verdugo, M. A. (1989b). *Programas conductuales alternativos: I. Habilidades sociales* [Alternative behavioral programs: I. Social skills]. Madrid: MEPSA.

Verdugo, M. A. (1993). Normalización e integración de las personas con minusvalía psíquica [Normalization and integration of people with mental retardation]. In Instituto Nacional de Servicios Sociales (Ed.), *Sexualidad en personas con minusvalía psíquica* [Sexuality in people with mental retardation]. [Proceedings of the First National Convention on Sexuality in People With Mental Disability.] Madrid: Editor.

Verdugo, M. A. (1995). El papel de la psicología de la rehabilitación en la integración de personas con discapacidad y en el logro de la calidad de vida [Rehabilitation psychology role in the integration of persons with disability and in the achievement of quality of life]. In Fundación Mapfre Medicina (Ed.), *Daño cerebral traumático, neuropsicología y calidad de vida* [Traumatic brain impairment, neuropsicology, and quality of life]. (pp. 3-22). Madrid: Editor.

Verdugo, M. A. (1997). *Programa de habilidades sociales (PHS). Programas conductuales alternativos* [Social skills program (PHS). Alternative behavioral programs]. Salamanca: Amarú.

Verdugo, M. A., Bermejo, B. G., & Fuertes, J. (1995). The maltreatment of intellectually handicapped children and adolescents. *Child Abuse and Neglect, 19*(2), 205-215.

Verdugo, M. A., Bermejo, B. G., Fuertes, J., & Elices, J. A. (1993). *Maltrato infantil y minusvalía* [Maltreatment and handicap]. Madrid: Ministerio de Asuntos Sociales, Instituto Nacional de Servicios Sociales.

Verdugo, M. A., Canal, R., & Bermejo, B. G. (1997, May). *Enhancing residential services for persons with mental retardation and extensive support needs.* Paper presented at the 121st annual meeting of the American Association on Mental Retardation, New York, NY.

Verdugo, M. A., Canal, R., Bermejo, B.G., Parte, J. M., López, A., & García, L. (1996). *Contexto residencial y calidad de vida. Hacia una mejora en los modelos de servicios residenciales para personas con retraso mental y necesidades de apoyo generalizadas* [Residential context and quality of life. Toward an improvement in residential service models for people with mental retardation and pervasive support needs]. (Research report). Madrid: Instituto Nacional de Migraciones y Servicios Sociales.

Verdugo, M. A., Canal, R., & Gómez, M. (1997). *¿Por qué no les preguntamos a ellos? Evaluación de la calidad de vida de personas con retraso mental desde su propia percepción* [Why not ask them? Evaluation of quality of life of persons with mental retardation from their own perception]. Manuscript in preparation, University of Salamanca.

Improving the Quality of Life of People With Disabilities in Least Affluent Countries: Insights From Guyana

Roy McConkey
University of Ulster at Jordanstown
Newtownabbey, County Antrim, Northern Ireland

Brian O'Toole
School of the Nations
Georgetown, Guyana

The World Health Organization (1985) estimated that three quarters of the world's population with intellectual disabilities live in the least affluent countries of the world, and at best only 10% of these people and their families receive any form of help. Many of the services available in these countries have been modeled on those found in the more affluent countries of the North. In the main they are specialized, segregated services such as special schools and residential institutions. Most are located in the major cities and towns, and they tend to serve more wealthy families. The vast majority of rural peoples receive little or no help from outside the family.

Although information is sparse, the incidence of intellectual disability in less affluent countries appears to be somewhat less than that found in the developed world, but there are marked differences in the causes. In poorer countries there is a much greater incidence of acquired disability as a result of childhood illnesses, such as meningitis, and a correspondingly lower incidence of genetic and birth defects. Poorer medical services are implicated in both phenomena. However, as these continue to improve, the numbers of people with moderate and severe disabilities is predicted to increase by upwards of 125% in the next 25 years (Helander, 1993).

The presence of a person with intellectual disability threatens a family's well-being on a number of fronts. First, local customs and beliefs about the causes of disability can threaten the relationship between husband and wife, as the mother is often blamed for the shame brought on the family. Moreover, the disability can threaten the marriage prospects of other siblings. Second, the family, but mothers especially, may become socially isolated within the community. In part this derives from avoiding critical comments from one's peers, but many mothers are so burdened by extra work that they have little time to socialize. Third, the family's economic well-being is affected if the mother (or other female relative) is diverted from income generating activities in either subsistence agriculture or employment in order to care for a child who cannot be left alone. Moreover, a lack of out-of-home services, such as nurseries and schools, means that families have to draw upon their own resources to care for a dependent relative. In addition, money has to be found for the expenses involved in consulting doctors or for visiting clinics.

In sum then, the quality of life of people with intellectual disability in the least affluent countries of the world is poorer than that enjoyed by their contemporaries in the affluent North. What then have services in affluent countries to learn from such countries? Simply this: *that more money and more resources do not in themselves purchase a better quality of life for people with intellectual disability.* This insight is hard to appreciate in countries where resources are so plentiful and the tradition of purchasing innovations is well established. This situation has not, and for a long time to come probably will not, pertain to the least developed countries. Hence, any improvements brought about in quality of life at minimal or no cost should clearly challenge the priorities and presumptions of service planners and purchasers in the West.

In this chapter we aim to identify the salient factors that have led to an improved quality of life for families in Guyana, South America. From this, we will argue that specialized, professionalized services offer limited scope to generate sustained improvements in people's quality of life and that alternative systems for doing so need to be nurtured and supported within local communities. We contend that experiences in least affluent countries offer a possible way forward.

At the outset we have to admit that our evidence for improvements comes from the information supplied from informants, mostly in an anecdotal manner, although a number of evaluations have been undertaken by external reviewers (Stout, 1996). Furthermore we concentrate on one country—Guyana—but there is a growing literature from other countries in the developing world that supports our conclusions (Coleridge, 1993).

Lessons From Guyana

Guyana is located on the Atlantic shoulder of the South American subcontinent. It is bordered by Suriname on the west, Venezuela to the east, and Brazil to the south. Guyana is a land of 83,000 square miles with an estimated population of 0.8 million, mostly African-Caribbean and East Indian with a small proportion of native Amerindians. Ninety percent of the population live on the narrow coastal region. Guyana achieved its political independence from Britain in 1966 and declared itself a cooperative republic along socialist lines in 1970. The economy is based primarily on the production of sugar, gold, rice, and bauxite and is very vulnerable to fluctuations in world trade.

An examination of social and economic statistics for the country reveals both positive and negative trends. Infant mortality is declining, from 69 per 1,000 in 1960 to 33 per 1,000 in 1985, and so is the crude death rate, from 10 per 1,000 in 1960 to 6 per 1,000 in 1985. Life expectancy has risen from 60 years in 1960 to 69 in 1985, and is now 12 years longer than the world average. The picture is however balanced by other indicators. The GNP per capita is falling from the 1982 figure of $670 (U.S.) to a figure of $590 in 1994. The percentage of the national budget allocated to health has been one of the lowest in the Caribbean.

Guyana has only one special school which is based in the capital Georgetown and serves the needs of children with hearing impairments and intellectual impairment. The city also has a center for children with physical handicaps, along with a unit for children with visual impairment, attached to a regular school. There are two very small units serving children with disabilities in two rural towns, and a residential home serving around 20 children and young adults. The capital, with approximately 23% of the population, has 90% of the provision in the area of special education.

Community-Based Rehabilitation

The gap between the need for and the provision of rehabilitation in countries such as Guyana cannot be reduced by developing, or even expanding, conventional services. Instead new patterns of services need to be developed, characterized by fewer paid specialists, less advanced forms of training, and simplified methods of intervention. As monies are not available to create new services, the challenge is to find ways of providing the most essential assistance to high numbers of people by using readily available and existing resources.

Community-based rehabilitation (CBR) has been promoted by the World Health Organization as a means for doing this (Helander, Mendis, Nelson, & Goerdt, 1989). The goal is to demystify the rehabilitation process and give responsibility back to the individual, family, and community. Rehabilitation becomes one feature of community development whereby the community seeks to improve itself. Once the community takes on the responsibility for the rehabilitation of their people with disabilities, then the process could truly be called community based. Hence rehabilitation must become one element of a broader community integration effort.

The philosophy of CBR is immediately persuasive, but can it be translated into practice? Experiences worldwide have been mixed, but, as a generalization, the programs that have been more successful in their impact on the lives of people with disabilities have tended to emphasize community empowerment, and they have worked from the "bottom-up" rather than setting up national structures within existing health services and trying to deploy or redeploy professional workers to undertake the work (McConkey & O'Toole, 1995).

The CBR program in Guyana has been based around specially trained volunteers from the local communities who have come from a range of backgrounds (e.g., nurses, midwives, and school teachers) and also family members of people with disabilities who volunteered their services. Up to three times as many people have applied to be accepted as volunteers on the 150-hour training program as could be accommodated, and the drop-out rate over the course of 2 years was no more than 5%. The volunteers have proved to be a committed group of individuals who have given generously of their time in visiting and supporting families and people with disabilities. Their input has included devising training programs, obtaining equipment and aids, promoting social integration, and giving advice and counsel. Over 70% of the volunteers have remained deeply involved in the program 3 years later. The volunteers are generally accepted by the families, and they have generated a high degree of wider community involvement through their awareness-raising activities.

The volunteers are supported by 12 regional coordinators who come from a range of backgrounds and work on a part-time, paid basis. The present complement consists of three people with disabilities, two parents of children with special needs, three special educators, two head teachers in nursery schools, one physiotherapist, and one teacher of the deaf. The coordinators have undertaken various training courses in community-based rehabilitation, ranging from a 9-month, full-time course in London to short, 2- to 6-week courses in Sri Lanka, Indonesia, and Sweden. Four of the coordinators were themselves volunteer participants in the Hopeful Steps CBR Training program in Guyana.

Rehabilitation committees have been set up in all five regions of the country where the program is active. Each committee consists of volunteer workers, family members, and people with disabilities. Increasingly the committees are responsible for the management of the program in their locality; organizing training courses, social events, fund-raising endeavors; and opening local resource centers where families can meet and where income-generating activities are promoted. A further development of late has been the devolving of funds from the international funding agency to the regional committees. Ten years have now elapsed from the inception of the program and at present it is involved with some 700 people with disabilities and their families. Some 300 volunteers are actively working on the program and committees are operative in 7 of the 10 regions of the country.

A broad consensus from local people and from external evaluators is that the quality of life for many people with disabilities and for their families has improved. In particular, they point to changed attitudes among communities. When the project began working in the interior region of the Rupununi, local headteachers assured project personnel that there were no people with disabilities in their villages. Three years later upwards of 60 people have been identified and helped locally (Stout, 1996).

Greater social integration has also resulted. For example, some 47 children with disabilities are now enrolled in local schools, whereas before they remained at home, and a group of musicians with disabilities has come together to perform at local events. Parental confidence has increased, five preschools have been started by the project in partnership with mothers, and 26 income-generating projects have been initiated for people with disabilities. What then have been the key factors in the success of the program?

Factors Contributing to Improved Quality of Life
Our analysis suggests that six elements are key to the improved quality of life the program has brought to people living in rural areas of Guyana.

Community Volunteers. In Guyana circumstances demand the use of interested people from the community who freely give of their time and talents to assist the local people with disabilities. Experience has demonstrated that they play three key roles:

1. providing emotional and practical support to families through regular visits;
2. acting as advocate for the family in dealing with others in the locality; for

example, volunteers have approached local headteachers about the enrollment of children with disabilities in nursery and preschools;

3. providing education for their community either through individual neighborhood contacts or more systematically through community events such as puppet shows and art competitions, organized by groups of volunteers within a neighborhood.

Hence a major improvement in a family's quality of life can come about through building a network of community connections. This process can be started by enlisting the assistance of just one person in each locality.

Social Inclusion. The essence of CBR is working with families in their own neighborhood, rather than transporting people to centers located some distance away. Moreover, the volunteers are encouraged to complement their home visits by using their social networks and contacts to provide opportunities for families and people with disabilities to join in community events. Professionals within traditional disability services often distinguish between their work and private lives. Ironically this tends to perpetuate the social isolation of people with disabilities within specialist services. The extent to which a professional workforce can create opportunities for social inclusion within communities in which they themselves are not active members is questionable.

Healthy Environments. The physical well-being of families in developing countries is often jeopardized by poor housing, inadequate sanitation, and poverty. Communities are often well aware of their needs. For instance, in the interior region of Guyana, consultations with village leaders identified the following concerns:

- improved water and sanitation;
- training in health and education;
- improved methods of agriculture;
- improved health centers;
- development of kitchen gardens.

A project that is truly community based must attempt to address the needs of the wider community and not just those of families with a disabled member. In Guyana this has been achieved by forming Village Health Boards in nearly all villages of the Rupununi (35 in all), consisting of elected representatives who have been trained and supported in undertaking their own self-improvement initiatives. For instance, one village has built a new health center using monies obtained from an international aid agency. An integrated playgroup also uses the premises 3 days a week. Sustainable improvements in the health of people with disabilities in developing countries is much more likely to come about through initiatives that benefit the whole community. Moreover, the needs of people with disabilities should be incorporated into all community development projects in addition to energies being focused specifically on people with disabilities and on designating special agencies to meet their needs. Such agencies have very limited power to influence wider societal policies, as evidenced from experiences in the affluent North on issues such as accessibility in housing and public transport.

Poverty Reduction. Enabling people with disabilities and their families to generate an income must be a major priority for disability projects in the developing world. The creation of sheltered workshops similar to those in the West have singularly failed to do this. Such workshops quickly fill up; they create dependency in the workers; and the work undertaken is often repetitive and low paid, with frequent "lay-offs" when contract work in not forthcoming (McConkey, 1996). A more promising alternative is encouraging self-employment and the development of cooperatives (Neufeldt, 1995). In rural Guyana more than 30 income-generating projects have been established using a revolving loan fund to help families obtain start-up materials and capital equipment. These include boat building, chicken rearing, peanut farming, selling charcoal, pottery, petty trading, sewing, and baking.

Similar strategies, such as supported employment, are now advocated in affluent countries. These schemes appear to produce greater feelings of self-esteem, as well as giving people with intellectual disabilities the opportunity to forge social relationships with workmates and customers. Moreover, community perceptions change as people with disabilities are seen doing productive and valued work (Beyer & Kilsby, 1997). Once again the essence of success is building partnerships with community enterprises rather than creating special solutions for the "disabled."

Building Solidarity and Empowerment. Although individuals with a disability are at the heart of the CBR Program's work in Guyana, the primary means for assisting them is through building solidarity among three groups. First, the community volunteers share a common training course, totaling more than 150 hours of talks, workshops, and practical sessions. Videos, recorded in Guyana, are a main medium of instruction (O'Toole & McConkey, 1997), but a major emphasis throughout is on problem solving based around local people and resources.

Second, the program has built solidarity among families, primarily through the formation of local resource centers where parents (mostly mothers) and their children can meet together once a week. The centers are "managed" by local committees and embrace a range of activities including play for children, talks for parents, and income-generation activities.

A third emphasis of late has been the promotion of self-advocacy organizations with the assistance of consultants from Africa and Europe who are activists with disabilities. These groups have focused mainly on developing a sense of solidarity among people with disabilities, promoting disability issues in the media and with politicians, encouraging social and sporting activities, and establishing income-generating projects.

Nurturing the formation of local groupings such as these not only removes feelings of isolation, but also creates a sense of power and purpose among people who may otherwise feel demoralized. As Schalock (1996) has noted, participation in civic processes is an important element in one's quality of life, yet it is a feature arguably attended to more actively in poorer countries, where needs are greater and shared, than in more affluent countries where individual differences and priorities are much more to the fore.

People First, Disabled Second. The dearth of disability specialists and resources in a country such as Guyana means that people lose out in a number of obvious ways. Aids and appliances, such as wheelchairs and hearing aids, are scarce and expensive. Therapeutic operations are infrequent, as are remedial therapies such as physiotherapy. Special teachers are few, and residential facilities are almost nonexistent. There is no system of welfare benefits.

In the absence of comparative scales for measuring quality of life across cultures and continents, it is impossible to estimate objectively how much the presence or absence of these factors actually contributes to people's quality of life. But our guess, having worked in both rich and poor countries, is that their contribution possibly fuels the "disability industry" more than it significantly changes the quality of an individual's life. After all, O'Brien's (1986) five accomplishments—community presence, relationships, competence, choice, and image and status—are in fact the celebration of human achievement within communities rather than the products of a rehabilitation process, as they have come to be interpreted. Indeed we rather suspect that a disability service system is actually biased against achievement, because its overt focus, indeed raison d'être, is based on *dis*ability rather than ability.

Rather, a community-building model that recognizes people's humanity and rights of belonging could be much better placed to enable even the most handicapped of citizens to attain basic life accomplishments. In a sense then, countries such as Guyana need not be concerned to replicate Western models of disability provision; rather they should continue to respond to people's specific disabilities within a broader "life-building" context.

Lessons for the West

And is this not the same challenge we face in the West? Our rehabilitation personnel, technologies, and resources have undoubtedly brought a better quality of life to many people with disabilities, at least in terms of their physical well-being, medical, and housing needs. Nevertheless, a recurring theme in much of the recent literature on intellectual disability is their social isolation, lack of control over their lives, and dearth of paid employment (Emerson & Hatton, 1996).

Requesting more money to bolster failing services is a popular but possibly misguided option when we look at what has been achieved in countries that have only a fraction of the resources we enjoy. It is not, however, a question of either-or; rather it is both-and.

Our specialist service models urgently need to be complemented by approaches that are truly community based and socially inclusive (Schwartz, 1992). The leaders and instigators may emerge from existing disability services, but their identity has to be more community focused, and certainly their allies will have to be drawn from the localities in which they work. Arguably such work is even more challenging in postindustrial urban societies that are experiencing the breakdown of families and geographical communities. Indeed pessimists may argue that it is not worth attempting such approaches.

Idealists that we are, this argument only reinforces the need urgently to develop community-building approaches that will enhance the quality of life not just of people with disabilities, but also of other vulnerable groups within our society. Self-help, self-determination, and social justice have been the cornerstones of the democracies that have flourished in this century. Perhaps the next millennium will see the application of these same principles to all the world's citizens with disabilities, wherever they live.

References

Beyer, S., & Kilsby, M. (1997). Supported employment in Britain. *Tizard Learning Disability Review, 2,* 6-14.

Coleridge, P. (1993). *Disability, liberation, and development.* Oxford: Oxfam.

Emerson, E., & Hatton, C. (1996). Deinstitutionalization in the UK and Ireland: Outcomes for service users. *Journal of Intellectual and Developmental Disability, 21,* 3-16.

Helander, E. (1993). *Prejudice and dignity: An introduction to community based rehabilitation.* Geneva: UNDP.

Helander, E., Mendis, P., Nelson, G., & Goerdt, A. (1989*). Training in the community for people with disabilities.* Geneva: World Health Organization.

McConkey, R. (1996). A valued life in the community. In R. I. Brown, D. Baine, & A. Neufeldt (Eds.), *Beyond basic care: Special education and community rehabilitation in low income countries.* North York, Ontario: Campus Press.

McConkey, R., & O'Toole, B. (1995*). Innovations in developing countries for people with disabilities.* Baltimore: Paul H. Brookes.

Neufeldt, A. (1995). Self-directed employment and economic independence in low-income countries. In R. McConkey & B. O'Toole (Eds.), *Innovations in developing countries for people with disabilities.* Baltimore: Paul H. Brookes.

O'Brien, J. (1986). A guide to personal futures planning. In G. T. Bellamy & B. Wilcox (Eds.), *The activities catalog: A community programming guide for youth and adults with severe disabilities.* Baltimore: Paul H. Brookes.

O'Toole, B., & McConkey, R. (1997). *A training strategy for personnel working in developing countries.* Paper submitted for publication.

Schalock, R. L. (1996). Reconsidering the conceptualization and measurement of quality of life. In R. L. Schalock (Ed.), *Quality of life: Vol. 1. Conceptualization and measurement* (pp. 123-139). Washington, DC: American Association on Mental Retardation.

Schwartz, D. B. (1992). *Crossing the river: Creating a conceptual revolution in community and disability.* Cambridge, MA: Brookline.

Stout, S. (1996). *An evaluation of the Guyana CBR Programme.* Unpublished thesis, University of California, Berkeley.

World Health Organization. (1985). *Mental retardation: Meeting the challenge.* Geneva: Author.

Author Note
We gratefully acknowledge the funders of this project: the European Community and Amici di Raoul Follereau. Additional financial assistance has been provided by the Canadian International Development Agency and UNICEF.

The Right to Be Treated as a Human Being: A Finnish Perspective on Quality of Life

Leena M. Matikka
Finnish Association on Mental Retardation
Helsinki, Finland

In the last few years, hundreds of articles and essays have been written with international interest in conceptualizing quality of life. Several structures of quality of life have been developed, such as quality of life as a sensitizing concept, as an organizing concept, and—my favorite at the moment—as a social construct (Allardt, 1975, 1993; Goode, 1994; Matikka, 1994, 1996a; Schalock, 1997a, 1997b). We need international discussions to find common definitions of quality of life and to find international policies that will enhance the quality of life of people with disabilities (Goode, 1994, 1997; Keith, 1996). The crucial point in this international deliberation is how successful we are in taking into account all the diverse cultural contributions that make up the quality-of-life movement or process.

Schalock (1996, 1997a) has aided considerably in defining eight core dimensions of quality of life. Three of these dimensions are self-determination, social inclusion, and rights. In this chapter I describe some Finnish perspectives on these three core dimensions and discuss some current developmental work in Finland on improving living conditions and the quality of life of people with disabilities. It is impossible, in this chapter, to give the whole picture of Finnish social policy or services provided for people with disabilities. The examples I include reflect my personal opinion of what is most important in Finnish quality-of-life issues at the moment.

Human Rights: Fundamental Issues of Quality of Life

It would be interesting to study the origin of the quality-of-life concept, which has been used in many fields, such as philosophy, psychology, and in medical and social sciences. However, if our purpose is to use the term cross-culturally, the most important uses are seen in the efforts to bind countries to the improvement of the human rights of all people in every country through worldwide treaties.

Here it would seem necessary to include both basic and additional dimensions of quality of life in our studies, because people's situations in different countries vary greatly. What is normal in the United States and in Finland is not as obvious in Zambia or in India. Also, what is usual among ordinary people is sometimes very rare among people with disabilities. However, the strong core of quality of life—human rights—could be shared in every country.

Rachels and Ruddick (1989) say: "Without liberty, a person cannot have a life ... at all" (p. 226). For them, being alive is to be a functioning, self-preserving organism. Having a life is, by contrast, a notion of biography rather than biology. Through the discussion "Can a slave have a biography?" Rachels and Ruddick show the importance of liberty. By exercising their capacities to make choices, people create their lives. Liberty makes lives possible; it constitutes our lives through the free choices and actions that are embodied in it. On the basis of the work of Rachels and Ruddick, we can conclude that liberty is an inalienable condition of quality of life.

In addition, we assume that people need opportunities to make choices in order to create their own will. Aristotle (1952), in his *Nicomachean Ethics*, described the relation between will and choice:

> Choice cannot relate to impossibles, and if anyone said he chose them he would be thought silly; but there may be a wish even for impossibles, e.g. for immortality. And wish may relate to things that could in no way be brought about by one's own efforts, e.g. that a particular actor or athlete should win in a competition; but no one chooses such things, but only the things that he thinks could be brought about by his efforts. Again, wish relates rather to the end, choice to the means; for instance, we wish to be healthy, but we choose the acts which will make us healthy, and we wish to be happy and say we do, but we cannot well say we choose to be so; for in general, choice seems to relate to things that are in our own power. (p. 357)

According to these sentences, if people do not have alternatives from which to choose, they do not have power over their life conditions, and they cannot develop their will.

In a Finnish discussion on the so-called coercive measures employed in services for people with intellectual disabilities, we have been obliged to analyze the profound roots of human rights and, in this context, the implications of our rehabilitation methods. I propose that thinking about philosophic origins of human rights would also be useful for other nations and to guarantee these fundamental rights is the necessary starting point for all measures planned for assessing quality of life in all countries.

The Legal Framework

Finland has signed some 40 worldwide treaties called conventions of human rights, most of which are composed by the United Nations, the Council of Europe, or the International Labor Organization. International conventions become a part of the Finnish national judicial system by laws prescribed by the Parliament. Human rights have total, international protection against any kind of national decision or procedure.

Of the covenants composed by the United Nations and enforced in Finland, the most important are the International Covenant on Economic, Social, and Cultural Rights and the International Covenant on Civil and Political Rights. Since they came into force in 1976, they have played a more and more prominent role in prescribing laws, in administration, and in courts. By accepting the International Covenant on Economic, Social, and Cultural Rights, Finland undertook a principle of continuous improvement in these issues. Accordingly, we have to do our best to allocate resources to provide better living conditions and quality of life for all citizens.

The conventions drafted by the Council of Europe are as important as the United Nations conventions. For example, the Convention for the Protection of Human Rights and Fundamental Freedoms (i.e., the European Convention on Human Rights, which came into force in 1990) and the European Social Charter (came into force in 1991) have also impacted our legal framework. Joining the European Convention on Human Rights was a turning point that brought into general knowledge the international monitoring system of human rights and opportunities in court decisions to adapt the convention articles, which are enforced as a part of the Finnish judicial system.

The 1971 United Nations Declaration on the Rights of Mentally Retarded Persons and the 1975 United Nations Declaration on the Rights of Disabled Persons were not given as much legal power as the international covenants, but they have been useful in political discourse.

The Finnish system of constitutional rights was changed in 1995. The aim was to attain a better correspondence with international development of human rights. For example, some inadequacies in basic social rights were amended.

Discussion of realization of human rights and the corresponding basic rights of people with mental retardation has focused recently on coercive measures and on the legislation concerning them. The deputy parliamentary ombudsman is responsible for inspecting institutions and controlling the care of people in these institutions. This new provision of the law took effect in 1995. Concern has also been directed toward institutions for people with intellectual disabilities, because these people have been seen to need very special protection.

After visiting several institutions, the deputy parliamentary ombudsman gave a decision (Decision of the Deputy, 1996) in which she demanded that the Ministry of Social Affairs and Health take measures to develop legislation and practices in the institutions. At the moment, this legislation is being prepared. The most striking issue was that coercive measures were used in many institutions to punish people with intellectual disabilities for aggressive or inappropriate behavior. This is against conventions of human rights, and, more important, today there is no excuse for violating any individual's human rights. Compare this with the situation 7 years earlier, when a task force of the National Board of Social Welfare identified the same problems but could only hope that the national legislation would someday be changed (Matikka, 1990).

Another significant problem concerns the freedom to choose a place to live (Parkkari, 1996). In Finland people with disabilities are bound to their home municipality in order to receive the social and health care services they need, because the municipality is responsible for providing public services for its own residents but not for other people. Furthermore, a municipality can, in a way, choose its inhabitants and is usually not willing to accept people who are known to need a lot of services and thus cost more money. These problematic examples show how the organization of local welfare services can restrict individual rights, even those the service system feels are necessary.

Instruments for Developing Rights

Perhaps the most important aspect of the philosophy of the international movement to guarantee the rights of people with disabilities is the equalization of opportunities, which means the process through which the various systems of society and the environment are made available to everyone, particularly to people with disabilities (Degener, 1995). The United Nations General Assembly adopted *The Standard Rules on the Equalization of Opportunities for Persons With Disabilities* (StRE) in 1993 (United Nations, 1994). Although the StRE are not compulsory, they can become *international customary rules* when they are applied by a great number of states with the intention of respecting a rule in international law (Newman, 1995). The StRE will someday get this status if we promote their application in our countries. Combining the ideas of the StRE with efforts to improve quality of life would help us in achieving the goals of a better life for people with disabilities. To do this we have to move from political concepts to research concepts and accept the StRE as an embodiment of current ideas of the quality of life in the field of disability. If we do this, we will solve one problem of quality-of-life research: Who has the right to define the concept of the quality of life?

In 1994 the Finnish Association on Mental Retardation designed scales for the assessment of service quality in an action research project (Kaipio, 1996) and had an opportunity to adapt the StRE target areas for our scales. The task was not easy but interesting and promising. We found that the StRE can also be tested at individual and service unit levels, not only at a state level (Matikka, 1996b).

In working with the StRE, we felt that, in addition to the international guidelines, we also needed a national discussion of the underlying ethical values of our services. As a result, at the general meeting in 1995 (Finnish Association on Mental Retardation, 1995) our association adopted a report that included the basic values of the service system. These values are listed in Table 25.1.

Thus far, I have addressed quality-of-life issues and instruments to improve the quality of life at international and national levels. However, the most important level for an individual is the local level or, narrowly speaking, the closest social environment in which a person lives and realizes his or her opportunities to create

Table 25.1

Basic Values of the Service System Adopted by the Finnish Association on Mental Retardation

Human dignity

Supports and services based on individual abilities and opportunities

Equal opportunities

Freedom of choice

Interaction and membership

The fairness of the delivery of welfare services to all citizens

Table 25.2

A Framework for Enhancing Quality of Life Using Different Instruments at Four Levels

Level	Actors	Instruments	Examples From Specific Tools

International	United Nations
	European Union
	non-governmental
	  organizations
	World Health Organization
	International Labor
	  Organization
	Rehabilitation Interna-
	  tional
	Disabled People Interna-
	  tional
	politicians
		covenants
		worldwide treaties
		international customer
		  rules
			United Nations Standard Rules on
			  Equalization of Opportunities
			  for Persons With Disabilities
			World Health Organization
			  International Classification of
			  Impairments, Disabilities, &
			  Handicaps
			International Organization for
			  Standardization-Quality
			  Management & Quality System
			  Elements. Part 2: Guidelines
			  for Services

National	parliament
	government
	national organizations
	politicians
	administrators
	researchers
		legislation
		committees
		evaluation of service
		  systems
		quantitative research
		  methods
		comparative statistics
			laws pertinent to disability
			  problems
			national standards for services
			special projects in Finland:
			  1. QOL survey
			  2. Quality of Services—
			     project with a nationwide
			     comparative data base

Local	local government
	politicians
	administrators
	citizens
	staff
	recipients
	supervisors
		action plans
		service system
		quality assurance
		action research
		qualitative & quantitative
		  research methods
		personnel education
			outcome-based performance
			  measures of the Council
			Malcom Baldrige National
			  Quality Award
			Quest, in Finland: Assi and
			  Asseri-Assessment Services

Individual	recipients families staff	individual plans case studies education supported living & employment	AAMR's needed supports personal quest

a personal lifestyle. Table 25.2 shows a conceptual framework of ideas (Matikka, 1996b) that could be used in analyzing and combining several useful instruments to enhance the quality of life of people with disabilities.

One can see that there is a general agreement about the very fundamental human rights and the international tools to promote these rights. This is the universal part of quality-of-life issues. When operating at the national level, other kinds of tools are needed, because cultures and situations vary in different countries. In monocultural countries such as Finland, it is easy to link culture with national politics. Also strategies developed to improve the quality of life of citizens are culture-bound and are the result of the long (emic) history of our national state. Our national culture and common Finnish language today function as the common ground for enhancing the quality of life of people with disabilities in our country. The situation is, however, changing due to our recent membership in the European Union. The importance of the state is diminishing, and the local municipalities are strengthening their status, as are European governmental bodies.

Social Inclusion and Self-Determination

In Finnish culture, self-determination has a very important meaning that differs from the Anglo-American definition often used in quality-of-life studies (see, e.g., Sands & Wehmeyer, 1996; Schalock, 1996). Wehmeyer and his colleagues define self-determination as the primary causal agent in one's life; making choices and decisions regarding one's quality of life free from undue external influence or interference. In operational terms, self-determined actions reflect autonomy, self-regulation, psychological empowerment, and self-realization (Wehmeyer, Kelchner, & Richards, 1996). In the psychological tradition of viewing life from a very individualistic perspective, many concepts have been removed from their social aspects; "social," in turn, has been seen as a distinct factor in an individual's life. Another reason for this type of categorization might be the multivariate statistics often used to construct quality-of-life measures.

In the Finnish tradition, a life is a collective story, and self-determination is firmly bound to social cooperation. To be a member of the collective and to have collective influence on circumstances that have an impact on things perceived as important to collective life is more important than to behave independently. (I am not sure this opinion is shared by the majority of Finns. My arguments come from experiences in developmental work to enhance the quality of life in the field of intellectual disabilities.) Every meaningful change has to be started from a grass-roots level and must be done with the people whom it concerns. Research (see, e.g., Engeström, 1987; Kärkkäinen, 1993; Tolman & Maiers, 1991) has guided developmental work and furthered education in our field for a long time. Into this framework we have adapted quality-of-life studies and worked closely with staff members and, in recent times, more often with recipients. To influence the collective life of the group living or acting together, the first step is to define quality of life together, to analyze it in the frame developed, and then to work toward the determined goals. By doing this, the important aspects of quality of life, social inclusion, and self-determination can become reality in everyday life.

By accepting this view of the improvement of the quality of life, we can achieve goals meaningful for people with disabilities. However, there are problems. We have to consider how we transfer the knowledge about quality of life to national and international levels. How can we convince politicians about issues that need to be improved, if we only have stories or experiences to tell them instead of empirical, comparative research data? My suggestion is that we need to work at all levels and with multiple methods simultaneously.

Conclusions

I have tried to illuminate some quality-of-life issues that I deem important in Finnish discourse and practices, and that I assume also exist in other countries. My viewpoint is perhaps pragmatic rather than scientific. Still, I believe that researchers in the field of disabilities have contributed and will contribute significantly in finding more core issues of the quality-of-life concept that will help us globally and locally. Briefly, I would like to stress the following aspects for further collaboration in quality-of-life issues:

1. Quality of life is a worldwide, social construct that could be viewed both as an outcome and as a process of pursuing equal opportunities for all people in choosing the lives they want.

2. Quality of life has *a universal aspect* that includes human rights, *a specific aspect* that gets its content within a collective discourse of the group of people living in the same community, and *an individual aspect* that is unique for every person and includes the person's individual preferences to create a personal lifestyle.

3. To enhance the quality of life, we have to work at international, national, local, and individual levels with specific and effective tools appropriate to different processes and strategies of levels.

4. A cross-cultural perspective on the quality of life is needed to construct common concepts useful in comparative studies and international politics.

References

Allardt, E. (1975). *Dimensions of welfare in a comparative Scandinavian Study* (Research Rep. No. 9). Helsinki: University of Helsinki Research Group for Comparative Sociology.

Allardt, E. (1993). Having, loving, being: An alternative to the Swedish model of welfare research. In M. C. Nussbaum & A. Sen (Eds.), *The quality of life.* New York: Oxford University Press.

Aristotle. (1952). Nicomachean ethics (W. D. Ross, Trans.). In *The works of Aristotle* (pp. 339-444). Chicago: Encyclopedia Britannica.

Decision of the Deputy Parliamentary Ombudsman concerning coercive measures in institutions for people with intellectual disabilities 16.12.1996, Dnro 121/2/95. Parliament of Finland.

Degener, T. (1995). Disabled persons and human rights: The legal framework. In T. Degener & J. Koster-Dreese (Eds.), *Human rights and disabled persons. Essays and relevant human rights instruments.* Dordreht, The Netherlands: Kulver Academic Publishers.

Engeström, Y. (1987). *Learning by expanding. An activity-theoretical approach to developmental research.* Helsinki: Orienta-Konsultit.

Finnish Association on Mental Retardation. (1995). *Life—a collective story. The underlying ethical values of the services provided for people with developmental disabilities.* Helsinki: Author.

Goode, D. (Ed.). (1994). *Quality of life for persons with disabilities: International perspectives and issues.* Cambridge, MA: Brookline.

Goode, D. (1997). Quality of life as international disability policy: Implications for international research. In R. L. Schalock (Ed.), *Quality of life: Vol. 2. Application to persons with disabilities* (pp. 211-222). Washington, DC: American Association on Mental Retardation.

Kaipio, K. (1996). *The project of quality of services provided for people with developmental disabilities: Final report* (Research Rep. No. 23). Helsinki: Finnish Association on Mental Retardation.

Kärkkäinen, M. (1993). *Toisenlaiseen toimintaan. Kehittävän työntutkimuksen sovellus kehitysvammatyöhön* [For another kind of activity. An application for developmental work research in care for disabled persons] (Mental Handicap Research Unit Pub. No. 65). Helsinki: Finnish Association on Mental Retardation.

Keith, K. D. (1996). Measuring quality of life across cultures: Issues and challenges. In R. L. Schalock (Ed.), *Quality of life: Vol. 1. Conceptualization and measurement* (pp. 73-82). Washington, DC: American Association on Mental Retardation.

Matikka, L. M. (1990). Pakko kehitysvammahuollossa [Coercive measures in care for people with intellectual disabilities]. In *Pakosta pois. Sosiaalihuollon pakkokeinoja selvittäneen työryhmän muistio* [Away from coercion]. Helsinki: National Board of Social Welfare, Reports 4/1990.

Matikka, L. M. (1994). The quality of life of adults with developmental disabilities in Finland. In D. Goode (Ed.), *Quality of life for persons with disabilities: International perspectives and issues* (pp. 190-210). Cambridge, MA: Brookline.

Matikka, L. M. (1996a). Effects of psychological factors on the perceived quality of life of people with intellectual disabilities. *Journal of Applied Research in Intellectual Disabilities, 9,* 115-128.

Matikka, L. M. (1996b, July). Measuring quality of services for people with developmental disabilities. Paper presented at 10th world congress of the International Association for the Scientific Study of Intellectual Disabilities, Helsinki, Finland.

Newman, F. (1995). Introduction. In T. Degener & Y. Koster-Dreese (Eds.), *Human rights and disabled persons: Essays and relevant human rights instruments.* Dordreht, The Netherlands: Kulver Academic Publishers.

Parkkari, J. (1996). *Vammaisten ja vanhusten ihmisoikeudet* [Human rights of disabled and elderly people] (Rep. No. 200). Helsinki: National Research and Development Centre for Welfare and Health.

Rachels, J., & Ruddick, W. (1989). Lives and liberty. In J. Christman (Ed.), *The inner citadel: Essays on individual autonomy* (pp. 221-233). New York: Oxford University Press.

Sands, D. J., & Wehmeyer, M. L. (eds.). (1996). *Self-determination across the life span: Independence and choice for people with disabilities.* Baltimore: Paul H. Brookes.

Schalock, R. L. (1996). Reconsidering the conceptualization and measurement of quality of life. In R. L. Schalock (Ed.), *Quality of life: Vol. 1. Conceptualization and measurement* (pp. 123-139). Washington, DC: American Association on Mental Retardation.

Schalock, R. L. (1997a). Can the concept of quality of life make a difference? In R. L. Schalock (Ed.), *Quality of life: Vol. 2. Application to persons with disabilities* (pp. 245-267). Washington, DC: American Association on Mental Retardation.

Schalock, R. L. (1997b). Considering culture in the application of quality of life. In R. L. Schalock (Ed.), *Quality of life: Vol. 2. Application to persons with disabilities* (pp. 225-244). Washington, DC: American Association on Mental Retardation.

Tolman, C. W., & Maiers, W. (Eds.). (1991). *Critical psychology: Contributions to an historical science of the subject.* Cambridge: Cambridge University Press.

United Nations. (1971). *Declaration on the rights of mentally retarded persons.* New York: Author.

United Nations. (1975). *Declaration on the rights of disabled persons.* New York: Author.

United Nations. (1994). *The standard rules on the equalization of opportunities for persons with disabilities.* New York: Author.

Wehmeyer, M. L., Kelchner, K., & Richards, S. (1996). Essential characteristics of self-determined behavior of individuals with mental retardation. *American Journal on Mental Retardation, 6,* 632-642.

Author Note

The author gratefully acknowledges Esa Makkonen for his help in designing a legal framework of Finnish discourse of human rights.

The Rights and Social Inclusion of People With Mental Retardation in Argentina

Diego González Castanón
Monica González Buján
Buenos Aires, Argentina

We have chosen to discuss the rights and the social inclusion of people with mental retardation in our country, because these concepts are very important to quality of life of these people. In this chapter we include a short demographic description of our country, a qualitative and quantitative description of characteristic elements of legal rights and social inclusion, and a number of proposals based on our personal experience and perspective.

Socio-economic Description of Argentina

Argentina has a population of more than 33 million and an area of 2,790,000 square kilometers (close to the area of India). Two thirds of these people live in an area of 60,000 square kilometers near Buenos Aires. Another 10 million people are scattered throughout an enormous territory, in 23 sparsely inhabited states (in which 65% of the population is located in the urban centers), with few human resources and communications. Further, the population's concentration around Buenos Aires does not guarantee that communications are facilitated or that accessibility to resources is ensured for those people. Argentina is a developing country, one that has experienced long periods of unconstitutional governments and a shorter history of evolution of the government's economical transformation process. The public institutions, parent associations, and nongovernmental organizations are not exempted from those conditions, and the connection among various groups is minimal. Even in the same city, providers of different services sometimes don't know each other, and although some data bases for disabilities are being developed, access is still limited. Reliable data about the percentage of disabled people in the country do not exist. Different organizations take as a reference the standard percentage of 10%; alternatively, based on regional and state studies, some accept that 6.8% of the population experiences some sort of disability (sensory, motor, intellectual, visceral, or psychiatric). Recent surveys indicate that the unemployment rate in the country varies between 15% and 20% of the working population. Depending on the region, from 7% to 39% of the population have their basic needs unsatisfied; 15% of the Argentine people lack minimum resources. This situation influences programming plans for assistance, with poverty and unemployment being pressing factors limiting the possibilities of developing help for other needy groups, such as citizens with mental retardation. Monthly pensions for those with disabilities are approximately $120 U.S. During the past few decades, those pensions were given with a great dose of bureaucracy and/or politics; now they are conditioned on the existence of indicators of social risk. The political decisions involved may be illustrated by the following: If a person lives in a state institution, the government contributes $2,000 for that service; but if the institution belongs to a nongovernmental organization, the state contributes $230. Four million citizens depend on the same partially regulated state social security entity. In its beginning, the system was designed for medical and social assistance to pensioned and retired people. This agency is obligated by law to give assistance to the majority of people with disabilities, and because it is the principal purchaser of services, it has a decisive role in design and regulation of the services provided. Because this agency long depended on the government, the plans and standards it established varied according to the preferences of the government in power. This brought inconsistency in planning and administration of resources; for this reason people with disabilities had no policy specifically centered on them.

Legal Rights of People With Disabilities

If the necessary legal and institutional structures are not created to achieve and protect people's rights, these turn out to be no more than a well-intentioned expression. In Argentina, laws protecting rights of people with disabilities are relatively recent, and although they are clearly recognized, their success varies. For full rights to be realized, these laws must be integrated into community life, and development of a social conscience for the problems of people with disabilities requires time. Although legislation can impose sanctions for noncompliance, it cannot make the society change its attitude toward minority groups. Only after years of effective implementation and education of the population, from schools to public campaigns, will these rights become a natural part of the Argentine culture.

People with mental retardation and their families do not yet feel these rights as their own. The majority are unaware of the legislation that protects and helps them, and even when they know about it, they often do not petition authorities for help. Without their participation, societal change will not occur, and people with disabilities will remain dependent.

Institutions that work with individuals with disabilities should include, as curriculum, knowledge of rights and techniques for speaking out—in the media or to authorities. Perhaps reading and writing about the issues of discrimination and citizen participation should be a vehicle for learning. The result may be awareness, not only on the part of the majority, but also the minority with disabilities, about their own condition.

National Constitution

The national Constitution expresses the equality of all citizens and recognizes the Universal Statement of Human Rights; the American Statement of Man's Duties and Rights; the American Convention About Human Rights; the International Agreement of the Economic, Social, and Cultural Rights; the United Nations International Covenant on Civil and Political Rights; and the Convention of Children's Rights, among others.

Integral Protection of Disabled People Law
This law determines that a person is to be considered disabled if he or she "suffers a functional alteration, for a long time or permanently, physical or mental, that, in relation to his/her age and social environment, implies considerable disadvantages for his/her familial, social, educational, or labor integration." It declares that the government's function is to promote equality of opportunities in educational, sanitary, and working areas. The government's duty is to guarantee social benefits in those areas.

Antidiscrimination Law
This law penalizes all types of discrimination.

National Labor Law
This law encourages employment opportunities for groups with inclusion difficulties. For example, it extends the contract period for those with disabilities, reducing the employer's contribution to both the employees' income taxes and retirement funds. It states that workplace accident insurance will not be more burdensome for workers with disabilities, and it indicates that people with disabilities should make up 4% of the government's employees.

Accessibility Legislation
There are several laws that require elimination of any architectural, urban, or transportation barriers.

National Penal Code
This law makes clear that those who are not capable of recognizing the criminality of their acts are not liable. This must be proved in each case by a judge, and not by any predetermined pathology or even by a certification of mental illness.

National Civil Code
This code establishes the civil incapacity of those who are declared by a judge, in accordance with the evaluation of specialists, incapable of administering their affairs. These people lose all their civil rights: They are not allowed to vote, marry, or execute contracts. A guardian is assigned to these people to look after their health and to safeguard and administer their resources. This responsibility generally falls on a family member. The intent is to prevent individuals losing their material goods through their own mistakes or due to the dishonesty of others. The guardian must report annually to the judge his or her work on behalf of the individual with disabilities.

The declaration of incapacity has been used in an indiscriminate way in Argentina, without consideration for the long-term consequences for the individuals affected. In fact, many people with mental retardation do not belong to a social strata that would allow them to accumulate wealth that should be protected by a guardian, but they nevertheless are declared incapacitated. This declaration complicates even the most simple decisions because of the requirement for supervision by a judge. This implies time and bureaucratic steps to keep the judge informed and to receive the judge's decision.

On the other hand, the declaration of incapacity facilitates (in practice, not in the regulations) the declaration of disability and the granting of pensions and subsidies: a $120 monthly pension and health coverage. Declarations of incapacity can, in theory, be reversed, although few are.

Social Inclusion

Social integration and disintegration processes can be examined in four areas: the working environment, institutional participation, collective representation, and association with peers.

Work

Through our institutional work, we know the realities of life of adults with mental retardation. Special and postelementary education do not guarantee a job in adult life. The enormous majority of adults with mental retardation are unemployed. This means they must depend on the government's economic contribution ($120 U.S. monthly) or on their families. In many cases, the disability of a member of the family is exaggerated to guarantee economic assistance. Even more, this economic assistance is limited to those families found in a poverty situation or at social risk, and home ownership excludes them from the benefit of social assistance.

Two strategies have been generated to treat this situation. One is schools and work training programs, which have proven, in most cases, ineffective for those who participate. They do not guarantee people a job after finishing the program, although they have other effects, like institutional belonging. The reason is that general training is given for different tasks or possible jobs, such as general office tasks, cadets, kitchen, computer operator, machine operation, simple tools, and maintenance. This way, the training is prolonged (the age of individuals when they leave or graduate is no less than 25 years), expensive (because it needs a large number of resources), in groups (not individually), and not centered on a concrete job. This program includes graduation with a certificate of qualification, but this certificate is worth less than a high-school certificate (which is the standard requirement to apply for any job).

The second strategy is sheltered workshops. These workshops, designed in the 1970s as an alternative to long-term inclusion in huge institutions, are not sufficient to nourish social inclusion of individuals with mental retardation, nor are they a bridge to a normal job. For the present, they are institutions that are economically supported by the state. Of the 200 sheltered workshops that exist in the country, only 2 finance themselves. The protection offered by state support is not for the participants but for the workshop itself: Out of the competitive circuit, it would disappear without the state's help.

Given the slow work speed of the workers, the only way to support production is to increase the number of workers. Following this strategy, the money given to this protected group of employees is reduced to $20 per month. The supervisors, who are also disabled but with more experience, earn $100 per month. Absent the need to compete, workers are not stimulated to develop and maintain any specific capacities. However, those who participate in sheltered workshops frequently get trained in a specific area (e.g., ceramic, carpentry, smithy) that, in some way, makes their inclusion into a similar area in the future easier.

The National Program of Working Integration for Disabled (PRONILAD) has as one of its goals to transform these workshops into competitive enterprises that can finance themselves. The government will finance the marketing analysis and feasibility study so these institutions can have a precise aim in the market. This group hopes to generate a connection among all the workshops, so they can benefit from each other's experience. As is usual in our country, the administration of the resources is centered in the capital, Buenos Aires, by an organization that includes a variety of groups (the Ministries of Labor, Economy, and Education). This first phase, that will last 3 years, has as a mission to provide each of these workshops with telephones and computers. Only in a second phase will retraining start. Thus far, little progress has been made in the first phase.

The Consultant Commission on Disabilities for the Senate sends observers to every public meeting to encourage that 4% of public jobs be given to people with disabilities. For several years, however, these public meetings have been reduced, and the government is also in the process of reducing the number of employees, with the agreement of the International Monetary Fund. For this reason, the jobs obtained in public organizations are very few. Further, both the law and this Senate commission deal with all the disabilities, of which people with mental retardation make up only a percentage. Thus they frequently have a lower training rate compared to others with disabilities. A recent study showed that, of public employees, the percentage of those with disabilities is between 0.3% and 1.65% (but never the 4% stated by the law), depending on the program considered. There is no information about how many of these are individuals with mental retardation. Few of them have finished primary school and all of them occupy low-paying positions.

As noted before, assistance for citizens with disabilities in Argentina has been based on a psychiatric or educational view; it has not been viewed as a transdisciplinary phenomenon. To guarantee the right of education, special schools try to adapt and to be at the same level as the conventional ones, without calculating the costs that could appear in the future. Their plans are based on failures: if a person doesn't obtain his or her goal or doesn't adapt within the curriculum, he or she is kept indefinitely in the educational system.

Our opinion is that education is an inalienable right. But it is a naive interpretation of that right to propose that the contents of education should be the same, without consideration of cognitive limitations, age, or the social condition of the person. Upon entering adulthood, it will be important for the person to know how to manage money or how to use public transportation. However, the time assigned to money management, or the emphasis put on autonomy, does not change even if the individual is 18, 20, or 22 years of age. Even with the best intentions to help them, the system is determined to make these students stay in school until they learn. And when that day arrives, we must ask, will they have the same opportunities as their peers?

Based on our experience, in many cases what is obtained is the overadaptation of the person: After years, he or she learns tasks only to please the educator; to solve arithmetic problems, but not to manage money or talk on the telephone; to read, but not to use the telephone directory; to write, but not to fill out a bank form.

Recent years have seen an increasing rate of unemployment in the country, in some places reaching 20% of the active population. As a result, the requirements and mechanisms of personnel selection have increased, and at least a high-school certificate is required to get a job. As a result, people with mental retardation can get a job only by chance. And socially, support systems are principally destined for the unemployed who are head of a family, because several people depend on that job. This is not the case for people with mental retardation.

Plans have been developed in India and Egypt to lessen social exclusion due to unemployment. The World Bank recommends that institutions should be competitive, with a specific marketing target: They should produce goods or services with a proven demand in the local market. We propose that a company formed from the beginning as a place where people with mental retardation can work according to the specific needs of the local market could have a promising future as a specific workplace inclusion device.

Institutional Participation

The dynamics of social inclusion or exclusion can be seen also in the collective representations by which a society thinks about and labels its own people and experience. People with mental retardation in Argentina are declared, by the law itself, as different and in worse conditions than other citizens. That is the motive for legislation about their specific rights. We can say that they feel radically different when they compare themselves with their parents, educators, and neighbors. Confronting the pregnancy of a peer, a person said spontaneously in a group meeting: "I thought only professors could get pregnant." This was a person with a good intellectual and adaptation level, and her words don't reflect a lack of information or magical ideas; they reflect her perceived distance from a role like motherhood.

Being "different" gives people with mental retardation primary and secondary benefits; that "different" label permits them to belong to a group, get better medical assistance than that given in the public service to the general population (because they have access to special services), and receive a guarantee that the government will make all possible efforts to assist and improve them. However, this also means they are trapped by images of sick people or childish adults who need education.

Participation in religious activities by people with disabilities in Argentina is also very strange. While there are a few synagogues and some Catholic parishes that recognize the need to include people with mental retardation in their communities, they are not characteristically considered part of the community; their situation is one of social isolation. Neither the institutions nor the families imagine a person with mental retardation to be like other members of the community. Perhaps what is unthinkable is the "difference" itself. If the "difference" is not in itself an entity, it is at least thought of as a shortage of "normality." This makes it difficult for individuals to find, in meaningful others, a representation of themselves.

Collective Representations

A third place to discuss the dynamics of social inclusion or exclusion is the distance from, and the level of participation of individuals in, the dynamic of the institutions. Let's begin by saying that the distance from the specific institutions comes from the centralization of community actions in Argentina. We oscillate between "great national plans" and almost personal small efforts. But the breach between planning at a large level and concrete actions is enormous. The National Center of Community Organizations (CENOC) has the intention of articulating the efforts made by all sectors—community organizations, companies, foreign and international organizations, and the government—to promote and make more efficient a complementary public-private model. For example, "joint focused and universal programs" are promoted (without acknowledgment of the contradiction of those purposes).

Efforts are not concentrated on regional and zone solutions, but on national plans that later have to be implemented and adapted to the particular requirements of every state. And even though every state has autonomy to decide which plans it will adopt in its territory, in practice the differences between national and regional plans are very few. The majority of the resources are concentrated around the capital city, for which the suitability of the national plans is more apparent. The majority of Argentine states, however, have serious economic difficulties, and depend on the federal government's contribution, which will logically finance those programs that match with the state's plans and designs. We further illustrate this situation with the CENOC, where it is declared that "The structure of control to accomplish the social goals that are proposed in this plan, must be developed from the establishment of a Unique Social Account in all the jurisdictions and of a Centralized System of Social Audit, universal and focused programs, regional adaptation and centralized control."

The administration of the government's resources in Argentina was formed during years of political favors and clientelism. Social sectors compatible with the government in office (democratic or military) received more benefits. Further, the bureaucratic structure in general, and more particularly in the case of people with mental retardation, is exhausting and discouraging when a family has to "walk" through it. Procedures take months, and to obtain any kind of benefit it is necessary to repeat the ritual of procedures in each office. In some cases, families must lose a day's pay to carry on with the procedures for their child.

Direct contact with a high official always makes the procedures go faster, so families from higher socioeconomic levels (who have better access to these officials) obtain benefits with much more speed, even though they may not have the greatest need. It is not only true that the number of people with disabilities is greater among the poor, but also that the presence of a disabled family member frequently limits economic resources of the family.

It seems to us that the system is at the service of the everlasting bureaucracy, as it is known, and that it postpones and discourages entrance of citizens with disabilities into the system. The system would explode if it had to cover the real size of the demand. The performance of the government in Argentina may be described in this way: Due to social-cultural differences, successive government changes, marked centralism, physical and social barriers, and poor coordination, there is a lack of systematic and specific planning, inconsistent programs, improvisation and superimposition of actions, lack of operative decentralization, poor use of human and economic resources, incoherent actions, idiosyncratic management, and institutional sectarism. The decentralization of the government's actions to give more autonomy to the municipality has been proposed, but we are, for the moment, only at the beginning of that process.

On the other hand, people with mental retardation and their families as a group do not have intrinsic power over the institutions providing service. They are a minority that, even when unsatisfied, doesn't change significantly the market or the political scene.

Association of Peers

People with mental retardation who have reasonable autonomy frequently form small affinity groups in which they share recreation and free time within their schools or institutions. The characteristics of these associations among peers serve as another area for discussion of inclusion and exclusion. The precariousness of these associations is in direct relation to the level of social exclusion. Once they are out of the institution, or even when they simply stop attending the association, individuals' social bonds become poor and are reduced to the family circle. We believe this phenomenon is important when imagining life after the institutions.

Institutions for people with mental retardation are closed in themselves, with strong emotional bonds between individuals and their teachers or other professionals. Secondary bonds, based on the function they serve beyond the affective tie, are typical of the "outside" (where we can also find discrimination and isolation). These bonds are difficult to establish in a context in which the outside is feared, not only because there are demands, but also because it involves loss of the constant reassurance that the group brings inside the institution.

Nongovernmental organizations that work with people with mental retardation come, in many cases, from programs started by their families. With very poor communication among them, there is a mosaic of conceptions in their actions, from philanthropic goals and compassionate help to advocacy for full social integration. The majority of these organizations concentrate on creating, organizing, and supporting services through all the phases of the lives of people with mental retardation. In only a few cases have they developed goals to create the possibility that in the future people could become independent from the institutions. Independent housing, personalized planning assistance, and investigations and publications about the issue are practically nonexistent.

We should mention that, culturally, disabilities are seen as an individual disadvantage, a problem that each family should solve. There is no social conception that the well-being of the members of the society is a matter that involves all its members. This conception exists in the culture of limited political participation as much as in the support of the institutions by their creators.

We would like to illustrate the government's functioning in relation to people with mental retardation. At the beginning of 1990, Professor Ana Silvia Robert Fanjul created an extensive program to reform regulations for sports competitions for individuals with mental retardation. Fanjul, of the Office of Physical Education for the Schools and Culture General Office in the state of Buenos Aires, believes that regulations should be based first on categorization of athletes according to age and sex, and second, according to their record or maximum mark for a determined competition (without consideration of intellectual ability, IQ, or any other classification). This means the principle of "yes" to possibilities and "no" to the limitations of labels is reaffirmed.

In 1997 the Ministry of Government and Justice organized the Youth Tournament of Buenos Aires, a series of events of great magnitude intended for all the teenagers of the state. In the section on Special Athleticism (designed to regulate the competition of people with mental retardation) we can find the following levels:

Level A: In this category will participate those athletes with mild disability, whose IQ doesn't exceed 75, and who are certified by the educational organization they attend.

Level B: Those athletes with moderate disability certified by their educational organization.

Level C: Those athletes whose disability is Down syndrome.

We want to point out how, in the same state, two governmental organizations can have such different conceptions about the same issue. At the same time, we can observe that it is normal to use the IQ level as a method of qualification of a person's athletic classification.

Quality of Life and Mental Retardation in Argentina

We would like to conclude this chapter by suggesting a number of ways that are worth exploring in our country to improve the quality of life of citizens with mental retardation. In some cases, the strategy should be implemented by the government; in other cases, by those who are directly involved. These strategies are:

- Assure accessibility to resources.

- Increase the connections among different groups of providers.

- Make a reliable census of the number of people with disabilities in the country.

- Decrease levels of unemployment and poverty.

- Increase pensions for people with disabilities.

- Design a mechanism granting social benefits to people with disabilities and their families, without waiting for them to be demanded.

- Simplify administration of resources for people with disabilities.

- Regulate and monitor the accomplishments of laws for people with disabilities.

- Simplify the financial mechanisms of assistance programs.

- Decentralize hiring mechanisms and control of the evolution of services.

- Promote joint participation in planning and management of services, communication media, and intermediate organizations.

- Transform sheltered production workshops into competitive programs.

- Integrate education and rehabilitation approaches and services.
- Promote the responsibility of the community to assist people with disabilities and the understanding that it is not just the family's responsibility.

Quality of Life of People With Developmental Disabilities in Italy: A Note on Legal Foundations

Giorgio Albertini
Casa di Cura San Raffaele
Rome, Italy

In many cultures the concept of quality of life is a milestone toward a new consideration of the dignity of every person, from childhood to adulthood and old age. Among these people are those with developmental disabilities, whose adjustment must be considered from a life-span perspective. Children, older people, and individuals with disabilities are especially vulnerable and at risk in many societies, and it is our responsibility to protect these groups.

In Italy we have a very important law granting people with disabilities the same rights as other citizens. This law has permitted significant progress toward the integration of people with developmental disabilities in society, and it is the prerequisite to reaching a good quality of life for these citizens. The law provides the framework for a functional organization that allows us to help these individuals toward a global solution to their problems.

The Law

This 1992 law, Legge quadro per l'Assistenza, l'Integrazione ed i Diritti delle Persone Handicappate (Base Law No. 104 on Services, Integration, and Rights of Handicapped People) serves as a guide for these citizens to the goal of an independent, pleasurable life in an integrated context. In this chapter I will try to explain the concept of quality of life for people with disabilities in Italy, summarizing the principles granted by this law. The law is directed toward the social integration and the rights of people with handicaps. After defining aims and general principles, it provides a definition of handicapped individuals. The 4th article emphasizes diagnosis and evaluation, and the 5th summarizes the rights of citizens with disabilities. Prevention and early diagnosis, description of the characteristics of assistance and rehabilitation, and the definition of social integration are emphasized in the 6th, 7th, and 8th articles. In the 10th article we find a description of intervention strategies for severe disabilities (sociorehabilitative services).

Education

The Italian law recognizes that the right to receive an individualized developmental profile and an individualized educational plan through integration in regular schools is important in Italy. This has been a very important change, allowing the majority of children the possibility of receiving a good level of education and a very good level of socialization. Integration in regular schools is considered by many authorities to be a resource not only for children with developmental disabilities, but for all children. And there are not only learning disabilities, but also teaching difficulties, forcing us to define new aims and strategies for teachers of children with learning difficulties. A cooperative model versus a competitive model; a school that tries to teach cognitive processes and strategies; and a school where it is possible to teach how to learn—These are the basic concepts of this important experience. In this area we are narrowing the gap between theory and practice.

Vocational Training

Vocational and professional training, integration, and employment are also key issues in the Italian law. At the age of 18 a person may be certified as affected by total or partial disability and consequently added to a special list for employment. Even so, in this area we continue to have a gap between the contents of the law and its achievement. There is much work to be done to avoid making fruitless the results obtained through integration in education, by not allowing adults with disabilities to enter the "real" world. Currently in Italy, the employment situation is difficult for all workers, so it will be particularly difficult to reach this goal.

Nevertheless, jobs for people with disabilities are very important, both for the quality of their lives and for economical reasons. If they do not have jobs, they will cost more to the society, and they will not have the feeling of belonging to the active society. If they do have jobs, they can go on learning and developing, planning their lives, promoting socialization, and improving their behavior. If they do not have jobs, they may have to live with parents, without social interaction and at neurological and psychiatric risk.

Related Issues

The law also describes the possibility of creating supports to promote participation in sports and recreational activities, with the consequence of eliminating architectural barriers, as well as the rights of families of children with significant needs to request financial aid. The quality of life of the latter group is also, of course, improved by cooperation with private and parent associations, access to information and communication, and transportation facilities.

Other articles in the law define the right to vote for people with handicaps; the role of regions (Italy is divided into 21 regions), town councils, and the Ministry of Social Affairs; and access to the Medical Social System and Rehabilitative Services which are free and available to all people, including those with developmental disabilities, with a certification of "civil disability."

The Future

The needs of citizens with disabilities differ according to their specific medical, functional, and social problems. In Italy we need to define a developmental profile in a life-span perspective, with more effective integration among institutions: Ministry of Health, Ministry of Education, Ministry of Social Affairs, regions, and local councils.

To improve the quality of life for people with disabilities in Italy, we must improve coordination of services, and we must use economic resources more efficiently. In fact, in our country we have a lack of change-oriented organizational culture; it is time to change, especially in this field, where there are not simple answers to complex problems.

It should be possible for individuals with different types of developmental disabilities to be part of the society, with rights to physical health, education, vocational training, and jobs. This would help to develop a sense of identity, which is the basis for emotional and affective life. In Italy the role of the local town council will be more and more important in supporting families toward this end. Taking part in all the activities of the community, including social and recreational activities, and having access to information and communication, will prepare individuals for old age with the concept of "aging in place." Provision of the necessary economic, emotional, and social support to make this possible is our aim in Italy.

Reference

Legge quadro per l'Assistenza, l'Integrazione ed i Diritti delle Persone Handicappate No. 104 del 5 febbraio 1992 – Supplemento ordinario G.U. No. 39 del 17 febbraio 1992 (Base Law No. 104 on Services, Integration, and Rights of Handicapped People).

Quality of Life and Social Inclusion

Patricia Noonan Walsh
University College Dublin
Dublin, Ireland

On the west coast of Ireland, a field stretches under clouding skies toward the Atlantic. This windswept place, removed from the sight of neighbors, is still marked on local maps as "the Infants Burial Ground." Now half-hidden, it is the resting place of a host of outliers—strangers to the nearby villages, unbaptized infants, seamen washed ashore. Even in death, these nameless individuals earned no more than a place apart from the established community. But customs change, seasons pass. Today it is no longer the practice to isolate individuals in this way, no matter how poor, friendless, or without grace they may be. Ireland at the end of the 20th century defines itself as an inclusive society with a welcome for diversity. National purpose thus echoes the tone of current political discourse in Europe, a community of nations united to promote the social inclusion of all citizens.

In Ireland today, it is widely assumed that people with disabilities, or those who may be disadvantaged in other ways, must first find their place in society if they are to pursue an enhanced quality of life (Schalock 1996). How are these worthy assumptions expressed in national policy, in social and economic practices and, most important, in the personal experiences of Irish people with developmental disabilities?

This chapter explores recent social and political developments in Ireland that have had an impact on the current status of Irish citizens with developmental disabilities. It also addresses the ways in which new experiences and expectations among people with developmental disabilities may, in turn, leave their mark on Irish society. I here suggest that opportunities for enhanced quality of life arise at points of confluence where individuals are included in society as students, employees, and citizens.

A Place in Irish Society

Ireland is a small country with a population of 3.6 million, distinctive among its European neighbors for its buoyant economy and youthful population. Its promotional literature extols a quiet pace, a desirable quality of life, and a clean, green physical environment. Yet it is haunted by long-term unemployment, contemporary social ills, and deeply rooted political conflict (Walsh & Linehan, 1997). The island of Ireland has recently become the terminal point of a path worn by refugees and asylum seekers, people displaced by shifting political forces to its east and south. Suddenly awash in ethnic diversity, this tightly knit society faces a disturbing phase of self-examination. Ireland has long been accustomed to the outflow of its citizens through emigration. By contrast, extending a welcome to eager newcomers from Central and Eastern Europe and much farther afield is a fresh challenge. Today Ireland shares the aspirations of the European Union for greater social cohesion.

Common policies are shaped so that cohesion may be achieved without compromising the distinctive identities of the Union's 15 diverse member states. Policies are enacted through a range of economic, social, and educational interventions devised to overcome social disadvantage and exclusion.

European Identity

Although religious, historical, and cultural ties with the Continent have been forged over many centuries, Ireland has become more European in the last quarter century. Living in Ireland means something different these days: not least, Irish people—like Swedish, Greek, or Spanish people—travel with dark red passports that identify them as citizens of Europe. Changes in every aspect of social, cultural, and economic life have swept Ireland since its eager entry to the (then) European Community in 1973. Primarily focused on economic cooperation at its birth, the European Union today has matured to exert a profound influence on the fabric of social policy within its member states and among its neighbors.

Today the European Union is vast in scope and resources, a complex organization with an explicit set of social policies. For example, broader goals of social policy have converged in many parts of the Union as countries enact their own national health and insurance systems. This social democratic, yet non-Marxist, tradition is a hallmark of postwar European social policy development. The European Union's foremost social aim is to achieve social inclusion by integrating those Europeans who are disadvantaged or who are perceived to be peripheral—women, the long-term unemployed, people with disability. Inclusion into society and to working life is a fundamental right expressed in the Social Charter drawn up in 1989 (Walsh & Linehan, 1997). If a socially inclusive Europe may be an overarching construct, it is expressed in a range of complex interventions at the national level. Thus Ireland, along with the other 14 member states of the Union, strives to achieve social inclusion for its own people through its own institutions and—in part—with its own finances.

In this way, the Union recognizes the preeminent competence of the constituent countries in education, health, and housing. Member states retain responsibility for teaching, caring for, and sheltering their own people. But training and employment are domains in which the European Union legitimately intervenes to promote a high-quality labor force and economic integration. When inclusive European policies bring matched funding in their wake—for example, in community initiatives such as Employment/HORIZON—fresh opportunities arise for advocates and service providers to try out new local programs of support. Ireland retains its competence—as do the other 14 Member States—in determining how best to provide health care and homes for its own people. But there are striking differences among countries in how well they do so.

Current Trends

The old world is not a static world. Population patterns continue to shift and change as birthrates decline. Overall, Europeans are aging: Ireland is distinctive in having a relatively low percentage of people aged 65 years and a relatively high percentage of those aged under 14 years (Council of Europe, 1995).

Employment. Rates of unemployment are relatively high—about 12% in France, Germany, and Ireland—compared with current rates of about 5% in the United States and 6% in the United Kingdom. Pockets of long-term unemployment endure despite interventions specifically targeted at those who have been out of the work force for years, and who as a consequence have become detached from active participation in society. Whether social inclusion bears a price tag too high for those without earned incomes, or whether those who have been unemployed for many years form a group largely self-excluded from society—these are themes that will continue to fuel an often-rancorous political debate.

Migration. Free movement across borders is at once a worthy ambition and a source of political friction throughout Europe. Migrant workers cross borders to find a better life in a host country. Their rates of fertility are typically higher than those among their host population, feeding social resentments. In Ireland today, debates thicken as to whether particular groups are economic or political refugees, and the former are less warmly welcomed by thrifty providers of social services. By contrast, well-to-do professional groups devise guidelines to promote their mobility and mutual recognition of their qualifications to practice in other countries.

Aging. Demographically, the European population is aging, and the proportion of older people is such that crude death rates have risen even though health conditions have improved. What are the implications for social policy and for funding of the costs of state-entitled payments such as pensions? In countries with growing populations of those who are not at work and whose health needs are substantial, is it feasible that groups will compete for state funds (e.g., the elderly and those with significant disabilities)?

Health and Quality of Life. Irish government policy is to develop a health strategy that will bring accountability, quality, and health and social gains for all of its citizens with available resources. The government's health strategy aims to achieve optimal health and social gain:

> Health Gain is concerned with improvements in the health status or life expectancy of individuals or populations. Social Gain is concerned with broader aspects of the quality of life of groups, such as the elderly or disabled and their carers or vulnerable children. (Institute for Public Administration, 1997)

Disadvantaged Groups. Currently, European social policies aim to achieve the social and economic integration of all citizens, whether they have long been unemployed or belong to groups that are deemed to incur disadvantage, such as the poor, women, migrants, or people with disabilities. Social inclusion is the desired outcome of these policies. It has been demonstrated that long-term unemployment diminishes the chance of reentry to the regular workforce. In Ireland, for example, recent data indicate that three quarters (74%) of people unemployed for more than 2 years are likely to remain so (Murphy & Walsh, 1997, p. 17).

Social Policy

The European Union (European Commission, 1996a) published a *White Paper* on Social Policy, whose broader principles are in harmony with a statement of the Union's position on the needs of Europeans with disabilities. Equality rendered as equal opportunities is the cornerstone of the new rights-led approach that forms the Union's current strategy on disability (European Commission, 1996b). People with disabilities are viewed within a new conceptual framework. The emerging model is rights led. It replaces earlier models of disease, care, or an assumption that people with disabilities have such special needs that these may be met only in seclusion (European Commission, 1996a). Europeans with disabilities are citizens with equal opportunities, including the right to pursue an enhanced quality of life.

Within this approach, equality is the benchmark against which economic and social structures must be assessed. Mainstreaming brings benefits for all people with disabilities, and a person-centered approach to welfare systems is encouraged. Taking a global perspective, the European Union also endorses the 22 *United Nations Standard Rules on the Equalization of Opportunities for Disabled Persons* (United Nations, 1993). These Rules form a comprehensive statement about human rights and participation in society by people with disabilities. Ireland has endorsed these Rules, as have the other 14 member states of the Union. What determines social inclusion? Are these forces the same forces that bear on an individual's satisfaction and contentment—core aspects of quality of life?

Irish People With Developmental Disabilities

In recent years, the number of people with intellectual disability in Ireland has grown. This trend is especially marked among those aged over 35 years where, as shown in Table 28.1[1], numbers have risen by 67% in the past 23 years.

Patterns of living reflect a move away from institutional care. Today more individuals in Ireland enjoy the increased longevity of people with intellectual disability which has been documented widely across the developed countries of the world (Seltzer, Krauss, & Janicki, 1994). More people of the current population of about 27,000 enjoy a life in their own communities, either in family homes or in small group homes. Yet pockets of institutional care persist in psychiatric hospitals and large, remote residential centers.

During the past year, three events cast light on the place of people with developmental disabilities in Irish society. First, the Commission on the Status of People With Disabilities, established by the minister for equality and law reform, concluded 3 years of deliberation. Members of the Commission compiled advice from experts and debated issues in thematic working groups. For the first time, they had consulted directly people with disabilities themselves in a series of small, face-to-face meetings conducted throughout the country. The Commission's major report, *A Strategy for Equality*, leads with the sentence, "People with disabilities are the ne-

---

[1] Data from Mulcahy, Mulvany, and Timmons (1996). Note that individuals with mild disability and those whose disability was "not verified" have been omitted in order to allow multiyear comparisons.

Table 28.1

Number of Irish Individuals With Moderate, Severe, and Profound Intellectual Disability in 1974, 1981, and 1996

Age	1974	1981	1996
0–34 Years	8,048	9,049	9,124
35+ Years	3,208	3,255	5,373
Total	11,256	12,304	14,497

glected citizens of Ireland" (Commission on the Status of People With Disabilities, 1996, Sec. 1.1).

Second, the parents of a young boy with developmental and physical disabilities entered a plea in the courts on his behalf, in order to secure his entry to school. They believed he was so entitled, in the wake of recent High Court and Supreme Court decisions that upheld the right of all Irish children to primary education provided by the state. And they believed, too, that their son's current day-care and activity program with a voluntary agency, however benign, did not meet his educational needs.

Third, in the same month, a small household in Dublin was broken irreversibly. The elderly and ailing parent of a man with intellectual disability died. The father's death changed utterly and irreversibly the life of his middle-aged son, for whom he was the primary caregiver. Despite all attempts to find a suitable home, the son was swiftly placed, sight unseen, in a residential home for elderly people with dementia. The plight of the man provoked a short, sharp public outcry. In its wake, familiar tales persist of the hundreds of Irish men and women whose life stories are being played out on a residential services priority list—not so much living at home each day, as in limbo, waiting to be somewhere else.

Neglect, exclusion, homelessness: Each sorry state confounds the spirit of the people of goodwill who framed the report *(A Strategy for Equality)* of the Commission (1996). This apparent disarray is perplexing to observers. How is it that governmental policy and national goodwill are not reflected in the daily experiences of individuals with disabilities? It prompts a fundamental question about how the quality of an individual's life, and that of the culture of which he or she is a part, may be attuned to each other. It is important to recall that—as individuals do—cultures live their lives in times, revealing themselves at various stages of development within their own social and political context (Elder, 1994). For example, recent evidence suggests that for Irish people with disabilities, exclusion, disability, and poverty are interwoven to form a barrier to their full participation in society (NRB, 1994).

How do the roles adopted by people with developmental disabilities in Irish society at the close of the 20th century relate to the quality of life available to them? To date, people with such disabilities and their families have relied on the consensus gained through social contracts, on a charitable tradition of goodwill, and on the informal networks that thrive in a small, relatively homogeneous culture. Indeed, in 1984 the authors of a government policy document on services for people with disability concluded that, while other countries may indeed have introduced legislative safeguards, Irish people would not necessarily benefit from similar provisions. On the contrary, they went on to say, "The most important thing which any disadvantaged minority needs is good-will and understanding" (*Towards a Full Life,* 1984, 10.18).

These words seem naive today. Certainly, goodwill and understanding are necessary. But if these two worthy sentiments have indeed flourished, they have not sufficed to attain widespread social inclusion. Is there evidence for positive change?

Social Inclusion in Ireland—A Critique

Quality of life, although conceptualized by many contributors as being essentially subjective (Goode 1994), is typically measured across domains of everyday life. Various scales differ in their taxonomy (Felce 1997; Schalock, 1996), but many agree that social well-being (i.e., relationships, support, family life), productive well-being (i.e., job, homelife, education), and material well-being (i.e., housing quality, income) are key dimensions of quality of life. Each setting offers the elements that individuals may seize in order to find and indeed to shape their satisfaction in a fitting environment. Distinctive barriers to inclusion also abound in each setting. The place where an individual lives may be at once a safe, friendly haven and source of delight—or a grim shelter removed from neighbors.

These obstacles were documented in the report of the Commission on the Status of People With Disabilities in Ireland (1996). Its very title, *A Strategy for Equality*, expresses a stance toward the rights of people with disability that had been dismissed only a decade earlier. The new report, the product of 3 years of intense consultation and debate, identified current barriers to social inclusion as well as the actions required if people with disabilities are to play a central role in their country's life. It contains hundreds of recommendations—far too many, some say—for improving the quality of life, the range of opportunities, and the extent of assistive services available to all people with disabilities through enhancement of their legal, economic, social, and civil rights. Its authors urge a fundamental redress of the relative disadvantage of people with developmental and other disabilities through antidiscrimination legislation—a bold and unprecedented strike.

The report of the Commission reflects the stated needs of individuals with disabilities. It is a tangible sign of the influences that Irish people with developmental disabilities may bring to bear on governmental policy, and hence on the social and political environment in which they live. How does this policy instrument map onto charts of the quality of life—the same charts available to all Irish citizens whether or not they have developmental disabilities? When key domains of life are examined—education, employment, community living—it seems that threats to social inclusion persist tenaciously.

Education

> If I accepted defeat in my efforts to have my daughter educated with her peers she would follow so many other children from the west of Ireland…there seems to be unlimited money to send my child away from home but none to enable her to stay at home with her family and friends. (Commission on the Status of People With Disabilities, 1996, p. 170)

Traditionally, children with severe and profound disabilities in Ireland have not been eligible for state-funded education, as it had traditionally been assumed that they could not benefit (Gash, O'Reilly, & Walsh, 1996). As a consequence, children described in this way might or might not avail of day or activity programs supported by local voluntary agencies. The vagaries of annual budgets and indeed of administrative goodwill held sway. There was no statutory obligation on the children's regular attendance. Neither was a national curriculum developed for educating children with severe and profound disabilities.

In 1992 a young boy in County Cork, Paul O'Donoghue, took a case against the state to establish his right to education under the Constitution. His mother acted on his behalf. Paul had attended day-care and activity centers for some of his childhood when the service agency to which he was attached had sufficient funds. But often he had a part-time placement in a setting in which there was neither classroom, teacher, nor curriculum. In the High Court, witnesses for the plaintiff cited legal precedents in the United States and current educational practice in the United Kingdom. Mothers testified in detail about years of neglect, contrasting this with the obvious benefits that followed any educational experience for their children with significant disabilities. On their part, the Departments of Health and Education in Ireland argued that, while the state provided primary education, Paul and children like him were unable to avail themselves of education, and because of these children's limited ceiling in mental age, they never could do so.

One year later the High Court judge who had heard the case decided firmly in Paul's favor. He declared that the state had not fulfilled its constitutional obligation to provide free primary education for Paul, rolling back arguments that supported a view that sporadic if benign day activities were equivalent to education: "I am of opinion that it is not sufficient for the Respondents to grant as a matter of grace and concession, educational benefits which the Applicant is entitled to claim as of right" (Judicial Review, 1993, p. 81).

The state lodged an appeal based on what they perceived as overly prescriptive elements in the decision, requesting constitutional clarification. This action delayed a final decision a further 4 years. While the Department of Education officials waited, parents and advocates continued to lobby on behalf of their children. A handful of teachers were allocated to work with groups of 12 children in day-care and activity centers. Four years later, the Supreme Court handed down a decision that addressed the original plaintiff's case alone and hence set no precedent that may be applied to the hundreds of children who remain excluded from classrooms

(*Sunday Business Post,* 1997). Today only a few children with severe or profound intellectual disabilities, or other disabilities such as autism, may look forward to a rightful school place. Access to education rises and falls, depending on geography, on the goodwill of individual school principals, and on the energy of service providers and parents.

Despite the heroism of such measures, they have as yet not sufficed to ensure the ready access of all Irish children to education. Exclusion is meted out arbitrarily, filtered through long-established traditions tightly knitted by statutory funders and voluntary providers. Service agencies vary considerably in their commitment to promote educational, as opposed to day activity or care, environments. School principals and teachers diverge in their passions for or against integration, falling back on the perennial outlets of defining what is "appropriate" and insisting that fresh funds accompany any change. If education is the critical path to social inclusion for children with developmental disabilities, how do Irish children fare? It seems that their right to education has been recognized by the Irish courts and tirelessly promoted by parents and advocates. Their position has been endorsed by international, European, and national statements of policy. And yet it is still the case that not every Irish child has access to school. For most of those with severe or profound disabilities, September marks another year of systematic exclusion.

Employment

In Ireland inclusive employment is for the few. Most adults with developmental disabilities who are available for work attend day activity or training centers, or centers providing sheltered employment. In recent years, the lure of funding from European Union initiatives has spurred service agencies to offer more inclusive employment alternatives. Supported employment has grown through operation of time-limited projects and is promoted by the Irish Union for Supported Employment (Walsh & Linehan, 1997). In a few cases, host agencies have embraced conversion in order to extend the obvious benefits of supported employment to other service users.

While many targets for widening inclusive employment opportunities for Irish people with disabilities have been set, not all have been met. For example, although considerable sums from the European Social Fund (ESF) have been spent on Irish projects, the authors of a recent evaluation study concluded that:

> In terms of employment and work outcomes only, although there is general agreement that the rates of placement to integrated employment are very low overall, it is presently impossible to definitively conclude on the impact of ESF training. (Department of Enterprise and Employment, 1996, p. 35)

Recent efforts to pass antidiscrimination legislation, an initiative endorsed by the Commission on the Status of People With Disabilities (1996), failed on constitutional grounds. It is likely that new legislation will be drafted. During this impasse, there is no mandate for employers and workplaces to ensure reasonable accommodation for employees with disabilities.

Life in the Community

There is a consensus that, for Irish adults with intellectual disability, community living may be a success when it happens. Led by voluntary service agencies and in some cases by parents, ordinary houses with staff supervision have proliferated. But there is far too little community living, and it is available far too late in the lives of family members. Residential waiting lists are distressingly large, and abrupt homelessness is a constant threat:

> Many parents of people with disabilities, some very elderly, live in great stress because of the size of the waiting lists and the uncertainty of their child ever having an alternative option to living at home. Respite care places relieve some of the problems for parents but the future residential needs of their child are a constant source of preoccupation and worry. This is particularly the case in relation to children and young adults. (Commission on the Status of People With Disabilities, 1996, p. 192)

Most Irish adults with intellectual disability live at home. Many do so long past the time when the family home is the preferred option for either parent or son or daughter. As a result, aging parents, especially mothers, continue in their role as primary caregivers for three, four, or five decades. Life in the community may be the ultimate goal of social policy for Irish people with developmental disabilities. But whether driven by virtue or necessity, most community living takes place within the family:

> Without the support of family carers, public policy for old people and disabled people would be very different. Family care also reflects public policy. The inadequate nature of community care in many countries means that families must care. There is a moral imperative, which goes beyond altruism and reciprocity, to provide assistance, since, without extensive family support, life would be intolerable for people with disabilities living at home. Residential care would probably be the only option. (O'Shea & Kennelly, 1995, p. 9)

Perhaps it is so that in Ireland family care continues to thrive because it must. Without such scaffolding, opportunities for people with developmental disabilities to enjoy community inclusion might well diminish. But with family care so firmly in place, will governments be slow to assume greater responsibility and pay the price?

Future Developments

Today Irish people with developmental disabilities must share the fortunes of a youthful, energetic country rooted in European social and political tradition. These fortunes are mixed: The boom in the information technology sector is matched by robust claims on health and social service budgets, changed family patterns, and the commonplace range of urban ills. What developments comprise the best hopes for the future?

First, financial resources must be reallocated—a change that will not come readily. Human rights are laudable, but they tend to cost money when implemented. Increasingly, other worthy groups of citizens (e.g., seniors) clamor for a fair share. It is more than likely that the Irish government has costed the extension of education to hundreds of children with severe and profound disabilities with some dismay. The push from European social policies imbued by the new human rights approach to disability will be widely felt and perhaps resisted on financial grounds.

Second, national priorities must be merged with the aspirations and needs that people with disabilities have struggled to publicize in the last few years. It remains to be seen how quality-of-life indicators for Irish people with developmental disabilities will converge with, or diverge from, those of other citizens. Inclusion is an overarching principle for national, not merely disability, policies. Irish people with and without disabilities are numbered among the long-term unemployed who are disadvantaged by being excluded from the workforce.

Third, changes will also arise from the bottom-up, on the small scale where individuals live their lives. Community development initiatives work in partnership with service agencies. Supported by local people, and converted to inclusive practices, a local service provider may become the agent of change for the whole community, not only for those individuals who have developmental disabilities.

And finally, individuals have already changed. It is far too late to reinsert them into yesterday's molds. Today's Irish citizens with developmental disabilities form a new generation, showing marked cohort differences. "Especially in rapidly changing societies, differences in birth year expose individuals to different historical worlds, with their constraints and options. Individual life courses may well reflect these different times" (Elder, 1994, p. 5).

Today's toddlers will never be separated from their parents, dressed in institutional garb, and consigned to decades of sheltered work. They and their family members want more than this and will work to achieve it by advocating for equality and inclusion. In Dublin, Kildare, Galway, and elsewhere around Ireland, the advocacy movement has taken root. At first closely nurtured by service agencies, advocates have gradually taken the lead in speaking up for themselves as citizens. They have heightened the expectations that others hold for them and they now hold for themselves.

Summary

The quality of a person's life ultimately reflects the equal opportunities that are his or her gift, day after day, as a member of an inclusive society. No one goes to school in a court of law; no one works in an abstraction; no one lives a life precariously balanced on ideological lines. Points of confluence—moments when individuals act as students, employees, or neighbors—make inclusion a reality. The scaffolding that society erects must lend enough support so that people may embrace these opportunities optimally. Irish people with developmental disabilities, their family members, and advocates build from known strengths. They share common traditions and values in a small country which claims global influence through a history of emigration, European identity, and a distinctive cultural life. Their task, already begun, is not merely to carve space for themselves in existing structures, but also to create a society that is generous enough and wise enough to include each person.

References

Commission on the Status of People With Disabilities. (1996). *A strategy for equality.* Dublin: Department of Equality and Law Reform.

Council of Europe. (1995). *Recent demographic developments in Europe.* Strasbourg: Council of Europe Press.

Department of Enterprise and Employment. (1996). *Training for people with disabilities: Summary report.* Dublin: ESF Programme Evaluation Unit.

Elder, G. H. (1994). Time, human agency, and social change: Perspectives on the life sourse. *Social Psychology Quarterly, 57*(1), 4-15.

European Commission. (1996a). Doc 020F/96. Brussels: Author.

European Commission. (1996b). *Promoting a social Europe.* Catalogue No. CC-91-5-EN-D. Brussels: Author.

Felce, D. (1997). Defining and applying the concept of quality of life. *Journal of Intellectual Disability Research, 41*(2), 126-135.

Gash, H., O'Reilly, M., & Walsh, P. N. (1996). Educational services for students with intellectual disabilities in rural and urban areas of the Republic of Ireland. *Rural Special Education Quarterly, 15*(3), 20-24.

Goode, D.(Ed.). (1994). *Quality of life for persons with disabilities.* Cambridge, MA: Brookline.

Institute for Public Administration. (1997). *Health strategy.* Dublin: Government Publications Office.

Judicial Review. (1993). Opinion of Mr. Justice Rory O'Hanlon in the matter of O'Donoghue v. the State. Dublin: High Court.

Mulcahy, M., Mulvany, F., & Timmons, B. (1996). Preliminary report from the Irish Intellectual Disability Database. *Irish Medical Journal, 59*(3), 101-103.

Murphy, A., & Walsh, B. (1997*). Aspects of employment and unemployment in Ireland.* Dublin: National Economic and Social Forum.

NRB. (1994). *Disability, poverty, and exclusion.* Dublin: Author.

O'Shea, E., & Kennelly, B. (1995). *Caring and theories of welfare economics.* (Working Paper No. 7).Galway: University of Galway; Department of Economics.

Schalock, R. L. (1996). Reconsidering the conceptualization and measurement of quality of life. In R. L. Schalock (Ed.), *Quality of life: Vol. 1. Conceptualization and measurement* (pp. 123-139). Washington, DC: American Association on Mental Retardation.

Seltzer, M. M., Krauss, M. W., & Janicki, M. (Eds.). (1994). *Lifecourse perspectives on adulthood and aging.* Washington, DC: American Association on Mental Retardation.

Sunday Business Post. (1997, February 9). Dublin.

Towards a full life. (1984). [Green paper on services for disabled people.] Dublin: The Stationery Office.

United Nations. (1993). *United Nations standard rules on the equalization of opportunities for disabled persons.* Geneva: Author.

Walsh, P. N., & Linehan, C. (1997). Factors influencing the integration of Irish employees with disabilities in the workplace. *Journal of Vocational Rehabilitation, 8,* 55-64.

The Concept of Quality of Life in the United States: Current Research and Application

Robert L. Schalock
Hastings College
Hastings, Nebraska, United States

Kenneth D. Keith
University of San Diego
San Diego, California, United States

The concept of quality of life is not new; the discussion of what constitutes well-being or happiness dates back to Plato and Aristotle (Mackie, 1977). However, over the past two decades, quality-of-life-related research and application have increasingly become a focus in the United States in the field of mental retardation and developmental disabilities.

To fully appreciate the importance of this concept, it is necessary to understand its semantic meaning and use. In reference to its meaning, *quality* makes us think of the excellence or "exquisite standard" associated with human characteristics and positive values such as happiness, success, wealth, health, and satisfaction; whereas, *of life* indicates that the concept concerns the very essence or essential aspects of human existence (Lindstrom, 1992). This semantic meaning explains why the concept of quality of life is having such impact on the field of disabilities; it shifts our focus away from principles (e.g., normalization and mainstreaming) and processes (e.g., community living and inclusion) to considering how these principles and processes *change* peoples' lives and their perception of a life of quality.

Specifically in the United States, the concept of quality of life is critically important to people with disabilities for the following reasons:

1. Quality of life is a social construct that impacts program development and service delivery in the areas of education (Halpern, 1993; Snell & Vogtle, 1997), health care (Coulter, 1997; Oliver, Holloway, & Carson, 1995; Renwick, Brown, & Nagler, 1996), mental retardation (Brown, 1997; Schalock, 1996b, 1997a), and mental health (Lehman, Rachuba, & Postrado, 1995).

2. Quality of life is being used as the criterion for assessing the effectiveness of services to people with disabilities (Felce & Perry, 1996, 1997; Gardner, Nudler, & Chapman, 1997; Rapley & Hopgood, 1997; Perry & Felce, 1995; Schalock, 1995b).

3. The pursuit of quality is apparent at three levels of today's human service programs: individuals who desire a life of quality (Ward & Keith, 1996; Whitney-Thomas, 1997), providers who want to deliver a quality product (Albin-Dean &

Mank, 1997; Schalock, 1994, 1997a), and evaluators (policy makers, funders, and consumers) who want quality outcomes (Gardner & Nudler, 1997; Schalock, 1999).

How did we in the United States get to where we are in reference to the concept of quality of life, and where might we be going as we embark on the 21st century? In this chapter we suggest that we got here by embracing the concept of quality of life during the 1980s, and that during the 1990s we clarified the concept and its measurement. In the final section, we predict that during the next decade the concept of quality of life in the United States will be pursued even more intensely by individuals advocating for a life of quality, service and support providers focusing on quality enhancement techniques, and evaluators analyzing quality outcomes.

Embracing the Concept

During the 1980s the field of mental retardation and closely related disabilities embraced quality of life as both a sensitizing notion and an overarching principle for service delivery. Why? Because the concept captured the changing vision of people with disabilities, provided a common language for people across disciplines and functional statuses, and was consistent with the larger "quality" revolution.

Captured the Changing Vision

Over the last two decades, there has been a significant change in the way we view people with disabilities. This transformed vision of what constitutes the life possibilities of people with mental retardation is reflected in terms and phrases such as *self-determination, strengths, and capabilities, the importance of normalized and typical environments, the provision of individualized support systems, equity, enhanced adaptive behavior,* and *valued role status.* As a term and concept, *quality of life* became during the 1980s a *social construct* that captured this changing vision and thus became the vehicle through which consumer-referenced equity, empowerment, and increased life satisfaction could be achieved. It was also consistent with the rapidly emerging individualization and person-centered focus in the field. Most assumed that if adequate and appropriate supports were available, the person's quality of life would be enhanced significantly.

Provided a Common Language

Anyone who was involved in the field of disabilities remembers the 1980s as a time during which the field was expanding and trying to adjust to the major upheavals caused by normalization, deinstitutionalization, and mainstreaming. As important as these movements were, they were more process than outcome oriented, and thus failed to provide a clearly articulated goal for the people involved. Quality of life became attractive as a universal principle providing a common goal across environments and people. Thus the statement "to enhance one's quality of life" became our goal. This *sensitizing notion* went beyond the processes of systems change, to the outcomes of those processes. The desire for a life of quality, and quality outcomes from services, was characteristic of everyone. Thus a common language was born.

A second aspect of the common language was that the quality-of-life concept fit the increasing need for accountability in rehabilitation programs. Increasingly, programs were being asked to evaluate their efficiency and effectiveness. The notion that one's quality of life could be enhanced became a mantra for many who were looking for a way to provide services and supports and to evaluate program outcomes across a vast array of people and services. So the quality-of-life concept provided a common language to guide program services and set outcome standards for those services and supports.

Consistent With the Quality Revolution

The quality revolution, with its emphasis on quality products and quality outcomes, was emerging rapidly during the 1980s. One of the main products of this revolution was a "new way of thinking" about people with disabilities that was guided significantly by the concept of quality of life, which became the *unifying theme* around which programmatic changes and "the new way of thinking" were organized. This new way of thinking stressed person-centered planning, the supports model, quality enhancement techniques, and person-referenced quality outcomes (Schalock, 1999). More specifically, this new way of thinking allowed:

- service providers to reorganize resources around individuals rather than rearranging people in program slots (Albin-Dean & Mank, 1997; Albrecht, 1993; Edgerton, 1996; Gardner & Nudler, 1997; Schalock, 1994);

- consumers and service providers to embrace the supports paradigm (Schalock, 1995a);

- program evaluation to shift its focus to person-referenced outcomes that could be used to improve organizational efficiency and enhance person-referenced services and supports (Clifford & Sherman, 1983; Mathison, 1991; Schalock, 1995b; Torres, 1992).

- management styles to focus on learning organizations (Senge, 1990), reengineered corporations (Hammer & Champy, 1993), entrepreneurship (Osborne & Gaebler, 1992), and continuous quality improvement (Albin-Dean & Mank, 1997).

Thus by the end of the 1980s we in the United States had embraced the quality-of-life concept because it captured the changing vision of people with disabilities, provided a common language for consumers and providers alike, and was consistent with the quality revolution with its emphasis on quality products and quality outcomes. Embracing the concept of quality of life had two significant impacts on the field of disabilities.

First, the concept became a *sensitizing notion* that gave us a sense of reference and guidance from the individual's perspective, focusing on the person and the person's environment; a *social construct* that was an overriding principle to improve and enhance a person's perceived quality of life; and a *unifying theme* that provided a systematic or organizing framework to focus on the multidimensionality of the concept.

Second, a number of quality-of-life principles emerged around which was organized the 1990s work on quality-of-life conceptualization, measurement, and application. The most important of these principles included (Goode, 1990; Schalock, 1990):

- Quality of life for people with disabilities is composed of those same dimensions that are important to people without disabilities.

- Quality of life is experienced when a person has the same opportunities as anyone else.

- Quality of life is related to a person's and group's cultural and ethnic heritage and is based on a set of values that emphasize consumer and family strengths.

- Quality of life has both objective and subjective components, but it is primarily the subjective view of the individual that determines the quality of life that he or she experiences.

- Quality-of-life variables and outcomes should play a prominent role in program evaluation.

Clarifying the Concept and Its Measurement

During the 1980s the field of mental retardation embraced a concept that was neither well defined (hence the presence of more than 100 definitions of quality of life) nor completely understood. Thus the 1990s began with investigators and advocates attempting to answer a number of questions about conceptualizing and measuring quality of life. Chief among these questions were the following (Raphael, 1996; Schalock, 1996c):

- Conceptual issues: How should we refer to the term *quality of life?* Is quality of life a single, unitary entity, or a multidimensional, interactive concept? How is it best to conceptualize indicators of quality of life? Is quality of life the same for all individuals?

- Measurement issues: What should be measured? How do we measure quality of life? What psychometric standards need to be considered? How do we overcome measurement challenges?

At the close of the 1990s, these questions are beginning to be answered, thanks largely to a number of significant conceptual shifts regarding how we view and assess quality of life. These shifts include: (a) the multidimensional nature of quality of life; (b) the use of multiple methods (i.e., methodological pluralism) to assess one's perceived quality of life; and (c) the use of multivariate research designs to study important correlates of quality of life.

Multidimensional Nature

There is increasing agreement that quality of life is a multidimensional concept that precludes reducing it to a single "thing" of which the person may have considerable, some, or none. On the basis of recent quality-of-life research (e.g., Cummins, 1996, 1997, 1998; Felce, 1997; Felce & Perry, 1996, 1997; Hughes & Hwang, 1996; Parmenter & Donelly, 1997) Schalock (1996c) identified *eight core quality-of-life dimensions*: emotional well-being, interpersonal relationships, material well-being, personal development, physical well-being, self-determination, social inclusion, and rights. The configuration of these core dimensions varies slightly among investigators. Even so, reaching consensus on these core dimensions is important because they give focus to the values and human characteristics referenced in the semantic meaning of *quality of life* and to efforts to improve the life conditions (and by inference quality of life) of people with disabilities. Investigators also agree that these core dimensions are valued differently by individuals, and that the value attached to each core dimension varies across one's life.

Methodological Pluralism

One of the most significant changes during the 1990s was the shift toward outcome-based evaluation and the use of multiple methods (i.e., qualitative and quantitative) to assess a person's perceived quality of life. This emerging focus on person-referenced outcomes and methodological pluralism reflects not just the subjective and objective components to one's perceived quality of life, but also:

- the quality revolution that we are currently experiencing;
- consumer empowerment with the associated expectations that human service programs will result in an improved quality of life for service recipients;
- the increased need for program outcome data that evaluate the effectiveness and efficiency of intervention and rehabilitation programs;
- the supports paradigm—based on the premise that providing needed and relevant supports will enhance one's quality of life;
- the pragmatic evaluation paradigm—emphasizing the practical, problem-solving orientation to program evaluation.

The approach to methodological pluralism that is emerging in the United States uses *personal appraisal* and *functional assessment* strategies to assess one's perceived quality of life. These two strategies represent the historically based qualitative (personal appraisal) and quantitative (functional assessment) methods.

Personal Appraisal. This strategy addresses the subjective nature of quality of life, typically asking the person how satisfied the person is with various aspects of life. For example, this is the approach we have used in the *Quality of Life Questionnaire* (Schalock & Keith, 1993) wherein we asked questions such as, "How satisfied are you with your current home or living situation?" or, "How satisfied are you with the skills and experience you have gained or are gaining from your job?" Although the person's responses are subjective, the person's responses need to be measured in psychometrically acceptable ways. Thus a 3- to 5-point Likert scale can be used to indicate the level of expressed satisfaction. There are advantages to this approach to measurement: it encompasses the most common dependent measure used currently in quality-of-life assessments; it allows one to measure those factors that historically have been considered to be major subjective indicators of a life of quality; and it allows one to quantify the level of expressed satisfaction.

Increasingly, we are seeing that a person's measured level of satisfaction (i.e., personal appraisal) is a commonly used dependent measure in evaluating the person's perceived quality of life. One might well ask, "Why this emphasis on satisfaction?" Reasons include:

- It is a commonly used aggregate measure of individual life domains (Andrews, 1974; Campbell, Converse, & Rogers, 1976).

- It demonstrates a trait-like stability over time (Diener, 1984; Edgerton, 1990, 1996; Heal, Borthwick-Duffy, & Saunders, 1996).

- There is an extensive body of research on level of satisfaction across populations and service delivery recipients (Cummins, 1998; Halpern, 1993; Harner & Heal, 1993; Heal & Chadsey-Rusch, 1985; Heal, Rubin, & Park, 1995; Schalock & Faulkner, 1997).

- It allows one to assess the relative importance of individual quality-of-life dimensions and thereby assign value to the respective dimensions (Campbell et al., 1976; Cummins, 1996; Flanagan, 1978, 1982; Felce & Perry, 1996, 1997).

Thus the major advantages of using satisfaction as a common indicator of one's perceived quality of life are in (a) comparing population samples; (b) providing a common language that can be shared by consumers, providers, policy makers, regulators, and researchers; (c) assessing consumer needs; and (d) evaluating organizational outcomes. Its major disadvantages are (a) its limited utility for smaller group comparisons that might provide only a global measure of perceived well-being and (b) its discrepancy with current multidimensional theories of quality of life (Cummins, 1996). For these reasons, other dependent measures of one's quality of life are needed, such as those obtained from the functional assessment strategies discussed in the next section.

Functional Assessment. The most typical formats used in functional assessment are rating scales, participant observation, and/or questionnaires (Schalock, 1996c). Each attempts to document a person's functioning across one or more core quality-of-life dimensions and the respective quality-of-life indicator(s) suggested in Table 29.1. To accomplish this, most instruments employ some form of ordinal rating scale to yield a profile of the individual's functioning. For example, one might ask (or observe), "How frequently do you use health care facilities?" or, "How many civic or community clubs do you belong to?"

There are a number of advantages in using functional, more objective assessments of one's perceived quality of life: (a) Objective measures can confirm results from the personal appraisal (i.e., satisfaction) strategy; (b) adding objective measures to personal appraisal overcomes the commonly reported low correlation between subjective and objective measures of quality of life (Schalock, 1996c); (c) their use allows for the evaluation of outcomes across groups; and (d) objective measures provide important feedback to service providers, funders, and regulators as to how they can change or improve their services to enhance the recipients' perceived quality of life.

But there are also some disadvantages: (a) Functional assessment must be balanced with other considerations (e.g., it is clear that not all outcomes related to one's perceived quality of life can be measured). (b) Functional assessment can have more cost than benefit. One needs to be cautious that the functional assess-

Table 29.1

Quality-of-Life Indicators

Dimension	Exemplary Indicators	
Emotional Well-Being	Safety	Freedom From Stress
	Spirituality	Self-Concept
	Happiness	Contentment
Interpersonal Relations	Intimacy	Interactions
	Affection	Friendships
	Family	Supports
Material Well-Being	Ownership	Employment
	Financial	Possessions
	Security	Social Economic Status
	Food	Shelter
Personal Development	Education	Personal Competence
	Skills	Purposeful Activity
	Fulfillment	Advancement
Physical Well-Being	Health	Health Care
	Nutrition	Health Insurance
	Recreation	Leisure
	Mobility	Activities of Daily Living
Self-Determination	Autonomy	Personal Control
	Choices	Self-Direction
	Decisions	Personal Goals and Values
Social Inclusion	Acceptance	Community Activities
	Status	Roles
	Supports	Volunteer Activities
	Work	Residential Environment
Rights	Privacy	Due Process
	Voting	Ownership
	Access	Civic Responsibility

ment system does not consume in resources more than its information is worth. (c) The usefulness of functional assessments varies by their use. Functional assessments are only useful to the management or decision-making process to the extent that they are used and that they answer the right questions. (d) Organizations are sometimes limited in their ability to influence outcomes. Users of functional assessment data need to understand the role that many factors play in one's perceived quality of life and not focus exclusively on the service or supports provider.

In summary, methodological pluralism has become an integral part of the assessment of one's quality of life. Its major advantages include more than simply resolving the quantitative-qualitative debate in the literature; rather, it allows researchers and practitioners alike to meet the following objectives of using mixed-method evaluations:

- *triangulation* or the determination of correspondence of results across personal appraisal and functional assessment strategies (Cooke, 1985);

- *complementarity* or the use of qualitative and quantitative methods to measure overlapping, but distinct facets of the quality-of-life phenomenon (Greene, Caracelli, & Graham, 1989);

- *initiation* that allows one to recast questions or results from one strategy with questions or results from the contrasting strategy (Caracelli & Greene, 1993).

Multivariate Research Design

The third conceptual shift during the 1990s has involved changing the research and statistical design used to study the quality-of-life concept. Specifically, we have seen a significant shift from a "between" to a "multivariate or within" approach. Historically the study of quality of life was approached from a "between groups" or conditions perspective; investigators sought to find factors such as social-economic status and large demographic population descriptors that could discriminate between those people or countries with a high and those with a lower quality of life. This "between" mentality spilled over to our early work on quality of life in subtle ways, as reflected in the attitude expressed by some: *We need to have different measures or quality-of-life indexes for those who are higher functioning from those who are either nonverbal or lower functioning.*

Shifting to a multivariate research design has a number of heuristic and practical advantages. First, it allows one to focus more on the correlates and predictors of a life of quality rather than comparing quality-of-life scores or status. More specifically, one can use multivariate research designs to determine the relationship among a number of measured predictor variables and one's perceived quality of life. This approach has been one that we have used to evaluate the relative contribution to one's assessed quality of life of a number of personal characteristics, objective life conditions, and provider characteristics. Across a number of studies (e.g., Schalock, Lemanowicz, Conroy, & Feinstein, 1994; Schalock & Faulkner, 1997; Schalock, Bonham, & Marchand, 2000) personal factors (e.g., health status and adaptive behavior level), environmental variables (e.g., perceived social support, current residence, earnings, home type, and integrated activities), and provider characteristics (e.g., worker stress and job satisfaction) are significant predictors of individuals' assessed quality of life.

Second, once these significant predictors are identified, programmatic changes can be made to enhance the person's quality of life through techniques such as personal development and wellness training, quality enhancement techniques, and quality management techniques (Schalock, 1994; Schalock & Faulkner, 1997).

Third, multivariate research designs help us understand better the complexity of the concept of quality of life and the role that a number of contextual variables play in the perception of a life of quality.

And finally, these designs shift the focus of our thinking and intervention from exclusively personal to personal *and* environmental factors as major sources of quality-of-life enhancement.

The Future: Pursuing Quality

By embracing quality of life and clarifying the concept and its measurement, we in the United States are on the verge of seriously pursuing quality and implementing the concept of quality of life to improve the lives of people with disabilities. In the near future, we anticipate that the concept of quality of life for people with disabilities in the United States will be pursued from three perspectives: (a) individuals pursuing a life of quality, (b) service and support providers implementing quality enhancement techniques, and (c) evaluators (policy makers, funders, and consumers) analyzing quality outcomes.

Individuals Pursuing a Life of Quality

We foresee at least three major thrusts by people pursuing a life of quality. First, we will continue to see strong advocacy for increased opportunities to participate in the mainstream of life, associated with increased inclusion, equity, and choices. Related efforts will involve advocating for increased individual supports within regular environments and inclusion in major activities such as decision making (Wehmeyer & Schwartz, 1998), person-centered planning (Butterworth, Steere, & Whitney-Thomas, 1997), and participatory action research (Whitney-Thomas, 1997).

Second, consumers will work jointly with researchers in determining the relative importance or value of the core dimensions. For children and youth, for example, the most important dimensions may well be personal development, self-determination, interpersonal relationships, and social inclusion (Schalock, 1996a; Stark & Goldsbury, 1990); for adults, the dimensions of emotional well-being, personal development, interpersonal relations, and material well-being may well be most important; and for the elderly, physical well-being, interpersonal relationships, and emotional well-being may be the most important dimensions (Schalock, DeVries, & Lebsack, 1998).

Third, consumers will increasingly become involved in assessing their own quality of life. For example, we (Schalock et al., 1999) have shown recently that consumers are excellent surveyors and can assess other consumers' quality of life with highly acceptable reliability and validity. When such is done, the major predictors of a life of quality from the consumers' perspective is having a job and the sense of dignity experienced in interactions with others.

Service Providers Implementing Quality Enhancement

Looking ahead, we also foresee service and support providers implementing quality enhancement techniques that focus on quality-of-life-related outcomes from education and rehabilitation services and supports. These techniques will be either environmentally or program-based.

Environmentally Based Enhancement Techniques. Environmentally based quality enhancement techniques will involve the implementation of three concepts: (a) the belief that an enhanced quality of life is the result of a good match between a person's wants and needs and their fulfillment, and that reducing the discrepancy between a person and that person's environment increases the person's assessed quality of life (Cummins, 1996; Michalos, 1985; Murrell & Norris, 1983; Schalock, Keith, Hoffman, & Karan, 1989); (b) the corollary that it is possible to assess the match between individuals and their environments (Schalock & Jensen, 1986); and (c) the proposition that the higher the imbalance between the person and the person's environment, the greater the person's support needs.

Environmentally based enhancement techniques involve designing environments that are user friendly and reduce the mismatch between individuals and their environmental requirements. Examples include (Ferguson, 1997):

- opportunity for involvement (e.g., food preparation);
- easy access to the outdoor environment;
- modifications to stairs, water taps, door knobs;
- safety (e.g., handrails, safety glass, nonslip walking surfaces);
- convenience (e.g., orientation aids such as color coding or universal pictographs);
- accessibility to home and community;
- sensory stimulation (e.g., windows, less formal furniture);
- prosthetics (e.g., personal computers, specialized assistive devices, and high technological environments);
- opportunity for choice and control (e.g., lights, temperature, privacy, and personal space).

Program-Based Enhancement Techniques. Once the core dimensions of quality of life are understood and their correlates assessed, it is possible to implement program-based quality enhancement techniques such as the following (specific to the eight core dimensions proposed by Schalock, 1996a):

- emotional well-being: increased safety, stable and predictable environments, positive feedback;
- interpersonal relations: friendships, intimacy, family support;
- material well-being: ownership, possessions, employment;
- personal development: education and functional rehabilitation, augmentative technology;
- physical well-being: health care, mobility, wellness, nutrition;
- self-determination: choices, personal control, decisions, personal goals;

- social inclusion: community role, community integration, volunteerism;
- rights: privacy, voting, due process, civic responsibilities.

Service providers will also need to evaluate the impact of these implemented strategies. This means service providers will need to pursue quality outcomes related to both individuals and organizations, such as the efficiency and value outcomes discussed in the next section. Evaluations should look at where they are, where they want to be, and what organizational changes will be required to increase both person-referenced outcomes and program outputs.

Evaluators Analyzing Quality Outcomes

Human service organizations throughout the world are currently being challenged to provide quality services that result in quality outcomes. This is a difficult task because of two powerful, potentially conflicting forces: (a) person-centered, quality-of-life-focused values and (b) economically based accountability and efficiency standards (frequently called economic rationalism). The focus on person-centered values stems from: (a) the quality-of-life movement; (b) the human rights and self-advocate movements' emphasis on equity, inclusion, empowerment, respect, and community living and work options; (c) numerous public laws that stress opportunities and desired person-referenced outcomes related to independence, productivity, community integration, and satisfaction; and (d) research demonstrating that people can be more independent, productive, community integrated, and satisfied when quality-of-life concepts are the basis of individual services and supports. Conversely, the focus on increased accountability and efficiency stems from economic restraints and the movement toward a market economy in health care and rehabilitation services.

How can service providers adapt to these two conflicting forces and still focus on valued, person-referenced outcomes? A heuristic model for doing so is presented in Figure 29.1. The model has three components: standards, focus, and critical performance indicators.

- *Standards* reflect the current emphasis on efficiency and value. Efficiency standards are based on the economic principles involved in increasing the net value of goods and services available to society; value standards reflect what is considered as good, important, or of value to the person.

- *Focus* represents the current accountability emphasis on programmatic outputs and person-referenced outcomes. In the model, *outputs* reflect the results of organizational processes, and *outcomes* represent the impact of services and supports on the person.

- *Critical performance indicators* for the organization include service coordination, financial stability, health and safety, program data, staff turnover or tenure, access to service, customer satisfaction, staff competencies, family or consumer supports, and community support. Critical performance indicators for the person (which are keyed to the eight core quality-of-life dimensions proposed by Schalock, 1996c) include physical well-being (health status, wellness

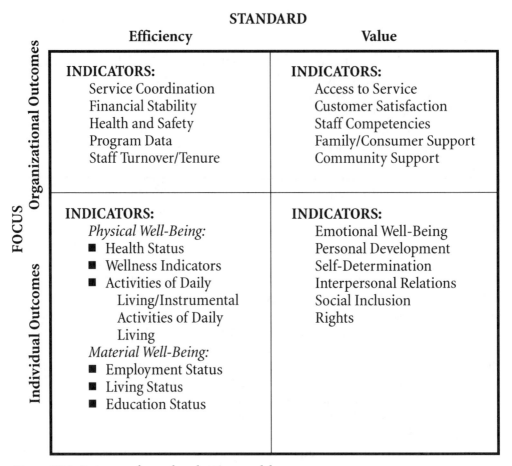

Figure 29.1. Outcomes-focused evaluation model.

indicators, activities or instrumental activities of daily living), material well-being (employment, living and education status), emotional well-being, personal development, self-determination, interpersonal relations, social inclusion, and rights.

The primary challenge to service providers and evaluators alike is to reach a balance among the four matrix cells of Figure 29.1, recognizing that different constituents will emphasize their respective desired indicators and outcomes. Funders, for example, will most likely focus on efficiency outputs; advocacy groups will stress the importance of evaluating value and efficiency outcomes. Those emphasizing public policy might well stress efficiency outcomes and value outputs. A second challenge will be to reach a reasonable balance between accountability demands and available evaluative resources so that we can use the resulting outcome data to: (a) determine whether functional limitations have been reduced and the person's adaptive behavior and role status enhanced; (b) provide feedback to decision makers about the effectiveness and efficiency of the respective services and/or supports provided; (c) provide the basis for program changes and improvements; (d) target those areas where increased resources can be applied to improve the match between individuals and environments; and (e) show a commitment to consumers that we are serious about program evaluation and willing to involve them in the evaluation activities.

Conclusion

In conclusion, the future will be an exciting and active time as we jointly "pursue quality." This pursuit will involve individuals desiring and advocating for a life of quality, service and support providers producing quality products, and evaluators analyzing quality outcomes. Despite this optimism, we should never forget that the future will probably continue to reflect the current value clashes regarding the dialectical issues of program efficiency and economic rationalism versus person-centered values and quality-of-life enhancement strategies. Thus considerable hard work, advocacy, and risk lie ahead.

Despite these value clashes, the last two decades have seen in the United States considerable progress in understanding the significant role and impact that the concept of quality of life has played in the lives of people with mental retardation and the systems that interact with those lives. Indeed, the concept of quality of life has extended beyond the person and has now impacted an entire service delivery system; this is because of its power as a social construct, unifying notion, and integrating concept.

As the United States embarks on the 21st century, we will continue to pursue both the concept of quality of life and an enhanced life of quality for people with disabilities. Given the value clashes and practical problems that we will undoubtedly encounter, what guidelines might assist our efforts? We offer these 10 suggestions for our readers' consideration:

1. Consider that quality of life for people with mental retardation is composed of those same core dimensions that are valued by all of a nation's citizenry.

2. Base public policies and service delivery principles on the concept of quality of life and the enhancement of a life of quality for all people.

3. Realize that the value ascribed to the various core quality-of-life dimensions will probably vary over the life span of the person, but, regardless of age, an enhanced quality of life is experienced when a person's basic needs are met and when a person has the same opportunities as anyone else to pursue and achieve goals in the major life domains and settings.

4. Focus evaluation activities on both consumer outcomes and system performance.

5. Stress that continuous quality improvement is a fundamental aspect of an organization's culture.

6. Have evaluation activities play a complementary and supportive role that is consistent with the changing concept of disability as resulting from the inter-

action of the person and his or her environment.

7. Identify the significant predictors of a life of quality and evaluate the impact of targeting resources to maximize their positive effect(s).

8. Assist consumers, policy makers, funders, service providers, and advocates to understand the multidimensional nature of the concept of quality of life and its assessment.

9. Use multivariate statistical and research designs to determine the effectiveness and efficiency of quality-of-life-focused education, rehabilitation, and/or health programs.

10. Integrate subjective and objective quality-of-life indicators into a unified concept of the core dimensions of quality of life, realizing that some aspects of each core dimension can be evaluated best via personal appraisal strategies and other aspects through objective functional assessments.

References

Albin-Dean, J. M., & Mank, D. M. (1997). Continuous improvement and quality of life: Lessons from organizational management. In R. L. Schalock (Ed.), *Quality of life: Vol. 2. Application to persons with disabilities* (pp. 165-179). Washington, DC: American Association on Mental Retardation.

Albrecht, K. (1993). *The only thing that matters: Bringing the power of the customer into the center of your business.* New York: Harper Business.

Andrews, F. M. (1974). Social indicators of perceived quality of life. *Social Indicators Research, 1,* 279-299.

Brown, R. I. (Ed.). (1997). *Quality of life for people with disabilities: Models, research, and practice.* Cheltenham, United Kingdom: Stanley Thornes.

Butterworth, J., Steere, D. E., & Whitney-Thomas, J. (1997). Using person-centered planning to address personal quality of life. In R. L. Schalock (Ed.), *Quality of life: Vol. 2. Application to persons with disabilities* (pp. 5-24). Washington, DC: American Association on Mental Retardation.

Campbell, A., Converse, P. E., & Rogers, W. L. (1976). *The quality of American life: Perceptions, evaluation, and satisfaction.* New York: Russell Sage.

Caracelli, V. J., & Greene, J. C. (1993). Data analysis strategies for mix-method evaluation designs. *Educational Evaluation and Policy Analysis, 15*(2), 195-207.

Clifford, D. L., & Sherman, P. (1983). Internal evaluation: Integrating program evaluation and management. In A. J. Love (Ed.), *Developing effective internal evaluation: New directions for program evaluation* (No. 20). San Francisco: Jossey-Bass.

Cooke, T. D. (1985). Postpositivist critical multipluralism. In R. L. Shotland & M. M. Mark (Eds.), *Social science and social policy* (pp. 21-62). Beverly Hills, CA: Sage.

Coulter, D. L. (1997). Health-related application of quality of life. In R. L. Schalock (Ed.), *Quality of life: Vol. 2: Application to persons with disabilities* (pp. 95-104). Washington, DC: American Association on Mental Retardation.

Cummins, R. A. (1996). The domains of life satisfaction: An attempt to order chaos. *Social Indicators Research, 38,* 303-328.

Cummins, R. A. (1997). Assessing quality of life. In R. I. Brown (Ed.), *Quality of life for people with disabilities: Models, research, and practice* (pp. 116-150). Cheltenham, United Kingdom: Stanley Thornes.

Cummins, R. A. (1998). The second approximation to an international standard for life satisfaction. *Social Indicators Research, 43,* 307-334.

Diener, E. (1984). Subjective well-being. *Psychological Bulletin, 95,* 542-575.

Edgerton, R. B. (1990). Quality of life from a longitudinal research perspective. In R. L. Schalock (Ed.), *Quality of life: Perspectives and issues* (pp. 149-160). Washington, DC: American Association on Mental Retardation.

Edgerton, R. B. (1996). A longitudinal-ethnographic research perspective on quality of life. In R. L. Schalock (Ed.), *Quality of life: Vol. 1. Conceptualization and measurement* (pp. 83-90). Washington, DC: American Association on Mental Retardation.

Felce, D. (1997). Defining and applying the concept of quality of life. *Journal of Intellectual Disability Research, 41*(2), 126-135.

Felce, D., & Perry, J. (1996). Assessment of quality of life. In R. L. Schalock (Ed.), *Quality of life: Vol. 1. Conceptualization and measurement* (pp. 63-72). Washington, DC: American Association on Mental Retardation.

Felce, D., & Perry, J. (1997). Quality of life: The scope of the term and its breath of measurement. In R. I. Brown (Ed.), *Quality of life for people with disabilities: Models, research, and practice* (pp. 56-70). Cheltenham, United Kingdom: Stanley Thornes.

Ferguson, R. V. (1997). Environmental design and quality of life. In R. I. Brown (Ed.), *Quality of life for people with disabilities: Models, research, and practice* (pp. 56-70). Cheltenham, United Kingdom: Stanley Thornes.

Flanagan, J. C. (1978). A research approach to improving quality of life. *American Psychologist, 33,* 138-147.

Flanagan, J. C. (1982). Measurement of quality of life: Current state of the art. *Archives of Physical Medicine and Rehabilitation, 63,* 56-59.

Gardner, J. F., & Nudler, S. (1997). Beyond compliance to responsiveness: Accreditation reconsidered. In R. L. Schalock (Ed.), *Quality of life: Vol. 2. Application to persons with disabilities* (pp. 135-148). Washington, DC: American Association on Mental Retardation.

Gardner, J. F., Nudler, S., & Chapman, M. S. (1997). Personal outcomes as measures of quality. *Mental Retardation, 35*(4), 295-305.

Goode, D. A. (1990). Thinking about and discussing quality of life. In R. L. Schalock (Ed.), *Quality of life: Perspectives and issues* (pp. 41-58). Washington, DC: American Association on Mental Retardation.

Greene, J. C., Caracelli, V. J., & Graham, W. F. (1989). Toward a conceptual framework for mixed-method evaluation designs. *Educational Evaluation and Policy Analysis, 11*, 255-274.

Halpern, A. S. (1993). Quality of life as a conceptual framework for evaluating transition outcomes. *Exceptional Children, 59*, 486-498.

Hammer, M., & Champy, J. (1993). *Reengineering the corporation: A manifesto for business revolution.* New York: Harper Collins.

Harner, C. J., & Heal, L. W. (1993). The Multifaceted Lifestyle Questionnaire (MLSS): Psychometric properties of an interview schedule for assessing personal satisfaction of adults with limited intelligence. *Research in Developmental Disabilities, 14*, 221-236.

Heal, L. W., Borthwick-Duffy, S. A., & Saunders, R. R. (1996). Assessment of quality of life. In J. W. Jacobson & J. A. Mulick (Eds.), *Manual of diagnosis and professional practice in mental retardation* (pp. 199-209). Washington, DC: American Psychological Association.

Heal, L. W., & Chadsey-Rusch, J. (1985). The lifestyle satisfaction scale (LSS): Assessing individuals' satisfaction with residence, community setting, and associated services. *Applied Research in Mental Retardation, 6*, 475-490.

Heal, L. W., Rubin, S. S., & Park, W. (1995). *Lifestyle satisfaction scale.* Champaign-Urbana: Transition Research Institute, University of Illinois.

Hughes, C., & Hwang, B. (1996). Attempts to conceptualize and measure quality of life. In R. L. Schalock (Ed.), *Quality of life: Vol. 1. Conceptualization and measurement* (pp. 51-62). Washington, DC: American Association on Mental Retardation.

Lehman, A. F., Rachuba, L. T., & Postrado, L. T. (1995). Demographic influences on quality of life among persons with chronic mental illness. *Evaluation and Program Planning, 18*(2), 155-164.

Lindstrom, B. (1992). Quality of life: A model for evaluating health for all. *Soz Praventivmed, 37*, 301-306.

Mackie, J. L. (1977). *Ethics: Inventing right and wrong.* Harmondsworth, United Kingdom: Penguin.

Mathison, S. (1991). What do we know about internal evaluation? *Evaluation and Program Planning, 14*, 159-165.

Michalos, A. C. (1985). Multiple discrepancy theory (MDT). *Social Indicators Research, 16,* 347-413.

Murrell, S. A., & Norris, F. H. (1983). Quality of life as the criterion for need assessment and community psychology. *Journal of Community Psychology, 11,* 88-97.

Oliver, N., Holloway, F., & Carson, F. (1995). Deconstructing quality of life. *Journal of Mental Health, 4,* 1-4.

Osborne, D., & Gaebler, T. (1992). *Reinventing government: How the entrepreneurial spirit is transforming the public sector.* Reading, MA: Addison-Wesley.

Parmenter, T., & Donelly, M. (1997). An analysis of the dimensions of quality of life. In R. I. Brown (Ed.), *Quality of life for people with disabilities: Models, research, and practice* (pp. 91-114). Cheltenham, United Kingdom: Stanley Thornes.

Perry, J., & Felce, D. (1995). Objective assessments of quality of life: How much do they agree with each other? *Journal of Community and Applied Social Psychology, 5,* 1-19.

Raphael, D. (1996). Defining quality of life: Debates concerning its measurement. In R. Renwick, I. Brown, & M. Nagler (Eds.), *Quality of life in health promotion and rehabilitation: Conceptual approaches, issues, and applications* (pp. 146-165). Thousand Oaks, CA: Sage.

Rapley, M., & Hopgood, L. (1997). Quality of life in a community-based service in rural Australia. *Journal of Intellectual and Developmental Disabilities, 22*(2), 125-141.

Renwick, R., Brown, I., & Nagler, M. (Eds.). (1996). *Quality of life in health promotion and rehabilitation: Conceptual approaches, issues, and applications.* Thousand Oaks, CA: Sage.

Schalock, R. L. (Ed.). (1990). *Quality of life: Perspectives and issues.* Washington, DC: American Association on Mental Retardation.

Schalock, R. L. (1994). Quality of life, quality enhancement, and quality assurance: Implications for program planning and evaluation in the field of mental retardation and developmental disabilities. *Evaluation and Program Planning, 17,* 121-131.

Schalock, R. L. (1995a). The assessment of natural supports in community rehabilitation services. In O. C. Karan & S. Greenspan (Eds.), *Community rehabilitation services for people with disabilities* (pp. 184-203). Newton, MA: Butterworth-Heinemann.

Schalock, R. L. (1995b). *Outcome-based evaluation.* New York: Plenum Press.

Schalock, R. L. (1996a). The quality of children's lives. In A. H. Fine & N. M. Fine (Eds.), *Therapeutic recreation for exceptional children: Let me in, I want to play* (2nd ed., pp. 83-94). Springfield, IL: Charles C. Thomas.

Schalock, R. L. (Ed.). (1996b). *Quality of life: Vol. 1. Conceptualization and measurement.* Washington, DC: American Association on Mental Retardation.

Schalock, R. L. (1996c). Reconsidering the conceptualization and measurement of quality of life. In R. L. Schalock (Ed.), *Quality of life: Vol. 1. Conceptualization and measurement* (pp. 123-139). Washington, DC: American Association on Mental Retardation.

Schalock, R. L. (1997a). The concept of quality of life in 21st century disability programs. In R. I. Brown (Ed.), *Quality of life for people with disabilities: Models, research, and practice* (pp. 327-340). Cheltenham, United Kingdom: Stanley Thornes.

Schalock, R. L. (Ed.). (1997b). *Quality of life: Vol. 2. Application to persons with disabilities.* Washington, DC: American Association on Mental Retardation.

Schalock, R. L. (1999). A quest for quality: Achieving organizational outputs and personal outcomes. In J. Gardner & S. Nudler (Eds.), *Quality performance in human services* (pp. 58-80). Baltimore: Paul H. Brookes.

Schalock, R. L., Bonham, G. S., & Marchand, C. B. (2000). Consumer based quality of life assessment: A path model of perceived satisfaction. *Evaluation and Program Planning, 23*(1), 77-87.

Schalock, R. L., DeVries, D., & Lebsack, J. (1998). Rights, quality measures, and program changes. In S. S. Herr & G. Weber (Eds.), *Aging, rights and quality of life: Prospects for older persons with developmental disabilities* (pp. 81-92). Baltimore: Paul H. Brookes.

Schalock, R. L., & Faulkner, E. H. (1997). Cross-validation of a contextual model of quality of life. *European Journal on Mental Disability, 4*(14), 18-27.

Schalock, R. L., & Jensen, M. (1986). Assessing the goodness-of-fit between persons and their environments. *Journal of the Association for Persons With Severe Handicaps, 11*(2), 103-109.

Schalock, R. L., & Keith, K. D. (1993). *Quality of life questionnaire.* Worthington, OH: IDS.

Schalock, R. L., Keith, K.A., Hoffman, K., & Karan, O. C. (1989). Quality of life: Its measurement and use. *Mental Retardation, 27*, 25-31.

Schalock, R. L., Lemanowicz, J. A., Conroy, J. W., & Feinstein, C. S. (1994). A multivariate investigative study of the correlates of quality of life. *Journal on Developmental Disabilities, 3*(2), 59-73.

Senge, P. (1990). *The fifth discipline: The art and practice of the learning organization.* New York: Doubleday/Currency.

Snell, M. E., & Vogtle, L. K. (1997). Facilitating relationships of children with mental retardation in schools. In R. L. Schalock (Ed.), *Quality of life: Vol. 2. Application to persons with disabilities* (pp. 43-62). Washington, DC: American Association on Mental Retardation.

Stark, J. A., & Goldsbury, T. (1990). Quality of life from childhood to adulthood. In R. L. Schalock (Ed.), *Quality of life: Perspectives and issues* (pp. 71-84). Washington, DC: American Association on Mental Retardation.

Torres, R. T. (1992). Improving the quality of internal evaluation: The evaluator as consultant-mediator. *Evaluation and Program Planning, 14,* 189-198.

Ward, N., & Keith, K. D. (1996). Self-advocacy: Foundations for a life of quality. In R. L. Schalock (Ed.), *Quality of life: Vol. 1. Conceptualization and measurement* (pp. 5-10). Washington, DC: American Association on Mental Retardation.

Wehmeyer, M., & Schwartz, M. (1998). The relationship between self-determination and quality of life for adults with mental retardation. *Education and Training in Mental Retardation and Developmental Disabilities, 33*(1), 3-12.

Whitney-Thomas, J. (1997). Participatory action research as an approach to enhancing quality of life for individuals with disabilities. In R. L. Schalock (Ed.), *Quality of life: Vol. 2. Application to persons with disabilities* (pp. 181-198). Washington, DC: American Association on Mental Retardation.

Quality of Life:
Challenges and Confrontation

Roy I. Brown
Flinders University of South Australia
Adelaide, South Australia, Australia

As discussed in the previous 29 chapters, the development of quality-of-life models and the application of quality-of-life concepts in the field of intellectual disabilities has raised some important issues for education and rehabilitation programs. Quality-of-life research, particularly that carried out by psychological and sociological researchers (e.g., R. I. Brown, 1997b; Renwick, I. Brown, & Nagler, 1996), has developed a wide range of ideas (Goode, 1994b; Schalock, 1996) now being consolidated. The theoretical construct of quality of life (e.g., Felce & Perry, 1994, 1997) and research and demonstration results (e.g., R. Brown, Bayer, & R. I. Brown, 1992) now need to be put into practice. This does not happen suddenly, for, as we have seen across countries, the concept of quality of life raises significant personal, social, and political concerns and issues (Taylor, 1994; Wolfensberger, 1994).

There are a number of clear and generally agreed views about the nature of the concept of quality of life (e.g., H. Brown, 1997; Goode, 1994a; Renwick et al., 1996). There is also a range of applied research studies examining quality of life among adults with disabilities (R. Brown et al., 1992; R. I. Brown, Bayer, & MacFarlane, 1989; Parmenter, 1997) and, to some lesser degree, children with intellectual disabilities (R. I. Brown, 1997a; Timmons & R. I. Brown, 1997). Many of these research projects, which over the years have increasingly used innovative methods (Velde, 1997), have direct relevance to applications in the field of intellectual disability.

The Challenge

Developing a concept of quality of life has been recognized as a sensitizing process and has, as it were, "rotated the prism" so that we have a different perception (R. I. Brown, 1997b; Taylor, 1994) of the nature of disability and the importance of choices, which need to be made from the perspective of individuals with disabilities. The application of quality of life is causing us to rethink available information and then to reassemble information to give us a new and different understanding of disabilities. This should influence our practice and particularly the involvement of people with disabilities within the community as reflected strongly in the self-advocacy focus of part 1 of this volume. Such developments will likely have implications for a wide range of services; if applied appropriately, they will likely affect both management and policy development (Bruggemann, 1997). They also have potential to assist us in reorienting our resources and services for people with disabilities. Inevitably these developments have ramifications for policy development and program management.

The present chapter is about the impact, real and potential, of the concept of quality of life on the field of intellectual disability.

Development of Conflict in Values

My arguments accept that quality of life is an enabling concept, with increasing potential for scientific investigation. Quality-of-life findings also impinge upon policy development and professional practice. It is gradually being recognized (see R. I. Brown, 1997b) that approaches to quality of life within the field of intellectual disability have application to society in general, including the way we manage a range of services in education, health, legal affairs, and social and community resources (see Renwick et al., 1996; chap. 1, this volume). This influence has impact on legal proceedings involving discrimination and rights tribunals (Andrews & Lupart, 1993), including areas such as inclusion (whether in education or the community), sterilization (e.g., *Lellani Muir and Her Majesty the Queen in Right of Alberta,* 1996), abortion, rights to employment, and sexuality (H. Brown, 1997).

It is probably not too extreme to suggest that such developments bring quality of life into confrontation, or potential confrontation, with a wide range of practices in society. However, it would be incorrect to believe that conceptualizing quality of life has brought this about on its own. It is, after all, a concept of its time, arising out of a zeitgeist that has gradually become sensitive to notions of well-being, individualization, and human rights. Quality of life is recognized as a concept at both scientific and popular levels, yet conflict arises, as its development occurs at a time when society is preoccupied with other concerns and ventures that in themselves have implications for services and society as a whole. As discussed throughout the chapters in part 3, economic rationalism is one such development (Bruggemann, 1997). Such societal thrusts result in confrontation. Resulting dilemmas are also discussed within this chapter, for they represent not only a confrontation between viewpoints, but also divergences in society. These divergences appear to be represented by two different value systems whose philosophical assumptions challenge and determine not only what we explore, but how we explore. At one level the issue of political correctness is raised along with the right to use, employ, and communicate in language that challenges and causes anxiety.

Quality of Life—Some Basic Concepts

I regard quality of life as a psychosociological construct influenced by anthropological (Dossa, 1989), sociological (Goode, 1994a), and psychological constructs (R. Brown et al., 1992). The resulting structure differs markedly from some health science and allied views of quality of life (Kaplan, 1994; Parmenter, 1994) that can be used to strengthen an economic rationalist view (see Parmenter & Donelly, 1997; Romney, R. I. Brown, & Fry, 1994). In addition, writers such as Sobsey (1994) have raised concerns that the health and economic rationalist views about quality of life can be used to bolster arguments in favor of eugenics and euthanasia. These arguments are often based on a professional assessment of patients' expected quality of life, but it is critical that these arguments about quality of life are separated from the psychological, sociological, and anthropological concepts that are the basis of the present discussion.

Although there are some disagreements about the definition of the social construct of quality of life, some common components have emerged. It is generally agreed that quality of life is concerned with factors associated with people's well-being. Felce and Perry (1997), summarizing the views of many other researchers, have suggested that there are five divisions of well-being. These relate to specific domains such as physical health, social living, education, productivity, and emotionality. Subcategories under each of these domains have been noted by Felce and Perry and have been put forward by a wide range of authors such as Cummins (1997a), Parmenter and Donelly (1997), and R. I. Brown et al. (1989). A number of studies have taken place in each of these domains. Those that espouse the notion of quality of life examine issues from a different perspective from those studies relating to the same domains at a previous point in time. These different perspectives relate to research methodology, individual outcome, measurement, variability, definition, choice, holism, and empowerment.

Research Methodology
As suggested in this volume, quality-of-life studies employ a wide range of methodologies and do not simply espouse positivistic, experimental research. Indeed if we view research on a continuum with positivism and constructionism as the two poles, much of the quality-of-life research takes a middle position and employs diverse methodologies often in a complementary manner (Crotty, 1996; Goode, 1994c; Stevenson & Cooper, 1997). Thus experimental, quasiexperimental, naturalistic, phenomenological, and ethnographic methods are employed. The adoption of a broadly based research agenda inevitably results in confrontation with the proponents of systems such as economic rationalism, for the values of quality of life are multidimensional, and truth is recognized as a concept determined by philosophical assumptions about the nature of social and behavioral constructs. Indeed, in research on quality of life, it becomes possible to hold different views equally accurately and strongly when it is recognized that the assumptions are relative. In pragmatic terms the outcome relates to what is deemed to be most appropriate in a particular situation for a particular person at a particular point in time, but the basic test is individual perceptions and individual concerns that are legitimate and critical within any advanced civilization (Andrews, 1974). This has far-reaching implications for policy and practice.

Using a range of research methods is productive in that it enables us to use the concept of triangulation to test the veracity of outcomes. But the concept of triangulation itself is also limited, for many of the parameters in quality of life (e.g., external, objective performance, participant perception, family perception) not only afford an opportunity for triangulation, but also in various instances (R. I. Brown, P. M. Brown, & Bayer, 1994) offer different results. This is due not to unreliability but to differences of perception or performance that may well be individually accurate and contribute to our understanding of behavior, intervention, and adaptation. Multimeasurement through linked variables is therefore not necessarily effective triangulation, but it can be a feature of a multidimensional view of disablement.

Individual Outcome

Quality-of-life studies accept choice and empowerment as both causes of behavior and outcomes of participant well-being. These two terms, *choice* and *empowerment,* reflect underlying structures within quality-of-life models (R. Brown et al., 1992; Goode, 1994a). It is recognized that the individual, if given opportunity, is able to effect changes that influence his or her development and growth. It is also recognized that if individuals become empowered, they will have increasing control over aspects of their environment. We need to understand that this internal locus of control provides a new dimension. We can no longer accept the idea of a linear stimulus-response relationship; behavior must be accepted as contextual. It also means that the perceptions of the individual become critical, independent variables in research—often more powerful than the researchers' self-imposed independent variables; that is, the traditional independent variables in social and behavioral research (e.g., intelligence and age) become less of a concern than the perceptual expressions of each individual. Indeed, what we formerly regarded as error, we now know includes important perceptual constructs.

Such perceptual expressions of each individual, if harnessed in change or intervention processes, can be potent. The question is whether research services and policies will permit these to be used. Obviously this has implications for the design of control and experimental groups. Either we have to employ strategies that view the individual as his or her own control, or we must construct groups employing knowledge of each participant's choices and perceptions. Thus an experimental group may first appear heterogeneous, but its commonality lies in the fact that each consumer made his or her own, but different, choices.

Both individual and societal constructs have roles to play in mediating and changing the environment to the individual's advantage. At a professional level it must be assumed that any two or more parties in an interaction or intervention have responsibilities. Society operates at different levels and has some responsibility to enable the individual to mold his or her local environment. These levels have been partitioned in various ways (Bronfenbrenner, 1979; Mitchell & Winslade, 1997), as reflected in the uses of the terms *micro, meso,* and *macrosystem* in this volume. However, at each level society operates to enable the individual to make effective responses, thus allowing him or her to interact positively in the societal-individual interchange. But the individual, having rights to choice and having accepted empowerment, must increasingly be responsible to society for his or her own actions. Implicitly, as well as explicitly, such notions imply degrees of interaction and raise issues of measurement.

Measurement

In quality-of-life studies, both objective and subjective data are recognized as critical components to an understanding of development (Felce & Perry, 1996, 1997). How well the attributes or dimensions of quality of life can be measured is still in doubt, but here again certain specific beliefs are developing. As we have seen, most scientists in the field of quality of life now accept the importance of objective and subjective measures of well-being. Although "hard" science has required external and calibrated measures of performance, it is recognized in quality-of-life models that subjective components are equally, if not more, important in determining consumers' motivation and adaptation (R. Brown et al., 1992; Cummins, 1997a; Felce & Perry, 1997). The question arises: How do we measure these so-called subjective attributes? And this represents a challenge that quality of life raises for research methodology in general.

In the past many of the data relating to individuals have been regarded as subjective (e.g., how an individual feels, what an individual thinks), yet as Andrews (1974) points out, these very perceptions are most important for determining people's behavior. Many of the quality-of-life instruments summarized by Cummins (1997a) have this feature. Yet many of the data from quality-of-life scales have qualities normally associated with objective measurement, even though aspects are said to be subjective (or perceptual). Many of the data are repeatable, not only in the sense that the same participants provide similar results on different occasions over short time periods—a requirement of reliability—but are repeatable across a sample despite variability among members of the sample. Indeed behavioral measurement should be interested in such variability, which, as indicated earlier, until recently was regarded as error of measurement or "noise" in the system.

The results from quality-of-life studies also have reasonable validity, in that different measures of the same attributes using different instruments show significant correlation. In the quality-of-life domain, this is known as triangulation, but there are notable and interesting differences between results taken from different perspectives, and this variability needs to receive comment.

Variability

Variation or differences among individuals often prove the most interesting aspects of research and practice. This notion of variability has implications for the nature of research and for practical application. In research it must be recognized that to treat different individuals the same way can result in very different effects. Therefore, traditional experimental paradigms involving control versus experimental groups are often inappropriate. There are many internal and external reasons for such interparticipant variability, and only when we know how this variability occurs can we begin to erect the types of control necessary for effective experimental research. The change in methodology this involves does not mean a weakness in the science that is being developed, but rather a strength, particularly in terms of research-to-practice paradigms. As suggested in preceding chapters, we are beginning to realize that the congregate care of individuals may be less appropriate than highly individualized programs that relate to internal parameters concerning the individual's perception of his or her own state in relation to the external world. Indeed, the personal perception and choices of individuals become independent variables and may have overriding importance in determining outcome. Thus intelligence and age (examples of traditional control and matching) may assume less importance. If this is correct, then in experimental research it becomes important to control such perceptual variables. Obviously, such an argument means that initially we must conduct research by different means. One example is Goode's (1994c) ethnographic account of an individual who was severely disabled and blind. A further example is the use of individual choice and intervention developed by R. Brown et al. (1992). In this longitudinal study, both group comparisons and individual case studies were carried out. Individual differences were recognized and specific and different interventions were employed.

Definition

Quality of life is already a well-worn term within society. Everything from clothes to condoms tends to be marketed from this perspective—a perspective where quality of life equates to pleasure. Yet in social and behavioral research, the use and definition is both more precise and more confusing. That there is some disagreement on terminology is valuable, as it helps us decide on the relevant boundaries of a concept. In biology Wills (1995) has argued that redundancy is a basic requirement for evolution. In the present context, multiple aspects of definition permit expansion and development of concepts within the field.

Definitions of quality of life nevertheless generally include a notion about people's needs and choices within the context of well-being. Some of the definitions relate to control by the individual of his or her environment, regardless of baseline (R. I. Brown et al., 1989). The notion that choices can be exerted over personal environments, regardless of disability level, is critical, for it alerts professionals and others to the need to examine the ways and nature of choice, and it exercises us in relation to modifying environments in the context of individual wishes. Other definitions contain concepts about discrepancies, and examine the difference between what individuals have and what they actually require and want. Some of the discrepancy definitions have been criticized by Cummins (1997a) on scientific grounds. Although there may be some problems regarding such definitions, at a practical level discrepancies between what people have and what they want often result in an interesting interplay of responses that constitute valuable information for program intervention (e.g., in a counseling context). As indicated earlier, measures from different viewpoints may not effectively constitute triangulation. Differences in perception between parents and a person with intellectual disability may represent different viewpoints. If we regard both as tenable (objective reality is not the issue), then we can use the differences to construct counseling, intervention, and measurement of progress. However, there are interesting anomalies.

As one example of the paradox of positive intervention within a quality of life model, R. I. Brown et al. (1994) have pointed out that happiness is often not increased through quality-of-life interventions, because when individuals gain the notion of exercising choice, they may become less satisfied. They thus become more active in attempting to control their environment and make further choices because they recognize it can be improved. This I see as a positive attribute, but often an unsettling one for professionals, policy makers, and managers. This increase in dissatisfaction can be a major challenge for family members. Indeed, many perceptual evaluations (e.g., Cummins, 1995) suggest the majority (around 70%) of individuals are happy in institutions. We are adaptive organisms, and only when different possibilities are available does disequilibrium or dissatisfaction tend to occur. In all these instances, adaptation is required by one's society.

Choice

Choice is a fundamental concept within quality of life. Issues of choice become critical if we know something about people's perceptions, their needs, and the methods by which they might fulfill these needs. Recent studies (R. I. Brown et al., 1989; R. Brown et al., 1992; Cummins, 1997a) in quality of life have used the dimension of choice to elicit information about individual preferences. These preferences are employed to design, develop, and apply specific intervention programs. Brown (1996) refers to three relevant characteristics of choice: choice of activity, choice of place where the activity occurs, and choice of the individual who carries out this activity with the participant. In the intervention and therapeutic world, this has relevance to whether interventions take place at all, and which interventions are employed, and where they are carried out (e.g., within an individual's home environment, in the community, or within a center). Choice also carries with it the right of the individual to have a dominant say in who carries out such interventions.

Interestingly enough, within the field of intellectual disability, most quality-of-life research has been carried out with adults, and generally adults make verbal responses and have some life experience (see Timmons & R. I. Brown, 1997). One of the challenges for a quality-of-life model is whether it can be applied effectively to people who have no language or to people very young who lack environmental experience. It is important to note that in the development of a quality-of-life model, the most empowered individuals have been given much attention; whereas those more controlled by society, and who make the least responses, have been given very little attention. This is one of the important aspects of the development of the quality-of-life model; the outlook it constructs raises questions about choices and individual attention for poorly empowered individuals. Indeed, one of the values of the model is to focus attention on the plight of individuals who are disempowered and severely disabled. This aspect makes the concept relevant to those who speak and have no "voice" (e.g., prisoners and aborigines).

Timmons and R. I. Brown (1997) have argued that concepts of quality of life must apply to children with intellectual disabilities, and therefore should be a consideration in the debate about inclusive education. Children (not just their parents) need to be consulted on the effectiveness and desirability of inclusive practices. Using the quality-of-life debate, inclusion does not center only on schools, but also on community and family practices. Further, individuals who have no language need to be assessed, in terms of their wishes, through demonstrated behavior (e.g., eye and hand movements). This new window provides a challenge to our scientific community to develop the appropriate types of tools to carry out acceptable, trustworthy, reliable, and valid assessments. The *Comprehensive Quality of Life Scale* (Cummins, 1997b) is an example of this, because it frequently substitutes the pictorial dimension for verbal statements.

There is a concern among some quality-of-life researchers that the very notion of choice, if misunderstood, may lead to an "anything goes" attitude. So within the area of choice, the notion of structure has also developed (R. I. Brown et al., 1994).

That is, individuals need information and knowledge in relation to their choices (i.e., experience). Further, it is recognized that choices may follow a developmental sequence. Experience suggests that most people with intellectual disability make reasonable choices about fairly local and minor matters, yet even these may represent a challenge within the existing systems for policy makers and management. However, issues that are minor to society may be perceived by the individual as major. Thus acceptance of choice has even greater ramifications. As the individual develops, choice making has an increasingly loaded impact for the individual and the system, and may eventually be seen as confrontation. Lack of experience should not be used as an argument for denying choice, but a reason for constructing opportunities for experience—a role that may be new and challenging for many professionals.

Holism

Quality of life involves the concept of holism. There are a number of domains of well-being, but unless those domains are interconnected and mutually supported, as shown in part 1 of this volume, rehabilitation is unlikely to be successful. For example, a program may run employment and vocational projects but not be supported by and supporting residential accommodation programs; such a program may represent a conflict for the individual, resulting in poor performance or poor development. At an extreme level, residential programs may be exclusive, sheltering, or controlling, whereas vocational programs may be outgoing, individualized, supportive but not overprotective (or overprotective but not supportive).

Individuals appear to function or attempt to function in an integrated fashion; this means that problems can arise when different systems are out of step. Indeed, we regard individuals as disturbed if different areas of their lives are antagonistic and cause stress. Not only does this argue for more links among different types of programs, but it argues fundamentally against the types of policy and administrative splits that we construct through governmental and social systems, which often have different departments or governmental institutions developing policy and rights for different areas of the person's life. This is true of governmental structure and policy in many English-speaking countries. There are, of course, justifications for such divisions, but these relate to the perceptions of policy makers and appliers, and very often run counter to the needs of consumers. This, then, is another area of actual as well as potential conflict.

Empowerment

As discussed in parts 2 and 3 of this volume, the aim of quality-of-life programs is to provide an environment where individuals can empower themselves—make their own choices and through these choice networks take command of the systems from which they require guidance, support, information, and so on. But rehabilitation and habilitation services as we know them tend to be controlling mechanisms and frequently do not enable these developments. In so doing, they imprison another component of quality of life, namely intra- and interconsumer variability. Recognition and response to this variability is thought to enhance development and adaptation. In some research in quality of life (R. I. Brown, Bayer, & P. M. Brown, 1988), I have referred to rehabilitation as "the art of keeping people quiet." The system prefers clients who do what they are told, do not ask too many questions, and do not raise problems when choices are imposed upon them. It is common knowledge that many programs reject clients who show what society or professionals regard as inappropriate or violent behavior. Yet much of this behavior may arise because the individual is attempting to gain control of his or her environment and is being frustrated in the process of carrying this out. We have demonstrated this in a number of studies carried out in the application of individualized choices and programs (e.g., R. Brown et al., 1992).

The above discussion suggests that traditional dimensions of service conflict with such a quality-of-life model. Indeed, if we are to accept quality of life as a model, the design, development, and delivery of services will need to change.

It should be noted that use of the term *quality of life* in the disability field now has application to people within a framework of behavioral and social constructs. As such, it is not particularly more relevant to disability than to other individuals. In social and psychological terms, the quality-of-life model can function effectively without the use of disability labels. The model requires that we respond to the individual in relation to the environment. We may, however, need labels to understand certain aspects of biomedical functioning.

In terms of the design and development of the environment and responding to the individual within a quality-of-life model, we need to apply a wide range of behavioral and social knowledge. It will not be necessary in most instances to classify the individual, but it will be important to describe behavior and define the environment. The quality-of-life model, then, does not destroy the notion of intervention; in fact it encourages more diversity in application. It accepts the need for social sensitivity and change, but also recognizes the need for assessment and intervention. In this sense it does not accept the extremes of social role valorization (choice may be nonnormalizing!).

Interaction of Quality-of-Life Models and Society: A Potential Confrontation

I sense the quality-of-life model, and those who promulgate it, are on a collision course with a number of strongly held views within our society, at both informal and formal levels. Definition and concept within quality of life raise issues for our understanding and our application of science. In accepting the concept of quality of life, we are agreeing that it includes concepts of research and measurement from the social sciences that do not conform with the standards and concepts held within experimental science. Yet there are bridges and insights that may improve experimental methodology in this context.

Societal models and practices are concerned with group behaviors, group needs, and group requirements. This, for example, is seen quite clearly in the education system. Yet a quality-of-life model suggests that we must be concerned and direct our structures toward individual choices and individual application. This is a far cry from an economic rationalistic view that is consistent with highly structured curricular, group standards, and performance benchmarks. In its undiluted form, the view argues that society cannot compete effectively unless such requirements are maintained. The explicit value system rests on notions of competition for heightening reward, status, and efficiency. The primary values of a quality-of-life model, which are particularly directed to individual and personal values, to choices, and to an acceptance that each person must be supported to progress along his or her individual path with individualized support, are not accepted. Economic rationalism does not provide for such processes, which are seen as wasteful. Inclusive practices, social role valorization, and individual program plans are logically "out of the window" in this model. The extent to which they continue to be practiced will be the degree to which the economic rationalists are prepared to compromise, and this is, in part, associated with the level of organization and strength of the quality-of-life model.

A collision course is also set between the policies of economic rationalism and quality-of-life values, for the latter favor individualism and promotion of protection for individuals with specific needs. The former implies monetary control backed by law-and-order concerns that override individual needs, including treatment, intervention, and therapy. What prevails is not what the individual needs, but what the economic rationalist will tolerate. Consistent with this is the collision course that arises between biological and (in particular) genetic views of disability, and a more behavioral and social-scientific view of the role that environment plays in the development of behavior. The all-pervasive view of genetics, accentuated by our dramatic increase in knowledge over the last few decades and the prospect of completion of the human genome project, at a public level tends to precipitate the notion that we can control disease and disability, and that we can modify genetic structures that are sensitive to promotion of diseases, such as Alzheimer's disease, endogenous depression, schizophrenia, and various types of genetically based impairment. This view, being compounded by sections of society, seems to be a more sophisticated version of the eugenics arguments at the beginning of the 20th century. The geneticist Haldane (1949) observed in the middle of the 20th century that it is not a matter of environment or heredity but how and to what extent the two components interact with one another. Indeed, he believed that neither an extreme environmental nor inheritance viewpoint was tenable. Genetics operates within environment. Change the environment to some considerable degree, and genetics changes its impact. At this point in time it is perceived, increasingly, to be easier and more desirable to assert genetics over environment. This leaves the door open to revisiting such issues as eugenics, sterilization, abortion, and genetic manipulation.

Again, the quality-of-life model, where it is socially and psychologically derived, is inconsistent with this oversimplification of the situation. Individuals have rights on their own merit. They are able to make choices and decisions at various levels. Experience and support increases their independence and internal locus of control, which in turn enhances further variation and choice. To ensure that this occurs, the environment needs to be changed. It needs to be changed not just in terms of its overriding ambience, but also in terms of the designer package for the individual in need. The values in this process are not supported by an economic rationalist argument. The latter is concerned that a procedure should be cheaper or more effective for the group and, in a utopian sense, for the common good. This approach, however, does not recognize (and in fact limits) the behavioral development of individuals.

There is a similar problem in relation to policy development and management systems. Although arguments have been given against top-down models of organization and management, organizations still pursue a largely controlling top-down approach toward their clients and view effectiveness from this standpoint. Indeed, governments often employ quality-of-life and quality-assurance language, while still promulgating centralist and economic rationalist policies based on market needs and benchmarks, which themselves link choice to volume, demand, and ability to pay. These are not client-based concepts and are the antithesis of a quality-of-life-based model of intervention and support. Thus policy and management-centered approaches are still largely insensitive to individual needs. These approaches assume that consultants, managers, and allied professionals know best and that they know how to treat and manage people's needs without major controls from the individual. They do not accept requirement of a model that is accented by personal perception. But then science has deprecated such variables and viewed them as soft or even unmeasurable!

I also note issues regarding quality on the one hand and differences in behavior on the other. At this level, quality of life raises issues of discrimination. Quality-of-life models are entirely consistent, conceptually, with the development of human rights. The formation of antidiscrimination legislation in many Western countries and the development of ombudsmen to oversee the appropriateness of the delivery of rights in relation to individuals and governments are consistent with human rights statements, such as the UNESCO Salamanca Agreement of 1994, concerned with the inclusion of all children within regular schools. The problem, of course, is that although there is a will among many people to develop a system of rights consistent with notions of well-being, in practice there are legislative loopholes that allow exclusionary principles to apply. This is seen clearly within the area of education, where on economic grounds it is argued that individuals cannot be accommodated in particular inclusive settings, because there are insufficient numbers of trained teachers, insufficient teaching aids or support systems. Such arguments are interesting, because it is within the poorest communities that inclusion is often applied most effectively. For example, in Canada it is among the poorest of the provinces that inclusive principles are particularly effectively applied.

Some governments are now arguing in many instances that the balance has gone too far in the direction of discriminatory control. Strictures on native and aboriginal societies in Australia and the move to restrict inclusive behavior because of its expense (e.g., government cuts in some countries to the ombudsman office) are examples of this. The issues are portrayed as economic ones, but in reality they have far more to do with the value systems that one maintains than with the costs that are involved. Indeed, where values are accepted, costs are generally met. The Mars space probe, the large amount of funds expended on AIDS research, and current arguments in relation to the needs of the older population are examples of this. Power influences values, and the values of the powerful control the behaviors of the disenfranchised. The quality-of-life model argues for asserting the rights of the individual, particularly over social choices, including the types of environment they wish to live in, and the types of supports and controls they need. However, unlike many of the social valorization arguments, the quality-of-life model does not argue for the total application of a social-perspective values argument. It is based on both social and behavioral principles, and choice is viewed as a construct within a structure. Yet to implement it through research and demonstration models requires basic changes in values of society, policy makers, and scientists. In a nutshell, quality of life is about maximizing awareness of issues surrounding and impacting the individual, the very issues that are often seen as minimal for society as a whole (e.g., Barnes, 1991; Oliver, 1990).

References

Andrews, F. M. (1974). Social indicators of perceived life quality. *Social Indicators Research, 1,* 279-299.

Andrews, J., & Lupart, J. (1993). *The inclusive classroom: Educating exceptional children.* Scarborough, Ontario: International Thomson.

Barnes, C. (1991). *Disabled people in Britain and discrimination: A case for anti-discrimination legislation.* London: Hurst.

Bronfenbrenner, U. (1979). *The ecology of human development.* Cambridge, MA: Harvard University Press.

Brown, H. (1997). Sexual rights and sexual wrongs in the lives of people with intellectual disabilities. In R. I. Brown (Ed.), *Quality of life for people with disabilities: Models, research, and practice* (pp. 228-250). Cheltenham, United Kingdom: Stanley Thornes.

Brown, R., Bayer, I., & Brown, R. I. (1992). *Empowerment and developmental handicaps: Choices and quality of life.* London: Chapman & Hall.

Brown, R. I. (1996). People with developmental disabilities: Applying quality of life to assessment and intervention. In R. Renwick, I. Brown, & M. Nagler (Eds.), *Quality of life in health promotion and rehabilitation: Conceptual approaches, issues, and applications* (pp. 253-267). Thousand Oaks, CA: Sage.

Brown, R. I. (1997a). Legislation in Australian special education intent and effect: The impact on child, family, and teacher. In D. Mitchell & J. Kugelmass (Eds.), *The view finder: New models for re-forming special education, Vol. 4* (pp. 41-45). Reston, VA: DISES.

Brown, R. I. (1997b). Quality of life: The development of an idea. In R. I. Brown (Ed.), *Quality of life for people with disabilities: Models, research, and practice* (pp. 1-11). Cheltenham, United Kingdom: Stanley Thornes.

Brown, R. I., Bayer, M. B., & Brown, P. M. (1988). Quality of life: A challenge for rehabilitation agencies. *Australian & New Zealand Journal of Developmental Disabilities, 14,* 189-199.

Brown, R. I., Bayer, M., & MacFarlane, C. (1989). *Rehabilitation programs: Performance and quality of life of adults with developmental handicaps.* Toronto: Lugus Productions.

Brown, R. I., Brown, P. M., & Bayer, M. B. (1994). A quality of life model: New challenges arising from a six year study. In D. Goode (Ed.), *Quality of life for persons with disabilities: International perspectives and issues* (pp. 39-56). Cambridge, MA: Brookline.

Bruggemann, R. (1997). Pitfalls for purchasers and providers. *Australian Disability Review, 1,* 3-14.

Crotty. M. (1996). *Phenomenology and nursing research.* Melbourne: Churchill, Livingston.

Cummins, R. A. (1995). On the trail of the gold standard for life satisfaction. *Social Indicators Research, 35,* 179-200.

Cummins, R. A. (1997a). Assessing quality of life. In R. I. Brown (Ed.), *Quality of life for people with disabilities: Models, research, and practice* (pp. 16-150). Cheltenham, United Kingdom: Stanley Thornes.

Cummins, R. A. (1997b). *Comprehensive quality of life scale: Intellectual/cognitive disability* (5th ed.). Melbourne: Deakin University.

Dossa, P. A. (1989). Quality of life: Individualism or holism? A critical review of the literature. *International Journal of Rehabilitation Research, 12*(2), 121-136.

Felce, D., & Perry, J. (1996). Exploring current conceptions of quality of life: A model for people with and without disabilities. In R. Renwick, I. Brown, & M. Nagler (Eds.), *Quality of life in health promotion and rehabilitation: Conceptual approaches, issues, and applications* (pp. 51-62). Thousand Oaks, CA: Sage.

Felce, D., & Perry, J. (1997). Quality of life: The scope of the term and its breadth of measurement. In R. I. Brown (Ed.), *Quality of life for people with disabilities: Models, research, and practice* (pp. 56-71). Cheltenham, United Kingdom: Stanley Thornes.

Goode, D. A. (1994a). The national quality of life for persons with disabilities project: A quality of life agenda for the United States. In D. Goode (Ed.), *Quality of life for persons with disabilities: International perspectives and issues* (pp. 139-161). Cambridge, MA: Brookline.

Goode, D. A. (1994b). *Quality of life for persons with disabilities: International perspectives and issues.* Cambridge, MA: Brookline.

Goode, D. A. (1994c). *A world without words: The social construction of children born deaf-blind.* Philadelphia: Temple University Press.

Haldane, J. B. S. (1949). Preface. In L. S. Penrose, *The biology of mental defect.* London: Sidgwick & Jackson.

Kaplan, R. M. (1994). Using quality of life information to set priorities in health policy. *Social Indicators Research, 33,* 121-163.

Lellani Muir and Her Majesty the Queen in Right of Alberta, Court of Queen's Bench of Alberta. (1996). Decisions of the Hon. Madam Justice Joanne B. Veit. Edmonton, Canada: Queens Printer.

Mitchell, D., & Winslade, J. (1997). Developmental systems and narrative approaches to working with families of persons with disabilities. In R. I. Brown (Ed.), *Quality of life for people with disabilities: Models, research, and practice* (pp. 151-182). Cheltenham, United Kingdom: Stanley Thornes.

Oliver, M. (1990). *The politics of disablement.* London: MacMillan.

Parmenter T. R. (1994). Quality of life as a concept and measurable entity. *Social Indicators Research, 33,* 9-46.

Parmenter, T. R., & Donelly, M. (1997). An analysis of the dimensions of quality of life. In R. I. Brown (Ed.), *Quality of life for people with disabilities: Models, research, and practice* (pp. 91-115). Cheltenham, United Kingdom: Stanley Thornes.

Renwick, R., Brown, I., & Nagler, M. (Eds.). (1996). *Quality of life in health promotion and rehabilitation: Conceptual approaches, issues, and applications.* Thousand Oaks, CA: Sage.

Romney, D. M., Brown, R. I., & Fry, P. S. (1994). *Improving the quality of life: Recommendations for people with and without disabilities.* Dordrecht, The Netherlands: Kluwer.

Schalock, R. L. (Ed.). (1996). *Quality of life: Vol. 1. Conceptualization and measurement.* Washington, DC: American Association on Mental Retardation.

Sobsey, D. (1994). Reflection on the holocaust: Where did it begin and has it really ended? *Developmental Disabilities Bulletin, 22*(2), 121-135.

Stevenson, C., & Cooper, N. (1997). Qualitative and quantitative research. *The Psychologist, 10*(4), 139-140.

Taylor, S. J. (1994). In support of research on quality of life, but against QOL. In D. Goode (Ed.), *Quality of life for persons with disabilities: International perspectives and issues* (pp. 260-265). Cambridge, MA: Brookline.

Timmons, V., & Brown, R. I. (1997). Quality of life—Issues for children with handicaps. In R. I. Brown (Ed.), *Quality of life for people with disabilities: Models, research, and practice* (pp. 183-200). Cheltenham, United Kingdom: Stanley Thornes.

Velde, B. P. (1997). Quality of life through personally meaningful activity. In R. I. Brown (Ed.), *Quality of life for people with disabilities: Models, research, and practice* (pp. 12-26). Cheltenham, United Kingdom: Stanley Thornes.

Wills, C. (1995). *The runaway brain: The evolution of human uniqueness.* London: Flamingo.

Wolfensberger, W. (1994). Let's hang up "quality of life" as a hopeless term. In D. Goode (Ed.), *Quality of life for persons with disabilities: International perspectives and issues* (pp. 285-321). Cambridge, MA: Brookline.

Cross-Cultural Perspectives on Quality of Life: Trends and Themes

Kenneth D. Keith
University of San Diego
San Deigo, California, United States

Robert L. Schalock
Hastings College
Hastings, Nebraska, United States

Editing this book has been both challenging and rewarding: Challenging because of the need to integrate culturally based terms and concepts and rewarding because of the similar cross-cultural patterns that have emerged regarding the concept of quality of life. Indeed, throughout these 30 chapters the reader has found that within the 21 countries represented, quality of life is currently being used in three important ways in the field of mental retardation and closely related disabilities:

- as a sensitizing notion that is giving us a sense of reference and guidance from the individual's perspective, focusing on the person and the individual's environment;

- as a social construct that is being used as an overriding principle to improve and enhance a person's perceived quality of life;

- as a unifying theme that is providing a systematic framework to apply the quality-of-life concept.

The book's ecological perspective has also allowed us to understand better the multiple levels of influence on one's perceived quality of life. We saw in part 1 regarding the microsystem (the immediate social setting), for example, a number of common trends and themes including the emergence of self-advocacy and People First organizations, a person-centered approach to understanding and applying the concept of quality of life, the importance of friends, family, and associates, and the key role that dignity and meaningful work play in a person's perceived quality of life.

In reference to the mesosystem (the neighborhood, community, or organization), we saw in part 2 a number of common themes including how organizations and their leadership can apply quality-of-life principles to the services and supports they provide people with disabilities, the impact that different environments have on perceived quality of life, the need to recognize individual differences in factors contributing to a positive quality of life, and the importance of partnerships between service providers and service recipients.

And finally, in reference to the macrosystem (the overarching patterns of culture and society), we saw in part 3 the use of quality of life as a unifying theme to improve the quality of life of people with disabilities within a number of countries that have their unique history, culture, challenges, and opportunities. Throughout these three sections of this book, the authors have shared with the reader not just the promises of quality of life as a social construct, but also the importance of being sensitive to culturally based trends and themes that will impact significantly the future of both the concept and its application.

Our concluding chapter challenges each of us to think about the future of the concept of quality of life, and how a number of trends and themes will impact that future. To that end, the chapter has two major sections. The first section discusses four trends that emerge from the preceding chapters and other quality-of-life literature that will impact significantly the future of the quality-of-life concept: (a) searching for the core quality-of-life domains; (b) using methodological pluralism to assess quality-of-life indicators; (c) embracing an ecological model of quality enhancement; and (d) implementing an outcomes-based approach to quality-of-life evaluation. The second section discusses four themes that analogously will impact significantly the future of the quality-of-life concept: (a) community, (b) aesthetics, (c) the importance of culture, and (d) the self-advocacy movement.

Trends Impacting the Future of the Quality-of-Life Concept

Over the last several decades, health and human services have embraced quality of life both as a sensitizing notion and an overarching principle of service delivery. As a sensitizing notion, the concept gives us a sense of reference and guidance from the individual's perspective, focusing on the person and the individual's environment. As a sensitizing notion, *quality* makes us think of the excellence or "exquisite standard" associated with human characteristics and positive values such as happiness, success, wealth, health and satisfaction; whereas *of life* indicates that the concept concerns the very essence or essential aspects of human existence (Lindstrom, 1992).

As reflected in the preceding chapters, the concept of quality of life has become a social construct that is used as an overriding principle to improve and enhance a person's perceived quality of life. In that regard, the concept of quality of life is impacting program development, service delivery, management strategies, and evaluation. The information shared in these chapters has also increased significantly our understanding of this important concept and its use. Simultaneously, this increased understanding has come about with the application of participatory action research, consumer-oriented evaluation, and empowerment evaluation (Schalock, in press). There is no reason to assume that the concept of quality of life will not continue to influence personal desires and social policies. As this occurs, quality of life and its application will be influenced significantly by the four trends discussed in this first section of the chapter: (a) searching for the core quality-of-life domains; (b) using methodological pluralism to assess quality-of-life indicators; (c) embracing an ecological model of quality enhancement; and (d) implementing an outcomes-based approach to quality-of-life evaluation.

Searching for the Core Quality-of-Life Domains

Despite the subjective nature of quality of life, the field of mental retardation and developmental disabilities will continue to search for the core quality-of-life domains, because the movement to apply the concept as a sensitizing notion, social construct, and unifying theme is too strong to preclude its assessment, application, and evaluation. It is safe to predict that the search will evolve within the context of the various levels of the system (i.e., micro, meso, and macro) that affect each of us. For example, Renwick, Brown, and Raphael (chap. 1, this volume) and Lin (chap. 18) remind us that a full picture of quality of life includes the interactions among factors at various degrees of immediacy to the person and that it is necessary to understand how factors at all levels affect an individual's experienced quality of life. As stated so well by Rapley (chap. 15), quality of life is "the product of interaction in community with others."

Two concepts regarding core quality-of-life domains have emerged in this volume, as well as the wider quality-of-life literature: person-centered quality of life (PCQOL) and health-related quality of life (HRQOL). A brief discussion of each is relevant, because as we continue the search for core quality-of-life domains, a fundamental question arises: Do we need to make a distinction between PCQOL and HRQOL, or can the two concepts be integrated into one?

Health-Related Quality-of-Life. The term *quality of life* was first used in medicine in connection with life or death situations. Now, however, the evaluation of one's quality of life is routinely used in all kinds of medical decisions and evaluations, with the term *health-related quality of life* used to reflect how well individuals function in daily life and their perceived well-being. Within the HRQOL literature, there is a consensus that quality of life is a multidimensional phenomenon encompassing physical, mental, and social functioning and well-being (World Health Organization, 1997). More specifically, and depending on the clinical population and methodology used, health-related core quality-of-life dimensions include general satisfaction and feelings of well-being, physiological state or symptoms of illness, neuropsychological functioning, interpersonal relationships, performance of social skills, and economic and employment status (Schalock, in press).

Person-Centered Quality of Life. Over the last two decades, there has been a significant change in the way we view people with disabilities. This transformed vision of what constitutes the life possibilities of people with disabilities is reflected in concepts such as self-determination, strengths and capabilities, the importance of normalized and typical environments, provision of individualized support systems, equity, and enhanced adaptive behavior and role status. As a term and concept, person-centered quality of life has become the unifying theme around which one can organize programmatic changes, person-centered planning, the supports model, quality enhancement techniques, and person-referenced quality outcomes. As discussed in this volume, this unifying theme has also allowed (a) service providers to reorganize resources around individuals rather than rearranging people in program slots, (b) consumers and providers to embrace the supports paradigm, and (c) program evaluation to shift its focus to person-referenced outcomes that can be used to improve organizational efficiency and enhance person-referenced services and supports (Gardner & Nudler, 1999). As with HRQOL, there is an emerging consensus, as discussed in this volume and in the PCQOL literature, that quality of life is a multidimensional concept involving at least eight core dimensions: emotional well-being, interpersonal relationships, material well-being, personal development, physical well-being, self-determination, social inclusion, and rights (Schalock, 1996).

Need to Distinguish Cross-Culturally? In thinking cross-culturally, is there a need to distinguish between PCQOL and HRQOL? In this volume chapters by Groulx, Doré, and Doré (chap. 2), Watson, Barreira, and Watson (chap. 7), Otrebski (chap. 9), Baum (chap. 10), James (chap. 13), Felce (chap. 16), Pengra (chap. 17), and Goel (chap. 20) suggest not. For example, the recent work on measuring quality of life by the World Health Organization (1997) suggests that the following six core quality-of-life dimensions reflect both PCQOL and HRQOL:

- physical health (i.e., energy and fatigue, pain and discomfort, sleep and rest);
- psychological state (i.e., bodily image and appearance, negative feelings, positive feelings, self-esteem, thinking, learning, memory, and concentration);
- level of independence (i.e., mobility, activities of daily living, dependence on medicinal substances and medical aids, work capacity);
- social relationships (i.e., personal relationships, social support, sexual activity);
- environment (i.e. financial resources, freedom in physical safety and security, health and social care, home environment, opportunities for acquiring information and skills, participation in recreation or leisure, physical environment, and transport);
- spirituality or religious or personal beliefs.

Thus our future search for the core quality-of-life domains will undoubtedly identify five to eight core domains, with a number of indicators for each that will be used to assess the individual's level of satisfaction, the person's functional status, and a number of person-referenced social indicators reflecting individuals' lifestyles vis-à-vis the nation in which they live. The assessment of those core domains will require the use of methodological pluralism such as described in the next section.

Using Methodological Pluralism to Assess Quality-of-Life Indicators

The ecological approach to quality of life presented in this volume makes a strong statement about assessing quality-of-life indicators across all systems levels: micro, meso, and macro. The approach is also consistent with (a) the history of quality-of-life assessment that has focused on subjective, functional (i.e., objective), and social indicators; (b) the strategy of methodological pluralism that combines quantitative and qualitative assessment and research methodologies; and (c) the realization that a complete picture of quality of life includes the interaction among factors at various degrees of immediacy to the person.

A model that reflects this ecological approach to quality-of-life assessment is presented in Figure 31.1. As noted in the figure, the core quality-of-life dimensions are listed across the top of the matrix, with the three levels of ecological assessment down the side. Exemplary indicators can be identified for each cell of the matrix,

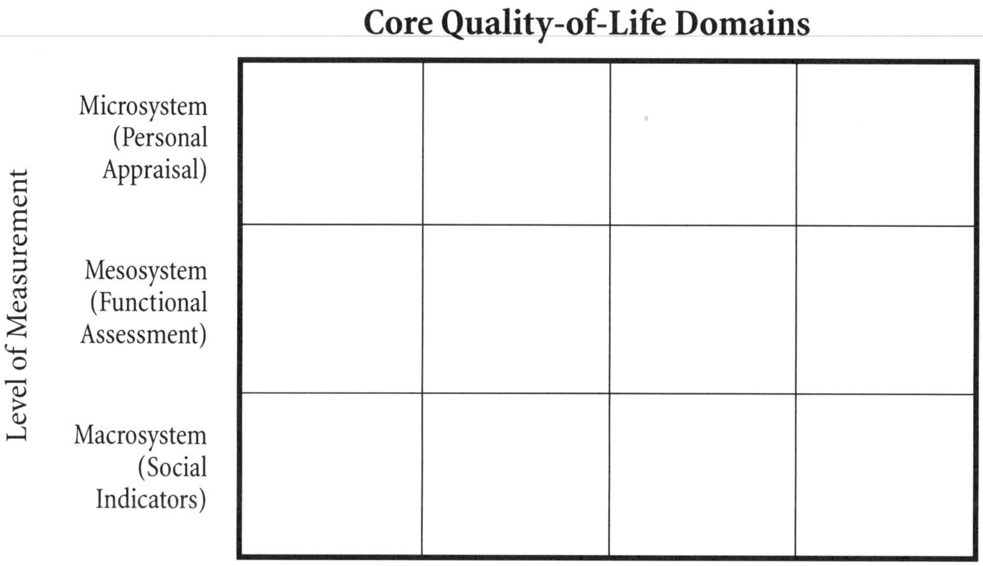

Core Quality-of-Life Domains

Figure 31.1. An ecological approach to quality-of-life assessment.

based on culture-specific personal, environmental, or larger societal factors. Implementing the model requires that these exemplary indicators be assessed on the basis of personal appraisal (generally via satisfaction measures), functional assessment measures, or by using one or more social indicators.

Microsystem: Personal Appraisal. This level of assessment addresses the subjective nature of quality of life, typically asking people how satisfied they are with the cell-specific exemplary indicator. For example, one can ask, "How satisfied are you with the skills and experiences you have gained or are gaining from your job?" or, "How happy are you with your home or where you live?" Although the person's responses are subjective, responses need to be measured in psychometrically sound ways. A 3-point Likert scale can be used both to indicate the level of expressed satisfaction and to demonstrate reliability and validity of measurement.

Increasingly, a person's measured level of satisfaction (i.e., personal appraisal) is a commonly used dependent measure in evaluating core quality-of-life dimensions. Its advantages include (a) satisfaction is a commonly used aggregate measure of individual life domains and demonstrates a trait-like stability over time (Andrews, 1974; Edgerton, 1996); (b) there is an extensive body of research on level of satisfaction across populations and service delivery recipients (Cummins, 1997, 1998); and (c) satisfaction as a dependent variable allows one to assess the relative importance of individual quality-of-life domains and thereby assign value to the respective domain. The major disadvantages of using only satisfaction as a measure of quality of life include (a) the reported low or no correlation between subjective and objective measures of quality of life; (b) its limited use for smaller group comparisons; (c) its tendency to provide only a global measure of perceived well-

367

being; and (d) its discrepancy with the multidimensional nature of quality of life (Schalock, in press). Because of these disadvantages, the general recommendation among quality-of-life researchers is to include both personal appraisal (i.e., subjective) and functional assessment (i.e., objective) measures of the core quality-of-life dimensions.

Mesosystem: Functional Assessment. This level of assessment addresses the objective nature of quality of life, and reflects individuals' interactions with their neighborhood, community, or organization. The most typical formats used in functional assessment are rating scales, participant observation, and/or questionnaires. Each attempts to document a person's functioning across one or more core quality-of-life domains. To accomplish this, most instruments employ some form of an ordinal rating scale to yield a profile of the individual's functioning across major life activity areas, such as home, work, school, or community. There are a number of advantages to using functional assessments to evaluate the core quality-of-life domains: (a) objective measures can confirm results from the personal appraisal strategy; (b) adding objective measures to personal appraisal overcomes the commonly reported low correlation between subjective and objective measures of quality of life; (c) their use allows for the evaluation of outcomes across groups; (d) objective measures provide important feedback to service providers, funders, and regulators as to how they can change or improve their services to enhance the recipient's functioning level.

However, there are also some disadvantages to functional assessment: (a) functional assessment must be balanced with other considerations (e.g., it is clear that not all outcomes related to one's perceived quality of life can be measured; (b) functional assessments can have more cost than benefit; one needs to be cautious that the functional assessment system does not consume in resources more than its information is worth; (c) the usefulness of functional assessments varies by their use; they are useful to management or the decision-making process only to the extent that they are used and that they answer the right questions; (d) organizations are sometimes limited in their ability to influence outcomes; users of functional assessment data need to understand the role that many factors play in one's perceived quality of life and not focus exclusively on the service provider.

Macrosystem: Social Indicators. Social indicators generally refer to external, environmentally based conditions such as health, social welfare, friendships, standard of living, education, public safety, housing, neighborhood, and leisure. These indicators may be defined as a statistic of direct normative interest that facilitates concise, comprehensive, and balanced judgments about the conditions of major aspects of society (Andrews & Whithey, 1976). Such indicators are good for measuring the collective quality of community or national life; however, they are probably insufficient to measure either an individual's perceived quality of life or functional behavior(s). Campbell, Converse, and Rogers (1976), for example, argue that social indicators reflect only an outsider's judgment of quality as suggested by external, environmentally based conditions. Thus "because we are accustomed to evaluating peoples' lives in terms of their material possessions, we tend to forget that satisfaction is a psychological experience and that the quality of this experience may not correspond very closely to these external conditions" (p. 3).

In summary, methodological pluralism that combines personal appraisal, functional assessments, and social indicators has become a widely accepted way to assess the core quality-of-life domains. It has two major advantages.

First, all assessment focuses clearly on the multidimensional, core quality-of-life domain. Thus one need not use different indicators for subjective versus objective measurement; rather, the core domains remain constant, and what varies is whether or not one focuses on micro-, meso-, or macrolevel of measurement (see Figure 31.1).

Second, methodological pluralism allows researchers to meet the following objectives of using mixed-method evaluations: (a) triangulation or the determination of correspondence of results across personal appraisal and functional assessment strategies (Cook, 1985); (b) complementarity or the use of qualitative and quantitative methods to measure the overlapping but distinct facets of the quality-of-life construct (Greene, Caracelli, & Graham, 1989); and (c) initiation, which allows one to recast questions or results from one strategy with questions or results from the contrasting strategy (Caracelli & Greene, 1993).

Embracing an Ecological Model of Quality Enhancement
The reader may be sharing two fundamental questions asked of those working in the quality-of-life field: Why? And so what? Why it is important to understand and assess the core domains of quality of life, and what is the proper and best use of such data? Many investigators in the field (e.g., Hatton, 1998) suggest that the insuperable problems in assessing subjective quality-of-life indicators preclude useful application of the data; furthermore, the quality-of-life movement, which claims to liberate people from a medical model, may paradoxically serve to extend the license of services to exert control over all facets of a person's life (Hatton, 1998, p. 104). Still others (e.g., Raphael, 1996) indicate the need to examine in more detail than has currently been done a number of issues regarding the measurement of quality of life and its application. Chief among these debates are sociological versus psychological perspective, quantitative versus positivist methodologies, value-based versus values-free approaches, social policy versus basic research orientation, systems versus individual data collection, objective versus subjective measurement, self-reports versus reports by others, and traditional versus participatory approaches.

Part 1 of this volume stressed the viability of enhancing consumers' perceived quality of life through the self-advocacy movement, the person-centered approaches to services and supports delivery, continued growth and development, and dignity and meaningful work. Similarly, part 2 emphasized the impact the quality-of-life revolution has had on (a) the demands of the consumer, (b) the quality-of-life-focused services and supports provided to people with disabilities, and (c) the organizational-change leadership and transformed leadership style required to implement the quality-of-life concept (see Lobley, chap. 14, this volume). In addition, chapters in this volume by Watson (chap. 21), Verdugo (chap. 23), McConkey and O'Toole (chap. 24), Matikka (chap. 25), Castanón and Buján (chap. 26), and Walsh (chap. 28) reflect how the concept of quality of life is increasingly being used as the basis for social policy and service enhancement. Together these efforts encompass an ecological model of quality enhancement the major components of which are depicted in Figure 31.2. As shown in the figure, quality enhancement can occur at any level of the system: micro, meso, or macro. Furthermore, the enhancement focus can involve personal growth and development opportunities, program- or environmental-referenced quality enhancement techniques, and/or social policies. The model indicates further that the specific quality enhancement technique needs to be referenced to the appropriate core quality-of-life domain. As with Figure 31.1, specific culture-specific quality enhancement techniques can be identified for each cell of the matrix.

Microsystem: Personal Growth and Development Opportunities. In the future there will be at least four major thrusts at the microsystem level to enhance a person's perceived quality of life: (a) we will continue to see strong advocacy for increased opportunities to participate in the mainstream of life, associated with increased inclusion, equity, choices, and self-determination (Wehmeyer & Schwartz, 1998); (b) consumers will work jointly with researchers in determining the relative importance or value of the core quality-of-life dimensions; (c) consumers will increasingly become involved in assessing their own quality of life (Schalock, Bonham, & Marchand, in press); (d) the area of personal development and wellness training will become a major thrust in service or support delivery (Schalock & Faulkner, 1997).

Mesosystem: Program and Environment Enhancement Techniques. The future will also see service and support providers implementing quality enhancement

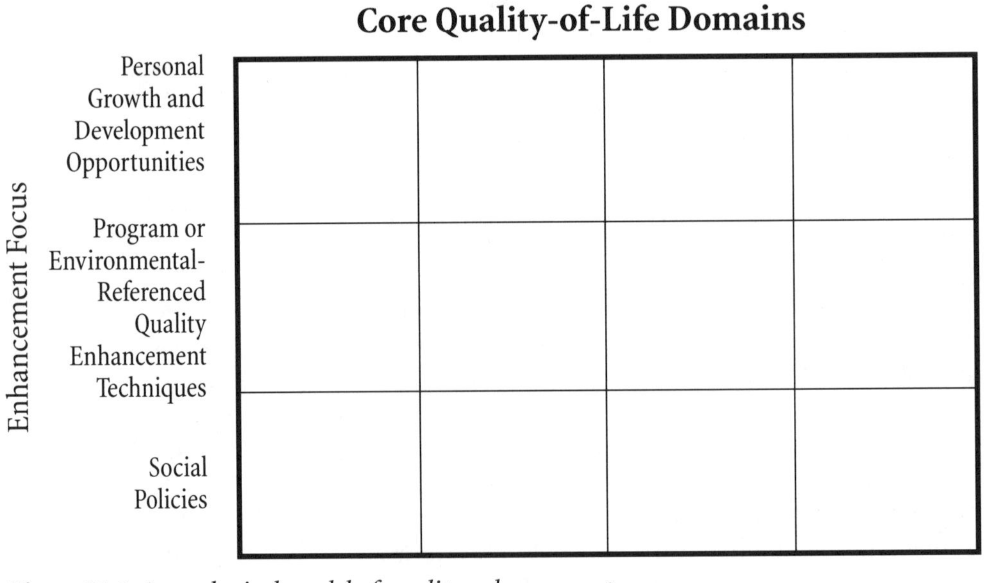

Figure 31.2. An ecological model of quality enhancement.

techniques that focus on either the environment or the service or support program. Environmentally based enhancement techniques involve designing environments that are user friendly and reduce the mismatch between the person and the environment. Examples include (Ferguson, 1997): opportunity for involvement (e.g., food preparation); easy access to the outdoor environment, modification to stairs, water taps, door knobs; safety (e.g., handrails, safety glass, nonslip walking surfaces); convenience (e.g., orientation aids such as color coding or universal pictographs); accessibility to home and community; sensory stimulation (e.g., windows, less formal furniture); prosthetics (e.g., personal computers, specialized assistive devices, high technological environments); and opportunity for choice and control (e.g., lights, temperature, privacy, and personal space).

Program-based enhancement techniques will most probably be built around the core dimensions of a life of quality. In reference to the eight core dimensions suggested by Schalock (1996), emotional well-being can be enhanced by increased safety, stable and predictable environments, and positive feedback; interpersonal relationships by fostering friendships, encouraging intimacy, and supporting families; material well-being by supporting ownership, possessions, and employment; personal development by fostering education and functional rehabilitation and using augmentative technology; physical well-being by assuring adequate health care, mobility, wellness, and proper nutrition; self-determination by encouraging choices, personal control, decisions, and personal goals; social inclusion by emphasizing community roles, community integration, and volunteerism; and rights by ensuring voting, due process, and civic responsibilities.

Macrosystem: Social Policies. There are currently more than 40 worldwide treaties or conventions of human rights that address people with disabilities. The second half of the 1990s witnessed a major initiative by the international community to increase the legal status and situation of people with disabilities. Reflective of this initiative, the United Nations General Assembly adopted in 1993 the *United Nations Standard Rules on the Equalization of Opportunities for Disabled Persons* (United Nations, 1993). Eight of the 22 rules can be considered "enabler standards" that deal with issues such as international cooperation (technical and economic), information and research, policy making and planning, coordination of work, personnel training, and monitoring and evaluation. Significantly, the 14 "outcome standards" are congruent with the eight core quality-of-life dimensions mentioned earlier. As a cross-reference to the core dimensions and standards:

- emotional well-being: reflected in the rule regarding religion;
- interpersonal relations: reflected in rules related to family life and personal integrity;
- material well-being: employment, income maintenance, and social services;
- personal development: education and rehabilitation;
- physical well-being: medical care, recreation, and sports;
- self-determination: self-advocacy organizations;

■ social inclusion: support services;

■ rights: awareness raising, accessibility, equal rights to participate.

Summary. In summary, one cannot separate the quality of a person's life from the influence that factors at the micro-, meso-, and macrosystem levels have on that person's perception of a life of quality. By embracing an ecological model of quality enhancement, one becomes more sensitive to these factors. At the same time, one begins to realize that implementing quality enhancement techniques must of necessity focus on all three system-levels. The same principle is true of the evaluation of quality-of-life-related outcomes.

Implementing an Outcomes-Based Approach to Evaluation

In part 2 chapters by Tachi (chap. 8), Ninomiya (chap. 11), Elorriaga, Garcia, Martinez, & Unamunzaga. (chap. 12), and Lobley (chap. 14) indicated clearly that service and support programs for people with disabilities throughout the world are currently being challenged to provide quality services and supports that result in quality outcomes. As discussed by Brown (chap. 30) and further by Schalock (1999), this is a difficult task because of two powerful, potentially conflicting forces: (a) the desire for person-centered, quality-of-life-focused values and (b) the demands for economically based accountability and efficiency outcomes (frequently referred to as economic rationalism). These two forces necessitate an approach to quality-of-life evaluation that permits one to respond to both the accountability and value demands of each of the key evaluation players: consumers, policy makers, funders, service providers, and society at large. An outcomes-based approach to evaluation allows one to accomplish both tasks.

Outcomes-based evaluation is a rapidly evolving area within program evaluation that allows one to evaluate quality-of-life-related outcomes at multiple levels of a system (micro, meso, and macro), using a methodological pluralistic approach that combines personal appraisal, functional assessment, and social indicators (see Figures 31.1 & 31.2). In addition, outcomes-based evaluation allows one to employ participatory action research paradigms, be theory driven, measure both person-referenced and organization-referenced outcomes, and use outcome data for accountability, program improvement, and reporting purposes (Schalock, in press).

An outcomes-based evaluation model is presented in Figure 31.3. As shown in the figure, exemplary outcomes are arrayed in a matrix against the three levels of the system discussed throughout this volume: micro, meso, and macro. In addition, the listings in the figure represent a number of suggested exemplary outcomes for each level of the system. For example,

■ the microsystem involves personal appraisal of levels of satisfaction and well-being;

■ the mesosystem involves functional assessment of adaptive behavior, role status (in regard to living, work, and community), health status, and educational status;

■ the macrosystem involves the measurement of social indicators related to so-

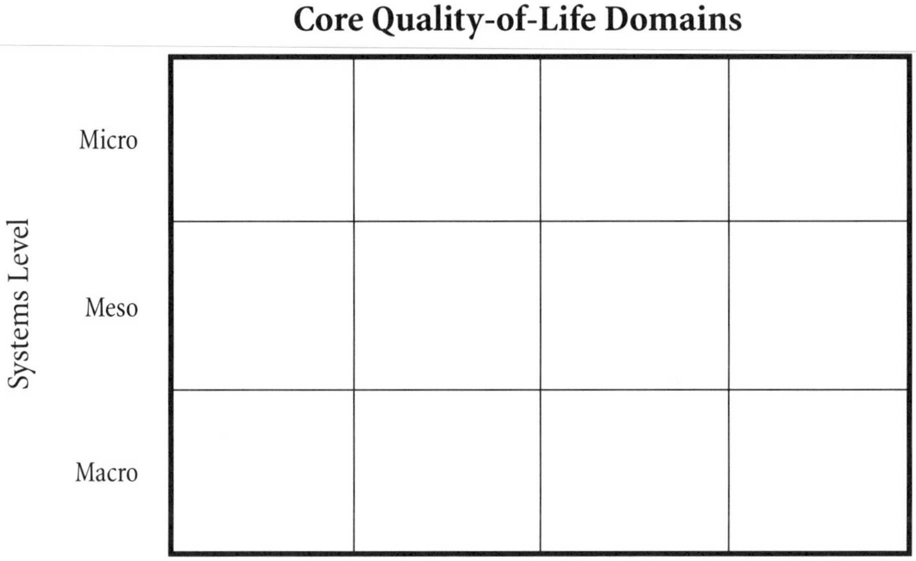

Core Quality-of-Life Domains

Figure 31.3. An outcomes-based evaluation model.

cial economic status, standard of living, housing, education, employment, health, social welfare, friendships, and public safety.

As reflected in the preceding chapters, a number of critical issues still need to be addressed in implementing an outcomes-based approach to quality-of-life evaluation. The following three are among the most important: First, we will need to develop strategies to weigh the relative importance of the individual core quality-of-life domains and determine changes in these weightings over the individual's life experiences and life span. Second, we will need to answer a very basic question: What is the "quality" in quality outcomes? For example, people with disabilities are increasingly becoming employed, but as shown in chapter 8 by Akio Tachi, there is considerable question and concern about their quality of work life. Similarly, as shown by Otrębski (chap. 9) and Felce (chap. 16), people with disabilities are living more independently within the community, but what is the quality of their community life? Quality-of-life investigators will need to become increasingly sensitive to knowing quality outcomes when we see them and to discerning outcomes from process. And third, we will need to pursue multivariate research designs and meta analysis integration strategies to determine the relationship among the three levels of outcomes depicted in Figure 31.3. It is reasonable to assume that changes in social policy will be reflected in outcomes experienced at the level of personal appraisal, functional assessment, and social indicators.

Summary
In summary, how these four trends—searching for the core quality-of-life domains, using methodological pluralism to assess quality of life indicators, embracing an ecological model of quality enhancement, and implementing an outcomes-based

approach to quality-of-life evaluation—play out over the next decade will definitely affect the impact that the quality-of-life concept will have as a sensitizing notion, social construct, and unifying theme. As discussed by Brown (chap. 30), there are not only challenges and confrontations that lie ahead, but tremendous opportunities as well. If quality of life is to remain a viable construct for the field of mental retardation and developmental disabilities, it will be so only if it reflects and is congruent with the four themes described in the next section of the chapter.

Themes Impacting the Future of the Quality-of-Life Concept

We believe that the future of the quality-of-life concept and its relevance to work in the field will likely be influenced significantly by four dominant themes, two of them well established (i.e., the concept of community and the self-advocacy movement) and two of them emerging (i.e., the importance of culture and the role of aesthetics).

Community

The aim of community integration of people with developmental disabilities has been deemed desirable for three decades or more (cf. Dybwad, 1969), and we have seen it as a fundamental theme in quality of life for at least the decade of the 1990s (Keith, 1990). In his review of major approaches to quality of life, Parmenter (1992) discussed a community adjustment model (Halpern, Close, & Nelson, 1986) as one important perspective. This model encompassed not only subjective and objective aspects of quality of life, but also attempted to take account of personal interaction with the environment—a notion that is extended eloquently by Rapley in chapter 15 of this volume.

A number of studies, from those conducted earlier (Keith, Schalock, & Hoffman, 1986; Schalock, Keith, Hoffman, & Karan, 1989) to those reflecting the present state of affairs (Otrębski, chap. 9, this volume; The ARC of Nebraska, 1998) have consistently shown higher measured quality of life in settings most nearly approximating ordinary community life, and this finding has also proven robust across cultures (Schalock et al., 1990).

Further, the importance to quality of life of community integration, and the resultant validation and recognition, is clearly identified by Groulx, Doré, and Doré (chap. 2, this volume), and was articulated by Ward (Ward & Keith, 1996) when she asserted:

> quality of life is related to being in the community, to personal empowerment, and to the opportunity to make personal evaluations of life experiences. The self-advocacy movement is clearly moving people in these directions, empowering them to evaluate their own experiences and to demand a place in the mainstream of community life. (p. 10)

Nevertheless, as Rapley's review (chap. 15) indicates, far too many individuals with disabilities remain isolated in their communities, neither interacting with nor enjoying connections to their environment and the people in it. If the concept of quality of life is to be a force for positive change in the lives of people with developmental disabilities, the theme of community integration must remain in the forefront. In fact, in some parts of the world, as McConkey and O'Toole make clear in chapter 24 of this volume, the power of community-based efforts may be most evident in the least affluent of countries, where expensive segregated services are both unaffordable and less effective.

Self-Advocacy
The notion that individuals with disabilities should advocate for their own rights and interests is not new. More than 30 years ago, Nirje (1969) reported on a 1968 Swedish conference in which people with mental retardation convened to discuss issues germane to their own life and work situations. As Nirje observed, "They wanted a stronger voice in their own leisure-time programs, student clubs, and labor union participation" (p. 184). Within 5 years, self-advocacy organizations emerged in Britain, Canada, and the United States (Williams & Shoultz, 1982), resulting eventually in local, state, and national movements (Beirne-Smith, Patton, & Ittenbach, 1994; Ward & Keith, 1996).

Self-advocacy is closely linked to self-determination and empowerment—concepts that contribute to a positive quality of life for individuals with developmental disabilities (Wehmeyer & Schwartz, 1998), and Taylor and Bogdan (1996) asserted that "without an understanding of how people with mental retardation view and experience their lives, quality of life becomes at best a hollow concept and at worst a justification for treating them in ways that we ourselves would not like to be treated" (p. 21).

The need to be heard and taken seriously is stated clearly by Helle (chap. 3, this volume), and has been translated into an international organizational program, as described by Ward in chapter 4. Individual involvement in planning from the very beginning, including research agenda (see Van Hove & Schelfhout, chap. 5, this volume), will remain a central theme for work in quality of life. A significant beginning is reflected in the American State of Maryland (Bonham et al., 1998), where the Ask Me! Project has employed individuals with disabilities as interviewers and data collectors in a statewide study of quality of life.

Role of Culture
Culture has been defined as "the set of attitudes, values, beliefs, and behaviors shared by a group of people" (Matsumoto, 1996, p. 16). Culture is a major factor in determining how individuals see the world, and, in the context of a worldview, it may determine how individuals judge the quality of their lives. Cultural characteristics may even influence the sense of self (Markus & Kitayama, 1991) and the ways in which individuals are taught the skills and behaviors that shape self. Myers (1992), for example, reported how parents in individualistic cultures raise their children to be independent, capable of making their own decisions and choosing their own friends. In contrast, in more communal societies children are taught interdependence and reliance upon the family and other groups.

These kinds of differences in worldview and in sense of self may also result in important differences in our notions of happiness, satisfaction, and well-being—key foundations of quality of life—across cultures (Keith, 1996). In this volume,

Watson, Barreira, and Watson (chap. 7) make clear the critical nature of cultural understanding in overcoming barriers to integration of individuals with disabilities in Brazil. Lin (chap. 18) describes the effect of hundreds of years of cultural tradition on current perspectives in Taiwan, and Pengra's (chap. 17) description of the Lakota worldview demonstrates that distinctive subcultural variations may remain influential within a larger cultural context.

If we are to advance our understanding of quality of life, and if we are to use our understanding to improve quality of life for people with disabilities, it will be imperative that we recognize, and become more sensitive to, the role of culture, cultural differences, cross-cultural similarities, and ways to improve our cross-cultural relationships. Matsumoto (1996) proposed seven guidelines for improvement of cross-cultural relationships:

1. Recognize that culture is a psychological construct that relies heavily upon subjective factors and can only be inferred from human behavior.

2. Recognize individual differences within a culture, understanding that this recognition will help us to avoid stereotypes and ethnocentrism.

3. Understand our own filters and ethnocentrism, realizing that each of us has been shaped by our own culture, with a worldview that may differ from others.

4. Allow for the possibility that conflicts are cultural, with the accompanying prospect that we can avoid personalizing misunderstandings that may arise due to our differing cultural experiences.

5. Recognize that cultural differences are legitimate, and that "different" does not necessarily mean "bad" or "wrong."

6. Have tolerance, be patient, and presume good intent, not being too quick to attribute ill will to behavior that may simply reflect differing cultural norms.

7. Learn more about cultural influences on behavior in order to enhance both research and the lives of individuals.

These guidelines provide an excellent foundation for our continued efforts in studying cross-cultural quality of life, and a careful reading of even a small sample of the chapters in this volume will affirm their importance.

Aesthetics
The idea of quality of life is closely entwined with the notion that life should be as pleasing and as beautiful as possible. The beautiful, Kupfer (1983) proposed, should permeate everyday life. In other words, the aesthetic should be present not only in obvious places—in works of art or in nature—but also in the day-to-day aspects of ordinary life: in education, work, relationships, athletic activity, decision making, sexual behavior, and even in how we die. This same beauty can be destroyed by violence, discrimination, hatred, and all the other acts and feelings that can do harm to satisfaction and personal well-being. This view has an intuitive appeal, but it presents certain problems for a researcher, not the least of which is the most obvious: How do we produce and/or measure the aesthetic quality of a life?

Some of the beauty of individual lives may lie in their personal stories. Taylor and Bogdan (1996), for example, used stories to illustrate significant aspects of the subjective experience of individuals with mental retardation. This is consistent with the perspective set forth by Coles (1989), who observed "Few would deny that we all have stories in us which are a compelling part of our psychological and ideological make-up" (p. 24). Just as Coles raises the question whether we really hear people's stories when we test them, interview them, or survey them, we too have noticed, in quality-of-life interviews, that people often want to do more than just answer the questions. We have come to believe we must hear the whole story—that we must encourage and record the stories individuals want to tell us and analyze these stories for themes, ideas, dreams, problems, aspirations, and so forth. This notion is consistent with the ideas of empowerment, personal choice, and the reality of people speaking for themselves.

It is not our place, as researchers, to impose a view of quality of life on people: It is our job to hear *their* stories, to help them make sense of them, and to help them use those stories to improve their own lives. This approach to research has potential in two ways: (a) it may help us to better understand the aspirations, frustrations, and realities of people, as embodied in their stories; and (b) it may help us to improve our picture of people's lives in community—the concept discussed by Rapley (chap. 15, this volume). Much of the research in the field has not dealt with the idea of relational communities—the ties and connections among people who may not live in the same locality, but who nevertheless share personal and community interests. At the same time, too much research has shown that too many people are isolated or dependent upon paid staff members for their psychological and social well-being, and thus not truly living in community. We must hear their stories—and help them to write new ones, when that is what they want.

Sanders (1997) believes that stories can entertain; create community; help us to see through the eyes of others; illuminate the consequences of our actions; educate our desires (e.g., generosity, greed, prejudice, compassion, etc.); give us a center for peace in home, family, and neighborhood; help us to dwell in time (showing how current choices may lead to new stories and experiences); help in dealing with suffering, loss, and death; teach us to be human (sharing in community, taking responsibility, coping); and aid appreciation of the beauty of the world and our place in it. Quality of life, at its core, is inseparable from individual notions of beauty and goodness. Consequently, if the concept of quality of life is to have meaning in the lives of individuals with disabilities, aesthetics is a theme that will be integral to the work of the coming decade.

Conclusion

These four themes—community, self-advocacy, culture, and aesthetics—are central to our understanding not only of disabilities, but of humanity in general. Our success in furthering the aim of improved quality of life will depend in large part upon the extent to which these themes are integrated with our efforts to conceptualize, measure, and apply the quality-of-life concept.

References

Andrews, F. M. (1974). Social indicators of perceived quality of life. *Social Indicators Research, 1,* 279-299.

Andrews, F. M., & Whithey, S. B. (1976). *Social indicators of well-being: Americans' perceptions of life quality.* New York: Plenum Press.

Beirne-Smith, M., Patton, J., & Ittenbach, R. (1994). *Mental retardation* (4th ed.). New York: Merrill.

Bonham, G. S., Pisa, L. M., Marchand, C. B., Harris, C., White, D., & Schalock, R. L. (1998). *Ask me! The quality of life of Marylanders with developmental disabilities receiving DDA funded supports.* Annapolis: The ARC of Maryland.

Campbell, A., Converse, P. E., & Rogers, W. L. (1976). *The quality of American life: Perceptions, evaluation, and satisfaction.* New York: Russell Sage.

Caracelli, V. J., & Greene, J. C. (1993). Data analysis strategies for mix-method evaluation designs. *Educational Evaluation and Policy Analysis, 15*(2), 195-207.

Coles, R. (1989). *The call of stories: Teaching and moral imagination.* Boston: Houghton Mifflin.

Cook, T. D. (1985). Postpositivist critical multipluralism. In R. L. Shotland and M. M. Mark (Eds.), *Social science and social policy* (pp. 21-62). Beverly Hills, CA: Sage.

Cummins, R. A. (1997). Self rated quality of life scales for people with an intellectual disability: A review. *Journal of Applied Research in Intellectual Disabilities. 10,* 199-216.

Cummins, R. A. (1998). The second approximation to an international standard for life satisfaction. *Social Indicators Research, 43,* 307-334.

Dybwad, G. (1969). Action implications, U.S.A. today. In R. B. Kugel & W. Wolfensberger (Eds.), *Changing patterns in residential services for the mentally retarded* (pp. 383-428). Washington, DC: President's Committee on Mental Retardation.

Edgerton, R. B. (1996). A longitudinal-ethnographic research perspective on quality of life. In R. L. Schalock (Ed.), *Quality of life: Vol. 1. Conceptualization and measurement* (pp. 83-90). Washington, DC: American Association on Mental Retardation.

Ferguson, R. V. (1997). Environmental design and quality of life. In R. I. Brown (Ed.), *Quality of life for people with disabilities: Models, research, and practice* (pp. 56-70). Cheltenham, United Kingdom: Stanley Thornes.

Gardner, J. F., & Nudler, S. (1999). *Quality performance in human services: Leadership, values, and vision.* Baltimore: Paul H. Brookes.

Greene, J. D., Caracelli, V. J., & Graham, W. F. (1989). Toward a conceptual framework for mixed-method evaluation designs. *Educational Evaluation and Policy Analysis, 11,* 255-274.

Halpern, A. S., Close, D. W., & Nelson, D. J. (1986). *On my own: The impact of semi-independent living programs for adults with mental retardation.* Baltimore: Paul H. Brookes.

Hatton, C. (1998). Whose quality of life is it anyway? Some problems with the emerging quality of life consensus. *Mental Retardation, 36*(2), 104-115.

Keith, K. D. (1990). Quality of life: Issues in community integration. In R. L. Schalock (Ed.), *Quality of life: Perspectives and issues* (pp. 93-100). Washington, DC: American Association on Mental Retardation.

Keith, K. D. (1996). Measuring quality of life across cultures: Issues and challenges. In R. L. Schalock (Ed.), *Quality of life: Vol. 1. Conceptualization and measurement* (pp. 73-82). Washington, DC: American Association on Mental Retardation.

Keith, K. D., Schalock, R. L., & Hoffman, K. (1986). *Quality of life: Measurement and programmatic implications.* Lincoln, NE: Region V Mental Retardation Services.

Kupfer, J. H. (1983). *Experience as art: Aesthetics in everyday life.* Albany: State University of New York Press.

Lindstrom, B. (1992). Quality of life: A model for evaluating health for all. *Soz Praventivmed, 37,* 301-306.

Markus, H., & Kitayama, S. (1991). Culture and the self: Implications for cognition, emotion, and motivation. *Psychological Review, 98,* 224-253.

Matsumoto, D. (1996). *Culture and psychology.* Pacific Grove, CA: Brooks/Cole.

Myers, D. G. (1992). *The pursuit of happiness: Who is happy—and why.* New York: William Morrow.

Nirje, B. (1969). The normalization principle and its human management implications. In R. B. Kugel & W. Wolfensberger (Eds.), *Changing patterns in residential services for the mentally retarded* (pp. 179-195). Washington, DC: President's Committee on Mental Retardation.

Parmenter, T. R. (1992). Quality of life of people with developmental disabilities. *International Review of Research in Mental Retardation, 18,* 247-287.

Raphael, D. (1996). Defining quality of life: Debates concerning its measurement. In R. Renwick, I. Brown, & M. Nagler (Eds.), *Quality of life in health promotion and rehabilitation: Conceptual approaches, issues, and applications* (pp. 146-165). Thousand Oaks, CA: Sage.

Sanders, S. R. (1997, Spring). The power of stories. *The Georgia Review, LI,* 113-116.

Schalock, R. L. (1996). Reconsidering the conceptualization and measurement of quality of life. In R. L. Schalock (Ed.), *Quality of life: Vol. 1. Conceptualization and measurement* (pp. 123-139). Washington, DC: American Association on Mental Retardation.

Schalock, R. L. (1999). A quest for quality: Achieving organizational outputs and personal outcomes. In J. F. Gardner & S. Nudler (Eds.), *Quality performance and human services: Leadership, values, and vision* (pp. 58-80). Baltimore: Paul H. Brookes.

Schalock, R. L. (in press). *Outcomes-based evaluation* (2nd ed.). New York: Plenum.

Schalock, R. L., Bartnik, E., Wu, F., Konig, A., Lee, C. S., & Reiter, S. (1990, May). *An international perspective on quality of life measurement and use.* Paper presented at the annual meeting of the American Association on Mental Retardation, Atlanta, GA.

Schalock, R. L., Bonham, G. S., & Marchand, C. B. (in press). Consumer-based quality of life assessment: A path model of perceived satisfaction. *Evaluation and Program Planning.*

Schalock, R. L., & Faulkner, E. H. (1997). Cross-validation of a contextual model of quality of life. *European Journal on Mental Disability* 4(14), 18-27.

Schalock, R. L., Keith, K. D., Hoffman, K., & Karan, O. C. (1989). Quality of life: Its measurement and use. *Mental Retardation, 27,* 25-31.

Taylor, S. J., & Bogdan, R. (1996). Quality of life and the individual's perspective. In R. L. Schalock (Ed.), *Quality of life: Vol. 1. Conceptualization and measurement* (pp. 11-22). Washington, DC: American Association on Mental Retardation.

The ARC of Nebraska. (1998). *1998 Nebraska developmental disabilities service provider profiles.* Lincoln: Author.

United Nations. (1993). *United Nations standard rules on the equalization of opportunities for disabled persons.* New York: Author.

Ward, N. A., & Keith, K. D. (1996). Self-advocacy: Foundation for quality of life. In R. L. Schalock (Ed.), *Quality of life: Vol. 1. Conceptualization and measurement* (pp. 5-10). Washington, DC: American Association on Mental Retardation.

Wehmeyer, M., & Schwartz, M. (1998). The relationship between self-determination and quality of life for adults with mental retardation. *Education and Training in Mental Retardation and Developmental Disabilities, 33*(1), 3-12.

Williams, P., & Shoultz, B. (1982). *We can speak for ourselves.* London: Souvenir Press.

World Health Organization. (1997). *Measuring quality of life: The World Health Organization quality of life instruments.* Geneva, Switzerland: Author.